Bearing the People Away

The Portable Highland Clearances Companion

June Skinner Sawyers

Bearing the People Away

The Portable Highland Clearances Companion

June Skinner Sawyers

CAPE BRETON UNIVERSITY PRESS
SYDNEY, NOVA SCOTIA

For the Macdonald clan of Skye and Inverness:
Roddy Martin, Sheena, Eileen, Tina, Roddy Angus, Morag

Copyright 2013 June Skinner Sawyers

All rights reserved. No part of this work may be reproduced or used in any form or by any means, electronic or mechanical, including photocopying, recording or any information storage or retrieval system, without the prior written permission of the publisher. Responsibility for the research and the permissions obtained for this publication rests with the author. CBU Press recognizes fair dealing uses under the *Copyright Act* (Canada).

Canada Council for the Arts   Conseil des Arts du Canada

Cape Breton University Press recognizes the support of the Province of Nova Scotia, through the Department of Communities, Culture and Heritage and the support received for its publishing program from the Canada Council for the Arts Block Grants Program. We are pleased to work in partnership with these bodies to develop and promote our cultural resources.

Cover design: Cathy MacLean Design, Chéticamp, NS
Cover photo (Assynt) by Mike Hunter, Port Hawkesbury and Sydney, NS
Author photo: Theresa Albini
Layout: Laura Bast, Sydney, NS
First printed in Canada

Library and Archives Canada Cataloguing in Publication

Sawyers, June Skinner, 1957-, author
    Bearing the people away : the portable Highland Clearances companion / June Skinner Sawyers.

Includes bibliographical references and index.
ISBN 978-1-927492-59-8 (pbk.)
ISBN 978-1-927492-60-4 (web pdf.)
ISBN 978-1-927492-61-1 (epub.)
ISBN 978-1-927492-62-8 (mobi.)

    1. Scotland--History--18th century. 2. Scotland--History--19th century. 3. Scots--Migrations. I. Title.

DA809.S28 2013   941.1   C2013-903767-5

Cape Breton University Press
PO Box 5300
1250 Grand Lake Road
Sydney, NS B1P 6L2 CA
www.cbu.ca/press

Table of Contents

Acknowledgments	1
Chronology	3
Introduction	7
Bearing the People Away	9
Appendix	260
Map of the Highlands (1804)	270
References	272
Index	301

I think ... every Highlander should have copies of the histories of the Clearances along with the Bible in his bookcase.
 —John Maclean, Inverness harbour master and father of artist Will Maclean

We have not become so civilised in our behaviour, or more concerned with men than profit, that this story holds no lesson for us.
 —John Prebble

Acknowledgments

My interest in the Highland Clearances began a long time ago, in the mid-1980s if I recall correctly, when I bought a copy of John Prebble's *The Highland Clearances* at the Inverness Museum in the capital of the Highlands. I read it from cover to cover numerous times (I still have that copy, but now it is a rather fragile state, held together by a rubber band). Around the same time I picked up an earlier version of Rob Gibson's *Highland Clearances Trail*, at that time it was just a small pamphlet (many years later, the Edinburgh-based Luath Press published a more elaborate edition). I remember the day too when Rob very generously gave me a black and white photograph that he took of the windowpane in the Croick Church in Glencalvie; the same diamond-shaped windowpane that has etched on its surface the troubling words, "Glencalvie people the wicked generation."

I still have that photograph.[1]

It wouldn't be the first time that a Lowlander was fascinated by Highland history and culture. Even today the Highlands is considered, by some, to be "exotic." When describing locations for the latest Bond film *Skyfall*, an American reporter referred to the numerous locations where the film was shot, including such "exotic" locales as Turkey, Shanghai and, yes, "the Scottish Highlands." The Highlands continue to fascinate the Scots and, especially, non-Scots public on so many levels.

A book of this kind is dependent upon the work of others. Thus, I would like to direct readers to the bibliography at the end of this volume. In addition to the scholars represented in the bibliography, I am also grateful for the feedback and input of the following people: Kenny Brill, Charlie Burns, Dr. Linda F. Carnes-McNaughton, Bill Caudill, Rob Gibson, James Hunter, Jacquie Aitkin, Tom Devine, Angus Peter Campbell, Michael Russell, David Woods, Tara Clark, Jennifer Williams, Anne Landin and Virginia Blankenhorn. I would also like to thank my editor, Mike Hunter, for his belief in the project and for his patience during the on-and-off again writing of this volume.

It is no exaggeration to say that this book could not have been written without the generosity of family and friends: my cousins Janet and Bert McFarlane in Glasgow, Drew and Lynn Campbell in Montrose, and John and Elspeth Campbell in Blairgowrie; Eileen Macdonald in Glenlomond, and Roddy and Sheena Macdonald in Skye, Diane and Robert Rae in Edinburgh, and Erlend and Hélène Clouston, also in Edinburgh.

I also have fond memories of of chasing the sun in the Outer Hebrides with the Canadian folk band Cowboy Celtic. A personal thanks to the ladies (Hannah, May and Jane) of the Lifestyle slimming club in Kelty for an entertaining evening.

As we go to press, the American filmmaker Guy Perrotta is working on a documentary about the Clearances, its legacy and the worldwide Scottish diaspora, which only proves, yet again, that the Clearances continues to be an endless source of fascination not only in Scotland but around the globe.

J.S.S.

Note

1. See page 269 for two views of the window at Croick Church.

Chronology

Major events in the history of the Highlands and Islands

ca. 500 Kingdom of Dalriada established

563 Columba lands at Iona

ca. 780-800 Norse settlement of Scotland begins

843 Union of the Kingdom of Picts and Scots under Kenneth MacAlpin

ca. 1100 Somerled of Clan Donald

1164 Death of Somerled, founder of the Lordship of the Isles

1296 Battle of Stirling Bridge

1314 Battle of Bannockburn

1408 Islay Gaelic Charter

1493 Forfeiture of the Lordship of the Isles

1513 Battle of Flodden

1603 Union of the Crowns of Scotland and England

1609 Statues of Iona

1645 Battle of Inverlochy

1647 Death of Alasdair MacColla

1689 Battle of Killiecrankie

1690 Establishment of the Church of Scotland

1692 Massacre of Glencoe

1707 Union of the Parliaments of Scotland and England

1715 First Jacobite Rising

1736 Settlement of Darien, Georgia, by Highlanders

1739 First migrations from Scotland to Cape Fear, North Carolina

1745 Second Jacobite Rising

1746 Battle of Culloden

1760 Introduction of large-scale sheep farming in the Highlands

1769-1774 Peak years of Highland emigration to Cape Fear, NC

1773 Voyage of the *Hector* from Loch Broom to Pictou, Nova Scotia; James Boswell and Samuel Johnson's tour of the Hebrides

1785, 1791, 1802 Emigration from Glengarry, Scotland, to Glengarry County, Ontario

1788 Death of Bonnie Prince Charlie

1792 Bliadhna nan Caorach (Year of the Sheep)

1802-1803 Some 8,300 Highlanders emigrate to North America

1803 *Passenger Act* passed, restricting emigration by raising the price of passage on emigrant ships

1803 Lord Selkirk settles Highlanders in Prince Edward Island

1807 Publication of the Gaelic Bible

1812 Red River Settlement in Manitoba begins

1814 The Year of the Burnings

1816 The trial of Patrick Sellar in Inverness

1819 Kildonan and Strathnaver evictions

1828-1838 Peak years of Highland emigration to Cape Breton

1843 Disruption; founding of the Free Church

1845 Glencalvie evictions; the *Times* (of London) sends a Special Commissioner

1846 Potato blight in Scotland; establishment of Destitution Relief Boards in Glasgow and Edinburgh

1847 Queen Victoria purchases Balmoral Castle

1849 Sollas evictions in North Uist

1851 South Uist and Barra evictions

1853 Boreraig and Suishnish evictions in Skye; Harriet Beecher Stowe, on her first visit to Britain, meets with the second Duchess of Sutherland

1854 Massacre of the Rosses

1856 Harriet Beecher Stowe's second visit to Britain; she stays in Inveraray and at Dunrobin Castle, gathering material on the Clearances, which she publishes as *Sunny Memories*

1857 Donald Macleod publishes *Gloomy Memories*, his account of the Strathnaver clearances

Chronology

1874 Bernera Riot in Lewis

1881-1882 The Crofter's War

1882 Battle of the Braes; Skye Rent Strike; Glendale Martyrs arrested

1882 Highland Land League formed

1883 Appointment of the Napier Commission

1886 *Crofting Act*; Crofter's Commission created by Act of Parliament

1887 Pairc Deer forest raid, Lewis

1888 Aignish Riot, Lewis

1891 Founding of An Comunn Gàidhealach (The Highland Association) in Oban

1892 Deer Forest Commission

1900 Land raids in Vatersay and Lewis

1920 Land raids in North Uist, Skye, Raasay and Sutherland

1948 Knoydart land raids

1951 Foundation of the School of Scottish Studies, University of Edinburgh

1955 Crofting (Scotland) Act

1965 Establishment of Highlands and Islands Development Board in Inverness

1968 Gaelic Books Council established

1972 *The West Highland Free Press* established in Skye

1973 *Crofting Reform Bill*; *The Cheviot, the Stag and the Black, Black Oil* tour

1975 Foundation of Comhairle nan Eilean, the Western Isles Council

1979 Radio nan Eilean goes on the air

1983 Sabhal Mòr Ostaig, the Gaelic College in Skye, opens

1984 Museum nan Eilean opens

1985 An Lanntair Art Gallery opens in Stornoway

1997 *Transfer of Crofting Estates Act* goes into effect

1998 National Museum of Scotland opens in Edinburgh

1999 The Scottish Parliament meets for the first time since 1707 in Edinburgh

2001 Scottish Land Fund established to encourage community buy-outs

2003 Passage of *Land Reform Act* by Scottish Parliament

2004 Opening of the new Scottish Parliament Building in Edinburgh

2007 The Scottish National Party (SNP) wins the most seats in the Scottish Parliament for the first time in Scottish history, governing as a minority administration with party leader Alex Salmond serving as First Minister of Scotland.

2011 The Scottish National Party (SNP) wins a landslide victory, forming a majority government in the Scottish Parliament for the first time.

2014 Referendum to determine Scottish independence from the rest of the United Kingdom set for September 18, 2014.

Introduction

The Highland Clearances generally refers to the forcible eviction of the indigenous Gaelic-speaking people of the Scottish Highlands and Islands roughly between 1790 and 1855 to make way for more profitable cattle and sheep farms and, later, sporting estates. The blunt result of these evictions was that of a culture fundamentally altered if not destroyed and the physical landscape transformed beyond all recognition. Many Clearance Highlanders emigrated to Canada and the United States as well as to Australia and New Zealand. Others were relegated to fishing villages on the Scottish mainland, such as Bettyhill on the Pentland Firth, where they were expected to make a living in a profession that they knew nothing about. Decade after decade, all over the Highlands and Islands the same scenes were re-enacted time and time again.

These evictions—The Clearances as they came to be called—occurred over a long period of time. There were many villains, and just as many heroes. A considerable number of books in the form of histories, novels, poetry, plays and memoirs have been written about this, the most transformative event in Scottish history, but it is a story that warrants retelling until its magnitude and sense of loss can be fully appreciated by everyone, especially those who know nothing or very little about it. It is a story that affected a particular subset of people in a particular part of a small northern nation, but it is also the larger story of the not always noble state of the human condition—the strong overwhelm the weak with their resources, their power and their cruel ambition. It is, in other words, a fundamentally human story and its casualty was people—not just cold statistics on a sheet of paper—but flesh-and-blood human beings, most of whom never had a choice to voice their opinion or had even a prayer's hope of improving their lot on this earth.

In recent years some scholars have tried to minimize the impact of the Clearances, referring to the historical accounts as being hyperbolic in nature, an exaggeration fuelled by anger as much as by wishful nostalgia. Others maintain that it was an inevitable part of economic history and a necessary, if painful, consequence of progress. But many more disagree, even going so far as to declare it an early example of what we now call "ethnic cleansing."

The Clearances is both an image and a concept; as such it has a profound symbolic resonance within Scotland but especially in the Highlands. *Bearing the People Away* is the only one-volume companion to one of the most defining moments in Scottish, and indeed, British history. As such, this is an invaluable guide to anyone who wishes to better understand contemporary Scotland and its place in the world. The book also serves as a reminder that the lessons of history are something that should be remembered, not forgotten, lest we repeat the same mistakes over and over again.

As the historian James Hunter so eloquently wrote: although Highlanders have done very well in their new homes outwith Scotland "that does not justify what was originally done to the people anymore than it makes sense to say that an American black today is better off financially than a person in West Africa and therefore the slave trade was a very good thing." Denis Rixson agrees. "The fact that in the long-term the people prospered in the New World is irrelevant to the issue of whether they were wronged in the Highlands."

A word about the title: I came across the phrase "bearing the people away" in an essay by David Craig that appeared in the May 24, 2001, issue of the *London Review of Books*. It stayed with me for days, weeks even, and continues to resonate with me as much for its disturbing imagery as for its phrasing which seemed to my ears as if it came directly from some Old Testament text.

Bearing the People Away barely scratches the surface of this very complex subject. Part handbook, part historical dictionary, it is not intended to be exhaustive (you will not find, for example, every Clearance site), but rather a stepping stone to greater knowledge. Many aspects of the Clearances will be addressed in this companion—the historians and the victims as well as the authorities who instigated it. Again, although not every Clearance site is listed in the book, the major Clearance "set pieces," as Eric Richards so memorably describes them, are here. And I have also included a listing of some of the so-called lesser sites ("lesser" is of course, a matter of perspective).

And for anyone who wants to know more about the Clearances, its impact and legacy, I would recommend browsing the references located in the back matter. The work of John Prebble, Rob Gibson, Eric Richards, James Hunter and Tom Devine were especially valuable.

A

Acair. Publisher of books of local interest in both Gaelic and English, Acair was established in Stornoway in 1977, and is the first bilingual educational publisher in Scotland. Since its inception, it has been at the forefront of the modern Gaelic cultural revival.

Act of Proscription (1746). Act of Parliament that banned Highland dress and the bearing of arms in an effort to assimilate the Highlands. Possible punishment included fines, imprisonment and transport to the penal colony of Australia. A subsequent law, the *Heritable Jurisdiction (Scotland) Act* of 1746 rescinded the feudal authority of clan chieftains. The laws were repealed on July 1, 1782.

"Address of Beelzebub." A satirical poem by Scotland's national bard, Robert Burns, condemning the behaviour of Alasdair Ranaldson Macdonell, clan chief of Glengarry known for his atrocious acts of evictions against his clanspeople.

Admiral (ship). A clear example of forced emigration during the Clearance era. In 1851, tenants on Gordon of Cluny's lands on Barra and South Uist agreed to accept assisted passage to Canada, but prior to embarkation they changed their minds. Police pursued them, handcuffing and forcing resisters onto the waiting vessel.
  See also emigrant ships

Agricultural Revolution. The mid-19th century transformed the Scottish Lowlands, changing individual estates into "models of farming efficiency and innovation." Aitchison and Cassell suggest that the Agricultural Revolution created two Scotlands: the consolidation of farms and the replacement of the primitive runrig system of subsistence farming with modern practices in the Lowlands; while in the Highlands and Islands similar policies left "a legacy of poverty, injustice and anti-landlordism which endures to this day."

agriculture. In 1750, according to Thomas Devine, only one Scot in eight lived in towns (that is, a community with a minimal population of 4,000). The majority of people made their living working the land and toiling in rural industries, such as spinning, weaving, fishing and mining. While there were some owner-occupiers, from Ayrshire to Fife the vast majority were under a tenant-landlord relationship.

By the early 18th century, tenants' right to the land was determined, according to Scots law, by a lease, or "tack," which typically lasted anywhere from nine to nineteen years. Tenants were often men of status in their own insular communities, especially in the *fermtouns* that were scattered across the Lowlands. Some were large enough to almost be considered villages while others were scattered haphazardly across the area. Either way, these communities had their own internal social structure, with tenants at the top, followed by cottars, farm servants and tradesmen. Cottars, in fact, formed the majority of the population in many of the rural communities. They held a few acres—Devine says less than five—but they also did much of the dirty work in the agricultural system of the time, such as the ploughing, harvesting and gathering of peat. In other words, the cottars of the Lowlands, like the crofters of the Highlands, relied overwhelmingly on the land for their livelihood.

The face of the Scottish countryside as well as the way the people lived, especially in the Lowlands, changed fundamentally from the 1769s to the 1820s. The needs and demands of the Scottish cities and towns for such staples as grain, butter, milk, cheese, eggs and meat transformed the agrarian system and led to basic changes in the social structure of rural life.

See also Agricultural Revolution; Lowland Clearances

Aird, Rev. Gustavus. Minister at Glencalvie, Aird forcefully criticized the landlords who cleared people from the land to make way for deer and sheep.

And the Cock Crew (1945). Novel written by Fionn MacColla, which criticizes Calvinist theology that played such a prominent role during the Highland Clearances. MacColla maintains that Calvinism left the Highlanders vulnerable to societal forces, paralyzed by an ideology that believed in a passive fate.

See also fiction of the Clearances

Antigonish Heritage Museum (Nova Scotia). A community museum that attempts to preserve and promote the history and material culture of Antigonish, both the town and the wider county. Housed in a former Canadian National (CN) railway station, the museum consists of two rooms. The resource room includes photographs; published materials;

community, church, school and family histories; census records; and school registers. Includes copies of the *Casket*, Antigonish's weekly newspaper founded in 1852, and *Mac-Talla* (The Echo), the Sydney-based Gaelic-language newspaper, published by Jonathan MacKinnon from 1892 to 1904.

apology. In 1998 Scottish landowners considered making a collective public apology for the Clearances in an effort to improve their public image. In September 2000, Jamie Stone, the Liberal Democrat member of the Scottish Parliament (MSP) for Caithness, Sutherland and Easter Ross, issued an apology on behalf of the victims of the Highland Clearances: That the Parliament expresses its deepest regret for the occurrence of the Highland Clearances and extends its hand in friendship and welcome to the descendants of the cleared people who reside outwith our shores.

Other MSPs supported Stone's motion and drew parallels between the Clearance Highlanders and Native Americans and Australian Aborigines even as others questioned whether Parliament was the right place for such an apology to be issued.

Ardnamurchan. In 1828 Sir James Milles Riddell cleared 26 families from the area around Ben Hiant. The clearances here have gone down in history as particularly cruel: a "half-witted" woman, according to Alexander Mackenzie, who refused to leave was locked up in her cottage. When there was no more food in the house, only then did she relent and agree to leave. Most of the families who were evicted went overseas, others settled on patches of barren land. More than 20 years later, in April 1852, 85 families scattered over 12 townships were cleared; some resettled on poor land at Sanna.

Argyll. As early as 1669, there were reports of mass evictions of tenants from the islands of Shuna, Luing, Torosay and Seil, to make way not for sheep but for commercial cattle production, according to Eric Richards. But many years on, Argyll continued to lose population, either directly or indirectly related to clearances. Indeed, notes Rob Gibson, Argyll lost half of its population between 1831 and 1911, "a total of 30,000 people."

Argyll Colony. Refers to the emigration in 1739 of Scots from Argyll, chiefly the islands of Jura, Islay, Gigha and the peninsula of Kintyre in Argyllshire, who settled in the Cross Creek area of North Carolina, now Fayetteville, and in and around present-day Cumberland, Moore, Hoke, Harnett and surrounding counties.

See also Cape Fear; "Fort Bragg Clearances"; North Carolina

Arichonan. Is located in mid-Argyllshire. By the late 18th century, the owners, the MacNeills, were on the verge of bankruptcy. Consequently, Daniel MacNeill of Gigha sold Arichonan to John Stevenson who in turn sold it to Neil Malcolm of Poltalloch. By the 1820s, large numbers of people were leaving for Upper Canada (what is now Ontario) and Australia. In 1848 Arichonan consisted of a multiple tenancy, that is, a group of families jointly sharing the land. That year Malcolm attempted to evict some of these small tenants from the land, offering assisted passage to Australia.

In April 1848 the owners terminated the leases of the remaining tenants in the township. They were given until late May to leave. In mid-June, the authorities attempted to enforce the writs of removal. Much to their surprise, though, the tenants did not go meekly; when police came to enforce the writs, the men and women of the township resisted, assaulting the officers with sticks and stones and showering them with threatening language. They were joined by roughly 100 to 200 people from the surrounding area. Another, more successful attempt, was made in early July when the superintendent of police for Argyll accompanied by a contingent of officers came to enforce the summons. Ultimately, five ringleaders were arrested and charged with mobbing, rioting and obstructing justice. They were found guilty and sentenced to several months in Inveraray Jail.

The ruins of Arichonan Clearance village are still visible. A plaque was erected to commemorate the site but, as of this writing, it is no longer there.

Armadale Castle and the Clan Donald Centre, Skye. Some 16 ha (40 acres) of woodland surround the remains of the castle, which also houses the Museum of the Isles, tracing the history of the Gaels generally and Clan Donald in particular. On site is the Study Centre, a valuable resource for people researching their Gaelic roots. The Armadale House, once the gardener's cottage, contains the archives and library of the Clan Donald Lands Trust, which operates the centre.

Aros Experience, The. Located on Viewfield Road and set on a hectare (4 acres) of mature woodland on the outskirts of Portree, Isle of Skye, this museum offers exhibits on the history and Gaelic heritage of Skye.

Arran Clearances. In the 1820s large swaths of the island were cleared for sheep: Glenree in 1825 and, more famously, Glen Sannox, in 1829. The landlord, the Duke of Hamilton, offered to pay half the fare of the tenants to Upper Canada (Ontario) along with the offer of 400 ha (100 acres) of Canadian land. Nearly twenty families accepted the offer, departing from Lamlash Bay.

Indicative of the time, farms on Arran were combined, ending multiple tenancies, leaving tiny holdings unable to sustain a family. Inhabitants who did stay were barely able to scrape by as labourers or fishermen, or went to the mainland in search of work. Residents who were able to hold onto their farms were given written tacks, or leases, which came with expiry dates; in 1829, all of the farm leases in Glen Sannox expired. The factor told nearly thirty families that they would have to leave (the Duke of Hamilton covered the cost of half of the people). Twelve families, or 86 people, chose to emigrate to Canada. They boarded the brig *Caledonia* in Lamlash Bay on April 25, 1829, as a Church of Scotland minister delivered a sermon on site. They arrived in Megantic County, Québec, on June 25, 1829, and received a 40-hectare (100-acre) plot of land there.

A cairn erected on Lamlash village green marks the spot where an open air church service was held for the emigrants who left on the brig for Québec.

MEMORIAL TO
THE ARRAN CLEARANCES

UNVEILED BY
MRS MYRTLE COOK MAXWELL
OF NEW BRUNSWICK, CANADA
ON 9th MAY, 1977

Also on the island of Arran, near Lochranza, is a site referred to as Cock Farm, where the Macmillan family (of Macmillan publishing fame) lived for generations. According to Rob Gibson, they were cleared from the island in 1814. The founder of Macmillan, Daniel Macmillan (1813-1857), was born at Achag in 1813; his great grandson, Harold Macmillan, was prime minister of Britain from 1957 to 1963. Two miles southwest of Lochranza is a series of twelve cottages (nicknamed the "twelve apostles") that were built at Catacol to house the people cleared from Glen Catacol to make way for deer shooting.

As an Fhearann (**From the Land**). Companion book to the exhibition of the same name, that originated at An Lanntair Gallery in Stornoway, in 1986, to mark the centenary of the *Crofting Act* of 1886. Both exhibition and book examine and offer commentary on the changing image of the Highlands from the Clearances to 1986. The book features essays by poets Sorley Maclean and Angus Peter Campbell, playwright John McGrath, author Finlay MacLeod, painter Alexander Moffat and writer John Murray. The tour made stops at the Royal Scottish Museum in Edinburgh, the Third Eye Centre in Glasgow, Artspace in Aberdeen, the Inverness Art Galley and Eden Court Theatre in Inverness and the Crawford Centre for the Arts in St. Andrews.

Ascherson, Neal (b. 1932). Journalist, born in Edinburgh. Educated at Eton College, Windsor, and King's College, Cambridge, Ascherson joined the *Guardian* as a reporter in 1956, and subsequently became the Commonwealth correspondent for the *Scotsman* three years later. In 1960 he was appointed foreign correspondent for the *Observer* before re-joining the *Scotsman* as a political correspondent covering Scottish events in 1975. He has also been a columnist on the *Observer* and the *Independent on Sunday*. In 2004 he published *Stone Voices: The Search for Scotland*, an astute and insightful modern-day travelogue that explores Scotland's past, present and future, including observations on the devastating effects of the Clearances on the Scottish mindset.

Assynt Clearances. In August 1811, the factor William Young recommended that most of the parish of Assynt be cleared to make way for sheep while "reserving accommodation for kelp makers, fisheries, lime burners, and other labourers." Further, in order to accommodate resettlement, he recommended village development on the west coast, around Lochinver.

In 1812 the factor Patrick Sellar carried out clearances in Assynt without incident, which he attributed to the "calming" influence of the tacksmen. Some though refused to resettle in the coastal villages, preferring instead to remain in the hills. Those who remained uncooperative were encouraged to emigrate. Lord Selkirk offered to take the married men among them to Canada to serve in regiments but the owner, Lady Stafford, rejected this idea as "totally inadvisible."

Subsequent, and uneventful, clearances took place in Assynt in 1819 and 1820. The evicted either went abroad (to America) or stayed in Scotland (in Ross-shire and Caithness). Despite clearances and emigration, though, the population of Assynt, notes Eric Richards, increased between 1811 and 1821, as some of the inhabitants worked in the kelp industry even as many more converted to fishing.

Assynt Crofters' Trust. In late 1992 an 8,600 hectare (21,132-acre) estate was repossessed by local crofters, including John MacKenzie, Bill Ritchie and Allan MacRae, whose great-grandfather of the trust's chairman, also named Allan MacRae, was cleared. MacRae remarked, "Assynt crofters have struck a historic blow." Membership in the trust was confined to crofters living within the estate. The purchase was made possible with assistance from, among others, the Highlands & Islands Enterprise Community Land Unit, Scottish Natural Heritage, Highland Regional Council, the John Muir Trust, the Tubney Charitable

Trust and the Big Lottery Fund (by agency of the Scottish Land Fund) as well as a public appeal for funds (those who contributed included the Gaelic rock band Runrig). In June 2005 the local community bought the Glencanisp estate, including Suilven and Canisp mountains and the neighbouring Drumrunie estate; the estates are managed by the Assynt Foundation on behalf of the Assynt community.

Assynt Foundation, The. Established prior to the landmark community land buy out of the Glencanisp and Drumrunie estates, in the parish of Assynt in the Northwest Highlands of Scotland. In June 2005, the community of Assynt bought nearly 18 ha (44,000 acres) of natural land, from the Vestey family, under provisions of the 2003 Scottish *Land Reform Act*. The area includes Suilven, Canisp, Cul Mor and Cul Beag mountains and the Victorian hunting lodge, Glencanisp Lodge. The objectives of the foundation are as follows:

> to create local employment and safeguard the natural and cultural heritage for the benefit of the community and future generations, and for the enjoyment of the wider public;

> to manage community land and associated assets for the benefit of the community and the public as part of the protection and sustainable development of Scotland's natural environment; and

> to educate the community about its environment, culture and history.

In addition, the foundation aims to create new employment opportunities and is working toward the creation of an environmentally-friendly local affordable housing.

Auchindrain. Township Museum in Argyllshire, an old farming township located six miles south of Inverarary that is now an open-air museum. It is the best remaining example of a typical Highland township that was common in pre-Clearances Scotland. It is open to the public between April and September. Auchindrain (in Gaelic, Achadh an Droighinn, or field of the blackthorn tree) was preserved in 1964 and has been open since then as an open-air museum.

Australia. Began its existence as a penal colony; Britain established Botany Bay in the late 1780s. The threat of being evicted to the strange and faraway land of Australia was sometimes used as a deterrent, such as at Strathrusdale in 1792, to those who dared to resist acts of removal. But there are many other instances where Highlanders were cleared and emigrated to Australia, either directly or indirectly. More than 600 people at Borve, on Harris, for example, moved to Australia in 1854. Other times the authorities, such as Sir Charles Trevelyan, believed that emigration was the only real solution to Highland poverty and destitution. Trevelyan proposed moving a massive amount, some 100,000 people from the Highlands to Australia (a fraction of that number did eventually leave). Quite often Highlanders experienced utter misery on the emigrant ships that left for Australia. One egregious example is the *Hercules* which, under the auspices of the Highlands and Islands Emigration Society, departed from Sollas, on the Isle of Skye, before Christmas 1852. When the ship docked at Queenstown (now Cove in Ireland), smallpox was already running rampant below deck.

B

Badbea. A deserted Clearance village in Caithness located about five miles north of the town of Helmsdale. A sign-posted public footpath leads to the site, which consists of a group of ruined crofts perched on a cliff-top high above the North Sea. The village was settled in the 18th and 19th centuries by families that were evicted from Langwell and from nearby Ousdale and Berriedale by landowner Sir John Sinclair of Ulbster to make way for sheep farms. (Some settlers also came from Auchencraig and Kildonan.) The evicted had to clear the land and build their new homes on steep slopes where they earned their living primarily in the herring trade and later salmon fishing. The village had a few cows, pigs and chickens and one horse; each house had its own spinning wheel. While the men worked, the children and even the livestock were tethered to the rocks to prevent them from being blown off the cliffs to certain death by the fierce winds.

The last inhabitant, John Gunn left in 1911. Although some emigrated to North America the majority went to New Zealand. David Sutherland, the son of Alexander Robert Sutherland of New Zealand, erected the monument, using the stones of the village, in honour of his father and the people of the village. The inscription on the monument reads in part:

> THIS MONUMENT WAS ERECTED IN 1911,
> TO COMMEMORATE THE PEOPLE OF BADBEA,
> BY DAVID M. SUTHERLAND OF WAIRRAPPA AND
> WELLINGTON, NEW ZEALAND,
> SON OF ALEXANDER ROBERT SUTHERLAND, BORN
> IN BADBEA IN 1806,
> AND WHO LEFT FOR NEW ZEALAND IN 1839, WHERE
> HE DIED IN 1877

An explanatory plaque also honours Badbea resident John Sutherland—doctor and preacher—who so personified the community that he was given the nickname of "John Badbea":

"John Badbea" stood out as a leader, acting as preacher and doctor, as well as owning the only watch in the village. Villagers left to find a more prosperous way of life, many of them emigrating to New Zealand. In 1911 they built the memorial (using the stone from John Badbea's cottage) to the community which once existed here.

All that is left of the village are ruins and several drystone walls; the outlines of buildings are clearly visible.
See also New Zealand

baile. Traditional township; consisting of settlements of multiple tenant farmers, cottars and servants, they formed the heart of Gaeldom for centuries. Over several generations, though, the baile was virtually eliminated. "By the 1830s and 1840s only a few remnants of a once universal pattern of settlement and cultivation remained," contends Tom Devine. In the crofting societies of the western Highlands and the Inner and Outer Hebrides, communal townships were replaced by individual smallholdings, or crofts; the arable land was held by single small tenants while the grazing land remained held in common. The new system consisted of separate holdings of a few acres. In effect, the fragile social structure of the baile were destroyed and replaced by small tenancies of these new crofting townships. Significantly, the tacksmen, or gentry class, were reduced. Devine calls the decline of the tacksmen "one of the clearest signs of the death knell of the old Gaelic society." The result was a new middle class usually comprised of southern sheep farmers and cattle ranchers who had little emotional connection with the indigenous people: an ominous omen for the Gaels.
See also townships

Baldoon. In Dover Township (Kent County) at western end of Upper Canada; Lord Selkirk settled Highlanders here. The first settlers consisted of 15 families, or 102 people, who came from the Argyll area. Sailing on the *Oughton* from Kirkcudbright in 1804; they arrived in Lachine, near Montreal, then made their way to the settlement. Lucille Campey calls Baldoon an "unmitigated disaster." But even as spiralling costs and mismanagement went wildly out of control, the settlers persevered. Because of its proximity to the American border, Baldoon was invaded and pillaged by American soldiers in 1812, and again in 1814 during the War of 1812.

The settlement is important because it consisted of the first large group from Argyll to reach Upper Canada and hence served as a catalyst for further emigration to the area. Named after an estate in Scotland, the settlement was sponsored by Lord Selkirk who later founded the Red River Colony in what is now Winnipeg. Located in a low-lying area, it was prone to frequent flooding. What's more, malaria killed many of the settlers while the incompetence of the superintendent, Alexander McDonell, further aggravated the situation. Eventually the settlers who stuck it out moved to higher ground. In 1818 Selkirk sold the property altogether.

Barra, Isle of. Major clearances occurred here at numerous times from 1848 to 1853. Among the most sensational were those instigated by Col. John Gordon of Cluny, a millionaire landowner from Aberdeen, who lived primarily in Edinburgh, and known for his "Scrooge-like eccentricity and meanness," as Eric Richards so evocatively describes him. Cluny's behaviour involved reprehensible acts of violence, deceptive practices and forced emigration.

In 1841, Cluny had bought Benbecula, South Uist and Barra from the bankrupt Clanranald. By that time the people of Barra were destitute, especially after the kelp prices dropped following the end of the Napoleonic Wars. Several years earlier trustees of the estate had recommended that two-thirds of the population be shoved off to Canada. Cluny himself concluded that with the growing population he could not afford to operate the estates—or would not—and thus chose to undergo a massive attempt of clearances and subsidized emigration. During the potato blight in 1847 the people suffered terribly from starvation even as Cluny insisted that he treated the people better than previous owners.

Also during these years Cluny used policies that combined both eviction and emigration. Some of the people went to the Lowland cities. In late 1850 a group of them arrived in Edinburgh and, with no money to their name, relied on the generoisity of the citizenry to avoid starvation. The city fathers, alarmed by the site of these poverty-stricken Highlanders, sought information regarding the causes of their dire condition. Others had gone to Glasgow, including, reports Richards, two widows and five children. "Their clothes were so appalling that they were burned," he notes. Some were suffering from smallpox and fever. Public and civic outcry ensued, as the Lowlanders blamed Gordon of Cluny for not accepting responsibility for the well-being of his people. But Cluny denied that he had cleared the people from the land. Still others from Cluny's lands on Barra went to Inverness where they stayed for two years when Sir Charles Trevelyan provided them with free passage to Australia. Only two families took up the offer. "The Barra account…," asserts Richards, "was a perfect juxtaposition of extreme wealth and poverty, of the power of the landlord and the impotence of the peasantry."

But conditions worsened when the people were tricked into emigrating on the understanding that their passage to Québec would be paid by Gordon and that they would be transported to their ultimate destination of Upper Canada (Ontario). In the summer of 1851, a number of people from Barra and South Uist were seized and dragged aboard emigrant ships waiting at the quay at Lochboisdale on South Uist en route to Québec. Men were struck with weapons and handcuffed. Those who managed to escape were chased by police and brought back to the waiting ship. When they landed in Québec, about 2,000 people strong, they were destitute and had nowhere to go. Two years earlier, Gordon had provided about 1,000 people free passage and clothing, but nothing of the sort had been arranged for the 1851 emigrants aboard the *Admiral*. Their pathetic condition prompted the medical examiner at Grosse Île, the quarantine station in Québec, to say that he "never, during my long experiences at the station, saw a body of emigrants so desitutute of clothing and bedding; many children of nine or ten years old had not a rag to cover them."

The memory of Gordon of Cluny remained strong on Barra where he was bitterly remembered as a "most tyrannical landlord." Subsequent landowners on Barra were not much better. Among the worst of the post-Gordon successors was Sir Reginald Cathcart. Under his tenure, the tenants were "little better than slaves."

Battle of Balaclava and the Thin Red Line. The Battle of Balaclava was fought on October 25, 1854, during the Crimean War. The three-year conflict was between the Russian Empire against the British, French and Ottoman empires as well as the Kingdom of Sardinia over the control of territories of the Ottoman Empire. Much of the action took place on the Crimean peninsula with smaller campaigns in Anatolia and the Caucasus.

For our purposes here, the Thin Red Line refers to an event during the Battle of Balaclava when the 93rd Highlanders, led by the Glasgow-born Sir Colin Campbell (1792-1863), and including Royal Marines and Turkish infantrymen, routed a Russian cavalry charge. Campbell's Highland Brigade had also taken part at the Battle of Alma (1854) and the Siege of Sevastopol from September 1854 to September 1855. The actual term, "thin red line," refers to the formation of the 93rd which Campbell formed into a line that was two men deep. The steely reserve of Campbell came to symbolize British composure while under pressure. The charge was portrayed by the Scots painter Robert Gibb (1845-1932) and entitled *The Thin Red Line* (1881). Some of men whose family were cleared in Greenyards served in the 93rd regiment at Sevastopol during the Crimean War. John Prebble notes that of 33 infantry battalions sent to serve during the Crimean War, only three were Highland regiments: the 42nd, the 79th and the 93rd. The national press, in Parliament, and in the church pulpits wondered where the Highlanders were. Of course, the answer was simple: lands that were once populated by young men had been emptied to make way for sheep.

Battle of the Braes. A major incident in Highland history as well as a turning point in the Land Agitation movement. It occurred in the district of Braes in Skye on April 19, 1882, on Lord Macdonald's estate, in which crofters, mostly women, clashed with a contingent of Glasgow police officers over the fundamental issue of land rights, specifically, over the loss of crofters' common grazing rights on Ben Lee. The conflict escalated to the point where troops and marines were called in to quell the disturbance.

The crofters had petitioned Macdonald to have their traditional grazing rights returned to them. Their request was rejected. In turn they responded by stating that they would no longer pay rent to Lord Macdonald until their rights were restored. Subsequently, writs of removal were issued on the grounds that the tenants were in arrears.

On April 7, 1882, the sheriff officer serving the summones was assaulted by a throng of about 500 people and the notices forceably removed from his hands and burned. As conditions escalated, a detachment of around 50 Glasgow police officers came to enforce the law under the command of Sheriff William Ivory. They arrested those who assaulted the sheriff officer but a dozen or so officers were injured by large crowd of men and women throwing stones and wielding sticks. In the ensuing melee, the police used batons against the people. Five men were arrested: Alexander Finlayson, Donald Nicolson, James Nicolson, Malcolm Finlayson and Peter MacDonald. The incident, which became known as the Battle of the Braes, precipitated a Royal Commission which ultimately led to the passage of the Crofters Act of 1886, allowing security of tenure and a fair rent.

A cairn commemorates the battle.

Battle of Culloden. On April 16, 1746, the Jacobite forces of Charles Edward Stuart—the Young Pretender, Bonnie Prince Charlie—fought loyalist troops commanded by William Augustus, Duke of Cumberland near Inverness in the Scottish Highlands. The Jacobites were routed by the government forces. It was the last pitched battle on British soil.

The government victory at Culloden halted the Jacobite plan to overthrow the House of Hanover and restore the exiled House of Stuart to the British throne. The Jacobite army consisted largely of Highlanders as well as some Lowlanders and French and Irish units, and even some Englishmen. The government force consisted mostly of English, along with a significant number of Scottish Lowlanders and Highlanders,

Ulstermen and Hessians from Germany and Austrians. The battle on Drummossie Moor lasted less than one hour.

Between 1,500 and 2,000 Jacobites were killed or wounded in the brief battle, while government losses were indicative of their decisive victory, with 50 dead and as many as 300 wounded. Culloden represented the beginning of the end of the clan system. Subsequent government acts led to the banning of the tartan and the kilt and the abolition of the hereditary rights of the chiefs.

The aftermath of Culloden was swift and brutal. The intent of the British government was clear: to pursue a policy designed to "civilize" Highland culture, to bring, in other words, Highland society into the modern era, as well as to pacify the region. The word "pacify" here had many meanings but none greater than to remove the military threat that the Highlands personified. If, as the government maintained, the Highlanders posed a barbarian threat, then that threat would have to be eliminated, no matter what the cost to Highland culture and heritage.

Before the Jacobite Rising of 1745 the chief granted tacks, or leases, on his property. All land was leased to his supporters. Many, but not all, were kin who in turn formed the bulk of the clan regiments and recruited companies among the sub-tenants who lived on the chief's land. Thus, the tenant was, for all intents and purposes, a warrior. Rents were paid in kind, or services. With the defeat at Culloden, and the subsequent reform of Highland society, the chief acted more as a landlord.

The half-century after Culloden was a traumatic period in the Highlands. Despite the impact of Culloden, the defeat could not destroy the social structure of the Highlands. Most historians conclude that cultural influence from the Lowlands and England, which had been at work long before the events that took place on Culloden Moor, were far more responsible for the decline.

Indeed, post-Culloden was a transitional phase in Highland history. Increasingly, in post-Culloden Scotland, more and more chiefs became absentee landlords. After Culloden, the landlords increasingly looked toward the south as their ambitions and business acumen led them away from their native land to the urban centres of the British Empire and her colonies, from Edinburgh and London and beyond to the New World.

See also *Culloden* (film)

Battle of Killiecrankie. July 27, 1689, between Highland clans supporting King James VII of Scotland (James II of England) and troops supporting King William of Orange. Although a victory for the Jacobite forces, it came at a great cost: their leader, John Graham of Claverhouse, 1st Viscount Dundee (1648-1689), otherwise known as "Bonnie Dundee," was killed in battle.

Battle of King's Mountain. A decisive battle between Patriot and Loyalist forces during the American Revolutionary War, the Battle of King's Mountain took place on October 7, 1780, when the Patriot militia defeated Loyalists commanded by the Edinburgh-born Major Patrick Ferguson (1744-1780) of the 71st Regiment of Foot, unofficially known as the Fraser Highlanders. The battle, which lasted a little over an hour, was a pivotal moment during the war—a surprising victory over the Loyalists that came after a string of rebel defeats by the British general Lord Cornwallis. After the Patriot victory, Cornwallis abandoned his plans to invade North Carolina and instead retreated into South Carolina.

Battle of Moore's Creek Bridge. Occurred during the American Revolutionary War, near Wilmington, North Carolina, on February 27, 1776, between Patriot and Loyalist forces. The Loyalists consisted of Regulators, a group opposed to the colonial government, and Scots loyal to the Crown. Allan Maclean lobbied King George III to recruit Scots throughout North America for the cause, including a battalion from New York and North Carolina and another from Québec and Nova Scotia. In the pre-dawn hours the Scots approached the bridge under the command of Lt. Col. Donald MacLeod. Asked by the opposing side to identify themselves, the captain, Alexander Maclean, referred to himself as a friend of the king. He in turn asked for the other side to identify their loyalties. With no reply, he ordered his company to open fire against the Patriot forces. Subsequently, Col. MacLeod and Captain John Campbell led a charge across the bridge. The Patriots had removed planking from the bridge, making it treacherous for the Loyalists to cross safely. Ultimately, the Patriot forces persevered.

In 1966 the site was listed on the National Register of Historic Places.

Battle of the Plains of Abraham. A pivotal battle in the Seven Years War (known in the United States as the French and Indian War) between Britain and France. The battle began on September 13, 1759, on a plateau outside the walls of Québec City, on land originally owned by a Scottish fisherman and river pilot named Abraham Martin (1589-1664), also known as Abraham the Scot. Although short—the battle lasted less than half an hour—it determined the political landscape of Canada. British troops under the command of General James Wolfe (1727-1759) defeated the French army under Louis-Joseph, Marquis de Montcalm (1712-1759). Both generals died during the battle: Wolfe within minutes of his injury, Montcalm the next morning. Among the regiments at the battle were the 78th Fraser Highlanders, which had the highest number of casualties of all British units.

The victory at the Plains of Abraham led to a successful assault on Montréal the following year. Although the French forces continued to fight, ultimately, France ceded its possessions to Great Britain, including Canada and the eastern half of then French Louisiana, after the signing of the Treaty of Paris in 1763. French sovereignty in Canada thus came to an end. Wolfe's heroics on the battlefield turned him into a national hero.

Earlier in his career, Wolfe served as aide-de-camp under General Henry Hawley at the Battle of Falkirk and the Battle of Culloden. At Culloden, he earned the respect of the Highlanders when the Duke of Cumberland ordered him to shoot a wounded soldier, which he refused (alas, Cumberland shot the soldier himself). Even so, after the Jacobite Risings were over, he remained in Scotland, taking part in the pacification of the Highlands. But it was also Wolfe who made the perjorative comment about Scottish soldiers, "they are hardy, intrepid, accustomed to a rough country, and no great mischief if they fall." The Canadian author Alistair MacLeod borrowed that line as the title of his highly acclaimed novel. In 1758, Wolfe commanded British and New England troops and militia for the final overthrow of Louisbourg.

The Plains of Abraham forms a part of the federally run Battlefields Park. The site where Wolfe purportedly fell is marked by a column.

Battle of Prestonpans. September 21, 1745, near the Lowland town of Dunbar during the 1745 Jacobite Rising. A Jacobite army led by Charles Edward Stuart defeated the government army commandeered by Sir John Cope (1690-1760). It proved to be a major victory and huge morale booster for the Highlanders. It is famous for another reason since the battle has been popularized in popular culture, especially in popular song. The rousing "Hey Johnnie Cope, Are You Awake Yet?" commemorates the Highland victory even as it promulgated a popular misconception: although Cope's men did indeed panic and flee the scene, taken back as they were by the Highland charge and the subsequent hue and cry, Cope himself did not leave.

Battle of Seven Oaks. A violent confrontation between the Hudson's Bay Company (HBC) and the North West Company, rival fur-trading companies, which took place on June 19, 1816, in what is now the city of Winnipeg. A plaque commemorating the battle was erected at the intersection of Main Street and Rupertsland Boulevard in the Winnipeg district of West Kildonan, the approximate centre of the battle site. The surrounding neighbourhood was named Seven Oaks after the battle.

Beamish, Sally (b. 1956). English composer, born in London; studied viola at the Royal Northern College of Music, where she received lessons in composition from Anthony Gilbert and Sir Lennox Berkeley. Beamish was a member of the Raphael Ensemble and played with the London Sinfonietta and Lontano. In 1989 she moved from London to Scotland, where she and cellist Robert Irvine founded the Chamber Group of Scotland with the Glasgow-based composer James MacMillan as co-director. In 1994 and 1995 she served as Sir Peter Maxwell Davies's assistant on the Scottish Chamber Orchestra (SCO) composers' course in Hoy, Orkney. In 2001 she received an Honorary Doctorate of Music from Glasgow University. Beamish has been commissioned by various organizations to write numerous major works, including *The Singing*, a concerto for accordion and orchestra that evokes the Clearances. During a particularly powerful segment she uses the accordion to recreate the sound of the bagpipes and evoke the elaborate variations associated with the pibroch, which prompted the composer and broadcaster John Purser to ask, "why not use the bagpipes themselves?"

Beaton Institute (of Cape Breton Studies). Repository of Cape Breton historical records at Cape Breton University in Sydney, Nova Scotia. The institute is also an archive whose purpose is to preserve the social, economic, political and cultural history of Cape Breton Island. Named after Sister Margaret Beaton, the Beaton Institute houses 3,000 manuscript collections, 60,000 images, 2,500 sound recordings, 1,599 videos and film reels, 1,500 reference books and 2,000 maps and plans, housed in a 17,000-square foot complex at the university. The manuscript collection emphasizes the island's industrial, labour and political history; the audio visual collection includes an oral history collection as well as material on Cape Breton's social life and songs. The Celtic Music Collection includes hundreds of recordings by Cape Breton fiddlers and pianists. The photographs include more than 60,000 images, dating from the mid-19th century to the present day. The Institute's special ethno-cultural materials include a large Gaelic selection, including original manuscripts, tapes, a small reference library and, significantly, the complete file of the important Gaelic newspaper *Mac-Talla*.

Beaton, Sister Margaret (1894-1975). Born at Broad Cove Banks, Cape Breton. In 1913 she became a sister of the Congregation of Notre Dame in 1913. She served as a librarian, archivist and Gaelic instructor at the College of Cape Breton (now Cape Breton University), where she founded the Beaton Institute.

Belfast, Prince Edward Island. Lord Selkirk sponsored a settlement of displaced Highlanders in 1803 to Belfast on Prince Edward Island. Today the area consists of numerous settlements, including Iona and Culloden.

Ben Bragghie, statue of. A monument in honour of the first Duke of Sutherland, it was erected in 1836 on Ben Bragghie, located northwest of the Highland town of Golspie; the statue overlooks the village and Dunrobin Castle. The statue was carved by Joseph Theakston, based on a model by the well-known English sculptor Francis Chantrey. Although James Loch sought out subscribers from the Duke's "grateful tenantry," not surprisingly his efforts were less than successful. Instead, the monies to build the statue came from Loch's own constituency, including the notorious factor Patrick Sellar himself. The Duke's back is turned against the land that he cleared. Nine meters in height, it sits on a plinth of sandstone, and remains a source of ongoing controversy. Over the years there have been calls to tear down the statue and to erect a commemorative plaque to the victims of the Highland Clearances in its place.

Benbecula. In 1841, Col. Gordon of Cluny, a wealthy landowner and entrepreneur from Aberdeen, bought Benbecula, South Uist and Barra from the bankrupt Clanranald. A decade later, Gordon evicted 1,500 people from these islands, after the potato famine and forced them—some were bound hand and foot—to board emigrant ships. Contemporary Canadian newspapers compared the poverty of these emigrants unfavourably with paupers from the Irish poorhouses.

Bennett, Margaret (b. 1946). Writer, folklorist, ethnologist, broadcaster and singer; Bennett was born and grew up on the Isle of Skye in a culture rich in singing, dancing and storytelling. In the late 1950s the family moved to the Isle of Lewis and then to Shetland in 1963. Soon thereafter her father, a civil engineer, emigrated to Newfoundland. Bennett worked as an elementary school teacher in St. John's between 1967-1968. She spent a year as a folklorist for the Museum of Man (now the Canadian Museum of Civilization). From 1984 to 1995 she was lecturer in Scottish Ethnology at the School of Scottish Studies at the University of Edinburgh. Since 1995 she has been a lecturer in folklore at the Royal Scottish Academy of Music and Drama in Glasgow. Her books include *The Last Stronghold: Scottish Gaelic Traditions in Newfoundland* (1989), *Oatmeal and Catechism: Scottish Gaelic Settlers in Quebec* (1999) and *Scottish Customs from the Cradle to the Grave* (1993). In 2007 she made available in digital form *Love and Loss—Remembering Martyn in Scotland's Music*, a homage to her son, the musician Martyn Bennett.

Bennett, Martyn (1971-2005). Musician; the son of the noted Scottish folklorist and Gaelic singer Margaret Bennett. Born in St. John's, Newfoundland, Bennett grew up among Gaelic-speaking farmers in

Newfoundland's Codroy Valley before his parents moved to Québec. When he was a young boy, his parents separated and he moved to Scotland, first to Mull and then to the Highland town of Kingussie.

A self-proclaimed musical alchemist, Bennett's interests were many, ranging from the oral tradition of Romany gypsies as well as the Gaelic bards and storytellers. At 15, he enrolled at the City School of Music in Edinburgh, which was affiliated with Broughton High School. In 1990 he was trained in classical violin and piano at the Royal Scottish Academy of Music and Drama in Glasgow while maintaining his interest in playing sessions in local pubs.

An idiosyncratic multi-instrumentalist—he played the pipes and the fiddle, among other instruments—Bennett blended a unique mixture of musical styles, including hip-hop and house music interspersed with traditional Scots music.

Bennett's first album, the eponymous *Martyn Bennett* was released in 1995. An influential album it fused folk melodies and sampling with pipes and fiddling. His most important work was the trailblazing *Bothy Music* (1998), an inventive hybrid of traditional Gaelic music, house and hip-hop sampling. One selection, "Hallaig," features a recitation of the poem by its author, the Gaelic poet Sorley Maclean. *Glen Lyon* consists of a song cycle exploring his family's history which also featured the singing of his mother, the noted folklorist Margaret Bennett, while *Grit* includes sampled speech and songs from Highland travellers. His last work, *Mackay's Memoirs*, was released on April 15, 2005, by the City of Edinburgh Music School. A composition for pipes, clàrsach and orchestra, the work was commissioned for the opening of the Scottish Parliament on July 1, 1999, and written in honour of the late Dr. Kenneth A. Mackay of Badenoch. The composition is built around a theme of the pibroch "Lament for Mary MacLeod" and opens with Psalm 121. It was recorded the morning after Bennett's death by students at Broughton High School.

Bennett was one of the finest of the younger generation of Scots folk musicians before his life was cut short by illness. Before graduating from the Royal Scottish Academy Bennett was diagnosed with testicular cancer and later with Hodgkin's lymphoma. He was only 34 when he died in February 2005.

Bentham, Jeremy (1748-1832). English philosopher and social reformer and founder of modern utilitarianism, a theory that believes in the greatest good for the greatest number of people, a philosophy that proved influential among the Improvers; that is, supporters of the Clearances. To follow this way of thinking to its logical conclusion, as many at the time did, is to believe that since the Highlanders were considered indolent, and hence "useless"; they were an obstacle to progress and, therefore, had to be removed.

Bernera Riot. Crofters on the island of Bernera, Loch Roag, Lewis, in the spring of 1874, resisted against the power of the landlords. It was considered a turning point in the Highland land wars of the 19th century, a "war" that ultimately led to agrarian reform. The dispute was over summer grazings used by the Bernera islanders in Uig, on the Lewis mainland.

The crofters lost their grazings in 1872 when it became part of a sporting estate and instead were given moorland that once belonged to the farm of Earshader. They were ordered to erect a dyke that would separate their grazings from another estate. This they did but then they were told that they would lose their grazings anyway and were to receive instead the grazings on a farm on Bernera. They refused to move, however. The factor, Donald Munro, tried to persuade them to accept the new offer. Allegedly, Munro even threated to evict them. In March 1874, a sheriff-officer from Stornoway, Colin MacLennan, served 58 summons of removal. Later that night he was attacked by a crowd of youngsters. The following morning he was involved in another conflict, this one with a group of men. The authorities decided to arrest the men who assaulted the officer.

The Bernera Riot thus refers to the time when the authories tried to arrest one of the men accused in the assault, Angus MacDonald, and were prevented from doing so. Later some 130 Bernera men travelled to Stornoway to try to free MacDonald. The group later went to Stornoway and sought a meeting with the landlord, Sir James Matheson. With their request granted, they told Matheson about the threats of eviction by Munro. Three Bernera crofters were tried at Stornoway Sheriff Court in July 1874, and acquitted. Derick Thomson has called Bernera a "breakthrough in the crofters' struggle for security." At another trial the sheriff officer was fined for assault. After the trials, the grazings in Earshader were returned to the men.

A cairn commemorates the conflict.

Bettyhill, Sutherland. Coastal village in Sutherland where many Clearance Highlanders settled following the evictions at Strathnaver.

Black House Museum. On the Isle of Lewis is located in the township of Arnol. Fully furnished, it consists of an attached barn, byre and stockyard. A peat fire burns in the open hearth while a three-legged pot hangs over the flames. The low-lying blackhouse was the traditional dwelling in the Highlands and Islands until fairly modern times. Indeed, the last occupants of this particular black house left as recently as 1964.

blackhouse. A traditional dwelling in the Highlands and Islands that typically had double dry-stone walls with thatched turf roof. The floor consisted of flagstones and a central hearth for the fire. People shared their living quarters with animals: the people at one end, the animals at another with a partition between them.

Black, Rev. John (1818-1882). First Presbyterian minister in the Canadian West; born in the parish of Eskdale Muir in the Scottish borders, the son of a shepherd farmer. After immigrating to New York in 1841, he entered the ministry and attended what later became Knox College in Toronto. Black was persuaded to go to the Red River settlement in what is now Manitoba even though he did not know Gaelic. Prior to his arrival the Hudson's Bay Company provided a plot of land to the Presbyterian community. In 1853 Kildonan Church was built on this property. Black established a school next to the church which later became known as Manitoba College and eventually the University of Manitoba. The John Black Memorial Church is located in North Kildonan.

Blackie, John Stuart (1809-1895). Born in Glasgow and educated at Aberdeen Grammar School and Edinburgh and Aberdeen universities, in 1834 Blackie was called to the bar although he never actually practised law. A scholar of considerable renown, he was Professor of Humanities at Aberdeen from 1841 to 1852 and of Greek at Edinburgh until 1882. A Scottish nationalist, he helped raise funds for the endowment of a Celtic chair at Edinburgh. Blackie famously championed the Gaelic language in the 1870s and 1880s.

Blair, Rev. Duncan Black (1815-1893). Born in 1815 in Strachur, Argyllshire, Blair moved in early childhood to the Ardgour area and subsequently to Badenoch. He entered Divinity Hall in Edinburgh in 1840 and was licensed to preach in 1844. He was in Mull in 1845, but moved to Pictou, Nova Scotia, the following year. He was in Ontario from May 1847 to October 1848. He returned to Scotland and married Mary Sibella MacLean in 1851, then came back to Canada as minister of the Presbyterian congregation of Barney's River and Blue Mountain, Pictou County.

Alexander MacLean Sinclair described Blair as "an excellent linguist, a good poet, and a devout man. As an accurate writer of Gaelic he had no superior." In Gaelic, Blair composed sacred poems, laments and secular poems and songs, totalling some 16,650 lines. Articles on the Clearances, poems and travelogues were published in *Mac-Talla* and other Gaelic publications.

blame. A sensitive and controversial topic when it comes to the Clearances. Even today people still take sides. In one corner, sat the Clearance deniers; in another the Clearance revisionists. The deniers believe that state "intervention" would make the situation worse. Let the free market play out in its own good time. According to this theory, the landlords were not villains but rather the agents of inevitable change who tried in their own, imperfect way to lessen the blow. On the other hand, revisionists offer nothing but criticism toward landlordism, declaring the Clearances an avoidable tragedy whose causes, according to Neal Ascherson, "were stupidity and improvidence as much as greed for cash."

See also Fry, Michael

Bliadhna nan Caorach (Year of the Sheep) (1792). *See* Year of the Sheep

The Blood Is Strong (film). Influential Grampian television documentary (1988) about the Clearances and the subsequent Gaelic diaspora co-written by Angus Peter Campbell. The soundtrack contains music written for three television programs. In addition to *The Blood Is Strong*, it includes *A Prince Among Islands*, a documentary about Prince Charles Edward Stuart's return to the Isle of Bernaray, off the coast of Lewis and *Highlanders*, a program celebrating the history and heritage of the Highlands, narrated by Sean Connery.

Boreraig, Skye. The 1853 clearance of Boreraig in southwest Skye is considered among the most ruthless. First, it occurred during the bitter cold. Women and children with their possessions were thrown out in the snow and their doors nailed up. Worse, the people had been moved at least twice, in 1849 and 1852. Subsequently, they were unable to support themselves and were thus in arrears. In 1853 the tenants were offered assisted emigration or removal to yet another part of the Macdonald estate. Although no one wanted to emigrate, according to Richards, eight families chose to move to another location on the estate. The remaining families, ten of them, were ordered to leave in October 1853. The little resistance that the tenants put up was quickly resolved (even so, three people were brought to trial and charged with obstruction of justice) and, as was the usual custom, the dwellings were razed so that the tenants would not return.

"Boston States." A Canadian term referring to the migration that has taken place over the decades from Nova Scotia to New England.

Boswell, James (1740-1795). Man of letters and biographer of Dr. Samuel Johnson. Born in Edinburgh, Boswell was the eldest son of a judge, Lord Auchinleck, and was educated at the University of Edinburgh. A man of often insatiable appetites—for knowledge as well as sexual experience—he wrote a remarkably frank and at times shockingly explicit account of his early days in London. It was there where, in the backroom of Tom Davies's bookshop on May 16, 1763, he met Dr. Johnson. It was Johnson of course who accompanied Boswell to the Highlands and Islands of Scotland in 1773. Boswell published his version of the famous journey as *The Journal of the Tour of the Hebrides* in 1785. He is best known as being the author of the magisterial *Life of Samuel Johnson* in 1791.

In his *Journal*, Boswell recalls a memorable incident while on Skye, that reflected the "epidemic of emigration" engulfing the island:

> In the evening the company danced as usual. We performed, with much activity, a dance, which, I suppose, the emigration from Sky has occasioned. They call it America. Each of the couple, after the common involutions and evolutions, successively whirls round in a circle, till all are in motion; and the dance seems intended to show how emigration catches, till a whole neighbourhood is set afloat.

The emigration that Boswell witnessed was more or less organized by displaced and unhappy tacksmen, the gentry of Highlands and Islands society, who chartered ships and often arranged for the mass departure of entire communities.

Brahan Seer. (Coinneach Odhar or "Sallow Kenneth") The archetypal seer of Gaelic tradition. A plaque on the shore near Chanonry Lighthouse near the town of Fortrose commemorates the burning at the stake in 1660 of Kenneth MacKenzie, the Brahan Seer, Scotland's equivalent of Nostradamus. He made many prophecies about the Highlands. A book of his prophecies was published in 1896.

His name derives from Brahan Castle, a Mackenzie stronghold in Ross-shire. His legend was carried from Ross-shire to Lewis, where he was allegedly born. Among his prophecies included the coming of the "black rain," which came to be interpreted as acid rain or, more likely, North Sea oil.

See also Thomas the Rhymer

Brill, Kenny (b. 1950). Singer-songwriter born in St. Andrews; composer of the 1985 Clearances song, "Gilmartin." Although the character of Gilmartin is modelled after the notorious factor Patrick Sellar—"there were many others who would fit the bill," said Brill—he was actually inspired by a real person. During the 1960s, Brill's ex-wife was working as a "tattie howker" in Fife under the supervision of a certain farmer named Gilmartin. A fellow worker, a woman from a travelling family, looked up at the stern farmer and uttered the memorable phrase, "You're a hard man, Gilmartin," a line which is repeated throughout the song. As it turns out, Brill's forebears, the Mackays, had moved from Strathnaver to the Loch Carron area prior to the infamous Sutherland Clearances so "the link was there." Brill spent half a dozen years working in Sutherland, which only fortified the connection. "Scotland is a small country with an uncomfortable history," he says, "and natives with long memories." The song has been in circulation among Scots singers since the 1980s. It was sung by Christine Kydd in a production by Janet Fenton at the Edinburgh Theatre Workshop. More recently, the Scots singer-songwriter David Ferrard sings it on his 2009 recording *Across the Troubled Wave*.

brochs. Circular dry-stone structures.

Bruce, James (1808-1861). Journalist and author; a native of Aberdeen, Bruce was editor of the *Fifeshire Journal* from 1840 to 1847. He was also the editor of several other papers, including the *Northern Whig*. In 1847, the *Scotsman* hired him as a "special commissioner" to investigate the conditions and causes of destitution in the Highlands. In a series of letters published in the newspaper, which were later published in pamphlet form under the title "Letters on the Present Condition of the Highlands and Islands of Scotland," he wrote about what he witnessed firsthand. On his journey, he toured the isles of Mull and Skye and Ross-shire on the mainland between January and March; from this he wrote fifteen letters. One inhabitant of Skye complained about mile after mile of sheep farms "and no room for any work at home." While stuck on Mull during some bad weather, Bruce expressed contempt for "the ugly and offensive language of Ossian" and visited several "miserable huts." The more he saw, the less apparently he liked.

> I know that what is called working in the Highlands would be called play in the Lowlands ... it is a fact that morally and intellectually they are an inferior race to the Lowland Saxon—and that before they can in a civisiled age be put in a condition to provide for themselves and not to be throwing themselves on the charity of the hard-working Lowlander, the race must be improved by a Lowland intermixture; their habits ...must be broken up by the force of Lowland example....

The Highlanders, in other words, were useless in a civilized Britain. The solution to their predicament: to intermingle with a better quality of people, that is, Lowlanders; or, better yet, change their nature altogether. He suggested two ways: (1) by abolishing the cottar system and (2) through education (although he was skeptical about the intellectual qualities of the Highlander). Like many non-Gaels of his generation and class, he equated the Gaels with the savage tribes of other lands.

Burt, Edmund (d. 1755). served with General Wade in Scotland from 1724 to 1728 as an army contractor. His visit to the Highlands occurred some forty years before Samuel Johnson although his *Letters from a Gentleman in the North of Scotland* was not published until 1754. He described the terrible conditions under which they lived. Burt considered the Highlanders lazy, yet his account is not entirely unsympathetic. In fact, it was rather generous for its time. Their situation did not derive from their nature, he believed, but rather due to a lack of opportunities. At one point, he even compared their plight to that of "negroes" rather than "natives of Britain."

C

Caithness. Like its southern neighbours, Caithness has its share of abandoned villages, including Broubster. In 1838, 27 families were evicted from Broubster and 31 families from Shurrery. Additional evictions in Caithness took place at Buldoo and Achreamie in the 1840s. In addition, some 67 families were evicted around Dounreay, now the site of the nuclear test site, as well as at Skiall and Borrowston. In sum, approximately 170 families were cleared between the late 1830s and 1860. In 1835, Sinclair of Freswick cleared 107 families at Badfern. Other clearance sites in Caithness included Olrig, just south of Castletown, Dunnet, West Greenland, Lochend, Hollandmake and Reaster.

The most notorious Clearance site in Caithness took place at Babdea.

See also Badbea

Caledonian Canal. Considered one of the greatest public works of its time, the 100 km (62 mile) Caledonian Canal connected the east and west coasts of Scotland by way of the Great Glen, from Inverness on the east to Corpach near Fort William on the west, making it possible for ships to sail through to and from these destinations. From a Clearances context, the Canal was intended to create employment in the Highlands and thus to reduce emigration. Constructed by the great Scots engineer Thomas Telford, the canal took twenty years to complete, employing as many as 3,000 workers.

Calgary, Isle of Mull (*Cala ghearraidh*, or beach of the meadow) Cleared in 1812; many of the evictees emigrated to what came to be known as Calgary, Alberta. Above Calgary Bay are ruins of the deserted Clearance village of Inivey.

See also Mull, Isle of

"Calum's Road" (Capercaillie). An original tune written by the Scots folk rock band Capercaillie inspired by the Raasay crofter Calum MacLeod, it appears on the soundtrack of the Scottish television documentary *The Blood Is Strong*, originally released in 1988 and reissued in 1995.

See also Calum MacLeod

Calum's Road (novel and play). In 2011, the National Theatre of Scotland and Communicado Theatre Company presented *Calum's Road* by the Scottish playwright David Harrower and directed by Gerry Mulgrew, an adaptation of Roger Hutchinson's book of the same name about Calum MacLeod, the Raasay crofter and his Quixotic task to build a road on the edge of the world with his own two hands. MacLeod was portrayed by Iain Macrae. Written from the perspective of MacLeod's daughter, the play tells the story of a man who with a pick, shovel and wheelbarrow constructed the road that now bears his name. The play was performed to mostly positive reviews throughout Scotland, including the Tron Theatre in Glasgow, Eden Court in Inverness, and, most poignantly, culminating in a performance at the Raasay Community Hall on Raasay in November 2011. The play included a score by the Scots musician/actor Alasdair Macrae, who has also appeared in the National Theatre of Scotland's *The Strange Undoing of Prudencia Hart*.

Cameron, Hugh (1835-1918). Scottish painter; influenced by fellow Scot David Wilkie as well as Dutch and French genre painting. One of his works, *Toiler of the Hills*, depicts a female Highland labourer. Significantly, it appears on the Canongate Classics cover of Iain Crichton Smith's Clearances novel *Consider the Lilies*. His best known painting, though, is the poignant *A Lonely Life* (1873) in which a Highland woman, her face partly covered by a red scarf, holds twigs for the fire in one hand, while opening the door to her humble thatched-roofed Highland cottage under a twilight sky. A basket lies on the red-hued dirt.

Campbell, Angus Peter (b. 1952). Poet, novelist, journalist, broadcaster and actor; born and brought up in South Uist; taught English by Iain Crichton Smith at Oban High School. Campbell graduated in Politics and History from Edinburgh University where Sorley Maclean was a writer-in-residence at the time (he makes clear that although Maclean was never his teacher, he did encourage his work). In 2001 he was awarded the Bardic Crown for Gaelic poetry. The following year he received the Creative Scotland Award for Literature and in 2008 was nominated for a BAFTA Best Actor Award for the lead role in *Seachd: The Inaccessible Pinnacle*, a Gaelic-language film set on Skye.

He worked at various times as a lobster-fisherman, forester and a builder's apprentice. After graduating from Edinburgh he pursued a career in journalism. He worked for many years for the *West Highland Free Press*, as a radio journalist on BBC Radio Highland and as a television journalist and editor with Grampian Television. An internationalist poet in spirit and perspective, he uses poetry as a great international language.

Campbell, a Gael and self-proclaimed socialist and Christian, believes that language can be used as a political weapon. "If you really want to conquer and enslave a people you must first make sure that they lose a grip on that which gives them a sense of self: their culture and language," he has said. Campbell's first English language work of fiction, *Invisible Islands* (2006), was inspired by Italo Calvino and Jorge Luis Borges. It draws heavily on Gaelic culture and history as well as magic realism. He has also written a short English language novel, *Archie and the North Wind* (2010), a fable-like picaresque novel that combines elements of magical realism and Highland folklore.

Campbell sees a commonality in South American and Gaelic traditions, in that both cultures find truth in the doctrine of transubstantiation, referring to the belief in the Roman Catholic and Eastern Orthodox traditions that the Eucharistic elements at consecration become the body and blood of Christ. "You flung an apple behind you, and it turned into a forest, then into a lake, then into a fire, to separate you from the pursuing dragon," he told the *Scottish Review of Books*. "I grew up in a community where such stories were both real and true."

In 1992 Campbell published *The Greatest Gift*, an English-language collection and the first of several volumes of poetry. Subsequent poetry collections have appeared in English, Gaelic and Scots, including *One Road* (1994) and *Aibisidh* (2011), in which he considers the fragmentation of language and identity in the modern digitized age. He has also written several novels, *An Oidhche Mus Do Sheol Sinn* (The Night before We Sailed) (2003) and *Là a' Deanamh Sgeil Do Là* (Day Speaketh Unto Day) (2004).

As an actor Campbell has appeared in Iain Finlay MacLeod's play *Somersault*s, presented by the National Theatre of Scotland, about the survival of language—the Gaelic language in particular—as seen through the eyes of a wealthy banker living in London whose father is dying back home in Lewis. Campbell played the father in a performance that received critical acclaim. In addition, Campbell co-wrote the script for the Scottish television documentary *The Blood Is Strong* and wrote the text for the accompanying booklet.

Campbell's poetry is universal and particular; its timeless themes include identity, time and memory, faith, language, history and what it means to be a Gael in the contemporary world. The Clearances figure prominently in many of his poems, including "Human Rights," "Do Unto Others," "Speaking to Me of Culloden," "Conversion," "This Same Moon," "A Cave in Drumnadrochit" and, especially, "The Highlands."

Campbell, John Francis (1821-1885). Of Islay; as a boy he learned Gaelic from another John Campbell, a piper on his father's estate. He studied law, although he never practised it, and became a civil servant, including a position as Private Secretary to the Duke of Argyll in 1854, as well as other prominent positions. He is best known today as a collector of Gaelic tales and folklore. The most famous of his works is *Popular Tales of the West Highlands* (1860-1862).

Campbell, John Lorne (1906-1996). Historian, folklorist and pioneer preservationist of Gaelic song and Gaelic tales; the eldest son of Col. Duncan Campbell of Inverneill on Loch Fyne and Ethel Waterbury, of New Jersey. Campbell read Rural Economy at St. John's College, Oxford, under Professor Sir James Scott Watson, and Celtic under Professor John Fraser of Jesus College. He arrived on the Isle of Barra in August 1933, to study the crofting conditions there. Among his colleagues and acquaintances were Compton Mackenzie and John Macpherson, the Gaelic storyteller (as well as country councillor and postmaster), also known as "the Coddy."

Campbell's first book, *Highlands Songs of the Forty-Five*, was published in 1933. Among his other important works include *The Book of Barra* (1936), *Tales of Barra, as Told by the Coddy* (1960), *Stories from South Uist as Told by Angus MacLellan* (1961), *Canna: The Story of a Hebridean Island* (1986) and *Songs Remembered in Exile* (1990), based on the work he collected while in Cape Breton and eastern Canada. During a period of 30 or so years, Campbell gathered a sound recording archive of some 1,500 Gaelic songs and 350 folktales. In addition, he was instrumental in the founding of the Folklore Institute of Scotland (FIOS), whose purpose was to "lobby for" the official recognition of Gaelic as a valid oral tradition in Scotland. Ultimately, the FIOS led to the creation of the School of Scottish Studies at Edinburgh University in 1951. Campbell endowed copies of more than 300 of his own recordings of traditional Gaelic songs to the archive. Campbell's three-volume collection of Hebridean folk songs (with Francis Collinson), *Hebridean Folksong*, published between 1969 and 1981, is still considered a vital resource by musicians and folklorists alike. In 1938 Campbell bought the islands of Canna and Sanday. Four years earlier he met Margaret Fay Shaw, a native of Glenshaw, Pennsylvania, while in South Uist where she was collecting traditional Gaelic songs. He married her the following year.

In 1981 Campbell bequeathed the Isle of Canna to the National Trust for Scotland (NHS), along with his library, archives and sound recordings, even as he and Shaw continued to live on the island. She remained at Canna House until her own death in 2004 at the remarkable age of 101. Ray Perman published a biography of Campbell, *The Man Who Gave Away His Island*, in 2010.

"**Canadian Boat Song.**" Anonymous poem that appeared in *Blackwood's Edinburgh Magazine* in 1829; it epitomizes the alleged inconsolable suffering of the Scottish exiles that pined for the homes they left behind in the Hebrides. Lines from the poem have been used numerous times for titles of documentaries on the emigrant experience (*The Blood Is Strong*) to memoirs (Vivian Innes Letson's *The Heart Is Highland: A True Story of Scots in Early Wyoming*). Another memoir, *The Highland Heart in Nova Scotia*, by Neil MacNeil uses the song as an epigraph, citing the Scots-Canadian novelist John Galt as the author. Robert Louis Stevenson quoted it in his California travelogue, *The Silverado Squatters* (1883) while, closer to our own time, Alistair MacLeod quotes from it in his novel *No Great Mischief* (1999).

> From the lone shieling of the misty island
> Mountains divide us, and the waste of seas—
> Yet still the blood is strong, the heart is Highland,
> And we in dreams behold the Hebrides.

The author of the song remains a bone of contention. Although said to have been translated from the Gaelic when it was first published, there is no evidence to indicate that is the case. Numerous names have been attached to it over the years, including Sir Walter Scott, John Galt, James Hogg, John Wilson, David Macbeth Moir and John Gibson Lockhart. The poem was set to music later. In June 1849 the poem appeared again, in slightly altered form, in *Tait's Edinburgh Magazine*. The fourth stanza of the poem referred to the Clearances:

> When the bold kindred, in the time long-vanish'd,
> Conquer'd the soil and fortified the keep,—
> No seer foretold the children would be banish'd,
> That a degenerate Lord might boast his sheep:
> Fair these broad meads—these hoary woods are grand;
> But we are exiles from our fathers' land.

An alternate version reads:

> When the bold kindred, in the time long vanish'd,
> Gather'd on many a Scottish battle-field,
> No seer foretold the children would be banish'd
> Proscrib'd the tartan plaid and studded shield.

Canna, Isle of. In 1938 the Gaelic scholar and folklorist John Lorne Campbell bought the Isle of Canna for £9,000. Many years later, in 1981, he bequeathed the island to the National Trust for Scotland (NTS) in perpetuity. The island experienced an early case of the Clearances in 1793, when several hundred people were evicted to make way for sheep. A'Chill, the island's main settlement, was cleared in 1851. In 1881, the owner, Donald MacNeil sold the island to Robert Thom, a Glasgow ship owner who in turn sold the island to Campbell in 1938.

Cape Breton Island. Almost 20,000 Highlanders immigrated to Cape Breton from 1802 to the early 1840s. Roman Catholics from West Inverness-shire and South Uist, Barra, Eigg and Canna began arriving as early as 1791. Direct migration from Scotland to Cape Breton began in 1802, with the arrival of 340 Catholic emigrants from the Clanranald estate in Moidart on the ship *Northern Friends*, which arrived in Sydney Harbour (a cairn and plaque commemorates these first arrivals from Scotland to Cape Breton). According to Michael Newton, parts of eastern Nova Scotia and Cape Breton "became solidly Gaelic in composition, so much so that even English merchants learnt Gaelic in order to conduct business." Indeed, by 1814 Highlanders comprised about half of the island's population. Many, if not most of these Highland Scots, came from Sutherland, Inverness-shire and the Western Isles. Cape Breton's Scottish population grew rapidly. By 1871, notes Lucille Campey, people of Scots descent outnumbered the rest of the island population by as much as two to one. Once they settled in their new home, most Scots emigrants segregated themselves according to their faith. Earlier to arrive, Catholics generally settled along the Western Shore and the east side of Bras d'Or; Presbyterians, who as a group arrived later, settled mainly in the backlands.

Overall, then, the vast majority of Cape Breton's Scottish immigrants came from the Western Isles, particularly Barra, North Uist and Harris as well as Rum and Skye.

See also the *Hector*; Nova Scotia

Cape Fear, North Carolina. Among the first of the Gaels to immigrate to the Cape Fear region of North Carolina was Neil MacNeil of Kintyre. Conservative at heart and loyal to authority, the Carolina Highlanders enlisted under the banner of King George III. Around 1767 another and larger Highland migration from Arran, Jura, Islay and Gigha began to settle in the Cape Fear Valley region.

But the best known of the early Highland settlements to the region was the Argyll Colony, when the first of the settlers arrived in 1739. The Argyll Colony was for some time the largest settlement of Highlanders outside of Scotland. New emigrants continued to arrive in the area until the early decades of the 19th century.

Leaders of the Argyll Colony petitioned in 1739 for a Presbyterian clergyman who could speak Gaelic. According to Michael Newton, a total of ten Gaelic-speaking ministers were brought over from Scotland. But the church tended to promote English which led to the further decline of Gaelic in the region.

Campelltown, now called Fayetteville, was the largest Highland settlement in the Carolinas. The city continues to remember its Highland roots with a plaque that commemorates "the settlement of the Upper Cape Fear by the Highland Scotch."

See also Argyll Colony

Capercaillie Scottish folk rock band founded in Argyll during the 1980s by keyboardist and accordionist Donald Shaw, but best known for the haunting vocals of singer Karen Matheson (b. 1963). The band takes its name from the capercaillie, or wood grouse, a native bird of Scotland. Their first album, *Cascade*, which was released in 1984, was emblematic of their style: a fusion of traditional Gaelic songs and music with modern and often highly innovative arrangements. Their 1992 recording, *A Prince Among Islands*, was the first Scots-Gaelic song to reach the U.K. Top-40 singles chart.

Among their other recordings include *Crosswinds* (1987), the soundtrack to the Scottish television documentary on the Highland diaspora *The Blood Is Strong* (1988), *Sidewaulk* (1989), *Delirium* (1991), *Secret People* (1993), *To the Moon* (1996), *Beautiful Wasteland* (1997), *Glenfinnan (Songs of the '45)* (1998), *Nàdurra* (2000), *Choice Language* (2003) and *Roses and Tears* (2008). Matheson has also recorded several solo albums, including *the dreaming sea* (1996), *Time to Fall* (2002) and *Downriver* (2005). Matheson is featured on the soundtrack to the motion picture *Rob Roy* (1995), and even performs on screen in the film.

Carinish (North Uist). A major centre of learning in the Middle Ages, the area today consists of the ruined 13th-century remains of an importiant ecclesticial site founded by Beatrice, the daughter of Somerled, Lord of the Isles. Further south is the Field of Blood, the site of the last battle fought in North Uist, which took place in 1601 and consisted of a skirmish between the Macdonalds of North Uist and the MacLeods of Harris.

Carmichael, Alexander (1832-1912). Born in Lismore; Scottish writer and folklorist best known for his important multi-volume work *Carmina Gadelica*, a collection of prayers, hymns, charms, incantations, blessings, runes and folkloric poems and songs collected and translated by Carmichael in the Gàidhealach between 1855 and 1910. Originally published in six volumes over many decades, a one-volume, English-language edition was released in 1992. Although criticized by some for its somewhat arch-Victorian tendencies—others also questioned its accuracy and authenticity—it is nevertheless still considered a major achievement in Scottish folklore. An interesting sidenote: Carmichael testified before the Napier Commission in 1883 on farming customs in the Outer Hebrides.

Carruthers, Robert Mackay. Influential editor of the medium-sized newspaper, the *Inverness Courier*, which dubbed itself as the "newspaper of the Highlands." Carruthers was a great advocate of the Clearances. In an editorial that appeared in the *Courier* on August 20, 1845, he argued that the Clearances were beneficial because they gave Highlanders "the same chances of improvement as the rest of the civilised world," instead of allowing them to exist in "the same semi-barbarous state in which they slumbered for ages."

Unlike other journalists of his time, though, Carruthers had no patience for race-baiting. Whereas many blamed the Highland problem on the traits of the Highlanders themselves, Carruthers disagreed with reports in the *Times* in the mid-1840s—and other newspapers—that the Highlanders were "unimprovable." Although, like others of his class and status, Carruthers believed the Highlanders were inferior and lazy he blamed their condition on their circumstances not on their inherent nature. His paper, thus, advocated land improvement. The remedy to the intractable "Highland problem," he offered, was not eviction or emigration, but rather to "cultivate the waste lands, drain, trench, and improve, and thus create food and labour."

caschrom. Foot plough, a tool used in the Highlands and Islands for the preparation and cultivation of the soil.

Celtic revival. *See* Highlandism

Central Board of Management for Highland Relief. Established in February 1847 to coordinate the work of existing relief committees, it was led by Sir Charles Trevelyan, Assistant Secretary to the Treasury. It consisted of three charities, the Free Church of Scotland, the Edinburgh Relief Committee and the Glasgow Relief Committee. Two main committees were based in Glasgow and Edinburgh: Glasgow managed relief operations in Argyll, western Inverness and the Outer and Inner Hebrides (except Skye); Edinburgh handled Skye, Wester Ross, Orkney, Shetland and the eastern Highlands. Food was distributed primarily through the landlords. It was not given freely, however, but rather as a form of payment for labour; that is, there would be no food without labour. "The fact that no great mass of people died from starvation was largely due to the efforts of the committees, the Free Church, charities and landlords," argues Krisztina Fenyö.

Centre for History. Located in Dornoch; part of the University of the Highlands and Islands (UHI). The Centre offers courses and programs at the undergraduate and postgraduate level as well as a wide range of short courses. During the 2012-2013 academic year it offered a postgraduate master (MLitt) in the history of the Highlands and Islands, including modules on "Contemplating the Clearances" by Dr. Elizabeth Ritchie. Other modules reference the Clearances. The "Arguments and Alternatives: Models, Interpretations and Debates in Highlands and Islands History" module by Dr. David Worthington, for example, discusses the Napier Commission as a case study while "(Re)Presenting Highland History" by Dr. Issie MacPhail explores the Clearances and Improvement. Another module, taught by Dr. Jim MacPherson, "The Diaspora," assesses the diasporized Highland and Island communities around the world, from the U.S. to Canada to Australia.

Centre for Mountain Studies. Established at Perth College, which is part of the University of the Highlands and Islands (UHI), in August 2000. Its objective is to create a centre for work in mountain areas within the Highlands and Islands region. Its primary goals include undertaking original research, disseminating and discussing knowledge to develop research agendas, contributing to policy-making processes and developing academic courses and training.

Cheviot sheep. Introduced to the Highlands by Sir John Sinclair of Ulbster, president of the Board of Agriculture, when he brought them to Ross and Cromarty in 1790. As its name suggests, the sheep came from the Cheviot Hills, the border country between England and Scotland. A breed of white-faced sheep, the four-footed clansmen, as they came to be called, was a sturdy mix that yielded more wool and meat—thus allowing sheep farmers to pay twice the rent on land previously grazed by blackface sheep—and had the stamina to survive the harsh Highland winters.

The Cheviot, the Stag and the Black Black Oil: A Ceilidh Play with Scenes Songs and Music of Highland History from the Clearances to the Oil Strike. A biting, clever, entertaining and satirical piece of agit-prop theatre, with songs and music, by the English playwright John McGrath. In thirty-three sharply written pages, McGrath argues that the legacy of the Clearances is still with us but instead of "improvers" and "improvement" we have "developers" and "development." If during the height of the Clearances, Strathnaver was exploited for its land, in the 20th century the oil from the North Sea has whet the appetite of business leaders. The messages may have changed, McGrath contends, but the attitudes have not.

The play, which was "given its first public airing" at the "What kind of Scotland?" conference in Edinburgh in April 1973 and first performed in Aberdeen at the Arts Centre, was conceived in the form of a traditional Highland ceilidh. The intent of the play is to show not only why the Clearances occurred ("because the forces of capitalism were stronger than the organisation of the people," McGrath writes) but also that the future is not necessarily pre-determined; that is, there are alternatives.

Many of the major figures of the Clearances era are featured as characters in the play, including Patrick Sellar, James Loch, Mary MacPherson, Harriet Beecher Stowe, Donald Macleod and Lord Selkirk while significant moments in Clearances history are reenacted or referenced, such as the resistance at the Battle of the Braes; evictions in Sollas, North Uist; Glencalvie; Greenyards; and Suisinish on Skye. The most chilling re-enactment is the eviction of Mrs. Chisholm by Sellar himself at Strathnaver, and Sellar's subsequent trial and acquittal in Inverness. The play concludes with a question, "Have we learnt anything from the Clearances?" asks one character. Various characters sum up Highland history with their responses. "When the Cheviot came, the landlords benefited," says one. "When the Stag came, only the upper-class sportsmen benefited," says another. Finally, "the Black Black Oil is coming," observes yet another. She fears that only the multinational corporations and local speculators will reap the rewards. *The Cheviot* was presented throughout the Highlands and Islands.

Although the play acknowledged the losses and tragedies of Gaelic culture, McGrath made clear than he did not want this play to be a long lament. He resolved "that ... for every defeat, we would also celebrate a victory, for each sadness, we would wipe it out with the sheer energy and vitality of the people, for every oppression, a way to fight back."

children's literature on the Clearances. Despite the dark subject matter a number of fine children's and/or young adult books have been written on the Clearances. They include *The Desperate Journey* by Kathleen Fidler, *A Pistol in Greenyards* by Mollie Hunter, *The Battle of the Braes* by Margaret McPherson and a trilogy by Allan Campbell McLean: *Ribbon of Fire, The Year of the Stranger* and *A Sound of Trumpets*. A book for very young children entitled *Children of the Clearances* by David Ross was first published in 2001 and reprinted several times, including as recently as 2008.

chiefs. Heads of clans.

chieftains. Heads of septs, or branches of clans.

Church of Scotland. With a few exceptions, most Church of Scotland ministers defended the landlowners, threatening the people with damnation if they did not obey. Indeed, ministers often told their congregation that the evictions were in fact God's will. Many parishioners took it to heart. Witness the famous etching that appears on the windowpane at Croick Church in Glencalvie in which they referred to themselves as being members of "the wicked generation."

Many Highlanders broke away from the church which eventually led to the establishment of the Free Church of Scotland. Even as landlords forbid the building of these churches and not to give Free Church ministers shelter or aid, the people continued to defy their orders, choosing to worship in a way they saw fit.

See also Croick Church

cianalas. The Gaelic word for a longing for home.

clachans. Highland townships that were so central to the society of the Highlands and Islands. The clachan formed the Highlander's sense of identity to a particular place and specifically to a particular community; oftentimes inhabitants of these clachans had been living there since time immemorial. Hence, to be evicted from their homes was both devastating and soul-crushing.

clan. Under Brehon law in Gaelic Scotland and Ireland, the term clan, is the anglicization of the Gaelic word for children, *clann*. The traditional relationships between chief and clan were straightforward: the chief would provide protection and a guarantee of land in exchange for allegiance and military service.

The land was owned by the chiefs for their relatives and those people who were affiliated with the chieftain's family. The primary function of the chief was to protect and hold onto the land in order to be able to be ready during times of war. On the other hand, during peacetime, the chief's role was to rear and herd the livestock. Consequently, the chiefs let out their lands as farms to their own relations. These tenants and their descendants held onto the land for generations. In return for the land the tenants were expected to pay a small cash rent and to supply cattle and sheep and free labour. In turn, they sublet part of their farms to their own near-relatives and to others as well. The subletting process culminated in the letting—of what amounted to as huts and grass for grazing goats—to the very poor among them, who actually were the majority. Thus, a large population was dependent on the chief but he was also dependent on them; it formed a complicated and symbiotic relationship. Traditionally, then, the clan system evoked a sense of continuity from generation to generation, the kinship of one generation to another.

The failure of the two Jacobite risings of 1715 and 1745, however, led to profound changes in the relationship between clan and chief. In truth, though, the commercialization of the Highlands and Islands had started long before Culloden. As far back as the previous century, in fact, landlord absenteeism, accumulation of debts and the raising of rents prompted criticism by numerous Gaelic poets.

Clan chiefs seemingly were more interested in acquiring fashionable clothing and fancy digs in Edinburgh and London. What's more, commercial markets down south increased for Highland products which included not only cattle but also timber and slate. The traditional social contract between chief and clan were growing apart. The new chiefs were becoming increasingly anglicized and since the threat of constant war was no longer hanging over their heads they no longer needed a standing army. Rather, more often than not, they needed money to maintain their now increasingly extravagant lifestyles. To be blunt: they acted more like landlords than chiefs.

But little else had changed. The living conditions remained the same as did the living arrangements of the tenants until the chiefs decided that in order to raise revenue they needed to terminate the old leases and made new ones, which usually involved doubling the rents. Many of those with means, commonly known as tacksmen, emigrated, taking their subtenants with them. Rents were doubled again and again; consequently, the majority of the people who remained—the landless poor—were reduced to abject poverty. They were not much better than serfs.

During the late-18th century, sheep farmers, mostly from the Lowlands, offered attractive rents to the Highland landlords. The chiefs usually accepted the generous offers but there was a catch: the sheep farmers demanded empty land to graze their sheep. Consequently, the tenants along with their subtenants and cottars were removed.

It was a perfectly legal procedure. The landless poor, though, still regarded their chief with deference and respect. Given the long-standing relationship between chief and clan, they believed—naively and foolishly perhaps, but apparently in all sincerity—that they had rights to the land. They were grossly mistaken.

They were evicted.

Clan Cameron Museum. Located near Spean Bridge, in the Highlands, has displays on clan and regimental history, a reconstructed 18th-century crofthouse and the ubiquitous presence of Bonnie Prince Charlie.

Clan Donald Centre. An 8,100-ha (20,000-acre) Highland estate located in Armadale, on the Sleat peninsula, on the Isle of Skye, that once part of the traditional lands of Clan Donald. The estate was purchased by the Clan Donald Lands Trust in 1971. The Centre houses the Museum of the Isles, which incorporates the library and study centre, as well as a visitor centre, nature trails and woodland walks, 16 ha (40 acres) of gardens and even accommodations.

clan museums. The first clan museum to open was the Clan MacPherson Museum in Newtonmore in 1952. Other clan museums include the Clan Gunn Museum in Latheron, Caithness; the Clan Cameron Museum in Achnacarry, Inverness-shire; and the Clan MacKay rooms at the Strathnaver Museum in Bettyhill, Sutherland. Although it originally started as a clan museum, the Clan Donald Centre in Armadale, on the Isle of Skye, is more than a museum.

clearance. Use of the word "clearance" dates to at least 1540. Webster's 11th edition offers a particularly urban American definition, calling it "an act or process of clearing" and uses as an example "the removal of buildings from an area (as a city slum)." The term "clearance" was not even used during the Clearances era; "removal" being the preferred terminology by the landlords and a word that was used until at least the 1840s. In fact, it wasn't until 1843 that the word "clearance" was used to refer to the Highland Clearances. The English journalist and social reformer, Henry Mayhew, offered his own definition of the word in 1851: "The clearing of land by the removal of wood, old houses, inhabitants, etc." Prior to that, many instances of "clearing" appeared in the literature of the time. James Loch, one of the instigators behind the Clearances, made reference, for example, to "clearing the hills of people, in order to make sheep walks" as early as 1821. Others, though, made a distinction between "removal" and "eviction." Richards, for one, notes that the Rev. Gustavus Aird, during his testimony to the Napier Commission in 1883, thought eviction meant to leave an estate altogether to go somewhere else while those that remained on the estate, even though in a different location, were merely removed.

A modern example of contemporary clearances is the illegal removals of the poorest residents of Rio de Janeiro's historic hillside *favelas*—the so-called shanty towns where more than 1.4 million people live—in order to make way for "improvements" leading up to the 2016 Summer Olympic games. If things go according to plan, almost a third of the community is expected to be threatened with destruction. As with the Highland Clearances, the anticipated removals in Brazil—whether they move forward or not—have the same result: a negative and quite often devastating impact on the community with its subsequent economic, social and psychological damage. At the same time, displacement for economic reasons often occur as a result of natural disasters, as the 2012 superstorm Sandy made evidently clear on the American east coast.

Because of the high cost of flood insurance and stricter requirements for rebuilding homes in a flood zone these changes posed a threat to middle-class and lower-income populations, which may inadvertently lead to a massive displacement, a major demographic shift, of these families from their historic beachfront communities.

Another modern term for clearance is "quick-take." Quick-take allows local governments to expropriate land for public projects, such as a highway, and thus avoiding often lengthy legal proceedings under eminent domain laws. Politicians have justified the concept of quick-take as being vital for job creation and economic development.

"The Clearances." Short story by Alistair MacLeod that appears in his 2000 collection *Island*.
See MacLeod, Alistair

Clearances studies. Although still in its infancy and thus nothing quite as comparable as, say, Irish Famine specifically or Irish studies generally, there is a movement afoot to study the Clearances on a more substantive and multidisciplinary level not only in Scotland but outwith Scotland. The Scottish Government, for example, is attempting to study the Clearances as part of a broader general education in which the Clearances era, and its legacy, is explored at length and from many perspectives. Further, Education Scotland has developed the online Scotland's History resource, which provides material on more than 200 topics, including information on the Highland Clearances. The Clearances is also an important part of the Higher History qualification for students as part of the Migration and Empire topic.

Colbost Folk Museum. By Dunvegan, on the Isle of Skye. An open-air exhibit established by a local man Peter MacAskill in 1969 (he also created the Giant Angus MacAskill Museum in Dunvegan). The highlight of the museum is the 19th-century blackhouse, a typical crofter's dwelling. The house consists of a sitting room, kitchen and bedroom; it has dry stone walls, a bare earth floor and a thatched roof. Inside is furniture of the time and clippings associated with the Clearances. At the rear of the garden are two small huts, one used for storage, the other containing a replica of an illegal whisky still.

Colonsay, Isle of. The ancestral home of Clan MacPhee (or Macfie) and the Colonsay branch of Clan MacNeill. During the Clearances era many people from Colonsay emigrated to Prince Edward Island and Ontario. The island's abandoned village, Riasg Buidhe, was inhabited up to 1918. Today the island is probably best known, in literary quarters as least, as being the ancestral home of the American writer John

McPhee. McPhee wrote about his stay on the island in *The Crofter and the Laird*.
See also McPhee, John

Columba Project. Or Iomairt Cholm Cille; formerly known as the Columba Initiative it is a programme for Gaelic speakers in both Scotland and Ireland. Named after St. Columba (521-597), it was launched by Mary Robinson, the then president of Ireland and Brian Wilson MP, the Scottish Minister of State for Education, Industry and Gaelic, to provide channels for interaction as well as cultural exchanges and relationship buildings "over complex geographical and political boundaries." Its activities include cultural events, language courses and an annual youth parliament. The Scottish office of the initiative is located at Sabhal Mòr Ostaig on Skye, where Robinson gave the Sabhal Mòr Lecture in 1997, in which she called the possibility of creating "an island space" for the Gaelic languages and their cultures.

Commissioners of the Forfeited Estates. Supervised eleven estates in thirty Highland parishes until the 1780s. They built schools, promoted the English language, developed the herring fishing industry and improved roads and communications. Improvers at heart, they attempted to introduce new ways of doing things to the recalcitrant Highlanders.

community buy-outs. Have occurred in various Hebridean island locations in recent years, including Eigg, Gigha, North Harris and South Uist. In addition, other areas have also reported increases in community acreages, including Knoydart, Melness, Abriachan, Glencanisp, Glenrunie, Galson in Lewis, Eriskay, Benbecula as well as Brove, Luskentyre and Scarista Mhòr on Harris (the latter three areas on South Harris were cleared in the early 19th century, and their families emigrated to Cape Breton). Indeed, as James Hunter notes, more than two-thirds of the population of the Outer Hebrides now live on community-owned land.

An Comunn Gàidhealach (Highland Association). Founded in Oban in 1891; an organization based in the whitewashed Abertarff House on Church Street, the oldest house in Inverness (it dates from ca. 1592) that preserves and promotes the Gaelic language and Highland culture. The organization also sponsors the annual Mòd (modelled on the Welsh Eisteddfod), a competitive festival of music, literature and spoken word. The first Mòd was also held in Oban, in 1892.

Comunn na Gàidhlig (CNAG). Established in 1985, CNAG acts as a clearing house for the larger Gaelic movement.

Connor, Ralph (Rev. Dr. Charles William Gordon) (1860-1937). Canadian novelist and Presbyterian minister who used Connor as a pen name. The most popular Canadian novelist of the early 20th century, he was born in Glengarry County, Ontario, and educated at the University of Toronto and the University of Edinburgh. He published several novels set in Glengarry, including *The Man from Glengarry* (1901) and *Glengarry School Days* (1902). To Connor, Glengarry was a special place, with its own customs and traditions and its own way of looking at the world, perhaps best expressed as a Canadian Highland perspective.

The Ralph Connor House, a National Historic Site of Canada, is located in Winnipeg, where he died.

Consider the Lilies (1968). Iain Crichton Smith's best-known novel, a deeply emotional work of the Clearances as seen through the perspective of an elderly Highland woman who is evicted by the factor Patrick Sellar (Smith uses real names). Sellar is depicted as an outsider ("His head wasn't Highland") who speaks in a rapid English and rides a white horse. In sharp contrast to the real Sellar, he appears as "a short fat man with piercing eyes and thin lips."

In a work that is utterly steeped in religious imagery it is no surprise that the title is taken from the Gospel of Matthew, Chapter 6: "Consider the lilies of the field, how they grow; they neither toil nor spin, and yet I say to you that even Solomon in all his glory was not arrayed like one of these." Like fellow author Fionn MacColla, Smith attacks the hypocrisy, and passivity, of the Presbyterian Church, especially the collusion of its ministers. The hero of the story, or to put in religious terms, the Good Samaritan of the story, is also a historical figure, the stonemason Donald Macleod, and the author of that seminal piece of anti-Clearances propaganda *Gloomy Memories*. Smith makes him an atheist "though," he notes, "there is no evidence that he was."

See also fiction of the Clearances

cottar. The landless agricultural labourer. Cottars and their families received small patches of land from tenants or subtenants in return for service. They were considered the backbone of Scotland: they did much of the menial but important work. "Most lived on the edge of poverty," notes Aitchison and Cassell. They had no legal right to hold land nor did the state and certainly not the landlords offer them any legal protection. Once they were evicted, they were on their own.

de Crèvecoeur, J. Hector St. John (1735-1813). In 1782, Crèvecoeur published *Letters from an American Farmer* and *Sketches of Eighteenth-Century America*, which painted vivid portraits of America after the Revolutionary War.

Born Michel-Guillaume Saint Jean de Crèvecoeur in Caen, France, Crèvecoeur received a Jesuit education in Latin, rhetoric, mathematics and theology. In 1755 he sailed for New France and served in the French colonial army as an artillery officer during the French and Indian War. He also fought under General Montcalm in 1759 at the famous Plains of Abraham siege in Québec. When the war ended, he immigrated to the New York colony, and changed his name to J. Hector St. John. In 1769 he married into a prominent Tory family in Orange County, New York. During the Revolutionary War, he was suspected of harbouring monarchist sympathies and thus imprisoned before managing to flee the colonies altogether. After the war, he published *Letters from an American Farmer* in 1781, which was a huge success in Europe. Subsequently, he was appointed as political and cultural liaison between France and the United States.

He died in Sarcelles, France, in 1813.

In *Letters from an American Farmer*, Crèvecoeur's essay, "What Is an American?," introduces the figure of Andrew the Hebridean, "an honest" man who emigrated from the island of Barra to Philadelphia in 1774. To Crèvecoeur, Andrew epitomized what the "Scotch can do wherever they have room for the exertion of their industry." He was impressed by the Highlander's strong work ethic and humble nature. "What a happy change it must be to descend from the high, sterile, bleak lands of Scotland, where everything is barren and cold, and to rest on some fertile farms in these middle provinces!" Crèvecoeur imagines Andrew's homeland to be "unfit for the habitation of men." In fact, when told that Andrew had come from Barra, the Frenchman looks at a map and, based on its latitude, concludes that it must be "an inhospitable climate." He then asks a series of questions. "What sort of land have you got there?" The Hebridean replies, "Bad enough" before adding, "[W]e have not such trees as I see here, no wheat, no kine, no apples." This leads Crèvecoeur to comment that the land must be hard for the poor to live on. "We have no poor," answers Andrew, "we are all alike, except our laird...."

Finally, in what can only be called a prophetic statement, Crèvecoeur concludes that the Hebrides "appear to be calculated only for great sheep pastures." But more than this, he also suggests that the Hebrides might be the perfect location to lodge "malefactors."

> ...it would be better to send felons [to the Hebrides] than either to Virginia or Maryland.... The English government should purchase the most northern and barren of those islands; it should send over to us the honest, primitive Hebrideans, settle them here on good lands as a reward for their virtue and ancient poverty, and replace them with a colony of her wicked sons. The severity of the climate, the

inclemency of the seasons, the sterility of the soil, the tempestuousness of the sea, would afflict and punish enough.

By doing the above, reasons the Frenchman, "two essential goods" would occur: "the good people, by emigration, would be rendered happier; the bad ones would be placed where they ought to be."
In the introduction to the Penguin Classics edition of *Letters*, Albert E. Stone contends that the parable of Andrew the Hebridean is nothing less than the story of a selfmade man and serves as the prototypes of the literary figures that subsequently would appear in the works of James Fenimore Cooper, William Faulkner (himself of Scots descent) and, "by implication, the whole tribe of gray-suited opportunists peopling the fictional Madison Avenue of the 1950s and 1960s."

Crimean War. Raged between October 1853 to February 1856; started in March 1854; "Where are the Highlanders?" the press asked. They were now needed to fight Britain's wars, but by this time there were few Highlanders left, or willing, to fight. Donald Ross, the crusading journalist, pointed out that whereas in 1745 there might have been 30,000 Highlanders joining the military by the time of the Crimean War, the Highlands could barely muster 3,000 men. Recruiting attempts in the Highlands were an utter failure. The Gaels of Skye and Sutherland were blunt in their response to the recruiting officers: they felt that since they no longer had a country to fight for; why should they fight for a country that in all likelihood would evict them from their dwellings after they returned home from battle? A committee of crofters thus announced that "we are resolved that there shall be no volunteers or recruits from Sutherlandshire," historically, the region of Scotland that had produced many if not most of the military recruits.

croft. A small landholding.

crofter. A tenant of a croft, or small land holding.

crofter colonies. Refers to the 79 families from Lewis and Harris who settled, with British government assistance, at the Killarney Colony and the Argyle Colony, respectively, near Pelican Lake, in southwest Manitoba, and the Lothian Colony at Saltcoats, in Saskatchewan, near the Manitoba border, in 1888 and 1889. Collectively, they are known as the Pelican Lake settlers. Although generally referred to as crofters, the majority of the adult males were in fact fishermen and landless cottars. In May 1888, the *Claymore* left Stornoway harbour bound for Canada. According to Wayne Norton, the passengers had accepted an offer by the British government for assisted emigration to the Canadian prairies. In exchange for a promise to repay a £120 loan, each family was to receive a grand total of 65 ha (160 acres) of Canadian farmland. The mastermind behind the emigration scheme, which was adopted by the Scottish Office in 1888, was Sir Malcolm McNeill (1839-1919), a native of Barra who was educated at Eton and Sandhurst. McNeill believed the only solution to the "Highland problem" of overpopulation and poverty was emigration. What's more, McNeill recommended the settlement of small, supervised groups of Highlanders.

The various crofter colonies experienced their share of difficulties. The settlers' resources were scarce, to say the least, and by the time they arrived public funds were virtually gone. They were often left to fend for themselves or with the assistance of the local communities. Although welcome committees and celebrations initially greeted the crofters upon their arrival it didn't take long for relations between the settlers and the locals to become strained. The problems, writes Norton, "were the logical outcomes of an emigration scheme that was flawed in conception and rushed in implementation."

Crofters' Holdings Act (Scotland) (1886). A piece of landmark legislation that marked the beginning of the modern era in the Highlands: it terminated landlords' right to evict and thus officially brought the Highland Clearances to an end. The *Act* granted security of tenure to the tenants and the right of inheritance and established a Land Court for the fixing of fair rents. Its major flaw was that it did not provide a solution to the crofters' most vexing problem: land shortage. That is, it did nothing to reform or fix the fundamentally unfair issue of land use and land redistribution. Since the 1880s the crofters had, usually unsuccessfully, demanded the return of their land. Essentially, the *Act* was designed to prevent future clearances and, thus, to solve the so-called Highland problem.

Still it was considered a revolutionary piece of legislation in that it created a foundation on which to build better and more laws. "It violated the sacredness of private property rights, smashed the sovereignty of Highland landlords ... this was the nearest Britain ever came to creating an independent peasantry, on the model of France, Poland or most other European nations in the late nineteenth century," writes Neal Ascherson. And yet it's greatest downfall was that it made no provisions for the landless cottars, the poorest members of the tenantry.

The *Act* applied to what were then the counties of Argyll, Inverness-shire, Ross and Cromarty, Sutherland, Caithness, Orkney and Shetland.

Crofters' Union. Established in 1985 to give crofters a collective voice.

Crofters' War. Refers to events of the 1880s when resistance to Highland landowners was at its zenith. As such, it was considered a triumphant example of popular protest, since it led to the creation of the Crofters' Party. This popular protest, or agitation, to use the parlance of the day, generally took the form of rent strikes (the withholding of rental payments) and land raids (crofter occupation of land that landlords had converted to sheep farms or deer forests). To most historians the success of the Crofters' War marked the end of the Highland Clearances.

crofting The heartland of the crofting region of the Highlands can be found from the western seaboard to the north of Fort William, including the Inner and Outer Hebrides. In the post-Culloden era the former communal townships, or clachans, were replaced by individual holdings, or crofts.

The system of crofting evolved from the 18th-century land system. A croft is not a house but, typically, a small piece of land with the tenant (called a crofter) paying rent to the landowner and sharing grazing rights with other crofters in what is referred to as a crofting township. Whereas the old clan system had been a *military* relationship between chief and clansman, crofting was an economic relationship between crofter and landlord—in other words, a fundamental shift in societal mores. To emphasize, the crofting system only developed after the clan system collapsed.

Crofting was a legacy of the Clearances. It was designed to reduce and, ultimately, to destroy the independence of the tenantry. Since the crofts were not productive enough to feed a family or offer a living, in order to survive men and women were compelled to work at occupations that did not suit them, such as fishing or working in the kelp industry or as estate labourers to supplement their meagre income.

Crofting continues to be the fundamental mainstay of the Highland economy, particularly the West Highland economy.

Croick Church, Glencalvie. The etchings on the pane glass windows of Croick Church in the parish of Glencalvie, Ross-shire, are among the most poignant reminders of the human tragedy behind the Clearances. Built in 1827 and designed by the renowned Scottish architect and engineer Thomas Telford, and one of forty parliamentary churches constructed with government grants, the little grey stone church is located ten miles west of the village of Ardgay in the county of Sutherland. Several attempts were made to remove people here, most famously, in 1845.

The Glencalvie Clearances were in fact also among the most publicized, the plight of the people appearing not only in the pages of the *Scotsman* but also in the *Times*. More than 400 families—as many as

2,000 people—received writs of removal in Glencalvie in 1845, according to Eric Richards.

The church congregation itself consisted of 18 families, or nearly 90 people, who lived in Greenyards and Glencalvie, which was located in the parish of Kincardine. They were evicted to make room for not only sheep farmers but also sportsmen or, in the words of the *Scotsman*, "to make way for strangers" even though their rents had been paid.

Their minister, the Rev. Gustavus Aird, was a particularly forceful advocate. "Matters have really come to an awful pitch," he wrote, "when beings possessed of immortal souls, originally created after the divine image, are driven out of their homes and fatherland to make way for fir and *larch plants, deer, roes, moorgame, partridges* and *hares*."

The self-contained community lived in modest means in Glencalvie at the time of the 1845 Clearances, growing barley, oats and potatoes and herding their sheep and black cattle. Outsiders may have seen in the surroundings nothing but bleakness, but the people of Glencalvie were attached to their small turf of land and everything associated with it—the rocks and flowers, even the brown hills surrounding them. Due to serendipity and good timing, the eviction of these particular people elicited wide publicity and a broader public outcry heretofore not heard. And in a bold and quite forward-thinking move the Glencalvie people appealed directly to the press for assistance, seeking public subscription for resettlement elsewhere. With the help of five Free Church ministers, they put together a petition and inserted it into the pages of the *Scotsman*.

But the times were changing, and these crofters were, to put it bluntly, in the way of progress. As early as February 1842, the efficiently efficient factor James Falconer Gillanders of Highfield near Beauly had placed an advertisement in the *Inverness Courier* making known the availability of farms to be let in the parish. Essentially, the people were told to leave to make way for sheep farmers and sportsmen.

Although the owner of the Glencalvie estate was Major Charles Robertson of Kindeace the actual dirty work of removing the inhabitants was left to Gillanders (Robertson was in Australia at the time with his regiment). It was he, Gillanders, who issued the writs of removal to the Glencalvie people. To Gillanders, and others like him, the indigenous population was in the way; to his way of thinking, the land could be put to better use, that is, more lucrative, as a single sheep walk. Gillanders had a reputation similar to another notorious factor, Patrick Sellar. In addition to Glencalvie, he evicted inhabitants from Newmore, Strathconon and the Black Isle.

The people had to go even though they were not in arrears and, in fact, were debt-free. Gillanders did allow the inhabitants to stay until late May 1845. Although initially destroying the writs of eviction, they eventually accepted the government compensation offer of £18 as an allowance per family—considered a substantial and, notes Eric Richards, "relatively generous" amount at the time—to assist their displacement. In truth, the authorities suggested emigration as the best solution to their plight. Either way, there was to be no further negotiation. Go they must.

Meanwhile, newspapers knew a good human interest story when they saw one. It didn't take long for the events at Glencalvie to come to the attention of the national press. John Delane, editor of the *Times* of London despatched a reporter, or Special Commissioner, to the Highlands to investigate. Although these special commissioners were usually anonymous, John Prebble has suggested that the identity of the reporter may have been Thomas Campbell Foster, a legal writer. In any event, the reporter travelled to the Highlands, staying at the Inn of Ardgay, and filed his devastating and quite remarkable stories, bringing to the attention of readers throughout Britain "a kind of slavery ten times worse than which for so long disgraced Britain."

The people of Glencalvie paid an annual rent of £55 and 10 shillings for poor land. Many Glencalvie men had served during the Napoleonic Wars. They pleaded with Gillanders to reconsider and even went so far as to ask for the assistance of their new minister, Rev. Aird. Still, in March 1843, attempts were made to issue writs of removal. As often happened during the Clearances, the women of Glencalvie refused to give up without a fight, setting the writs on fire and generally causing a commotion. In an effort to appease Gillanders, the Glencalvie folk even offered to pay a higher rent if they would be allowed to stay.

In 1844, Gillanders made another attempt to evict the Glencalvie people. Finally, he allowed them to stay until May 25, 1845. He even claimed that all of them had found alternative accommodation. But the *Times* reporter insisted that only 6of the 18 families had found shelter, mostly in the nearby villages of Bonar Bridge and Edderton. The rest, he concluded, were "hopeless and helpless." They did not know where to go.

The reporter arrived in Glencalvie in May 1845 just as the inhabitants of the glen were leaving. All of the houses were empty except for the cottage belonging to Hugh Ross, who lay dying. The remainder of the people, now homeless, were sitting on a brae, "the women all neatly dressed in net caps and wearing scarlet or plaid shawls; the men wearing their blue bonnets" with their plaids wrapped around them. Altogether, according to Richards, about 250 people from the nearby straths gathered. Two years earlier, the Disruption, as it was known (local ministers were at odds with the established church (*See* Disruption)) meant that the Croick congregation had no minister to manage their spiritual needs, since most of the families followed the Rev. Gustavus Aird to worship at the rival Free Church. For this reason, they chose to listen to the Psalms of David in the Gaelic in the open air, singing the reassuring words of Psalm 45.

Of the 250 who had assembled in the kirk yard, 80 were of the Glencalvie refugees: 23 were under the age of ten, 7 were in poor health, 10 were older than sixty and 8 were young single men. The reporter described the scene:

> Behind the church, in the courtyard, a long kind of booth was erected, the roof formed of tarpaulin stretched over poles, the sides closed in with horse cloths, rugs, blankets, and plaids.

The only shelter was a walled enclosure by the churchyard at Croick, protected, if that is the word, by several crooked trees. They started a fire in the churchyard to stave off the May chill. With them were all their meagre belongings and several carts filled with their infant children. When told that an Englishman from a great newspaper down south was there to visit them, they gathered around him, shaking his hand. The reporter later told Delane, "Their Gaelic I could not understand but their eyes beamed with gratitude."

Some of the people who took shelter in the churchyard at Croick scratched their names and left behind brief notes on the diamond-paned east window of the church. Significantly, they wrote in English rather than their native Gaelic. Their unbelievably poignant, disturbing and fatalistic words, even more than a hundred and sixty years later, remain:

> Glencalvie people was in the church here May 24, 1845 ...
> Glencalvie people the wicked generation ... John Ross shepherd ...
> Glencalvie people was here ... Amy Ross ... Glencalvie is a wilderness blow ship them to the colony ... The Glencalvie Rosses....

They marched out of the glen with their belongings, which consisted mostly of beddings and other bare essentials. Although the ultimate fate of the Glencalvie Highlanders after they left the relative security of the little churchyard remains unknown, their circumstances and the publication of the *Times* articles led to public sympathy and, more significantly, parliamentary debate on the poor laws in Scotland as well as to the short-lived formation of the Society for the Protection of the Poor. The larger impact, though, was the sense of outrage and disbelief that such conditions could be allowed to exist in Britain. The *Times* reports in particular were referred to in the House of Commons in June 1845.

In 1992, Alison Johnson, who for many years ran the small hotel Scarista House in Harris, wrote a novel, *The Wicked Generation*, about the Clearances (although not set in Glencalvie it most certainly was inspired by it). The name of Gillanders, the notorious Glencalvie factor, even was mentioned in Andy M. Stewart's song, "The Highland Clearances." Today, Croick Church is open throughout the year and holds monthly summer services beginning in May; every May a celebration takes place in honour of the Glencalvie people.

The church was restored in 1983. A plaque located across the road tells the story. See page 269 for a photo from Croick Church.

crusading journalists. During the Clearances era, several journalists lent their name to the cause of helping the Highlanders in their struggle to retain their rights. They included Thomas Mulock, Donald Macleod and Donald Ross. The pro-Highlander newspapers included the *Inverness Advertiser* and the *Northern Ensign*. Other supporters included Hugh Miller, editor of the *Witness* and Robert Somers, editor of the *North British Daily Mail*. The *Northern Ensign* and the *Advertiser* were among the most passionate of the papers; publishing, according to Krisztina Fenyö, more than 100 articles each on the Clearances between 1849 and 1855. In her research of the years 1845 to 1855 in the major Scottish newspapers alone, Fenyö reports that more than 2,000 articles were written about the Highlands; of those roughly 600 were about the Clearances. The circulation of the Highland newspapers though were woefully small—on average no more than 2,500—and could not compare with the hostile or less sympathetic articles that appeared in the mainstream press.

Culloden (film). Black and white docudrama 1964 written and directed by the English filmmaker Peter Watkins (b. 1935) for BBC-TV; Watkins is considered a pioneer of *cinema-verite* in Britain. In the early 1960s he was an assistant editor and director of documentaries at the BBC, where he honed his trade.

Culloden was Watkins's first full-length film. In the film he re-enacts the Battle of Culloden in the style of a modern television crew; that is, in the "you-are-there" style similar to the Vietnam War era reporting at the time when he made the film. In fact, Watkins intentionally drew parallels between Culloden and its brutal consequences and the Vietnam War. Although it was released years prior to the 1968 My Lai massacre, astute observers cannot help but make the connection.

Based on John Prebble's book of the same name (Prebble is listed as an historical adviser) it was noted for its use of non-professional actors—Watkins used an all-amateur cast from London and the Lowlands to represent the government forces and local people from Inverness to represent the Jacobite army—and its in-your-face Vietnam War-era honesty. It stands out for another reason. Much of the camera work was handheld which lends an air of immediacy. The actors portray historical characters who are being interviewed by the filmmaker on the spot as if it was happening then and there. At one point, the interviewer asks an emaciated Highlander, when was the last time he ate. He replies, "I can't remember." For all intents and purposes, this cinematic document looks like an 18th-century newsreel. It concludes with the famous statement often attributed to the chieftain Calgacus by the Roman historian Tacitus in *Agricola* after the battle of Mons Graupius, "They have created a desert and have called it peace."

Culloden was filmed in August 1964, near Inverness. According to Watkins's website, many of the actors who portrayed Highland soldiers were direct descendents of the Highlanders who were killed on Culloden Moor.

Culloden won a Society of Film and Television Arts TV Award for Specialised Programmes and the British Screenwriters' Award of Merit, both in 1965. In 2000, *Culloden* appeared on the 100 Greatest British Television Programmes by the British Film Institute. It is available on DVD (packaged along with another Watkins' film *The War Game*, which depicts the effects of nuclear war on Britain).

See also Battle of Culloden; Culloden Battlefield Visitor Centre

Culloden Battlefield Visitor Centre, Culloden Moor. Five miles south of Inverness. It was here that Prince Charles Edward Stuart and the Jacobite cause came to a crushing and devastating end on April 16, 1746. The battle itself lasted all of 40 minutes but it changed irrevocably centuries of Highland life and custom.

In 1881, the landowner of the time, Duncan Forbes erected a commemorative cairn as well as a series of stones marking the alleged burial places of the clansmen who fell at the battlesite. The battlefield passed into the ownership of the National Trust for Scotland over a period of years from 1937 to 1989. Highlights of the new Visitor Centre and its extensive grounds include: the Graves of the Clans, burial places with headstones lined along the main road; the Well of the Dead, a solitary stone with the inscription, plainly stated, "The English were buried here"; Old Leanach farmhouse, now a museum; and the Cumberland Stone, where the victorious Duke of Cumberland reportedly watched over the battle. The battlefield itself has been restored to how it probably appeared on that day.

See also Battle of Culloden; *Culloden* (film)

Culloden Moor Suite. A rarely performed jazz suite composed by Glasgow-born saxophonist Bobby Wellins. Originally written in the 1960s, fellow saxophonist the Edinburgh-born Tommy Smith commissioned new arrangements of the suite in 2011 by the Scottish National

Jazz Orchestra (SNJO), of which Smith is the director. Wellins was inspired to write the suite after reading John Prebble's books on the Jacobite Risings and the Clearances. Wellins himself was a guest saxophonist when the suite was presented at the Eden Court Theatre in Inverness in October 2011, just a few miles from the battle site.

"culture of victimization." Coined by the American historian Peter Novick (1934-2012), author of the controversial book *The Holocaust in American Life*. Refers to descendants and their sense of guilt and responsibility for perceived past injustices.

Culrain (Easter Ross). Anti-Clearance rioting took place here during the 1820 Clearances on the estate of Hugh Munro of Novar (who John Prebble refers to as "the young and rakish laird") after no provisions had been made for resettlement for the 600 people who were affected; reportedly 100 of them were aged and bedridden. The resistance was violent" and, as usual under these circumstances, troops were called in. Not anticipating such a reaction, the Sutherland authorities felt anxious about the possibility of similar revolts. But the little rebellion did not last long. Writes John Prebble, recalling the "wicked generation" etching on Croick Church in Glencalvie, "The old weaknesses of the Highlanders had ended it—their lack of leadership, their childish faith in the laird, who must now surely change his mind, and, most insidious of all, their melancholy belief that they had been a doomed race since Culloden."

Cumberland, William Augustus, Duke of (1721–1765). Born in London, he was the younger son of George II of Great Britain and Caroline of Ansbach, but he is best known for his role at the Battle of Culloden in 1746, where he earned the sobriquet of "Butcher" Cumberland for his brutal treatment of the Highlanders after the battle. Displaying no leniency, Cumberland ordered that his soldiers show no quarter toward any of the remaining Highland troops. Subsequently, the government forces engaged in the "pacification" of the Highlands by which the Jacobite rebels were hunted down and killed, their homes burned to the ground and livestock confiscated. South of the border he was hailed as a hero; in Scotland, though, an altogether different image of him emerged. The story goes, perhaps untrue but nevertheless poignant, that a flower, *dianthus barbatus* (Sweet William), is named after him; it is called "stinking Billy."

He died in 1765 in London and is buried at Westminster Abbey.

D

Darien, Georgia. A town in McIntosh County, Georgia, USA, founded in January 1736 by Highlanders, mostly from Inverness-shire, and consisting of about 170 men, women, and children. They were recruited by Gen. James Oglethorpe (1696-1785), the founder of Georgia. Most were soldiers who were recruited to fight on the American colonial frontier. Appropriately, its original name was New Inverness but changed, ironically, in honour of the ill-fated Scots settlement on the Isthmus of Panama in the late 1690s (and which, ultimately, led to the Scots to agree to *Act of Union* in 1707). Among the early settlers was Lachlan McGillivray (ca. 1718-1799 and born in Dunmaglass, Inverness-shire), an Indian trader, and Lachlan McIntosh (1725-1806, born in Badenoch), a Revolutionary War leader. The majority of the Highlanders spoke only Gaelic.

Darling, Frank Fraser (1903-1979). Naturalist, author and pioneer ecologist and educated at Midland Agricultural College and at the Institute of Animal Genetics at the University of Edinburgh. He was director of the West Highland Survey from 1944 to 1950, where he studied the ecological effects of the Clearances on the land. His Highland-related works include *Wild Country: A Highland Naturalist's Notes and Pictures* (1938), *A Naturalist on Rona: Essays of a Biologist in Isolation* (1939), *Island Years* (1940), *Island Farm* (1943), *Natural History in the Highlands and Islands* (1947), *West Highland Survey: An Essay in Human Ecology* (1955) and *Wilderness and Plenty* (1970). Another work, *Crofting Agriculture: Its Practice in the West Highlands*, was based on the two years he spent in the crofting regions of the Highlands and Islands.

The Death of General Wolfe (1770). Painting by the Anglo-American artist Benjamin West depicting the death of the British general James Wolfe at the Battle of Québec (1759) during the Seven Years War (known in the United States as the French and Indian War). Of particular interest is the inclusion of Simon Fraser, Lt. Col. of the 78th Fraser Highlanders, whom Wolfe admired; Fraser did not participate in the battle; he was recovering from wounds suffered from an earlier injury.

See also Battle of the Plains of Abraham

deer forests. By the mid-19th century the Highland Clearances were taking on a new look as sheep farms were being replaced by deer forests and elaborate Gothic mansions and shooting lodges were being erected for the shooting parties. The price of wool had decreased to such an extent that deer-stalking had become a more profitable, and reliable, source of income than sheep. In fact, after 1860, when the railways made the Highlands more accessible, much of the land was converted not into sheep farms but into deer forests, as shooting enthusiasts from England, but also Ireland, began to hunt the red deer, ptarmigan, black game and grouse. According to Eric Richards, some 28 deer forests were formed by as early as 1839, an additional 16 in the 1840s, 10 more in the 1850s and as many as 18 between 1855 and 1860. In other words, deer were effectively replacing sheep which, Richards notes in a particularly clever turn of phrase, "introduced a new type of bleating into the north of Scotland." By 1912, one-fifth of Scotland was under deer forest. Despite the abudance of deer, the tenants were not allowed to hunt them; that activity was reserved for the landowners and members of the aristocracy only. Ultimately, these restrictions led to what became known as deer raids, or incidents of rebellion. The most famous example was the Pairc Deer Raid on Lewis in 1887 where men slaughtered deer in order to feed their families.

Deeside (Aberdeenshire). Numerous removals took place in Deeside during the Clearances era. Among the Deeside Clearances, Glen Clunie was cleared of twelve families to make way for two large sheep farms. Glen Lui near the Lynn of Dee was cleared of four farms in 1726 by Lord Grange, the brother of John Erskine, "forfeited," asserts Rob Gibson, "as Earl of Mar for leading the 1715 Rising." Another clearance took place in 1776 in Luibeg for deer. Near Braemar, nine families were removed from Glen Ey around 1830.

Glen Gelder, part of the Balmoral estate, was leased to Prince Albert in 1848 and sold to him in 1852 by the Earl of Fife's trustees. He then, adds Gibson, "developed Balmoral Castle as the model for all aspiring wealthy sportsmen.... The removal of 13 families from the glen was organised under the Prince Consort's ownership of the estate." As an aside, Gibson also points out that the crofters in the upper reaches of the River Dee spoke Gaelic as well as some Doric.

In addition, around 1850 some 29 families were removed from the south side of Glen Tanar and other families were cleared between 1855 and 1858, along with their sheep to make way for the fashionable sporting preserves.

deforcement. Refers to the prevention, or attempt at prevention, of the use of force for writs of removal.

deforestation. Much of the Highlands has been deforested over the years, partly for timber and partly for grazing purposes, by both cattle and sheep. Consequently, without trees, many types of indigenous flora and fauna have vanished.

Destitution Road. Located in Dundonnell Forest, along the A832 road, east of Dundonnell in the Loch Broom area of the northern Highlands. Built in the late 1840s, the road provided employment and famine relief to more than 1,000 people.

Devine, T. M. (b. 1945). Born in Motherwell, educated at the University of Strathclyde, Thomas Martin Devine is among the leading authorities on the history of modern Scotland and the Scottish diaspora. In 1998 he was director of the Research Institute of Irish and Scottish Studies at the University of Aberdeen. In 2005 he was appointed to the Sir William Fraser Chair of Scottish History and Palaeography at the University of Edinburgh. Three years later he became director of the Scottish Centre for Diaspora Studies at Edinburgh. He is the author or editor of more than 30 books. His specialities include emigration, famine, the economic history of Scotland, the British (and Scottish) Empire, the Highland Clearances, the Irish in Scotland, rural social history and the Scottish Diaspora and its worldwide impact.

His books include *The Great Highland Famine* (1988, 1995, 2008), *Clanship to Crofters' War* (1994), *The Transformation of Rural Scotland* (1994), *The Scottish Nation: 1700-2000* (1999), *Scotland's Empire, 1600-1815* (2003, 2012), *Clearance and Improvement* (2006), *The Scottish Nation 1700 to 2007* (2006, 2012), *To the Ends of the Earth: Scotland's Global Diaspora 1750-2010* (2011, 2012) and *The Oxford Handbook of Modern Scottish History 1500-2010* (joint editor, 2012). *Scotland's Empire 1600-1815* formed the basis of a six-part BBC2 Scotland television series in 2005. In addition, in 2003, he was a consultant on the BBC Radio Scotland program, *The Lowland Clearances*, based on the book of the same name.

Disarming Act (1746) and subsequent **Disclothing Act** (1748). Had a profoundly negative impact on morale in the Highlands and Islands. Only the independent companies, the precursors of the famed Highland regiments, were allowed to wear the traditional Highland dress. The original *Act* was expanded two years later, in 1748. Essentially, the two *Acts* forbade the carrying or possession of weapons or bagpipes and the wearing of the traditional Highland dress. The *Acts* were repealed in 1782.

Disruption, The. Refers to the secession in 1843 of a large number of ministers and congregationists from the established Church of Scotland to form the Free Church of Scotland because of a disagreement over the issue of lay patronage. Other reasons included the increasing disaffection between the people and the clergy as well as the evictions, rising rents, emigration and poverty associated with the Clearances. The overwhelming majority of Protestants in the Highlands and Islands moved to the Free Church. In 1893, though, internal conflict led to secession once again, when members of the Free Church formed the Free Presbyterian Church, often given the patrynomic of "the Wee Frees."

The Diviners. Published in 1974, it was Margaret Laurence's final novel and the culmination of her celebrated Manawaka cycle. It is considered one of the classics of Canadian literature. The protagonist of the novel is Morag Gunn, a Scots-Canadian and fiercely independent woman who grows up on the Canadian prairie feeling dispossessed and lost.

Donn, Rob (also known as Robert MacKay) (1714-1778). Gaelic poet, born in Strathmore, Sutherland, and herdsman for the MacKay chief, Lord Reay. As a bard, he described rural life as well as the decline of clan society in Strathnaver and Strathmore after the 1745 Jacobite Rising. His poetry first appeared in published form in 1828.

Dunbeath Heritage Centre. In a harbour town in Caithness; the Centre is located in a mid-19th century school building, the Dunbeath Preservation Trust has a large collection of material on author Neil Gunn and his work. Gunn, an important 20th-century Scots author, was born and grew up there and attended school in the building that houses the Centre.

The Dunbeath Preservation Trust organizes a weekly guided tour of Dunbeath and the area and hosts programs of evening lectures. The trust features a substantial photography collection, a large collection of family history material, unpublished manuscripts and maps and a library of antiquarian, archaeological and local history books.

Dunrobin Castle, Golspie, Sutherland. Has been called the most politically incorrect museum in Britain. Commissioned in the mid-19th century by the 2nd Duke of Sutherland, it was designed by Sir Charles Barry who also designed the Houses of Parliament in London. The Duke of Sutherland envisioned this faux French chateau as the "Versailles of the North."

Originally a keep built ca. 1275 by Robert, Earl of Sutherland, it was for centuries the seat of the earls and dukes of Sutherland. Elizabeth, daughter of the 18th Earl of Sutherland, inherited her father's wealth and became the Countess of Sutherland. She married an Englishman, George Granville Leveson-Gower, and with their massive wealth they went about "improving" the lives of their impoverished tenants. He became the first Duke of Sutherland in 1833 and Elizabeth became the Duchess-Countess.

It is now a museum; open from May to September. With 189 rooms, it is the largest house in the northern Highlands. The Victorian Museum is located in a separate building that overlooks the gardens and includes exhibits on ornithology, archaeology, local history, geology, family memorabilia, and even Egyptology but, significantly, nothing on the Clearances.

See also Sutherland

Dunvegan Castle. Located in the northwest corner of Skye on Loch Dunvegan and, at 700 years old, is said to be the oldest inhabited castle in northern Scotland. Parts of the castle date back to the 9th century although the present exterior owes more to Victorian-era fancy. Among the pre-Clearances era artifacts on display include a lock of hair from Bonnie Prince Charlie and a pincushion belonging to Flora Macdonald. Open from mid-March to October, the castle also has extensive gardens. It is the seat of worldwide Clan MacLeod.

Durness Clearances. Systematic clearances occurred here in 1841. Ironically, the landlord, the 2nd Duke of Sutherland—son of the most notorious of Clearance landlords—tried to prevent evictions from taking place. In 1829 the new owners had acquired the bankrupt estate of Lord Reay. But by the time the son assumed control the Sutherland family had adopted a cautious approach to estate management. Thus, rather than evicting the people, incentives were offered to emigrate. The evictions that did take place at Durness in 1841 were undertaken by James Anderson, a leaseholder, who wanted to remove a large number of sub-tenants to convert his operations to sheep farming. Embarrassed by the situation and wary of opening old and still quite fresh wounds from the notorious clearances from the Sellar period, the Duke not only wanted no part of the proceeding, he also vehemently opposed Anderson's plans.

But because of the vagaries of the laws and the system of sub-letting in Durness, Anderson was completely within his rights and the evictions went forward—the tenant, not the landlord, held the power; the evictions were beyond the Duke's control. The Durness Clearances occurred in two phases: between 1839 and 1841 Anderson evicted 32 families, or 190 people. Some emigrated to Upper Canada (now Ontario) while others either resettled within the surrounding Sutherland estate or went to Caithness, Ross-shire or Inverness-shire.

In September 1841, Anderson made plans to evict an additional 31 families, or 63 people, which, according to Eric Richards, included shoemakers, coopers, fishermen, farmers and cottars, but also sickly children and an indigent and disabled elderly man. The people turned first to their minister and then to the Duke of Sutherland for help. Anderson, a businessman to the core, gave the people what he considered a reasonable amount of time: 48 hours notice. But when the authorities tried to proceeed with the evictions, they were met with an angry mob of about 300 people, including women, armed with sticks and stones. The people were momentarily triumphant. Several days later, though, the threat of military intervention changed their behaviour from, says John Prebble, "angry lions to timorous sheep." After the incident, a compromise was reached: the people were given an extra six months' notice.

But they still had to leave.

dùthchas. A Gaelic term that refers to the traditional, and hence moral, obligation of clan chiefs to provide protection for their people or, to put it succinctly, the hereditary right of tenure. But it also refers to the Highland belief that clansfolk were entitled to the lands associated with their clan.

E

Education (Scotland) Act (1872). Made school attendance compulsory to the age of fourteen. Because children were taught to read and write only in English with no provisions for Gaelic—indeed, there were prohibitions against the use of Gaelic, including corporal punishment—the English language became synonymous with education. Consequently, generation after generation grew up learning how to read and write in English but not in their native Gaelic. The *Act* was nothing less than a devastating blow to the future of Gaelic.

Eigg, Isle of. One of the Small Isles in the Inner Hebrides best known for its so-called singing sands. In 1828 it was sold to Hugh MacPherson, a former surgeon in the Indian Medical Service and later principal of King's College, Aberdeen. Like many of the Small Isles, in the mid-19th century most of the island was cleared to make way for sheep.

After a succession of absentee landlords in the 20th century, the Isle of Eigg Heritage Trust bought the island in 1997. The Trust consisted of a partnership between the residents of the island, the Highland Council and the Scottish Wildlife Trust. At the time of the sale the population had dwindled to sixty. By 2012, it had increased to 90 people.

Elgin Cathedral. Located in the royal burgh of Elgin in Morayshire. The notorious factor, Patrick Sellar, is buried there along with other members of his family amid the ruins of the 13th-century cathedral.

emigrant ships. The sea voyage on the emigrant ships during the Clearances era could take as long as six weeks, possibly more. The living conditions for steerage passengers on board the ships generally were cramped and unsanitary and, in a word, deplorable. There are countless tales of passengers who never made it across, who died during the long voyage and were buried at sea. Passengers typically paid £6-8 for a berth and food. However, berths lacked privacy and were meant to be shared by at least two people. Among the most famous of the emigrant ships that carried people away to the New World during the Clearances era were the *Hector* (see separate entry), the *Nancy*, the *Nestor* and the *Pearl*. The *Nancy* set sail for New York on September 17, 1773, with more than 200 people aboard. By the time the ship docked two months later, between 80 and 100 passengers had died. The *Nestor* is the ship that James Boswell so famously wrote about in his *Tour to the Hebrides*. Unlike many emigrant ships, Boswell was impressed with the accommodations, which he described as "very good." Of course, that is a relative observation from someone who did not have to make the long journey with hundreds of refugees.

Some other important emigrant ships of the Clearances era include the following:

Admiral	*Flora*	*Lady Kennaway*
Asia	*Georgiana*	*Liscard*
Celt	*Good Intent*	*Macdonald*
Ceres	*Hercules*	*Militiades*
Dove	*James*	*Pearl*
Eddystone	*John Gray*	*Prince of Wales*
The Edinburgh	*Kingston*	*Rambler*
	Sarah	*Sillery*

Emigrants, The (statue). Unveiled in the Highland town of Helmsdale by First Minister Alex Salmond in July 2007. Gaelic singer Eilidh Mackenzie from Lewis performed the Gaelic song, "O Teannaibh dluth" during the ceremony. A twin statue, enititled *Exiles*, is located in Winnipeg on the Red River.

The 10-foot-high bronze statue, which depicts a Highland family, stands at the mouth of the Strath of Kildonan and commemorates not only the Clearances but also people of the Clearances diaspora. The sculptor, the Black Isle-based Gerald Laing, used the expulsion from the Garden of Eden as his inspiration, which he considers the original archetype of displacement. The sensations, he said, "are loss, disorientation and anxiety," which he sought to express in the sculpture itself. "The man is tense, wary, anxious but determined," while the boy looks to his father for "guidance" even as he is "ready for adventure." Meanwhile, the mother holds her infant child, and looks back "longingly" at the familiarity of her homeland.

The plaque reads:

The Emigrants
Commemorates the people of the Highlands and Islands of Scotland who, in the face of great adversity, sought freedom, hope and justice beyond these shores. They and their descendants went forth and explored continents, built great countries and cities and gave their enterprise and culture to the world. This is their legacy. Their voices will echo forever through the empty straths and glens of their homeland.

The statue was commissioned by the Clearances Centre Ltd., a charitable company started by Dennis Macleod, a native of Kildonan, who now lives in Canada.

"It's my personal ambition," said Macleod, "to have the same statute erected in places where the Highlanders settled," including the United States and Australia.

At the ceremony, Minister Salmond made the following comments:

Today's unveiling of this remarkable new presence in the Highland environment marks an important moment for Scotland. The impulse to create this statue came from a desire to remember, but also to reconcile; to reflect on the past, but to draw on it for the future's strength.

The clearances that took place across Scotland in the eighteenth century were most acutely felt here in the Highlands—and rarely with such severity as in the communities like those around Kildonan.

There is a sadness of course in the recollection that this strath once played home to hundreds of families in dozens of small communities—a way of life that was transformed forever by the economic experiments of that period.

But we should take heart, and pride too, from the resilience of those that left this country and made their contribution, often a significant one, to the communities of other countries that showed generosity in receiving them.

Modern Scotland must learn from our history. Yes, we will continue to give our ideas and innovation and energy to the world, but will recognise too that our people are our country's greatest resource and they must always be treated as such.

Emigration Stone, The. At Cromarty in the Black Isle was designed and carved by Richard Kindersley and erected on October 10, 2002. It bears the names of the 39 emigrant ships that sailed from Cromarty in the 1830s and 1840s carrying Scottish emigrants to the New World, including Upper Canada (Ontario) and Nova Scotia. The stone commemorates Cromarty's role as the principal point of embarkation for emigrants who left the Highlands for the New World in the 1830s and 1840s. The ships were as follows:

Ami, Ann, Asia, Blagdon, Boyne, Brilliant, Canada, Cleopatra, Clio, Corsair, Dalmarnock, Diligence, Economist, George, Good Intent, Headleys, Industry, Isabella Simpson, John, Jane Kay, Kate, Lady Grey, Lady MacNaughton, Lamb, Lord Brougham, Planet, Poland, Robert & Margaret, Rover, Salamis, Theodora, Triton, Tweed, Vestal, Viewforth, XYZ, Zealous, Zephyr

enclosure movement. In England, turned small holders into landless agricultural labourers. The earliest round of enclosures in England occurred during the Tudor era. Maurice Beresford has referred to the "deserted villages" of England, which he argued were "a sign of men changing their view of the most profitable use to which land could be put.... It is the sign of a class of men who were able to pursue their own advantage to the point of annihilation of communities." In fact, nearly three-quarters of England was enclosed by 1760. The movement accelerated during the 19th-century Napoleonic Wars (1803-1815). Essentially, English gentry were placed on the same par as landlords in the Highlands. And, like the cottars, the lowest class of rural English society—the cottagers and squatters—suffered the most during the enclosure era.

Opposition in England to the forced enclosures varied. In *The Human Shore: Seacoasts in History*, John R. Gillis notes that the people who were displaced in the area of eastern England known as the Fens did not take lightly to the disruption. They regarded the marshes of their homeland "as a great common to which they had time-honored use rights." When turning to the courts seemed fruitless, they resisted: men and women armed themselves with scythes and pitch forks, ready to fight for what they considered belonged to them.

The enclosure movement also affected Wales. The rising price of wool during the Napoleonic Wars led to more so-called rational uses of land. Vast areas of mountain grazing were converted into private property. As in England, cottagers and squatters suffered the most. The Welsh responded by emigrating, but there were sporadic efforts of resistance. The enclosure movement affected Scotland as well where it was better known as the Lowland Clearances. Opposition was minimal with the possible exception of resistance in Galloway in the 1720s.

The main difference between the English enclosure movement and the Highland Clearances was that the Scots tenants enjoyed no security of tenure whereas their English counterparts at least had the right to the hereditary tenure of a farm under what was called the copyhold system. The landlord in Scotland held much more power over his tenants; in other words, the tenants were at the mercy of the landlord.

See also Lowland Clearances

Eriskay, Isle of. Two significant but quite different events took place on this small island in the Outer Hebrides. On August 2, 1745, Charles Edward Stuart accompanied by his "seven men of Moidart" landed here, an event that precipitated the 1745 Jacobite Rising. More recently, the *SS Politician* ran aground in 1941 with its precious cargo: whisky. The Anglo-Scottish writer Compton Mackenzie turned that story into a novel which became the basis for the 1947 film *Whisky Galore*. In 1934 the German filmmaker Werner Kissling made an early short film on the island, "Eriskay: A Poem of Remote Lives."

In November 2006 local residents took control of the island in a community buyout. The community-owned organization Stòras Uibhist manages 93,000 acres of land covering not only Eriskay but also South Uist and Benbecula as well as a number of other small islands. More than 95 per cent of the Stòras Uibhist lands consist of croft holdings.

ethnic cleansing. The brutal events following the loss at Culloden as well as the general after-effects of the Clearances themselves have led some historians and critics to use the term "ethnic cleansing" and its twin, "genocide." Among the followers of this line of thought is the historian Allan MacInnes. Others, such as Eric Richards, subscribe to a less severe interpretation. Richards points out, for example, that since there was no systematic effort to "extirpate and eliminate the indigenous population," the term should not apply. Others disagree. Krisztina Fenyö, for example, insists that in attitudes, ideology, motives and, "to some extent," practice, the Clearances was for all intents and purposes a form of ethnic cleansing.

The term itself was first used in 1991 during the atrocities in Bosnia even though the acts that took place there are as old as human "civilization." Acts of ethnic cleansing often forced emigration and are associated with deportation and genocide. Generally speaking, though, ethnic cleansing usually refers to the expulsion of people deemed "undesirable" elements of the population based on religious, ethnic, political or ideological reasons. To put it more bluntly, it can refer to the practice of removing minority populations.

Joseph L. Albini and Jeffrey Scott McIllwain define ethnic cleansing as "the displacement and dislocation of people whose property is confiscated by those who force them from their land...." Whether forced into refugee camps, like later generations of victims, or dispersed into vile urban slums, as many of the Clearance Highlanders were, the result is the same: anomie, chaos and trauma.

F

factor. An estate manager or property manager, the factor is responsible for the maintainance of the estate's income. Some of the most notorious historical figures associated with the Clearances were factors, including James Gillanders, William Young and, especially, Patrick Sellar. Tom Devine has called them petty tyrants "who ruled the people with an iron hand." Estate factors held all the power since small tenants held their meagre crofts on an annual tenure.

Gaelic poets often wrote scathingly of the factors. In "Lament for the Great Factor," the poet Eugene Rose (or Ross) celebrates with unbridled glee the death of John Campbell (1801-1872), the factor for the Argyll estates in Iona, the Ross of Mull and Tiree. This particular factor, writes the poet, "will be foremost in the pit owned by Satan ... with a flame of fire at his buttocks." When news of his death reached Canada, where many of the evicted were living, it was said that "bonfires were lit and banners fastened to the branches; their joy was then boundless...."

Faed, Thomas (1826-1900). Scottish painter, born in Kirkcudbrightshire; brother of John Faed, also a painter. Faed studied at the Edinburgh School of Design and was elected an associate of the Royal Scottish Academy in 1849 before moving to London in 1852. Several of his works have strong Clearances connections such as *The Last of the Clan* and *Oh Why I Left My Hame*.

The Last of the Clan is among the most famous images of the Clearances (along with Nicol's *Lochaber No More*) and has graced the covers of numerous Clearances books. A wildly romanticized and melancholy image that associates emigration with exile, the painting was first exhibited at the Royal Academy in London in 1865. An elderly clansman, sitting on a white horse, its head bowed, waits on the quayside as his family and friends leave Scotland on an emigrant ship. The following extract, a possibly apocryphal "Letter to a Kinsman in America" appeared in the Royal Academy exhibition catalogue:

When the steamer had slowly backed out, and John MacAlpine had thrown off the hawser, we began to feel that our once powerful clan was now represented by a feeble old man and his granddaughter; who, together with some out-lying kith-an-kin, myself among the number, owned not a single blade of grass in the glen that was once all our own.

Faed was one of the most successful painters of his time. His work was popular with the Victorian public who queued to see his latest paintings of often deeply romantic—many would say sentimental—Scottish themes. When *The Last of the Clan* was exhibited, the Royal Academy reportedly had barriers erected to control the curious crowds.

Faed excelled at still-life details, figures and especially landscapes. He died in London in 1900.

failed 1884 emigration to North Carolina. A little-known episode in North Carolina history. In 1884, promoters in Scotland as well as North Carolina recruited at least 180 Highlanders to emigrate to the old Scots settlement in Cape Fear. The promoters included James L. Cooley and the Rev. David Macrae as well as Margaret MacLeod from Dundee, who had relatives in the Upper Cape Fear and D. P. McEachern, a second generation Scottish American and a former Congressman from Robeson County. Others too were involved. Most of the emigrants came from Skye and Lewis although a second wave originated in Orkney and Glenelg on the mainland.

The 1884 emigration is significant for two reasons: it was the last organized emigration of Highland Scots to North Carolina and the only known Scottish emigration scheme to North Carolina during the Clearances era. The reasons for the emigration were also twofold: 1) to assist by relocating some of the impoverished and oppressed crofters in Scotland suffering from the ramifications of the Clearances and 2) to revitalize the ethnic identity of the original Scots settlement. The people of the Carolinas were well aware of the situation in Scotland. The St. Andrews Society of Charleston, South Carolina, for example, collected $8,000 for Highland relief efforts in 1847.

They were also aware of the resistance that was taking place in some parts of the Highlands and Islands, including the Battle of the Braes in 1882. Significantly, several of the emigrants, including Alexander Finlayson and Donald Matheson, had connections to the men arrested as "agitators" at Braes and were among the emigrants to North Carolina.

Unfortunately, resistance was futile. Most of the emigrants either returned to Scotland or moved elsewhere within just a few months of their arrival in North Carolina. Finlayson and Matheson were among the first to return to Scotland. By the time the new emigrants had settled in North Carolina, most Carolina Scots had become completely Americanized even as the Highland settlement was a culturally distinct community within North Carolina itself. The inhabitants, for example, continued to use Gaelic (Bill Caudill reports that Gaelic was still used in some areas as late as the early 20th century). But that was not enough to rise above the cultural chasm that existed between the Carolina Scots and the Highland Scots. Everything was alien: the weather, the food, the crops, the method of agriculture and the "gloomy forests." The fact that many of the newcomers did not speak English further complicated the situation. Also adding to the emigrants' dissatisfaction was the sense of isolation as emigrant families were separated from one another. They also maintained that promises were not kept and work was not forthcoming. Indeed, there are indications that the crofters may have found themselves working as labourers alongside African American slaves. The crofters thus thought they were simply a means to an end, and consequently were offended and humiliated by the situation they found themselves in.

Fairhurst, Dr. Horace (1908-1986). Senior Lecturer in Geography at the University of Glasgow and founder of the Department of Archaeology at the University of Glasgow. Fairhurst took part in various excavations with Professor V. Gordon Childe and excavated at numerous Scottish sites, including in Argyllshire, Glasgow, Stirlingshire, Perthshire, Sutherland and Caithness. He led the excavation at Rosal in Strathnaver, Sutherland, in 1962.

Ferrard, David. Contemporary Edinburgh-based Scots singer and songwriter of mixed ancestry (he is the son of an Italian-Scots father and an American mother from Appalachia) known for his affinity for protest songs. Blessed with a warm voice and pure diction, the charismatic Ferrard has released several well-received recordings. On *Across the Troubled Wave* (Alter Road Records, 2009), which was recorded in North Carolina, he performs "Gilmartin," a song about the Highland Clearances written by the Dunbar songwriter, Kenny Brill.

feu. Land held in perpetuity but, more generally for 99 years, in return for payment of an annual rent.

fiction of the Clearances. Numerous works of fiction have been written about the Clearances or inspired by the Clearances. Among the most important are Neil Gunn's *Butcher's Broom* (1934) and *Highland River* (1937), Fionn MacColla's *And the Cock Crew* (1945) and Iain Crichton Smith's *Consider the Lilies* (1968). The historical figure of Patrick Sellar is featured prominently in two of these works, *Butcher's Broom* and *Consider the Lilies*.

Much of Gunn's work, especially his novels, are set in and around the Caithness town of Dunbeath, the crofting and fishing village, where he was born and raised. In Gunn's *Highland River* (1937), the character of Kenn is an adult revisiting his Highland home where his father was a herring fisherman. One of the characters in the novel, Angus, is based on Gunn's real-life brother, Ben, who died in the trench warfare of the First World War. Another character is Gus, a Canadian of Highlands Scots descent whose ancestors were natives of Strathnaver. Although Gus has never been to Scotland, he is fully aware and knowledgable of Scottish history. He described himself as being a Mackay "out of the Mackay country." Gunn and his characters know Scotland from different perspectives, and Gunn seems to imply that they have equally valid perspectives: Gus, the outsider, filters his knowledge through heritage—he even has some knowledge of Gaelic—while the native son, Kenn, knows Scotland through direct experience by being intimate with its personal and natural history.

Highland River is an allegorical novel where a key image is that of the river of time, a river that goes back to the source of life itself. Gunn uses the image of salmon as a metaphorical symbol of Scotland, drawing upon the Celtic legend of Fionn and the Salmon—Fionn is given the wisdom of the ages when he inadvertently tastes the salmon. As a child, Kenn, fetching water from the river, plunges into the water to hunt the salmon. In a life-changing moment, Kenn becomes aware that there is something else beyond his immediate life; there are things in life that he cannot control. The salmon, notes Gunn, "is swimming back to the source of its life." In his own life, to walk the full length of his local river was, Gunn believed, the ultimate adventure "and the thought of it inhabited the mind with a peculiar strangeness."

Although there may be little of the Clearances actually depicted in *Butcher's Broom* (1934), Gunn's most famous novel, the impact and legacy of the Clearances is pervasive, as is the destruction of a way of life. The focus of the novel then is the changing conditions in a small Highland township before, during and after the removals. In *Butcher's Broom* the character of Heller is modelled after Patrick Sellar, the notorious factor and the figure most closely associated with the Strathnaver Clearances. The novel maintains the culture of the Highlands was destroyed by the Clearances.

Other Gunn titles associated with Dunbeath include his autobiography *The Atom of Delight* (1956), *The Green Isle of the Great Deep* (1944), *The Grey Coast* (1926), *The Serpent* (1943), *Sun Circle* (1933) and *Young Art and Old Hector* (1942).

Fionn MaCColla's *And the Cock Crew* explores the spiritual quandary of a minister whose congregation is forced to confront the inevitability of eviction. The minister must ask himself whether the Clearances are the "mark" of divine judgement, as his fellow ministers believe, or egregious examples of landlord oppression and tyranny. Finally, Iain Chrichton Smith's *Consider the Lilies* offers a psychological portrait of an elderly woman, Mrs. Scott, who is about to be evicted by Patrick Sellar.

All three of these Strathnaver novels, as they are often called, use similar themes: betrayal by the landlords, but also by the clergy. What's more, the very real threat of evictions is pervasive; indeed numerous portrayals of actual evictions appear in the novels. Other themes include a palpable sense of loss even as the inhabitants recall a more peaceful and secure time; if not quite a Golden Age, at least in those times they had little fear of being booted out of their homes without warning.

The novels also share similar imagery: use of fire; burning of houses; visions of hell and hell-fire. As Laurence Gouriévidis points out, the evictions represent hell on earth and factors as the "human expression of God's will"; resistance to the ministers were depicted as "acts and decisions" that are "deemed sinful or even 'satanic'."

Sheep too are part of the metaphorical imagery. The ministers, suggests Gouriévidis, have turned their human flocks into sheep who "meekly bow" to make room for "their animal counterparts." The portrayal of the factors in all three novels is uniformly malignant, even if sometimes bordering on caricature (especially, offers Gouriévidis, in *Cock Crew*). Historical figures sometimes appear in the novels. In addition to Patrick Sellar, the stonemason and journalist Donald Macleod is a major character in *Consider the Lilies*.

Other themes in the novels include scathing attacks on Calvinism, the Anglicization of the Gaels, and the binary of materialism and humanism.

"The importance of the three Strathnaver novels," asserts Gouriévidis, "lies in their being transmitters of a memory of the Clearances—a memory encapsulated in the Strathnaver evictions and saturated with moral outrage and condemnation" which in turn, argues Gouriévidis, "reinforces the memory of the Clearances as a formative event having shaped a country—let alone a region."

See also individual titles

Fire in the Glen (1991). A recording by two members of the Scots folk band Silly Wizard: lead vocalist and tenor banjo player Andy M. Stewart and accordionist Phil Cunningham, along with Irish singer Manus Lunny on acoustic guitar and bouzouki. The record includes two Clearances songs: the poignant "I Mourn for the Highlands," which Stewart set to music based on Henry Whyte's Gaelic song

"The Dispersal of the Glens" and the title track, Stewart's own composition. "I Mourn for the Highlands" is preceded by "Treorachadh" (Introduction), an original melody composed by Cunningham in the pibroch style. In "I Mourn for the Highlands," the protagonist, weary of witnessing the evictions and burning of crofters' homes, chooses to immigrate to America, a country which promises equality, rather than the tyranny of the Crown.

forfeited estates. Refers to lands on Highland estates which the Crown seized in post-Culloden Scotland. The estates were returned to their original owners in the 1780s.

Fort Augustus. Small Highland village built after the Jacobite Rising of 1715 and named after William Augustus, the infamous Duke of Cumberland. In Scotland he earned the sobriquet "the Butcher" because of his brutal behaviour at Culloden when he encouraged the hunting down and slaughter of countless Highlanders. The actual fort was erected in 1726.

"Fort Bragg Clearances," North Carolina. Home to the U.S. Airborne Corps and Special Forces, Fort Bragg occupies 160,000 acres on what was once an old Highland settlement. The inhabitants had names like McDiarmid, McNeill, McKay, McFayden, McInnis, Gillis, McLeod and Monroe; their people came from Argyll, the Isle of Bute, Skye, Islay and Jura.

After the First World War, the U.S. government purchased land that formerly belonged to a small community of North Carolina Scots, most of whom were of Highland descent. Their church, the Long Street Presbyterian Church, founded in 1756, was inactive as of the year in which the government bought it. The church building that stands today dates from 1847. With the military occupation, many of the civilian structures were razed. At the time of the government purchase, there were 170 families living on 135,000 acres of land. Of these, 108 were landowners and 62 were tenants. Their occupations were farmers, turpentiners (or coopers), millers, sawyers and craftsmen. According to Linda F. Carnes-McNaughton and Carl R. Steen, in 1918 the tracts were accessed for their value and proposals to the occupants were made. More than 60 per cent of the landowners refused the army's offer. Eventually the lands were condemned and taken and the farm buildings, mills, houses and sheds were cleared for future military activities.

Although not a clearance in the literal sense, one could argue that the removal of the North Carolina Scots was at the very least a metaphorical clearance. An archival postcard from 1918 depicts the demolishing and burning of a farmhouse located on Fort Bragg lands and echoes the original Highland Clearances. Eventually, the army agreed to maintain the church and the adjacent cemetery, which is now on the National Register of Historic Places. An annual family reunion service has taken place here since the 1950s. An offshoot of Long Street, Sandy Grove Presbyterian Church, also served the Scottish community until it was purchased by the U.S. Army in 1922.

See also Cape Fear; North Carolina

Fort George. Located eleven miles northeast of Inverness and built in the post-Culloden era from 1747-1763 as a Highland fortress, it was considered one of the most significant artillery fortifications in Europe. Today it houses the Regimental Museum of the Queen's Own Highlanders.

Fort William. Started as a garrison around the time of the Massacre of Glencoe in 1692. During the Clearances era, it was used as a port of emigration for those who were cleared from Inverness-shire and North Argyll.

Fraser, James Earle (1876-1953). American sculptor of Scots descent; the American muralist Barry Faulkner once described Fraser's character as being "like a good piece of Scotch tweed, handsome, durable and warm." Fraser's best-known work is his poignant sculpture, *End of the Trail*, which bears, intentionally or not, striking parallels with Thomas Faed's elegiac Highland portrait, *The Last of the Clan* (1865).

Born in Winona, Minnesota, Fraser worked as an assistant to sculptor Richard Bock and attended classes at the Art Institute of Chicago. During his time in Chicago he also helped with the production of architectural sculptures at the 1893 World's Columbian Exposition. He later studied at the École des Beaux Arts in Paris, where he met the great American sculptor Augustus Saint-Gaudens and became his assistant (among his tasks was assisting with the Saint Gaudens' sculpture of the Robert Louis Stevenson Memorial in St. Giles Cathedral in Edinburgh) before eventually opening his own studio at 3 Macdougal Alley in New York's Greenwich Village.

Fraser created *End of the Trail* for the Panama-Pacific International Exposition in San Francisco in 1915. Originally meant to be cast in bronze, the scarcity of metal caused by the First World War led it to be done in plaster instead. In 1968 the National Cowboy and Western Heritage Museum in Oklahoma City, Oklahoma, restored it where it remains today. The original bronze statue was purchased by inventor and sculpture Clarence Addison Shaler and is located in Shaler Park, in the town of Waupun, Wisconsin. Shaler donated it to the city in 1929.

In theme and presentation the *End of the Trail* bears a remarkable resemblance to Thomas Faed's equally doleful painting *The Last of the Clan*. Both works romanticize the indigenous peoples of their respective lands. By the time Fraser created his sculpture, Native Americans no longer presented a threat. Like the Highlander in Faed's canvas, Fraser's former warrior appears defeated, slumped on a horse with his head bowed, eyes downcast, resigned in other words to his fate.

Fraser-Mackintosh, Charles (1828-1901). Native of Inverness, a solicitor there from 1853 to 1867 and MP for Inverness burghs from 1874 to 1885. He was also a member of the Napier Commission and an avid supporter of the crofters and their cause.

Free Church of Scotland. Members of this church believe in a literal interpretation of the Scriptures. The Free Church was established in 1843 when 480 ministers of the Church of Scotland renounced the established church and set up their own. The Disruption, as it was called, was motivated by resistance to ministers being forced on congregations. Many congregations worshipped on the hillsides until they were able to build their own free-standing churches. Numerous Free Church ministers, such as the Rev. Gustavus Aird at Glencalvie, advocated for the rights of the indigenous population during the Clearances.

French and Indian War (1754-1763). Also known as the Seven Years War. The war was fought primarily between the colonies of British America and New France on the North American continent. The French and various Native American tribes opposed the British. Approximately 12,000 Highlanders fought under British command as members of such regiments as the Black Watch, Fraser Highlanders and Montgomery's Highlanders. The Fraser Highlanders fought most famously at the Battle of the Plains of Abraham in 1759. The Treaty of Paris ended the war in 1763. Among the long-term consequences of the war was British control of French Canada.

Fry, Michael. English author who has written extensively about Scotland. His books include *Patronage and Principle*, a political history of modern Scotland; *The Dundas Despotism*, a study of 18th-century Scottish government; *The Scottish Empire*, an examination of Scotland's imperial achievements; and *How the Scots Made America*, a look at the Scottish contribution to the United States. Educated at Oxford and Hamburg universities, he has been a weekly columnist for the *Scotsman*, the *Herald* and the *Sunday Times*. In 2005, he published his revisionist history, *Wild Scots: Four Hundred Years of Highland History*, a controversial work in which he argues that the Clearances were a sad but inevitable result of modernization. He went so far as to suggest that the Clearances were a myth and that claims of mass evictions were greatly exaggerated.

Fry believes in the Great Men approach to history. In his view, the lairds were well-meaning if misunderstood figures since as "improvers" they felt compelled to modernize land tenure because the land could not support the rising population. He maintained that the Duke of Sutherland moved tenants from their homes to the coast to provide them with new livelihoods, situations that were similar, he suggested, to the postwar Labour government moving people to, say, East Kilbride in the greater Glasgow metropolitan area.

Not surprisingly, the book raised a ruckus in Scotland. Fry has been vilified as a "Clearance-denier," among other less flattering descriptions. Alastair McIntosh called *Wild Scots* "a highly politicised attempt to turn back Prebble's and Hunter's tide of historical revisionism," concluding that it was nothing less than "buffoon history." Brian Wilson, the former editor of the *West Highland Free Press*, called him the "David Irving of the Clearances," referring to the famous Holocaust denier. Fry and his views were even condemned in the Scottish Parliament.

Not everyone reacted so negatively, however, especially south of the border. The *Times Literary Supplement*, for example, recommended *Wild Scots* as "prescribed reading" while the *Times* asserted that Fry "overturns the conventional demonology."

G

Gaelic Books Council. Founded in 1968 in the Celtic Department of the University of Glasgow to support Gaelic publishing. The Gaelic Books Council is now independent of the University, funded in part by *Bòrd na Gàidhlig* and *Creative Scotland*.

Gaelic College (Colaisde na Gàidhlig). Formerly the Gaelic College of Celtic Arts and Crafts, it was founded in Cape Breton in 1938 by Rev. A. W. R. MacKenzie and is devoted to the study and preservation of the Gaelic language and Celtic arts and culture. Once the only institution of its kind in North America, it offers programs in Gaelic language and song, music, fiddle, piano, guitar, dance and crafts. The Great Hall of the Clans features interactive displays, including a history of the first Scottish settlers to the area.

In 2013 the College celebrated its 75th anniversary.

Gaelic Society of London. Founded in 1777 to promote the Gaelic language and culture.

Gàidhealtachd. Refers to the Gaelic-speaking areas of the Highlands and Islands of Scotland.

Galloway Levellers. *See* Lowland Clearances

Gartymore Land League Cairn. Erected in 1981, about 3 km (2 miles) from the Highland town of Helmsdale, to commemorate the centenary of the first branch of the Sutherland Association, a branch of the Highland Land League.

See also Highland Land League

Gearrannan Blackhouse Village. Consists of nine refurbished traditional Highland blackhouses on the Isle of Lewis, some of which have been refurbished self-catering cottages to accommodate guests. They were completely modernized to include such amenities as underfloor heating, a shower room and fully fitted kitchenette—luxuries unimaginable to the original inhabitants. As recently as the 1950s the area was a flourishing community; the houses were occupied until 1974. After the last residents left, the community was declared a conservation area. In addition, there is a café, museum and resource centre.

Geikie, Sir Archibald (1835-1924). One of the pioneers of modern geology, Geikie was educated at the Royal High School in Edinburgh and at Edinburgh University. In 1867 he became director of the Geological Survey in Scotland and from 1870 to 1881 was Professor of Geology at Edinburgh University. Later he became Director-General of the survey of the U.K. and head of the Geological Museum in London. He is best remembered though for *Scottish Reminiscences*, an account of his travels as a geologist in the Highlands over a span of sixty years, from the 1840s to the early years of the 20th century. Most famously, he wrote about a village that he came across by accident ("after returning from my ramble") that was being cleared—Suishnish on Skye in 1854.

This corner of Skye had been occupied for ages by a community that cultivated the lower ground where their makeshift huts formed a kind of scattered village. The land belonged to Lord Macdonald, whose affairs were in a dire state. Since the main objective of the Macdonald estate was to wring as much rent out of the population as possible ("the interests of the crofters formed a very secondary consideration," admitted Geikie), Macdonald's trustees decided to remove the entire population in order to convert it into one large sheep farm.

As he tells it,

> a strange wailing sound reached my ears at intervals on the breeze from the west. On gaining the top of one of the hills on the south side of the valley, I could see a long and motley procession winding along the road led north from Suishnish. It halted at the point of the road opposite Kilbride, and there the lamentation became long and loud. As I drew nearer, I could see that the minister with his wife and daughters had come out to meet the people and bid them all farewell. It was a miscellaneous gathering of at least three generations of crofters, on their way to be "shipped to Canada."

His description of the leaving is among the most graphic and heartbreaking images in Clearance literature:

> There were old men and women, too feeble to walk, who were placed in carts; the younger members of the community on foot were carrying their bundles of clothes and household effects, while the children, with looks of alarm, walked alongside.... Everyone was in tears; as if they could not tear themselves away. When they set forth once more, a cry of grief went up to heaven, the long plaintive

wail, like a funeral coronach, was resumed, and after the last of the emigrants had disappeared behind the hill, the sound seemed to re-echo through the whole wide valley of Strath in one prolonged note of desolation.

He offers a final observation:

I have often wandered since then over the solitary ground of Suishnish. Not a soul is to be seen there now, but the greener patches of field and the crumbling walls mark where an active and happy community once lived.

genocide. In recent decades, the Highland Clearances has been described by some as an example of genocide. Ian Grimble, for example, compares the Clearances with the Holocaust and the genocide of the Gaels. And he's not the only one. David Craig compared the evictions to the "shipping-off of the Polish and other Jews in cattle trucks." Similarly, the poetry of Angus Peter Campbell finds parallels between the fate of the Jews and the fate of the Gaels.

The newspaper reports of the Clearance era sometimes employed horrendous imagery. In order to emphasize the urgency of the situation, several crusading journalists who supported the Gaels often used such incendiary words: "extermination," "annihilation" and "expulsion" being among the favourites. As Fenyö points out, language often was used as a "weapon" in order to make a point: that the Highlanders were in dire need of support.

Other scholars and writers viewed the Clearances as a form of cultural genocide that intentionally and willfully destroyed Gaelic society through what Ascherson has called "a prolonged act of 'ethnic cleansing'."

See also ethnic cleansing

George IV (1762-1830). A foppish king who led an extravagant and indulgent lifestyle. He was often the target of ridicule as much for his obesity as for his pretentious love of pageantry. He visited Scotland in 1822, the first visit of a reigning monarch since 1650. Sir Walter Scott organized the famous visit, down to the minute details, which included attending a Caledonian Hunt Ball and a theatrical adaptation of Scott's own *Rob Roy* at the Theatre Royal. David Wilkie's famous portrait depicted the king dressed in full Highland regalia, lending new-found respectability to the traditional Highland dress. The king's visit would have a long-lasting effect on Scottish identity as Scott ingeniously used the trappings of the defeated Jacobites to good effect. Essentially, Scott—the Lowlander extraordinare—in one fell swoop turned Scotland in its entirety into a nation of Highlanders.

A statue of the king, wearing a long cloak with a sceptre in his outstretched right hand, was unveiled at George and Hanover Streets in Edinburgh in 1831, where it remains to this day. Significantly, the sculptor, Sir Francis Chantrey (1781-1841), was the same sculptor who designed the controversial Ben Bhraggie statue in Sutherland.

Gibson, Rob (b. 1945). Politician, author and musician born in Glasgow. Convener of the Dingwall-based Highland Traditonal Music Festival, Gibson is a member of the Scottish National Party (SNP), for Caithness, Sutherland and Ross. He is the Deputy Convener of the Economy, Enterprise and Tourism Committee and a member of the Transport, Environment and Rural Affairs Committee. He was first elected to the Scottish Parliament in 2003, representing the Highlands and Islands and was re-elected in 2007. Before entering politics he was a secondary school teacher in Alness and Invergordon.

Gibson has written numerous books on the Highland Clearances, Highland history and Highland emigration, including *The Promised Land, Power in Easter Ross, Toppling the Duke: Outrage on Ben Bhraggie?, Plaids and Bandanas, The Highland Clearances Trail* and *Highland Cowboys*. As a member of the band Ceilidh Ménage he released *Plaids & Bandanas: Song Links from Scots Drovers to Wild West Cowboys* in 1998.

Gigha, Isle of. A small island off the west coast of Kintyre on the Scottish mainland. Gigha has been inhabited since at least prehistoric times and is the ancestral home of Clan MacNeill. Like many of the smaller Hibredean islands, the population peaked in the 18th century before dwindling due to high rents, emigration, evictions and absentee landlords. Over the decades the island changed hands numerous times. Conditions improved considerably though when, in March 2002, the islanders, through the assistance of grants and loans from the National Lottery and Highlands and Islands Enterprise, purchased the island. The Gigha Heritage Trust now takes care of the daily operations of the island. Since the buy-out the population has increased by more than 50 per cent and, to paraphrase James Hunter, has experienced a "spectacular reversal" of fortune so much so that Hunter suggests that Gigha might be a good role model for other community buyout plans.

Gillespie, Thomas. Pioneered sheep farming in Glengarry. Gillespie came to Glengarry in 1782 with his business partner Henry Gibson at the invitation of Marjorie, the wife of Duncan Macdonell of Glengarry, whom John Prebble calls a "shrewd and ambitious social climber." She offered Gillespie the lease of a sheep-walk along Loch Quoich which ultimately led to the removal of some 500 people who left aboard the ship *Macdonald* in the summer of 1785. Their destination was another

Glengarry: in Upper Canada or what is now Ontario. The emigrant's minister, the Rev. Alexander Macdonell, accompanied them on the journey across the ocean, built a church there and stayed in the New World until his death.

"Gilmartin." A Clearances song written by the Dunbar, Scotland, songwriter Kenny Brill and recorded by David Ferrard on the latter's *Across the Troubled Wave* (2009). Coincidentally, Gilmartin is also the name of the protagonist in James Hogg's darkly psychological novel *The Private Memoirs and Confessions of a Justified Sinner* (1824), who may or may not be the devil. In Gaelic, "Gille-Màrtainn" is a nickname for the fox—in other words, a trickster.

Gladstone, William E. (1898-1898). British prime minister, born in Liverpool; he entered politics as Tory MP for Newark in 1832 before switching to the Liberal Party, and representing South Lancashire from 1865 to 1868, Greenwich from 1870 to 1880 and Midlothian from 1880 to 1895. In 1882, Gladstone appointed a commission to enquire into the conditions of the crofters of the Highlands and Islands. Two years later, the evidence was collected and published and, in 1886, Parliament passed the *Crofters' Act*, which addressed many, if not all, of the crofter's grievances.

Glasgow Argus. Established in 1833, the *Argus* was a liberal anti-landlord newspaper and among the first newspapers in Scotland to demand land reform, including redistribution of land and the abolition of outdated feudal laws. The paper also advocated the abolition of the *Law of Entail*, a feudal Scottish custom that supported a landed aristocracy at the expense of the common man. By the mid-19th century more than half of Scottish land was entailed. (*Entail* was finally outlawed in 1914.) In addition, the *Argus* refuted the often racist anti-Gael rhetoric of other Scottish newspapers, asserting that the people were "naturally as laborious and intelligent, and independent as any other people on the globe."

The paper went out of business in 1847.

Glen More. Near Aviemore, was cleared of its inhabitants around 1830 by the Duke of Gordon to make way for sheep and then, later, deer. The people were resettled to Boat of Garten, 11 km (7 miles) away.

Glencalvie Clearances. *See* Croick Church, Glencalvie

Glencoe. Running from Rannoch Moor to Loch Leven, Glencoe is among Scotland's most famous and wildest glens. But it is remembered also for more sinister reasons, for it was here on a cold February night in 1692 that visiting Campbells massacred their hosts, the MacDonalds, in one of the most notorious and violent episodes in Scottish clan history.

In the early morning hours of February 13, 1692, Robert Campbell of Glenlyon and nearly 130 soldiers, acting under the order of King William III, rose from their beds to massacre their hosts, the MacDonalds, where they had been staying for about twelve days. What led them to commit such an atrocity? The MacDonald clan chief, MacIain of Glencoe, had failed to take the oath of allegiance to the king before the rather arbitrary January 1, 1692, deadline, which upset, and threatened, the authorities to such an extent that they chose to make an example of the unfortunate chief and his clansmen. MacIain, as it turns out, was in no particular hurry to take the oath, not fearing that his life would be in any imminent danger. Moreover, he mistakenly had travelled to Fort William to sign the oath rather than Inveraray. Consequently, he did not sign his name until January 6, a little less than a week after the deadline had elapsed.

Nearly 40 people died that night, but many more escaped into the Highland hills and subsequently died of hunger and exposure. MacIain was buried on Eilean Munde, a small island at the head of Glencoe in Loch Leven, his grave surrounded by the shelter of trees.

The Glencoe and North Lorn Folk Musuem is located in the village of Glencoe, along the old Glencoe Road. At the top of the village is the MacDonald Monument, a tall Celtic cross erected in memory of MacIain. The Glencoe National Trust Visitor Centre examines the area's geological history as well offers exhibits on the infamous Massacre of Glencoe.

Glendale. A Land League monument east of Glendale, on the Isle of Skye, that was unveiled in 1970 to honour the site of a confrontation that took place between marines who were attempting to arrest the so-called ringleaders of the Glendale land league movement. Led by John MacPherson, the crofters demanded the return of common grazing land that they believed had been taken from them. Defying court orders, they began grazing cattle on the land. One of the factors was assaulted when he tried to remove the cattle. Warrants were issued for the arrest of about 20 Glendale men. Ultimately, five crofters, including MacPherson, agreed to stand on trial as a token. For this reason they were given the sobriquet of the Glendale martyrs. They were sentenced to two months in jail.

The plaque reads:

To commemorate
The achievement of
THE GLENDALE LAND LEAGUERS
1882-1886
locus where 600 crofters challenged
the government forces
imprisoned
John MacPherson, Glendale Martyr
Rev. D. MacCallum, Donald Macleod
John Morrison

Glenelg. Situated on Loch Hourn, Skye, formerly in Macleod country; in the early 19th century the inhabitants were removed to overcrowded townships on the Sound of Sleat. In 1837 the owner, Charles Grant, president of the Board of Trade, sold his estate to James Baillie of Dochfour (originally from Bristol), a sheep farmer. With each successive sale of the property, more and more small tenants were removed. In 1849, 500 were offered assisted emigration on the ship *Liscard* to Québec by a grant from Baillie and the Destitution Board.

Glenfinnan. A pillar, built in 1815 by Alexander MacDonald of Glenaladale, positioned dramatically at the head of Loch Shiel, is topped by a statue of a kilted Highlander; it commemorates the raising of the standard by Prince Charles Edward Stuart on August 19, 1745. The Glenfinnan Visitor Centre is located directly across the road from the monument. The Jacobite Risings of 1715 and 1745 attempted to restore James Edward Stuart, known as the Pretender, to the British throne (James Edward Stuart was the son of the deposed James VII of Scotland, or James II of England). The 1745 Rising began when James Edward Stuart's son, Charles Edward Stuart, the Young Pretender (otherwise known as Bonnie Prince Charlie), came ashore at Glenfinnan after sailing from the continent.

Glengarry Clearances. In 1782 Thomas Gillespie came to Glengarry, Inverness-shire, with his business partner Henry Gibson, at the invitation of Marjorie, the wife of Duncan Macdonell of Glengarry. She leased him a sheepwalk along Loch Quoich that resulted in the removal of some 500 people. The tenants left on the ship *Macdonald* in the summer of 1785, bound for Canada. "They were leaving one Glengarry for another, for this was the name given to a Canadian settlement made by earlier Macdonell exiles who had left the United States at the end of the American Revolution," writes John Prebble. But Macdonell was not quite done. She evicted more tenants in 1785, again in 1787 and then again in 1788.

After her death, the evictions continued under her son Alasdair Ranaldson Macdonell (1773-1828), a clan chieftain who was as full of himself as anyone in the entire history of the Highland Clearances. He is the very same Highland chieftain that Sir Henry Raeburn painted in his famous portrait of 1812 and who served as the inspiration of Fergus MacIvor in Sir Walter Scott's novel *Waverley*. Prebble describes Macdonell as "an absurd" figure of a man. He lived the role of the noble Highland chieftain to the hilt (pun intended), even if he was far from noble and barely a chieftain. He wore the traditional Highland dress and kilt most everywhere he went and maintained a chief's retinue of bard, piper and gillies. (Macdonell of Glengarry made several highly publicized appearances when George IV visited Edinburgh in 1822).

In 1794, Macdonell raised the Glengarry Fencibles regiment; young men who refused to fight for him were threatened with eviction. When he disbanded the Fencibles in 1802, the soldiers returned to discover that their chief was in the process of evicting their parents. They quite reasonably chose to emigrate to Canada, rather than stay, much to Macdonell's apparent chagrin. He tried to prevent them from leaving (although he had no provisions for them had they chosen to remain), which earned him the eternal enmity of Robert Burns, who, in his poem "Address of Beelzebub," called him a tyrant and compared him to no less than Satan himself.

Glengarry County, Ontario. Founded by Scots loyalists, mostly Lochiel, Glengarry, Knoydart and Glenelg, as well as other Loyalist Highlanders from the Mohawk Valley in New York, fleeing from the newly formed United States after the Revolutionary War. Subsequent emigrants from Glengarry, Scotland, came partly as a result of the Highland Clearances. Most of the Glengarry emigrants were from the Glengarry estates, a vast area that stretched from the Great Glen along Glen Garry and Loch Quoich to Knoydart and North Morar. Additional emigrants arrived in 1826 and during the Great Highland Famine from 1846 to 1855; many of the latter received financial assistance. Between 1773 and 1853, Marianne McLean estimates that approximately 3,500 people immigrated to Glengarry County from the Highlands. Contrary to J. M. Bumsted, who argued that the emigrations of 1770 to 1815 were an attempt by the clanspeople to maintain their traditional customs rather than a result of the clearances, McLean asserts that when the land began to be cleared to make room for sheep after 1780 the Glengarry folk—which consisted of families—made a conscious decision to leave; hence, the Glengarry Clearances, in McLean's estimation, directly affected emigration. The peopling of Glengarry, then, was the result of both chain and group emigration. "The creation of a Highland settlement in Upper Canada," notes McLean, "was an ambitious alternative to the crofting and kelping settlements developed by the landlords...." In 1815 the government-sponsored emigration to Glengarry took place; it was the last large-scale emigration of its kind from the Highlands to Glengarry County.

Glenorchy (Argyll). The property of the Marquis of Breadalbane until the mid-19th century. Over several decades, from 1806 to 1831, he arranged for numerous clearances which led to a substantial decrease in the population. Glenorchy was the home of the Gaelic nature poet, Duncan Bàn Macintyre (1724-1808).

Gloomy Memories was written by the stonemason and journalist Donald Macleod that originally appeared as a series of *Letters in the Edinburgh Weekly Chronicle*. A seminal and influential piece of muckraking journalism, the letters were published in book form in 1841.
See also Donald Macleod

Gordon of Cluny, Col. John (ca. 1776-1858). An Aberdonian, ranks with Patrick Sellar, James Gillanders, Alasdair Ranald Macdonell of Glengarry and the Countess of Sutherland as among the most evil of the Clearance villains and certainly has one of the worst reputations of any of the landlords during the era. Indeed, he was responsible for some of the most brutal Clearances. Lucille Campey has called him a "tight-fisted, contemptible brute."

Cluny cleared inhabitants on Barra in the late 1840s, a Clearance that Eric Richards calls "the most sensational model of a Highland clearance." It combined violence with forced emigration but also "landlord trickery, starving peasants, conniving factors, premature deaths and the fawning collusion of the minster of the established church"—in other words, the Clearances in microcosm.

He also cleared his estates in South Uist and Benbecula in the late 1840s, from where some people went to Glenelg township in Grey County, Upper Canada (Ontario). He assisted some 3,000 Roman Catholics from South Uist to emigrate to Canada; they sailed to Québec between 1848 and 1851, most settled in Huron County, Upper Canada (Ontario). In 1851 some 1,700 inhabitants from South Uist came to Québec. They were so destitute that it prompted a Canadian immigration agent to declare, "I never during my long experience ... saw a body of emigrants so destitute of clothing and bedding; many children of 8 and 9 years old had not a rag to cover them."

Gordon, Seton (1886-1977). Naturalist, writer and wildlife photographer, born in Aboyne, Aberdeenshire, who studied the natural sciences at Exeter College, Oxford. Gordon published extensively on the natural history of Scotland. In particular, he wrote with great sensitivity and insight on the environment in rural Scotland. During his long lifetime he published more than 25 books. His masterwork, *Hebridean Memories*, originally published in 1923, is considered one of the most significant, and comprehensive, observations of bird and animal life on the islands as well as an insightful chronicle on the changing rhythms and customs of the various crofting and fishing communities. The book also offered firsthand and valuable accounts of the emigration of numerous islanders, specifically aboard the liners *Metagama* and *Marloch*, both of which were bound for Canada.

Grant, Elizabeth of Rothiemurcus (1797-1885). Born in Edinburgh, she was a notable diarist of Scottish social history. Her best known work in a Highland context is the posthumous *Memoirs of a Highland Lady* (1898).

The Great Glen. Divides the north and northwest Highlands from the central and southwest Highlands and runs from Lochaber to Inverness in a southwesterly to northeasterly direction. Large-scale sheep farming had reached the Great Glen by as early as 1790.

Great Highland Famine. Fear of famine was an omnipresent feature of life in the Highlands and Islands for much of the 18th and 19th centuries. As a result of the Great Highland Famine thousands left for Canada and Australia between 1846 and 1857 while many thousands more emigrated "internally" to Lowland cities. As in Ireland, the Scottish famine victims had relied too much on a single crop, the potato, since it could produce high yields from poor soil. Dependency on the potato would prove disastrous. The western mainland of Scotland and the Hebrides, the heart of crofting territory, were affected most severely.

The potato blight was caused by the fungus *Phytophthora Infestans*, the same fungus that led to so much human suffering in Ireland. Although the estimates of the number of people who were starving varied—it was estimated to be around 300,000—modern figures indicate that the more accurate number would be around 200,000. In total, the potato blight affected 70 per cent of parishes in the Highlands. Although the number of deaths did not approach that of the Irish Famine, the impact on the Highlands and Islands was still devastating. "Landowners took the initiative to rid their estates of populations that were no longer tenable and helped fund the passage of up to 20,000 Highlanders to Canada in the late 1840s," notes Aitchison and Cassell. What's more, many Highlanders remained destitute for many years after the initial emergency had ended even though very few actually died from starvation.

The *Times* of London sent a commissioner to report on the causes of the famine. His conclusion was less than sympathetic. And because his reports were reprinted in numerous Scottish newspapers, including the *Scotsman* and the *Glasgow Herald*, his impact was widespread, and profound. According to the reporter, the root cause of the Great Highland Famine lay not in the circumstances but in the character of the people. People in Scotland, as well as in Ireland, were destitute because they were lazy unlike their English brethren who were frugal and hard working, he wrote.

Charles Trevelyan, assistant secretary to the Treasury, supervised the relief efforts, much like he did in Ireland, although without the controversy that his tenure in Ireland provoked from the citizenry. The Free Church and destitution committees collected charity. Charity and philanthropy, after all, were entrenched as a part of Victorian society. Charity became almost fashionable, especially among middle-class women, and philanthrophy was part of the fashion for improvement. But charity was meant for the *deserving* poor; thus, the Free Church extended charity in exchange for work. This "food for labour" principal became prevalent throughout society. An editorial in the *Inverness Courier* summed it up: "No Relief Without Employment."

Greenyards, Strathcarron, Easter Ross. One of the bloodiest evictions in Clearance history was known as the Massacre of the Rosses. In March 1854, writs of removal were served to the tenants in the Greenyards estate in the parish of Glencalvie. According to John Prebble, 400 to 500 people lived in the strath. Most were Rosses or Munros. As in Glencalvie, their minister was the Rev. Gustavus Aird. The factor was James Falconer Gillanders.

The inhabitants refused to leave. When officers handed writs of removal to the women of the estate, the women threw them in the fire. With a shrug and a grin, the officers returned to Tain to wait for another day. They came again, this time with constables in force. A small group of mostly women, and some men, were ready, armed with cudgels and sticks.

Ultimately, the police charged with raised batons. After it was over, 26 women and girls were seriously wounded in the melee. According to Prebble, only two men and two boys were involved. One of the men, a veteran of Waterloo, was kicked and beaten as he lay on the ground. After it was over, the authorities returned to Tain, and brought with them four women who they referred to as the ringleaders. Two days later, they were released on bail. Of the four women arrested, only one, Ann Ross, was charged: with mob action, rioting and breach of the peace. Another "ringleader," a man, Peter Ross, was also arrested and charged. Ann Ross was sent to prison for 12 months; Peter Ross received an 18-month sentence with hard labour.

Donald Ross, the Glasgow lawyer, wrote about the incident and published in a small pamphlet with the intentionally provocative title of *The Russians of Ross-shire or The Massacre of the Rosses*.

The incident was dramatized in John McGrath's play, *The Cheviot, the Stag and the Black Black Oil*.

See also Croick Church, Glencalvie; Donald Ross

Grosse Île, Québec. Located on the St. Lawrence River, the main port of entry for emigrants to Canada between 1832 and 1937. Upon arrival immigrants were required to enter a quarantine station and have their bodies, clothes and belongings disinfected in order to stop the spread of disease; cholera, smallpox and typhus were especially prevalent.

Gruids Clearances. Located five miles north of Culrain, Sutherland. In April 1821 the people of Gruids resisted the sheriff-officers who came with writs of removal, stripped them of their clothing and threw away their papers. When soldiers from the 41st Regiment stationed at Fort George arrived, they retreated, surrendered the writs and left their homes behind to resettle in the village of Brora.

Gunn, Neil M. (1891-1973). Novelist, born in Dunbeath, Caithness, the son of a fisherman. He wrote about the ordinary life and habits of the Highland fishing and crofting communities. The Clearances are featured prominently in several of his novels, especially *Highland River* (1937). Educated at the village school, Gunn passed the Civil Service exam in 1907 and moved to London. As officer of customs and excise, he was a civil servant for most of his adult life, including a stint in Inverness. His first novel, *Grey Coast* (1926), was released to critical acclaim and was followed by *The Lost Glen* (1928) and *Morning Tide* (1931). His other works include *Sun Circle* (1933), *Butcher's Broom* (1934), *Highland River*, *The Silver Darlings* (1941) and *The Well at the World's End* (1951).

Gunn, Neil M. Memorial. A bronze sculpture in Dunbeath commemorates the birthplace of the 20th-century Scottish author. Located at the harbour, the sculpture depicts Kenn, the central character in Gunn's seminal Highland novel, *Highland River*, carrying home his first salmon. Erected by the Neil Gunn Society, it was unveiled by Diarmid Gunn, the author's nephew, in 1991.

Guthro, Bruce (b. 1961). Singer-songwriter, born in Sydney Mines, Cape Breton, and, since 1998, the lead singer of the Gaelic rock band, Runrig, having replaced the original singer Donnie Munro.

H

Hallaig, Raasay. Dun Caan (Dùn Cana) is the highest hill on the island and the hill made famous by James Boswell when, on his 1773 journey with Dr. Samuel Johnson, he danced an impromptu jig at the top; it overlooks the former township of Hallaig. In 1853 George Rainy removed the people to make way for sheep. Contemporary Gaelic scholar John MacInnes has called Raasay "a heroic landscape" with its "sweeping green plateaus down to the sea." In his *Journal of a Trip to the Hebrides*, James Boswell mentions descending a hill on the east side of the island and entering a farmhouse, "a Maclean's."

> It was somewhat circular in shape. At one end sheep and goats were lodged; at the other, the family. The man and his wife had a little bedstead. The place where the servants lay was marked out upon the ground with whinstones and strewed with fern. The fire was towards the upper end of the house. The smoke went out at a hole in the roof, at some distance and not directly above it, as rain would hurt it.

Gaelic scholars, including John MacInnes and Ronald Black, suggest that the farmhouse that Boswell visited that day would have been located at Screapadal, which Rainy cleared in 1852-1854. One hundred years later Sorley Maclean composed his magnificent poem "Hallaig" in which he mentions Screapadal ("in Screapadal of my people / where Norman and Big Hector were"). A memorial cairn to Maclean and to the memory of Raasay's people stands near the ruined houses of the township. The poem is reproduced on the cairn.

See also Hallaig (documentary); "Hallaig" (poem); Sorley Maclean.

"Hallaig" (poem). Sorley Maclean's "Hallaig" is concerned with time and nature. Perhaps it would be more accurate to say that it is about the nature of time, but also about tragedy, redemption and the very meaning of mortality. "Hallaig" was published in the Gaelic publication *Gairm* in 1954.

"Hallaig" is an elegy of a deserted township, the poet's birthplace, and in its use of nature imagery and its powerful application of incantation is reminiscent of Duncan Bàn Macintyre's nature poem "Beinn Dorain." More than this, though, it is a haunting reflection of what once was: a meditation on a now-empty landscape populated by the ghosts and shades of Maclean's own ancestors who lived there before being cleared for sheep. In Maclean's visionary words, the trees become girls who, in happier days, laughed under a Highland sky. Death haunts every line of the poem as the poet laments what became and what might have been of his people, the Macleans and the Macleods ("every single generation gone") although their spirit lives on. It ends with death too: the death of a deer in the woods but also of time itself.

The poem has been adapted into various musical scores, from classical to popular. "Hallaig" was incorporated into the lyrics for the vocal score of Peter Maxwell Davies's *The Jacobite Rising*, commissioned to commemorate the 250th anniversary of the Rising. The Glasgow-born composer William Sweeney (b. 1950) wrote a meditation for organ based on Maclean's poem.

Martyn Bennett included a sample of Maclean's own reading of it on the track of the same name which appears on Bennett's genre-bending 1997 album *Bothy Culture*. In 2011, "Hallaig," a musical celebration of Maclean's poetry, was presented at the annual Blas festival at St. Andrew's Cathedral in Inverness and at Sabhal Mòr Ostaig at Sleat, Isle of Skye. With Kenneth Thomson at the helm as musical director the program featured compositions by Stuart MacRae, Mary Ann Kennedy, Eilidh Mackenzie, Marie-Louise Napier, Allan Macdonald, Blair Douglas, Donald Shaw, Allan Henderson and Thomson himself. Performers included the Dingwall Gaelic Choir, Brian McAlpine, Gordon Gunn, Dougie Pincock, Jenna Cumming, Rhona MacKay, Alasdair Whyte, Mary McCarthy, Jack Evans and Su-a Lee.

See also *Hallaig* (documentary); Hallaig, Raasay; Sorley Maclean

Hallaig: The Poetry and Landscape of Sorley Maclean. A 63-minute documentary directed by Timothy Neat released in 1984 that examines the art and craft of Maclean's luminous, and profound, poetry in the context of the area's tragic past. The film includes commentary by Iain Crichton Smith and Seamus Heaney with poetry (mostly in English translation) read by Maclean himself.

See also Hallaig, Raasay; "Hallaig" (poem); Sorley Maclean

Handa. Small island off the northwestern coast of Sutherland; it was cleared in 1848; like St. Kilda, it had its own parliament for a time.

Harris Clearances. The Harris Clearances are notable because they occurred over a fairly lengthy period of time.

Lord Dunmore, the owner of land in Borve, had suffered great financial losses during the lesser known famine periods of 1836-1837 on his estate at Borve. In late 1839 and early 1840, while heavily in debt and therefore unable to pay his own expenses and with the people themselves reduced to abject poverty, he gave the people an unusually generous three years' notice to leave. According to Eric Richards, Dunmore offered to resettle the elderly and infirm elsewhere on the island and offered free passage to Canada for the rest. In addition, their rent arrears were forgiven and they were offered, notes Richards, a fair price for their cattle—all in all, a remarkably charitable package for the times.

Initially the people accepted the offer but then they changed their minds, refusing to emigrate. Dunmore's agents asked troops to help with their removal. The people stayed at Borve for an additional twelve months before they were ultimately removed, either resettled elsewhere on the island or outwith Harris. After some time had elapsed, those who remained reconsidered their options and asked Dunmore to help them emigrate to Canada. More than 600 left while another group departed for Australia in 1854. Notes Richards: "The Harris Clearances eventually dislodged all the people: emigration was a delayed (and perhaps fully considered) response some time after the original displacement."

Harrower, David (b. 1966). Born in Edinburgh, Harrower is a Scottish playwright whose most famous work is the critically acclaimed *Blackbird*, which has received productions in both London and New York. For our purposes here though, he adapted Roger Hutchinson's book, *Calum's Road*, about the Raasay crofter, Calum Macleod, into a play, which toured Scotland in autumn 2011.

Harvard University. The University's Department of Celtic Languages and Literatures was established in 1896 by Fred Norris Robinson. When he died in 1966, he left Harvard his collection of books on Celtic studies, which became the core of the collection. He also endowed Harvard with the Margaret Brooks Robinson Professorship of Celtic Languages and Literatures, named in honour of his wife. The department flourished under the leadership of Charles Dunn, from 1962 until his retirement in 1984. Born in Arbuthnott, Scotland, the son of a Presbyterian minister, Dunn is best known as the author of *Highland Settler: A Portait of the Scottish Gael in Nova Scotia*.

Heaney, Seamus (b. 1939). Irish poet, playwright and translator born in Castledawson, Northern Ireland. Among his many honours he won the Nobel Prize for Literature in 1995. For our purposes, though, the great Irish poet has been an advocate of Sorley Maclean for years. In his poem "To Sorley MacLean," he addresses the poet directly by stating, "Sorley, all I say is this: Your work and you have grown priceless." Indeed, "Hallaig," he continues, "survives the clearances. The wheel turns still." Filmmaker Timothy Neat in early 1984 travelled to Dublin to interview Heaney for the film *Hallaig*. Heaney considered Maclean among the most "exemplary" of poets. In the film Heaney explains,

> I first heard Sorley MacLean speaking his poems in Gaelic on the stage of the Abbey Theatre.... and that experience had the force of a revelation. MacLean is one of those writers whose actual physical voice adds a dimension to the written poem. The voice that I heard was really heightened and mesmeric and weathered and seemed to come in close from far away—rather like the drone of a pipe. And the performance had a terrific bardic dignity about it—it was a surrender of the self to the otherness of the poems, and, the resonance of the Gaelic language itself....

Heaney's translation of the poem was published by Urras Shomhairle in 2002.

Hector (ship). The *Hector*, a Dutch-built ship, departed from Ullapool at Loch Broom in July 1773 with 189 passengers on board and sailed to Nova Scotia, but did not arrive in Pictou until September 15, 1773. Sometimes called the *Mayflower* of Canada, it conveyed the first permanent Highland settlement in Nova Scotia and was the impetus for further emigraton from Scotland to British North America. Most of the passengers were from Wester Ross, Sutherland, East Inverness-shire and Assynt. They had been recruited by John Ross, an agent for the Philadelphia Land Company, which owned 81,000 ha (200,000 acres) of wilderness in Pictou. The ship was owned by John Pagan, a Glasgow merchant. Pagan and his partner in the enterprise, Rev. Dr. John Witherspoon (1723-1794), a Presbyterian minister from Paisley, recruited potential Highland emigrants, offering land at low rates in Nova Scotia. (Witherspoon was the first president of the College of New Jersey, later Princeton University, and would gain even more fame a few years later when he was among the signers of the Declaration of Independence.)

Barely seaworthy, a ship so rotten, wrote John Prebble, "that the emigrants were able to pick away its timbers with their finger-nails." The journey across the Atlantic was not only long and miserable—it had been expected to take six weeks but took eleven due partly to inclement weather—but also deadly: smallpox and dysentery claimed the lives of

18 children and many adults who were buried at sea before arriving in Pictou.

Their first winter was horrendous. The land they had been promised was in fact nothing but virgin forest. The newly arrived settlers had to chop down trees to build shelter before the winter set in. With the assistance of the indigenous Mi'kmaq and some New Englanders they managed to survive, adapt and, ultimately, flourish. In the next half-century or so, many thousands more Scots emigrated to Nova Scotia.

A fully-constructed replica of the ship is moored at the Hector Heritage Quay on the Pictou town waterfront. Each August the town sponsors the Hector Festival, which features Highland music and dance and a re-enactment of the arrival of the *Hector*.

Helmsdale. Established as a fishing community for those evicted during the Clearances. The boom years took place during the late 19th century when the herring industry was concentrated there. The village was laid out by the Duke of Sutherland ironically in an effort to accommodate those tenants that he himself had cleared during the Clearances era. He even chose the street names for the town, which range from Sutherland Street to Dunrobin Street. Helmsdale is home to one of the best historic museums in Scotland, Timespan Heritage Centre, which houses a museum and a gallery.

See also Timespan Heritage Centre

Highland Clearances. Refers to the forceable removal of the indigenous population of the Highlands and Islands to make way for sheep and, later, deer. Along with the massacre at Glencoe and the Battle of Culloden no other topic in Scottish history is as fraught with condemnation, or anger.

The Clearances affected every part of the Highlands and Islands, from St. Kilda in the far western fringes of the Hebrides to Aberdeenshire in the east, from Shetland and Orkney in the north to Perthshire in the south. Eric Richards refers to the "great set-piece Clearances"; that is, the often brutal evictions of Strathnaver in 1814, Gruids in 1821, Skye in 1853, Knoydart and Greenyards in 1855. These are the Clearances that have received the most attention and provoke the most anger.

The Clearances resulted in the radical transformation of the economic and social structures of Highland society during which a large proportion of the population was displaced, usually to make way for very large sheep farms. This occurred at a time when Britain itself was undergoing a massive transformation into an increasingly industrial society. The Industrial Revolution affected the Highlands in ways that were quite different from the rest of Britain, however. Agricultural Improvers cleared the land of people and replaced them with sheep pastures in order to accommodate the needs of a growing population to the south. In effect, the Clearances were a clumsy and misguided attempt at social engineering in order to replace an archaic system (feudalism) with another more modern system (laissez-faire capitalism).

The worse evictions involved the forced removal of entire communities with little or no notice and where no alternative accommodation, not to mention employment, was offered. They were simply pushed out and left to fend for themselves. Quite often the evictions were executed by estate officials reinforced by legal officers and members of the police or, in the worst cases, military personnel. At the same time, there occurred numerous instances of large-scale removals in which the landlord offered the people alternative accommodation on the same estate. Many of these less dramatic instances were, in other words, more relocations than evictions; nevertheless, they were still disruptive if not traumatic to those affected.

The Clearances occurred over a long period of time from roughly the 1750s to the 1880s, with the worse episodes taking place between 1790 and 1855. In the first decade of the 19th century large areas of the Highlands beyond the Great Glen were turned over to sheep farms and inland communities were forced to resettle on the coasts. To put it more bluntly: the Highland Clearances were the forced removal of Highlanders and Islanders during the 18th and 19th centuries. The Clearances led to mass emigration, externally as well as internally—to coastal communities, to cities and towns of the Scottish Lowlands and to the so-called new world. Part of a complicated process of agricultural change, the Clearances were particularly notorious due to the lack of legal protection for tenants under Scots law, the suddenness of change from the traditional feudal clan system and the brutality of many evictions. To put it yet another way, the Clearances were often cruel examples of not only rural transformation but also population displacement—the dispossession of a people conducted in fits and starts over a very long period of time.

Having said all of the above, it is important to note that some historians maintain that forced evictions were the exception rather than the rule. Lucille Campey, for example, insists that evictions amounted to "exceptional incidents and should not be allowed to distort the overall picture." Some maintain that the evictions were exaggerated even as evidence proves that those who were evicted suffered unnecessary cruelty. For the average Highlander, to be evicted from lands that their people had occupied for many generations in order to make room for sheep was foreign to their concept of loyalty and trust—*dùthcas*. That is, the Highlanders thought they had a moral right to stay by virtue of ancestral occupation. Others, such as Michael Fry, contend that, although tragic, they were the inevitable outcome of changing agrarian practices and rapid industrialization. Fry provocatively asked,

"Clearances? What Clearances?," contending that the condemnation of the landlords was grossly exaggerated. The Clearance landlords were no better or worse than landlords in other countries and situations, according to Fry. Others have suggested that Clearance sites are being exploited for commercial gain, on a par, suggests Richards, to the Loch Ness Monster museum at Drumnadrochit in the Highlands.

Still—no matter what side of the historical equation one stands on—the Clearances consist of a complex series of events that continue to raise numerous questions. Were the conditions that led to the Clearances a matter of too many people on too little land, as some maintain, or of failed economic and social policies that left a considerable portion of the British population vulnerable to greedy capitalists, as others insist?

But the Clearances are now, and have been for a long time, part and parcel of Scottish political identity and indeed national identity. Neal Ascherson refers to the Clearances as "a narrative of betrayal." In some quarters Highlanders as victims have become an integral part of Scottish identity. Many families who now live in the Lowland cities are the descendants of Clearance Highlanders. From a Scottish diasporic perspective the Clearances are looked upon as an acute example of cultural trauma that is often used, rightly or wrongly, to explain the worldwide dispersal of Scots; that is, the Clearances are the emotional and cultural equivalent of the Irish Famine: tragic in outcome if lacking the high fatalities of the latter event(s).

The mythic proportions of the Clearances is an integral part of Highland identity but also of the greater Scottish identity overall. Some observers find the Clearances to be grossly simplified in folk memory or in political rhetoric which lead to facile explanations. Still others divide the pro- and anti-Clearance factions into clearly delineated camps: the commercial, Protestant, Scots or English-speaking Lowlanders or Englishmen of the south on one hand, versus the feudal, tribal, Gaelic-speaking Highlanders and Islanders of the north on the other. As Eric Richards argues, "The Clearances stand for much more than a sheep invasion: they become emblematic of landlords versus people, of aristocratic power versus the rights of the community and, in extreme versions, of one civilisation against another."

What complicates the situation further is that many of the lairds who cleared tenants off the land were Highlanders themselves, though so suitably Anglicized that by the time of the Improvers they had lost much of the paternal interest in their clansmen that earliest generations had carefully cultivated.

One of the other myths associated with the Highland Clearances is the idea that pre-Clearance Highlanders lived an idyllic, Eden-like existence. This image appears in numerous poems and songs. David Stewart of Garth, the soldier and great defender of the old ways, once wrote that "a more happy and contented race never existed." Others such as Joseph Mitchell compared the Highland existence to that of an aristocracy, but without the wealth, as the "kindly affectionate people" enjoyed fishing and shooting and essentially lived a "half-idle life." But no one did more to romanticize the Highlands, and its inhabitants, than Sir Walter Scott in his series of Highland novels that portrayed a world that even in mid-19th-century Britain must have seemed like an exotic place far removed from the urban, industrial squalor of cities like Glasgow or London.

Another part of the Clearances myth, some believe, is that the emigrants were inconsolable exiles. But as scholar after scholar has indicated, many of the emigrants—especially during the early phases—willingly left Scotland to settle elsewhere. Most eventually became grateful residents, and later citizens, of their adopted homeland even as they looked back at Scotland with a sense of yearning and nostalgia.

Among cultural upheavals, the Clearances were unique for numerous reasons: governmental supervision was virtually nonexistent; it was perfectly legal for landlords to evict their tenants at will; the Clearances led to a destruction of a people, a completion of the process that began at Culloden. What also makes the Clearances different from similar rural transformations is the fact that it occurred over a long period of time, rather late in historical terms, and the brutality and callousness of the actual evictions—a callousness that shocked many people in Great Britain once the mainstream press brought it to the attention of the greater population. What also set it apart from other removals associated with agrarian change was the number of people evicted—quite often entire villages and townships en masse. Removals took place on an unprecedented scale. Another characteristic of the Clearances was the suddenness of it. The tenants had no time to prepare either physically or psychologically.

The reasons for the Clearances were varied and complex. Market forces produced or exacerbated the displacement of the Highland population. Landlords searched for new sources of revenue to fund their increasingly extravagant lifestyles. By clearing the population and resettling them along coastal areas they freed inland tracts of land for large-scale sheep farming and provided the landlords with a workforce to carry out the back-breaking work of harvesting, burning and processing of another profitable industry, albeit short-lived, kelp. Thus, up to about 1820 at least, landlords needed their tenants as a labour force to work in the kelp industry. During the Napoleonic Wars the price of kelp soared and the landlords did everything in their power to discourage emigration.

Competition for scarce land was fierce. Industrial demand down south for wool persuaded landowners to make an economic decision.

They soon realized that combining several small inefficient farms into one large sheep farm enabled them to do two things simultaneously: clear the land of a surplus population of poor people and thereby with one fell swoop eradicate poverty on their estate, while charging a higher rent. The big sheep farms, in other words, virtually guaranteed landlords regular and often lucrative incomes.

The Clearances can be divided into various phases. With the end of the Napoleonic Wars, the kelp market collapsed. The landlords began replacing more and more people with sheep, forcing the displaced families to shift to coastal communities. In the meantime, the population began rising, especially in the Islands. In this post-kelp phase of the Clearances, the tenants had become an albatross, a nuisance. To many, but not all, landlords they were a surplus and increasingly unnecessary populace.

Thus, this first phase took place from roughly the 1730s to the 1820s and consisted of the breakup of the traditional townships and the decline of the tacksmen in Highland society. They were replaced by individual tenancies in the form of sheep and cattle farms and followed by the emergence and spread of crofting.

The second phase took place from the 1820s to the 1880s, reaching its peak in the decade after the Great Highland Famine of the 1840s. Primarily it involved the spread of sheep and cattle farming and the collapse of the old economy combined with the troubles caused by the famine as well as incidents of forced emigration and depopulation. The most notorious and brutal of the Clearances took place in Sutherland and Glengarry from 1780 to 1820.

Finally, the third phase brought government assistance in the form of the subsidisation of emigration to reducing the power of the landlords. By 1837 when Victoria became queen, the South had become fascinated by Highlanders, who by now were harmless and exotic objects of curiosity since the Jacobite rebellions were now safely in the past. In 1859 Queen Victoria bought Balmoral Castle and helped foster the "Balmoralism" that continues to haunt the Highlands today.

Other historians describe the Clearances not so much as phases as distinct episodes. Thus, John Macleod asserts that the Clearances refers to (1) the brutal and notorious Sutherland Clearances during the early 19th century when hundreds of families were evicted so that the land could be rented to largely Lowland sheep farmers; (2) the Hebridean Clearances, which were precipitated by the Highland famine of the 1840s and which were particularly ugly in South and North Uist and Barra; and (3) the era of voluntary emigration which spanned both periods and which was especially strong during the kelp boom.

Despite emigration, the population of the Highlands rose through the worst years of the Clearances until the early 1850s. The medical advances of the 18th and 19th centuries and natural population growth are some of the factors that led to the increase in the population of the Highlands and Islands. According to Eric Richards, the rising population and the subsequent congestion in its glens and straths was the most important "single fact of life of the region" throughout the Clearances era but, he insists, it is rarely acknowledged. The population of the Highlands "was never greater than in the age of clearances." As the numbers increased, the population became particularly vulnerable to the vagaries of the economy. Or, to put it bluntly, the land was unable to support the number of people on it. There is a popular misconception that all Highland Scots were victims of the Clearances, but many Highlanders chose to either emigrate or move to bigger towns or into the cities to find employment in order to feed their families.

Still, determining the number of people cleared is difficult. Some estimate a million people in total were directly or indirectly affected by the Clearances over a 200 or so year period. Anecdotally others estimate the number to be closer to half a million. Others still disagree. There is perhaps no definitive number. "The situation was complicated and people left or were put off the land for different reasons at various times," James Hunter told the *Scotsman* in 2005.

Where did the evicted Highlanders go? That too varies greatly. Some moved to neighbouring estates or to nearby counties. Others went to work in the factories of Glasgow, Edinburgh or Dundee. Like their Irish counterparts, many of the women became domestic servants to the burgeoning new middle class emerging in newly urban Scotland. Others still went to newly created fishing villages on the coasts such as Bettyhill or Ullapool. And others emigrated to the United States, Canada, Australia, New Zealand and elsewhere.

Aitchison and Cassell note that the net Highland population loss between 1855 and 1895 was about 9 per cent. "But this conceals the difference between displacement and depopulation," they offer. Most of those evicted, they assert, did not board emigrant ships but rather were resettled within the Highlands itself, such as on barren strips of coastline where the only reliable crop was potatoes, which, as they would soon discover, led to another set of problems. But, as Richards suggests, statistics regarding the Clearance Highlanders is fleeting. "They figure much more in subsequent fiction than in the direct historical record."

Either way, the Clearances changed the Highland landscape. With the rise of sporting estates, by mid-Victorian times the Highlands were transformed into either a playground for the rich and, later, into what Richards describes as a "sort of national park of the nation at large and its tourists." The Clearances also coincided with the decline of Gaelic culture generally. The social consequences of the Clearances were many too. The Clearances destroyed the role of the tacksmen in Highland society. "Crofting predated the Clearances but was radically reinforced by the clearing landlords," maintains Richards.

In the late 20th and early 21st centuries the Clearances continues to fascinate and provoke debate, especially in the arts. There have been Clearances novels by such authors as Neil Gunn and Iain Crichton Smith; children's books on the Clearances, Clearance plays (most famously John McGrath's *The Stag, the Cheviot and the Black Black Oil*), Clearance documentaries (*The Blood Is Strong*) and Clearance songs by popular musicians (from Runrig to Capercaillie). As we go to press the American filmmaker Guy Perrotta is working on a new documentary, *Voices over the Water*, on the Clearances and the Clearance diaspora.

The Highland Clearances are part of a broader pattern of agricultural reforms that include the Lowland Clearances and enclosures in England. Clearances, in fact, have been a worldwide phenomenon over the centuries: in India today, rural populations are removed from their villages to make room for hydro-electric projects and in modern-day China populations were displaced by the damming of the Yangtze River. Whether then or now, the core question the Clearances have raised is: Who owns and who controls the land?

For these and other reasons, the Clearances remain a collective memory of Scots, in Scotland and abroad.

Highland Clearances Trail. In 1983 the organization Highland Heritage put together a slim but important 16-page pamphlet compiled by Rob Gibson that described Clearance sites throughout the Highlands and Islands. An expanded 36-page edition appeared later before the Edinburgh-based Luath Press published it in book form in 2006.

Highland drovers. Droving in the Highlands dates back centuries. Among the most popular trysts, or gathering places, for the sale of cattle were the Crieff Tryst, the Doune Tryst, the Portree Tryst and the Muir of Ord Tryst. The Falkirk Tryst in the Lowlands, though, is probably the most famous trysting site in Scotland. It consisted of 80 ha (200 acres) where drovers on small, shaggy ponies mingled among tents occupied by dealers, pedlars, jugglers, merchants, beggars and auctioneers, but also ballad singers. While the most famous cattle raider was undoubtedly Rob Roy MacGregor, the "Rob Roy" of legend, among the greatest drover, if not the greatest in Scotland, was a Highlander by the name of John Cameron of Corrychoillie (ca. 1780-1856), a Gaelic speaker from Lochaber. Cameron was also a sheep farmer. He was in fact the greatest sheep farmer in the north, according to Richards. Many of the Highland drovers were bards, such as John the Drover from Rannoch.

During the height of the cattle droving trade, Sir Walter Scott wrote a story called "The Twa Drovers," set at the Doune Tryst and involving the rivalry between a Highlander from Clan MacGregor and an Englishman as they drive the cattle to market south toward England.

In recent years, a number of songs have been written about the droving life. The Canadian folk band, Cowboy Celtic, for example, recorded *Cowboy Ceilidh* in 1997, which includes several songs that find numerous parallels between cowboy poetry gatherings in North America and ceilidhs in Scotland (many American cowboys were, after all, of Highland extraction). David Wilkie, the lead singer of the band, even goes so far as to call the Crieff Tryst the Scots' version of Abilene or Dodge City. More importantly, the record features the song "Farewell to Coigach" ("Mo Shoraidh Leis a Coigach"), sung by the Gaelic singer Arthur Cormack and reportedly the only surviving cowboy song composed in North America in Gaelic. Written by Murdo Maclean, a Gaelic-speaking Highlander who went out to the American West to work as a cattleman, it is a *paean* by a homesick Gael yearning for his sweetheart back in Coigach. Rob Gibson, who with his band Ceilidh Ménage made his own recording exploring the connection between the Scots drovers and the American cowboys on *Plaids & Bandanas* (1998), mentions "The Drovers Song," reportedly composed in the late 18th century by the evocatively named Murdoch of the Cows, a Mackenzie from Loch Broom.

On the outskirts of the Highland town of Dingwall is a bronze sculpture of a Highland drover accompanied by a Highland bull and the drover's trusted collie dog. *The Highland Drover—An Dròbhair Gàidhealach* monument, by Perthshire sculptor Lucy Poett, was erected by the Highland Livestock Heritage Society in 2010, and is located at the entrance to Dingwall and Highland Marts Ltd. The Highland Drover Exhibition is located at the Dingwall livestock mart while the Highland Drover Project collection is located at the Highland Archive Centre, a permanent exhibition and archive, on Bught Road in Inverness.

Highland Folk Museum (Newtonmore). Britain's first open air museum; the highlight of the museum for our purposes is the reconstruction of part of a ca. 1700 Highland township based on the archaeological excavation of nearby Easter Raitts and a ca. 1920 working croft. Opened in 1995, the museum now offers a variety of reconstructed buildings ranging from an 18th-century highland township to a traditional 1930s croft to a tin school originally from Knockbain and a corrugated church from Culloden.

Highland and Islands Emigration Society. Ended its operations in 1857. About 5,000 people emigrated through its efforts.

Highland Land League. Modelled on the Irish Land League founded by Michael Davitt; the Highland version was encouraged by public opinion which by the late 19th century was turning in favour of the Highlanders. They began to resist eviction, most famously represented by the Battle of the Braes on the Isle of Skye. The Land League used direct action protest tactics, which included rent strikes and land occupations (which came to be known as land raids) by crofters, cottars and squatters. Perhaps the Land League's best-known slogan was "*Is treasa tuath na tighearna,*" a Gaelic saying usually translated as "The people are mightier than a lord," and the title of Iain Fraser Grigor's seminal book on the Highlanders' struggle for land.

"Highland problem," the. Refers to the stubborn belief that the only solution to the intractable problems of poverty was emigration to other parts of the British Empire where Highlanders would learn the value of the Protestant work ethic and, thus, be cured of their inherent laziness. To put it in blunt terms, the only real solution to the so-called Highland problem essentially was to get rid of them, to force them to leave their native land. Since they were like a cancer in an otherwise healthy body, or so goes the theory, the only "cure" was for them to be removed altogether.

Among the most succinct summation of the solutions to the "Highland problem" was an editorial on the Glencalvie Clearances that appeared in May 1845 in the *Perth Constitutional*. In effect, the editorial supported the Clearances as the only solution:

> They merely vegetate in a state of poverty and inactivity, alike unprofitable to themselves and to their landlords, and in many instances a clearing of the kind has greatly advanced them in the scale of society, and by compelling them to acquire industrious habits, has rendered them happy and independent, instead of continuing to protract their existence in idleness and discomfort. (May 14, 1845)

Highland regiments. Historically, Highlanders had been a reliable source of soldiers to fight for the British Empire. The Highlanders have fought Britain's wars around the world for centuries. But the effects of the Clearances had a devastating impact on the military recruits. To cite just one example, Prebble notes that between 1793 and 1815, more than 72,000 Highlanders served in various battalions and regiments. He states further that "[p]robably no one district made a greater contributon of men than the Isle of Skye": some 4,000 enlisted between 1793 and 1805. But, when after the start of the Crimean War and the government had trouble recruiting enough men in the Highlands and Islands to staff their military they asked, "Where are the Highlanders?" The answer echoed prompt and profound: "We have no country to fight for. You robbed us of our country and gave it to the sheep. Therefore, since you have preferred sheep to men, let sheep defend you!"

Arguably the Black Watch continues to be the most famous of the Highland regiments. In 1740 General George Wade created six Independent Companies to police or "watch" the so-called rebellious areas of the Highlands. The Black Watch was raised and recruited from the so-called loyal clans—the Campbells, Grants, Munros and Frasers—to assist in the pacification of the Highlands. Originally raised on the orders of Charles II in 1667, only to be later disbanded, George II raised them again in 1725 after the Jacobite Rising of 1715 and used them in the pacification scheme of the Highlands. The regiment consisted of six companies and was officially called the 43rd Regiment of Foot (later the 42nd) even though it continued to be known by the more familiar name, the Black Watch. (The name derived from the distinctive dark colours of the regiment's tartan.) The Black Watch served in the War of the Austrian Succession, the French and Indian War (or Seven Years War) and other British conflicts around the world.

Devine reports that, by the time of the French Revolution and the Napoleonic Wars, the numbers of Highland regiments were unprecedented, with figures ranging from 37,000 to 48,000 men in regular, fencible and volunteer units, which he refers to as "an extraordinary figure, given that the population of the Highlands was only around 250,000 to 300,000 during this period." Once the Jacobite threat was over, the Highland regiments were permitted to wear the outlawed Highland dress and encouraged to maintain their own customs and traditions. All in all, between 1730 and the Battle of Waterloo in 1815, more than 80 Highland regiments were raised.

Significantly, between 1743 and 1804, 16 Highland regiments, including the Black Watch, mutinied against their commanders. (See Prebble's *Mutiny* for a full examination of the complicated reasons behind the insubordination.)

Other major Highland regiments include:

1757: 77th Regiment of Montgomerie's Highlanders (Frasers, MacDonalds, Camerons and Macleans) and 78th Regiment of Fraser Highlanders

1759: 87th and 88th Regiments of Keith's and Campbell's Highlanders and 89th Regiment of Gordon's Highlanders

1777: MacDonald's Highlanders, raised by the Chief of Sleat

1778: Argyll's Highlanders and Seaforth Highlanders

1793: Queens's Own Highlanders, raised by Sir Allan Cameron of Erracht.

1881: Argyll and Sutherland Highlanders merged

Finally, in a controversial move, it was announced in 2004—and implemented in 2006—that the Black Watch, the oldest of the Highland regiments, was to join with five other Scottish regiments, the Royal Scots, the King's Own Scottish Borderers, the Royal Highland Fusiliers, the Highlanders and the Arygll and Sutherland Highlanders to form a new single regiment, the Royal Regiment of Scotland. But even as the uniforms of the regiment changed over the years, the nickname remained.

In 2006 the National Theatre of Scotland premiered the critically acclaimed play *Black Watch* written by the Fife playwright Gregory Burke (b. 1968) and directed by John Tiffany (b. 1971) at the Edinburgh Fringe Festival. *Black Watch* seamlessly and intricately incorporates music and dance movements into its narrative. As seen through the perspective of ordinary soldiers, the play is set in the so-called Triangle of Death between Fallujah and Karbala during the Iraq War in 2004 just after the move was announced. The play toured throughout Scotland with subsequent runs in London, Dublin, New York, Los Angeles, Chicago, Washington DC, Chapel Hill, North Carolina and as far away as Seoul. The play features numerous traditional compositions, including most poignantly a rather obscure Jacobite song, "Theàrlaich òig a' chuailean chiataich" (Young Charles of the Bonnie Hair) performed by Margaret Bennett and her son Martyn Bennett.

Highland Settler: A Portrait of the Scottish Gael in Nova Scotia. Book by Charles W. Dunn. *See* Harvard University.

Highland Society. Starting in the 1790s the Society discouraged emigration from the Highlands and tried to regulate/oversee conditions on emigrant ships.

Highland Society of Glasgow. Founded in 1727 to educate children of Highland parents who had settled in Glasgow.

Highland Society of London. Founded in 1778 to promote Highland culture and traditions.

Highland Songs in North America. The following are some important Gaelic songwriters who emigrated to North America, along with their best-known songs:

North Carolina

Donald Matheson (1719-1782)
"Tha mi'Faicinn Iongantas" ("I See a Wonder")
John MacRae (Iain MacMhurchaidh (?-1780?)
"Sleep Softly, My Darling Beloved"
"Lonely Am I"
"I Have Been a Fugitive Since Autumn"

Nova Scotia

Michael MacDonald (Micheil Mor MacDhomhnaill) (ca. 1745-1815)
"Fair Is the Place"
Donald Chisholm (1735-1810)
"We Shall Go to America"
"I Was Young in Strathglass"
John MacLean (1787-1848)
"The Gloomy Forest"
"The Deception"
John "the Hunter" MacDonald (1795-1853)
"Song for America"
Allan "the Ridge" MacDonald (1794-1868)
"You Have Been Loud and Boastful"

Prince Edward Island

Rory Roy MacKenzie (1755-?)
"The Emigration"

Ontario

Anna Gillis (?-?)
"Canada Ard" ("Upper Canada")

See also individual songwriters; popular music of the Highland Clearances

Highland Village Museum. An outdoor living history museum dedicated to Gaelic culture and folkways located in Iona overlooking the Bras d'Or Lake in Cape Breton, Nova Scotia. The museum's mission is to research, collect, preserve and share the Gaelic heritage and culture of Nova Scotia with Gaels and non-Gaels alike.

Highland women. Played a prominent role in the resistance movement during the Clearances era. At Culrain, Gruids, Durness, Glencalvie and Greenyards or at the Battle of the Braes, among other places, they were the ones who often took the brunt of the violence directed at their people, often sustaining severe injuries in the process. Whether driving off sheriffs and factors or setting fire to eviction notices, they stood their ground, defending their homes and their children under the most difficult and strained of circumstances. It is surely no accident that the most influential poet of the Clearances was a woman, Mary MacPherson, or Màiri Mhòr nan Oran (Big Mary of the Songs).

Highlandism. Even as the inhabitants of the Highlands were being cleared, many Lowlanders and London society people appropriated the cultural traditions and traditional clothing of the Highlanders in their mock Highland society functions. In this way, Highlandism foreshadowed the Celtic Twilight of the late 19th century. What's more, the Highlander, once considered wild, was transformed into a noble creature. It is a situation that has been repeated elsewhere, from the Native Americans in North America to the aborigines in Australia. Jean-Didier Urbain (b. 1951), the French sociologist, has used the very appropriate term "desavaging" to describe the complicated process.

Highlandism became more popular, fashionable even, in the 1840s, especially in London. Increasingly, too the Lowland newspapers romanticized the Highlands: the emptier the land, the more romantic the images. "Grandeur" was a favourite word to describe the Clearances-era Highlands, but in the Highlandism context this was a good thing. By the 1850s, too, it became fashionable to "tour" the Highlands, much in the way that young European men of means participated in the Grand Tour of the Continent from roughly the 17th century to the mid-19th century. Thanks to the popularity of the novels of Sir Walter Scott, Loch Katrine and the Trossachs in the Central Highlands in particular, became a fashionable destination for city dwellers intent on getting away.

Going further back, Highlandism has its roots in the 14th century with the Anglicization of the Lowlands. In the aftermath of Culloden the creation of the Highlands as we know it today really began. The Highlander as a noble savage recalled Enlightenment ideals as well as the Romantic interest in so-called primitive themes and landscapes. "By the end of the eighteenth century Jacobite rebelliousness had been so thoroughly tamed and metamorphosed," notes Paul Basu, "that it provided the key iconography for a new unified, assimilationist, Protestant 'North British' identity."

When Queen Victoria began summering at Balmoral in 1848, the cult of the Highlands was in full swing. There would be no looking back.

Highlands. Geographically speaking, the Highlands are the vast area of Scotland that lies north of the Highland Boundary fault, which runs a jagged southwest to northeast along a geological rift, roughly from Helensburgh in the west to Stonehaven in the north. The name is a bit of a misnomer since a great deal of the land north of the Highland line is actually quite flat. Indeed, Scotland's highest villages, Leadhills and Wanlockhead, are located in the Lowlands. Several of the islands are also quite flat, such as Tiree and Benbecula. Further, the Highlands are separated into three distinct regions: the West Highlands, which includes the Hebrides; the East Highlands, from Nairn to Caithness; and the Central Highlands, which covers the inland districts of Inverness to the north and Perth to the south. The Highlands vary too in religious breakdowns. Historically speaking, the East Highlands were largely Episcopalian, the Central Highlands were Presbyterian and the area around Inverness was Roman Catholic.

The only city in the Highlands is Inverness, billed as the unofficial capital of the Highlands. Fort William, on the other hand, is the biggest community in the West Highlands. The only town of significant size in the Hebrides is Stornoway, the capital of Lewis. But the vast majority of Highlanders continue to live in villages and smaller towns such as Oban, Invergordon and Portree. The economy is based largely on agriculture and tourism.

The economy of the pre-Clearance Highlands was marginal at best. The region exported black cattle and illicit whisky to the south but otherwise the Highland economy produced very little. Communication with the outside world was virtually nonexistent. By the early 1850s, during the height of the Clearances, the Highlands were for all intents and purposes turned over to sheep farms with the possible exceptions of crofting and some fishing businesses in the coastal towns of, for example, Wick and Helmsdale. As a result of the extensive sheep farming, though, the Highlands contributed greatly to the success of British manufacturing in raw wool. In addition, the Highlands provided meat to the Lowlands and English markets.

Afer being known for its empty glens and small population, for the first time in modern Highland history, more people are moving into the Highlands and Islands than are moving out, which may be considered a positive development.

History of the Highland Clearances. Published in 1883 by the journalist and editor of the *Celtic Magazine*, Alexander Mackenzie, it was the first significant book on the Highland Clearances. It contained a reprint of Donald Macleod's *Gloomy Memories* and a verbatim report of the trial of the Braes crofters on Skye.

Holocaust. More than a few writers on the Clearances have hyperbolically evoked the Holocaust to describe the Clearances. In particular, Ian Grimble compared Patrick Sellar's behaviour in Strathnaver with Reinhard Heydrich's behaviour against the Jews in Prague during the Second World War (Heydrich was the mastermind behind the "final solution"). David Craig compared the evictions to "the shipping-off of the Polish and other Jews in cattle trucks" while the Gaelic poet, Angus Peter Campbell, has also inferred that the Clearances bears more than a passing resemblance to the Holocaust.

Using excerpts from popular histories of the Clearances, Paul Basu has put together a rather remarkable table comparing the Clearances with the Holocaust. Among the 14 points Basu has cobbled together, he quotes David Craig ("Sutherland's managers kept records of their shipments of people with the obsessional thoroughness of an Eichmann") and Michael Newton (when he refers to "the cultural genocide of the Highlands").

Even the passivity of the tenants has led some observers to compare the Clearances with the Holocaust, when the Jews in Nazi-occupied lands went quietly to the death trains with little resistance.

Holocaust effect. A term used to refer to an intentionally collective forgetting about a traumatic event or episode in a nation's history.

Hugo, Richard (1923-1982). In September 1977 the American poet Richard Hugo and his family spent several months on the Isle of Skye. The result was *The Right Madness on Skye* (1980), a finalist for the National Book Award. Hugo, a poet from Montana, found in Scotland (and especially in the Hebrides) an affinity with the American West. In its mythology, history, folklore and legends, he discovered a shared identity and a spiritual connection between those who were evicted from their lands and the emigrants and pioneers who settled on the American frontier.

Several poems in the collection refer either directly or indirectly to the Clearances and their aftermath. In evocative and plaintive language, Hugo writes about the importance of place and the legacy of oppression. In "The Clearances" ("When you can't read, not even a map / where does home end and Tasmania start?"), "The Braes" ("You have to know / this is where the poor woke up a nation") and "Letter to Garber from Skye" ("The fate of the Gael is to lose everything"), Hugo finds an emotional link, a shared destiny, between the Highlanders who were removed from their lands and the Native Americans who were dispossessed of theirs. In succinct sentences ("it took no more than the wave of a glove, a nod of the head over tea"), he captures the essence of the unfair relationship between the powerful (the landlords) and the powerless (the land-strapped inhabitants herded aboard the emigrant ships as if cattle being fattened for slaughter). "The Braes," on the other hand, honours the ordinary men and women—mostly women—who put up a fight. Meanwhile, back in America, he reflects that around the same time "in sand, in snow / where nothing grows / we started Indian reservations." Hugo died of leukemia in 1982. The Richard Hugo House, a non-profit community writing centre in Seattle, is named in his honour.

Hunter, James (b. 1948). Former director for the University of the Highlands and Islands Centre for History, Chairman of the Isle of Eigg Heritage Trust and formerly the chairman of Highlands and Islands Enterprise. Hunter is best known, however, as the author of numerous critically acclaimed books on the Highlands and Islands, including the seminal *The Making of the Crofting Community* (1976, 2010). His other books include *Skye: The Island* (1986), *The Claim of Crofting: The Scottish Highlands and Islands* (1991), *Scottish Highlanders: A People and Their Place* (1992), *A Dance Called America: The Scottish Highlands, the United States and Canada* (1994), *On the Other Side of Sorrow: Nature and People in the Scottish Highlands* (1995), *Glencoe and the Indians* (1996), *Last of the Free: A Millennial History of the Highlands and Islands* (1999), *Culloden and the Last Clansman* (2001) and *Scottish Exodus: Travels among a Worldwide Clan* (2007).

Hutchinson, Roger (b. 1949). An English author and journalist. Born in the north of England, he has written for the *West Highland Free Press* since 1977. He has also served as editor of the *Stornoway Gazette*. Hutchinson has written often about Scottish topics, including *Polly: The True Story behind Whisky Galore* (1990) and *The Soap Man* (2003), about the soap magnate Lord Leverhulme, which was shortlisted for the Saltire Scottish Book of the Year Award. *Calum's Road* (2006), about the Raasay crofter Calum Macleod who single-handedly built a road on Raasay, was shortlisted for the Royal Society of Literature's Ondaatje Prize. In 2011 it was adapted for the stage by the Scottish playwright David Harrower.

I

"improvements." Term that refers to the economic, political and social changes that applied to the Highland Clearances. Improvements came in a variety of forms: the introduction or extension of cattle and/or sheep farms, which led to many evictions. In fact, before 1770, cattle caused the greatest amount of disruption. But these earlier removals received little publicity. The basic concept behind the improvements was the reduction of the number of tenants and the increase in farm size.

Another influence on the so-called Age of Improvement was the ideas associated with the Enlightenment. Enlightenment advocates believed in progress. According to this theory, revolutions such as the American Revolution and the French Revolution were not only right but necessary, as they swept away the inequality and unfairness of the old with the modernizing tendencies of the new. Devine refers to the improvers as propagandists for the new order. To their way of thinking, the old ways were irrational and stubbornly conservative and hence needed to be changed in order to bring the living conditions of the Highlanders up to date.

Inveraray. Planned village near Inveraray Castle, seat of the Dukes of Argyll, and among the best examples of an 18th-century new town in Scotland. Most of the town was designed and built by the Edinburgh architect Robert Mylne (1733-1811), between 1772 and 1800, as a community for woollen mill and herring fishery workers.

Inverness Advertiser. A liberal weekly founded in 1849, and one of the two Highland newspapers, the other being the *Northern Ensign*, that were "dedicated to the Highlands." The paper hired its own commissioner to investigate the Highland famine and subsequent destitution, reporting from the actual scenes of the evictions, including, most significantly, the clearances that occurred in North Uist and in Greenyards (near Glencalvie), Sutherlandshire.

Islay, Isle of. The medieval capital of the (MacDonald) Lords of the Isles, who ruled most of the Hebrides from the capital, Loch Finlaggan. By the 19th century, though, landowners sought to improve their rental income by introducing sheep farming and subsequently removing tenants. Clearances took place in the 1820s and again in the 1830s and 1840s, particularly around the Oa peninsula. The largest exodus from Islay occurred during the 1860s when John Ramsay encouraged entire communities to leave; he helped 400 people emigrate to Canada in 1862-1863.

Isle of Arran Heritage Museum. Located in Rosaburn, near Brodick, the largest town on the island, the museum features exhibits of island life from the earliest times to the 1920s. Most of the items have been donated by residents. The museum itself is set amid a group of older buildings that were originally part of an 18th-century croft, consisting of a smithy, semi-detached converted cottage, coach house, stables and harness room. Of significance for our purposes are old photographs illustrating Clearance sites on the island, including photos of tombstones of Arran-born people who emigrated to New Brunswick.

J

Jacobite Rising. A 40-minute work for soprano, mezzo-soprano, tenor, baritones, chorus and orchestra by composer Sir Peter Maxwell Davies. Commissioned by a Scottish businessman, Alistair Grant, to commemorate the 250th anniversary of the Jacobite Rising, it was first performed in October 1997 at the Glasgow city hall. Its text includes Edwin Muir's sonnet "Dream and Things," a few lines from Wilfred Owen's "Spring Offensive" and the entire text of Sorley Maclean's poem "Hallaig." It also includes traditional songs "Hey, Johnnie Cope," written after the Jacobite victory at the Battle of Prestonpans, and "A Song of the Battle of Falkirk" by Duncan Bàn Macintyre.

Jacobite Rising of 1715. Also called the "Fifteen," refers to the attempt by James Francis Edward Stuart (also called "the Pretender"), the son of the deposed James II of England (James VII of Scotland), to regain the British throne for the exiled House of Stuart. His famous son, Charles Edward Stuart (Bonnie Prince Charlie), also attempted to take back the throne, but he too failed. James Francis Edward Stuart died in 1766.

Jacobite Rising of 1745. Also called the "Forty-five," the attempt by Charles Edward Stuart (Bonnie Prince Charlie, also called "the Young Pretender"), the son of James Francis Edward Stuart, to regain the British throne for the exiled House of Stuart. Like the previous Rising, this one too ended in failure. The "Forty-Five" culminated in the crushing defeat of Highland forces by a government army at the Battle of Culloden in April 1746.

Jacobite songs. A particular genre of Scots songs (both Lowland and Highland) that comments on or makes reference to the Jacobite Risings, culiminating in the Battle of Culloden. The songs tell of the familiar military battles and historical figures of the Jacobite era, including Killiecrankie, Sheriffmuir, the Jacobite Risings of 1715 and 1745, Culloden, and Bonnie Prince Charlie. Themes of exile and restoration are common. As William Donaldson points out, more than 50 years after Culloden, the topic of Jacobitism was verboten. Only with the publication of Sir Walter Scott's Waverley novels did it became acceptable, even fashionable, to broach the subject.

Most of the so-called Jacobite songs that we are familiar with today though were written by Lowlanders, including Robert Burns, James Hogg and Lady Nairne as well as at least one Englishman, Harold Boulton, and were essentially Lowland in language if not content. These songs were published long after the official Jacobite era had ended. They include "The Skye Boat Song," "Ye Jacobites by Name," "Come o'er the Stream Charlie," "Cam' Ye by Athol?" "Parcel of Rogues," "Loch Lomond," "The Massacre of Glencoe," "The White Cockade," "My Bonnie Moorhen," "Who'll Be King but Charlie?" and "Will Ye No Come Back Again?" and, quite significantly, are mostly written in the Scots vernacular.

For our purposes it is important to remember that the Jacobite song helped to change popular opinion in Britain generally and Scotland in particular toward the figure of the Highlander. Thus, the Highlander, previously a savage enemy of the Crown who spoke a foreign tongue, became romanticized and even eroticized in the figure of the Bonny Highland Laddie. The songs too indicated a sea-change in attitudes as Lowlanders began to slowly recognize Highlanders as fellow Scots. What's more, as the once reviled Highland soldiers gained acceptance as guardians of the Empire, renowned for their military prowess on the battlefield, the very image of Scotland was transformed from a Lowland country to a Celtic country.

The Highlanders that appear in these Jacobite songs that were written by Lowlanders were portrayed in a sympathetic manner, whether the figure of Donald MacGillivray or Bonnie Prince Charlie himself. During his tour of the Highlands in 1787, Burns was known to have collected Jacobite songs; he included nearly 30 in his seminal *The Scots Musical Museum* anthology (significantly, two-thirds of those songs were written by Burns himself). His famous song about the Battle of Bannockburn, "Scots Wha Hae," was inspired by the Jacobite rebellions; thus, as Donaldson notes, Burns ingeniously linked the Scottish Wars of Independence with the Jacobite Risings. On the other hand, although Burns set many of his songs to Highland airs and was familiar with Gaelic literature (in translation of course), he still harboured ambivalent feelings toward the Highlander. "There is little reason to doubt," notes the Canadian scholar Michael Newton, "that he saw them as a people apart from his own." In a journal entry from his Highland tour, he makes this striking observation as he makes reference to their essential Otherness: "I write this on my tour through a country where savage streams tumble over savage mountains, thinly overspread with savage flocks, which starvingly support as savage inhabitants."

Although the Clearances are not mentioned by name in these songs they do appear indirectly. James Hogg toured the Highlands during the Clearances era and was undoubtedly familiar with what was going on there. Indeed, one of his Jacobite songs, "The Highlander's Farewell," addresses the aftermath of Culloden and the theme of Highland depopulation. From a modern perspective it also seems to imply ethnic cleansing:

> Farewell, farewell, dear Caledon
> Land of the Gael no longer!
> A stranger fills thy ancient throne,
> In guile and treachery stronger.

In the elegiac but little known "Stuarts of Appin," Hogg's reference to the Clearances is even more obvious as the narrator equates the devastating loss at Culloden with the equally devastating effect that the Improvers had on Gaelic culture as he laments the passing of the clans while the Sassenach (the English or Lowland Scot) "sings on the hills of green Appin." Still, another Jacobite song, "Sound the Pibroch," commemorates the loss at Culloden and the deserted Highland glens as it eulogizes the men who "died for royal Charlie."

Gaelic songs also refer to the Jacobite Risings and Culloden, including "I Am Asleep, Don't Waken Me" ("Tha mi am chadal, na dùisgibh mi") and "The Silver Whistle" ("An fhideag airgid"). But perhaps the most celebrated, and beautiful, of the Gaelic Jacobite songs (Anne Lorne Gillies calls it "one of the great masterpieces of Gaelic song") must be "My Fair Young Love" ("Mo rùn geal òg"). Composed by Christina Fergusson for her husband, William Chisholm, standard bearer to Clan Chisholm at Culloden, it is both a lament and an elegy. The widow addresses Charles Edward Stuart directly ("O young Charles Stewart / it is your cause which has left me wretched / You took from me everything I possessed / in the war on your behalf") as she venerates the memory of her slain husband ("and there stood at Culloden / no man your equal, nor any more valiant").

Johnson, Alison. Grew up in Aberdeen and earned degrees from Aberdeen University and Oxford. After marrying Andrew Johnson, the couple worked as teachers on the Isle of Harris. They bought Scarista House, a decaying manse, and converted it into one of the most highly acclaimed small hotels in Scotland (they sold the hotel in 1989). In 1993 Johnson wrote a novel *The Wicked Generation* that was inspired by the Clearances. Although not strictly about the Glencalvie Clearances it does take its title from the words that the people etched on the windowpane at Croick Church in Glencalvie. As she makes clear in her author's note, she did not intend the novel to be an accurate account of the Clearances but rather to make an artistic statement about the inevitability of change with modern-day parallels: "as at Glencalvie, a traditional, static community is overwhelmed by the juggernaut of modern economic growth. It is still happening, every day, to ethnic peoples from Siberia to Sarawak."

Johnson, Samuel (1709-1784). In 1773, Dr. Samuel Johnson, the great English lexicographer, and James Boswell, his Scottish companion and eventual biographer, made a journey to the Western Isles. Subsequently, each wrote his own journal: Johnson's *Journey to the Western Islands of Scotland* appeared in 1775 and Boswell's *Journal of a Tour to the Hebrides* in 1785. Combined, they are considered among the finest literary accomplishments in the annals of travel writing.

Johnson was an insightful observer. He was especially aware of the conditions—the "general dissatisfaction"—that led so many Highlanders to leave for other lands: "He was going to America because his rent was raised beyond what he thought himself able to pay." When Johnson asked his host whether the people would stay home if they could, the Highlander replied, "No man willingly leaves his native country."

For someone of his class and period, Johnson was rather charitable in his attitude toward the Highlanders. Whereas later generations of British society (including newspaper editors on both sides of the border) saw the Highlanders as inferior barbarians, Johnson instead saw a culture whose manners and customs were determined not by their nature or race but by the social conditions of the Highlands at that time. Of course, Johnson's entire purpose for visiting the Highlands and Islands in 1773 was to observe their "antiquated" life. Even by as early as 1773, he admits that he arrived too late, for their ancient ways of living were already fast disappearing. The Highlands were in a state of transition. Increasing commercialization and the breakup of the clan system was already well under way and, in fact, widespread and clearly evident. Already the economy, long based on clans and clanship, was ending and becoming commercialized: the clan chiefs less paternal guardians and more ruthless landlords with an eye toward lining their pockets with money gained in the Lowlands or in London. They were, in fact, becoming newly minted members of the British landed class and, thus, eagerly accepted the "improvement mania" that was taking over the Highlands; this is to say that the post-Culloden measures had only accelerated a course already set upon.

Like many social critics of his generation, Johnson did not see beauty in the wildness of the Highlands but rather sterility and ugliness, nothing in fact but a "naked desert." On the other hand, Johnson was surprised by the Highlanders themselves. Impressed by the "hospitality" and exquisite manners of his Highland hosts that seemed to filter down from the lairds to the ordinary folk, Johnson concluded that civility was a "part of the national character of the Highlands...."

Nor did Johnson romanticize the old Highland way of life the way others did and would continue to do. What mattered most to him was not the romance associated with the clan chiefs but the reality of the here and now that he witnessed on his journeys. He was critical of the large-scale emigrations, the evictions of tenants—they were not yet being referred to as the Clearances—and especially the departure of Highland society's middle class, the tacksmen. Such a development did not auger well for the future he predicted.

Johnson, Sir William (ca. 1715-1774). Born in County Meath, Ireland; British Superintendent of Indian Affairs for the American colony of New York from 1756 until his death. He commanded Iroquois and colonial militia forces during the French and Indian War (also known as the Seven Years War) in the Mohawk Valley of New York. At least 20 Highland families who were veterans of the French and Indian War settled on his land at his invitation in 1763. That same year he built Johnson Hall, where he lived until his death. It is now a National Historic Site.

Johnson offered land on his estates in the Mohawk Valley to Highlanders who fought in the French and Indian War, including Hugh Fraser who was a lieutenant in the 78th Highlanders. Fraser helped establish one of the larger Scottish communities at that time in North America. In 1773 an additional 425 men, women and children arrived from Fort William on the *Pearl*. As it turned out, most of these Highlanders were Loyalists during the American Revolution. After the war ended, they moved north of the border in Upper Canada (Ontario) to a new land which they called Glengarry.

Jura, Isle of. During the Highland potato famine the township of Cnocbreac was cleared. Subsequent decades saw further population decline so that about a third of the inhabitants, according to Gibson, were removed between 1841 and 1851.

K

kelp. Seawood harvested and burned for fertilizer and used in the manufacture of soap and glass.

kelp industry. Highly profitable in the Western Isles from the late 18th century to ca. 1810. Because of the great demand for kelp as Britain's agricultural economy expanded, and the subsequent need for labour, the population in the Hebrides increased dramatically, from 40,000 in the mid-18th century to 90,000 by the 1840s. Kelp production was largely confined to North and South Uist, Benbecula, Barra, Harris, Lewis, Skye and Mull and on the mainland areas of Ardnamurchan, Sunart and Morvern in Argyll. Landlords sought to maximize their profits by encouraging their tenants to live on increasingly smaller plots of land, which led, in turn, to congestion, overpopulation and unhealthy living conditions.

Prebble notes that for close to 60 years kelp brought a "twilight prosperity" to the lairds, for it required no cultivation, just "a vast army of men, women and children to tear it from the rocks with hooks and sickles to carry it to great kilns and there burn it over peat until it became hard, brittle and multi-coloured." It was strenuous, gruelling and backbreaking work. When the Napoleonic Wars ended, though, and the Germans—who were among the greatest exporters of kelp—found alternative sources, the demand for the seaweed dropped precipitously, and the need for other products increased in the industrial south, especially wool and mutton. Consequently, sheep, the so-called four-footed clansmen, were said to be the saviour of the Highland and Hebridean economy, not kelp. Rents increased, and evictions accelerated while prices for kelp declined by as much as two-thirds between 1823 and 1828.

Kilbeg Village Project, Skye. A joint project of Sabhal Mòr Ostaig, the MacDonald Lands Trust and Sleat Community Trust, it will be a 21st-century example of community planning in the Highlands of Scotland and will consist of affordable housing, commercial and educational facilities, sports and recreational facilities, a conference centre and a hotel.

Kildonan. When Elizabeth, the Countess of Sutherland, married Lord George Leveson-Gower, first son of the Marquis of Stafford, in 1785, they inherited a huge family fortune, and thus made plans to improve their vast Sutherland estate. By the late 18th century wool prices had soared and the demand for good hill pasture land for the large flocks of sheep rose immeasurably. In keeping with the spirit of the age, the couple was now "seized with the rage of improvements." Many of the dispossessed tenants were offered allotments in the area's barren northern and eastern coasts.

In early 1813 a number of factors and shepherds arrived in the Strath of Kildonan to survey the area. Troops were ordered into Kildonan to evict the tenants but they were able to successfully ask for an extension. The reprise was temporary. Summons of removal were served again. This time the tenants directly appealed to the Countess and Marquis at their home in London. They were ready to pay as much rent as the sheep farmers, they told the couple. They further insisted that since their sons had served in the 93rd Sutherland Highlanders this entitled them to stay on what they considered their own land.

Meanwhile, Lord Selkirk, a director of the Hudson's Bay Company (HBC), approached the Countess and offered to take many of the married men to Canada to serve in the Highland regiments; their families would be allowed to follow after the war had ended. Lady Stafford rejected this idea but news of the proposal reached the Highlanders who were eager to sign up for the journey. Ultimately, some 80 tenants accepted Selkirk's offer.

In June 1813 the HBC ship the *Prince of Wales* set sail from Stromness, bound for Canada. Those who stayed behind were removed to the shore and given a small piece of land, or croft. A new fishing village was established, called Helmsdale, to encourage the displaced tenants to take up fishing; there was a great herring boom during the early years of the 19th century. But the crofters found the fishing life difficult and fishermen from Morayshire had to be brought in to teach them how to fish.

The evictions continued in Sutherland until 1821. By that time the land that had been used for sheep farming was converted into sheep walks, and most of the people removed. Large profits were made until the price of wool fell in the mid-19th century, and lodges were built along the Helmsdale River for tourists to make way for deer forests.

A small, unadorned church sits there, surrounded by a kirkyard that contains the pulpit of Alexander Sage—whose son the Reverend Donald Sage wrote *Memorabilia Domestica*, a scathing eyewitness account of his life in Strathnaver before and after the Clearances. In late 1812 and early 1813, the residents of the area were faced with eviction. In order to stay, they offered to agree to a rent increase, which was refused. They even went so far as to contact the Home Office in London but were still rebuffed. Consequently, the fifth Earl of Selkirk heard about their plight and offered what he felt was a reasonable solution: emigration. He was developing a colony on the Red River in what would later become Winnipeg. He offered land and generous credit terms. More than 700 applied but he could accept only 100 people. This group became known as the Selkirk Settlers. They asked for only one condition: that they be accompanied by their minister, Donald Sage, the son of the Kildonan pastor, Alexander Sage.

The first wave of emigrants left in 1813. Sage asked that his departure be delayed a year so he could improve his Gaelic. Unfortunately for the settlers, Donald Sage never did cross the Atlantic. Finally, in 1820, the Church Missionary Society of England sent an Anglican clergyman by the name of John West to the settlement. But West insisted on using the liturgy of the Church of England despite the Scots majority. Three years later West was replaced by Rev. David Jones, who offered a compromise between the rituals and trappings of the Anglican Church and the Presbyterian Church. Even so, the settlers continued to ask the Hudson's Bay Company and the Church of Scotland to send them a Presbyterian minister. Finally, the Presbyterian Church of Canada sent John Black, a Lowlander who did not speak Gaelic (this led to some initial disappointment but eventually the settlers were won over by his commitment and hard work). The settlers then formed the Kildonan Presbyterian Church, the first Presbyterian congregation in western Canada. In 1854, a church building similar to the original Kildonan church in Sutherland was built. It is still there, on John Black Avenue, in the Kildonan neighbourhood of Winnipeg. The Rev. Black died in 1882; he was buried in Kildonan Cemetery.

See also Red River Colony; Winnipeg, Manitoba

Kissling, Werner (1895-1988). German filmmaker and photographer; born into a well-to-do family, he was the second son of a family of brewers. Although he was the grandson of the founder of the Conrad Kissling brewers, established in Breslau (then in Germany) in 1935, he chose to follow less conventional pursuits. He is remembered today for his extensive photographic images of the crofters on Eriskay and South Uist as well as the farmers and fisherfolk of Dumfries and Galloway. His best known work is a short film, "Eriskay: A Poem of Remote Lives." The footage was shot in 1934.

Kissling's interest in the Western Isles was partly inspired by the experiences of his mother, Johanna, who toured the Outer Hebrides and as far away as St. Kilda in 1905. She sent a postcard back home to Kissling, who was then a 10-year-old boy. The memory of receiving that card remained an important talisman for him during his entire life. When he died at the age of 83 at Moorfields Nursing Home in Dumfries, it has been said that the postcard was found in a suitcase in his room.

In 1952, Kissling bought the Kings Arms Hotel in Melrose, which he ran, with some difficulty, for more than a decade. Between 1952 and 1961 he earned additional income as a part-time writer and photographer for the School of Scottish Studies. In 1968 he moved to Dumfries, where he worked as an honourary assistant at Dumfries Museum from 1969 to 1988.

Kissling had spent the summer of 1934 on Eriskay, taking photographs and recording video footage of Hebridean customs, including peat collecting, sheep shearing, the repairing of fishing nets and the waulking of the tweed. From this primary material he created a short film, "Eriskay: A Poem of Remote Lives." The film was shown in London in April 1935 as part of a so-called Hebridean Evening. In attendance were the Prince of Wales (the future Edward VIII), the Queen Mother, the sitting Prime Minister Ramsay MacDonald (who originally hailed from Lossiemouth), Macleod of Macleod and Cameron of Locheil. The funds collected that evening were to be used toward the building of the first major road on the island; part of the old road, Rathad Kissling (or Kissling Street) still remains. Although the film was largely forgotten—it lay in the archives of the School of Scottish Studies until the late 1970s—it has received a remarkable second life partly due to the work of Michael Russell, a former television producer and Cabinet Secretary for Education and Lifelong Learning in Alex Salmond's SNP administration. Russell not only produced a documentary about Kissling for BBC Alba, which was broadcast in 2009, he has also published two books on Kissling, *A Poem of Remote Lives: Enigma of Werner Kissling* (1997) and *Kissling, A Different Country: The Photographs of Werner Kissling* (2002). The latter consists of more than 100 of his Hebridean photographs. Among his most evocative photograph is one of two women walking home in the evening on Eriskay in 1936.

Kissling was buried in St. Michael's kirkyard, at Dumfries, in an unmarked grave. Two years after his death the town historian, Ralph Coleman, organized a drive to raise funds to finance a granite headstone. It reads: SOLDIER, DIPLOMAT, SCHOLAR, GENTLEMAN.

Knox, John (1778-1845). Scottish painter, born in Paisley. A follower of Alexander Nasmyth (1758-1840), considered by some to be the father of Scottish landscape painting, he is known for his romantic landscapes. His *Landscape with Tourists at Loch Katrine* (ca. 1820), probably his best-known work, was a direct response to Sir Walter Scott's popular poem, *The Lady of the Lake*, which spawned massive interest in the Trossachs as a popular destination spot for tourists and which led the way for further works, from literature to painting, that saw the Highlands as a playground for the wealthy. Knox's painting depicts an idyllic Highland landscape of almost Edenic proportions. In the foreground, travellers fish in a calm loch under moody mountains while a top-hatted aristocratic gentleman, accompanied by his equally well-coiffed female companion, points toward an unspecified view. Off to the side is a piper in tow.

Knox, Robert. Scottish anatomist; fellow of the Edinburgh College of Surgeons and author of *The Races of Men* (1850), which was based on his popular lectures. The book contains illustrations of the different races, including what Knox, and others of his social class and status, considered classical beauty; the fair Anglo-Saxon. Race was determined to be the epitome of attractiveness while the so-called dark races, which included Jews, Gypsies, aborigines and Celts, were said to represent ugliness and barbarity. Further, Knox believed the Celts of Caledonia were destined for destruction, and not soon enough apparently. Knox cheerfully promoted the eviction of the Celts from their native soil since there was no hope, in his way of thinking, that they would ever become good Saxons. Worse, they, along with their Celtic brethren, the Welsh and the Irish, were in the way of the progress of the English nation, to use Knox's terminology. The following quotation sums up Knox's beliefs:

> The really momentous question for England, as a nation, is the presence of three sections of the Celtic race still on her soil: the Caledonian or Gael; the Cymbri, or Welsh; and the Irish, or Erse; and how to dispose of them. The Caledonian Celt ... must be forced from the soil; by fair means, if possible; still they must leave. England's safety requires it.

Knoydart. The last major clearance to arouse public outcry and receive widespread coverage in the press took place at Knoydart in 1853. The Glasgow-based lawyer, Donald Ross, wrote an incendiary little booklet called *The Glengarry Evictions*, 31 pages that describe what occurred here during the summer and autumn of 1853. Ross was an investigative reporter before the term was even coined.

Knoydart was the fief of Clan Donald, at one time the largest and most powerful clan in Gaeldom. In the 16th century the Macdonells of Glengarry went their own way and assumed territorial rights. The debt of the Glengarry clan led to the land being cleared and sold in the

1850s. Josephine Macdonell, laird of Knoydart, evicted her tenants to make way for sheep and, later, deer.

Located in the parish of Glenelg, the Knoydart Clearances were the last remaining part of the Glengarry estate to be replaced by sheep. In the summer of 1852 the residents had been given writs of removal. They were told either to leave or be transported to Australia. (Later the destination was changed to Canada.) A ship that could transport the entire population of the five townships was chartered. Removals began on 2 August. Macdonells of Glengarry owned Knoydart. The clan chief had died in 1852. Subsequently, his widow and the trustees prepared to sell the estate to a sheepfarmer who informed them it would be more successful if all the tenants were evicted. The people were in the way and regarded as a liability, an impediment to progress.

About 300 people were forced to board an emigrant ship but some 20 families refused to go. In a scene all too familiar, officers burned down the houses of those who refused to leave. The inhabitants were exposed to the open air without any form of shelter to protect them from the elements; they spent several weeks from August to late October in the cold and damp. Some of the people hid in makeshift shelters even as elderly women clung to their huts and fought off the officers as best they could. Some who were evicted attempted to erect temporary shelters, but even these were destroyed. What's more, anyone who tried to help the evicted were themselves threatened with eviction. Even the previously less than sympathetic *Scotsman* considered such actions as "gross inhumanity."

Despite being a muckraking journalist of the first order, Donald Ross was also a man of his times. Thus, he did not attack the rights of the landowners to evict their tenants. He merely complained about and disagreed with their manner and practice—that is, he complained about the un-Christian conduct of the owners but never actually questioned their right to do so.

The entire population in Knoydart was not cleared; some 600 remained as of 1861. Like elsewhere in the Highlands when sheep farming in Knoydart became less profitable the land was converted to deer forest. By the late Victorian period the aristocratic activity of hunting had become a craze. Sporting estates and shooting lodges sprouted up all over the Highlands. "Shepherds became redundant," explains Denis Rixson, "although some locals found employment as ghillies and stalkers." For all intents and purposes, Knoydart became a "shooting estate."

Knoydart changed hands many times over the years. From 1893 until the early 1930s, Knoydart was owned by the Bowlby family, who were regarded as benevolent proprietors, until they sold the estate to Lord Brocket (1904-1967), a Member of Parliament, absentee landlord and known Nazi sympathizer. In November 1948 the Seven Men of

Knoydart staked claims to land on the Kilchoan and Scottas farms, in effect launching a land raid, and essentially squatted on the land. Lord Brocket successfully sought legal action against them which they in turn defied. Enormous public sympathy was generated toward them from all over Scotland even as they were evicted and then charged. But soon thereafter Brocket sold his property.

Finally, in 1999, the Knoydart Foundation bought the estate in a community buy out—a watershed moment in a checkered past. The Foundation owns about one-third of Knoydart. The partners of the Foundation that made the £750,000 buy out possible include, among others, the John Muir Trust (£250,000); the Highlands and Islands Enterprise (£75,000); Scottish National Heritage (£50,000); and the theatre producer Sir Cameron Macintosh (£75,000), who has a family connection to Knoydart.

Surrounded on three sides by the sea, Knoydart is bounded on the north by Loch Hourn, on the south by Loch Nevis and on the west by the Sound of Sleat. There are no roads into the Rough Bounds, as the Knoydart peninsula is known. Knoydart can only be reached by boat. Today it is, thus, a must-see destination, especially for adventure tourism enthusiasts and is being marketed as the Last Wilderness.

In September 1991, the Knoydart Land Raid Commemoration Committee erected a cairn at Inverie.

See also Seven Men of Knoydart

L

laird. Owner of an estate.

Lamlash, Arran. Located south of Brodick, Lamlash is a charming village overlooking a lovely bay. Situated prominently in the village green is a monument to the Arran Clearances, erected by Canadian descendents in New Brunswick, reportedly on the spot where the local minister preached his farewell sermon on April 25, 1829, as 12 families (86 people), mainly from the nearby village of Sannox, sailed on the brig *Caledonia* for Mégantic County, Québec.
See also Arran, Isle of

Lamond, Mary Jane (b. 1960). singer born in Kingston, Ontario, who performs Gaelic folk songs from Cape Breton, often with an innovative and contemporary twist. Lamond released her first album, *Bho Thir Nan Craobh* (From the Land of the Trees) (1994), a collection of traditional material while still a student in the Celtic Studies program at St. Francis Xavier University in Antigonish, Nova Scotia.

In 1995 Lamond provided Scottish Gaelic vocals on Ashley MacIsaac's 1995 hit single, "Sleepy Maggie" from MacIsaac's *Hi How Are You Today?* recording. MacIsaac (b. 1975) is the cousin of fiddlers Wendy MacIsaac and Natalie MacMaster and a distant cousin of White Stripes guitarist and vocalist Jack White (born John Anthony Gillis). Lamond had another hit single in Canada, "Horo Ghoid thu Nighean," from her 1997 album *Suas e!* (Go for It!). Her other recordings include *Làn Dùil* (Full of Hope) (1999), *Orain Ghàidhlig* (Gaelic Songs) (2001), *Stòras* (Treasure) (2005) and, with fiddler Wendy MacIsaac, *Seinn* (2012), which consists of traditional and original compositons.

Lamond is active in the ongoing preservation and revitalization of the Gaelic culture in Cape Breton. She is a member of the Gaelic Council of Nova Scotia and teaches Gaelic language and song workshops.

Land League movement. Started in the late 19th century when crofters voiced their concerns over their basic rights and, in particular, their desire to remedy past grievances. The Land League movement took the form of land raids, rent strikes, rallies, protests and, at its most egregious, confrontations with police and even military personnel. The Land League movement culminated in the founding of the Highland Land Law Reform Association in 1882, which a few years later became the Highland Land League and, ultimately, brought about the watershed *Crofters Act* of 1886.

land ownership and land reform. Traditionally, the old Highland order was based on a strict hierarchical social structure based on reciprocal obligations and duties. Indeed, traditional Highland culture was tribal in nature. Highlanders had a fierce emotional attachment to the land, so much so that during the era of the land raids many residents claimed they possessed an inherent right to own the land. The Highland economy thus was a rents-in-kind system that was based on an exchange of loyalty in return for security and protection. "A great many Highland estates currently survive because wealthy individuals are prepared to run them either at a loss or at paltry rates of return," notes Denis Rixson.

Land reform did not come easily. Most of the public as well as the press did not question the right of landlords to remove inhabitants from the soil. After all, it was their land, and it was legal. The exceptions were few, but they were important ones. Some were politicians, including Prime Minister William Gladstone; others were journalists and editors in London and a few were even Highlanders, including journalist John Murdoch, Clearances historian Alexander Mackenzie and professor John Stuart Blackie.

Even in our own day, land reform, especially in rural areas, continues to be in demand. Having access to the ownership of land is now considered a fundamental condition in order to achieve productive profitable land use. In early 2003 the Scottish Parliament passed a land reform bill that changed property rights in Scotland. The new law gave crofters the right to collectively purchase portions of the land they live on, even if the landowner did not want to sell. It also grants the public the right to roam virtually anywhere: landowners have restricted power to remove them from their property. Not surprisingly, critics have called it a type of Marxism and even compared it to the seizure of white-owned land in African countries. The sporting and leisure classes are fearful that they might lose their right to exclusivity. Advocates support the bill as a long overdue attempt to redress an imbalance in land ownership in Scotland that dates to before the Clearances. Even so, the most controversial aspect of the bill—allowing the crofters the right to buy—affects only 7 per cent of Scottish land.

Essentially, the *Land Reform Act* of 2003, as it is called, offered several important guarantees: (1) the right to roam on previously private land; (2) the right of pre-emptive purchase of rural land that is put up for sale; and (3) in crofting communities, the right of a community to buy their land at valuation even when the owner has not placed it on the market. James Hunter has called it a landmark piece of legislation.

landlords. "In no country in Europe are the rights of proprietors so well defined, and so carefully protected, as in Scotland," said Sir John Sinclair. Often painted in a broad swath as figures of hatred, landlords in fact came in all types. Some did their best to maintain the status quo and, invariably, ended up in bankruptcy. Some tried to improve their estates without evicting their tenants. But others modernized their estates to make way for more profitable sheep farms by evicting their tenants. These latter landlords of course came to epitomize the worst aspects of the Clearances. Most, though, adopted some aspect of the so-called improvements by employing a policy of population reduction, which quite often led to their support of emigration as the only solution for the seemingly intractable Highland problems of poverty and overpopulation. They often moved tenants in order to develop villages, especially along the coasts, but also for sporting purposes as well as to reduce congestion.

Unlike other agrarian changes in other parts of rural Britain, such as the enclosure movement in England or the Lowland Clearances, the Highland Clearances had devastating effects on the culture and societal structure of the Highlands. In the Highlands landlords had much more control over the land than in other parts of Britain. What the landlords did—remove people from their land—was perfectly legal; their behaviour required no parliamentary approval or the cooperation of the inhabitants of the land. Their power was near absolute; their tenants paid the price in a miserable existence at home, eviction or emigration.

Landseer, Edwin (1802-1873). English painter born in London known for his dramatic and highly romanticized Highland landscapes, especially *The Monarch of the Glen* (1851) and *Rent Day in the Wilderness* (1855-1868), which depicts Donald Murchison collecting rent from the Ross-shire estates of the exiled Earl of Seaforth. Landseer first visited Scotland in 1824. *Monarch* is arguably the most famous image of the Highlands. Not surprisingly it was originally intended to be displayed at the House of Lords, a fitting place perhaps for the Victorian ideals it expresses of the Highlands as a "man-made" wilderness. In 1828

Landseer was commissioned to produce illustrations for the Waverley Edition of Sir Walter Scott's novels.

He is buried at St. Paul's Cathedral in London.

"language of Eden." Gaelic is said to be the language spoken in heaven, according to William Gillies, professor of Celtic at the University of Edinburgh. The phrase was first used by the Rev. David Malcolm, minister of Duddingston (1705-1743) in the 18th century, but others too have put forth the claim, including the Gaelic enthusiast from Coll, Lachlan Maclean (ca. 1790-1848).

An Lanntair, Stornoway. The most prominent art gallery in the Outer Hebrides. It presents local, national and international exhibitions. It also sponsors a diverse program of music, from traditional and classical to jazz and rock as well as Gaelic events.

Laurence, Margaret (née Wemyss) (1926-1987). Born in Neepawa, Manitoba, a Canadian novelist and short story writer; best known for her Manawaka cycle of novels and short stories, which consist of *The Stone Angel* (1961), *A Jest of God* (1966), *The Fire-Dwellers* (1969), *A Bird in the House* (1970) and *The Diviners* (1974). In *The Diviners*, the culmination of the series, Laurence created the memorable character of Morag Gunn who during the length of the story seeks to uncover the historical and psychological truths of the country that she now calls home. Morag grew up in the fictional Canadian prairie town of Manawaka, modelled after Laurence's native town of Neepawa, Manitoba. Manawaka is a community of mostly Scots, as well as Ukrainians and Métis. At its most basic level, it is the story of dispossessed people in search of their birthright or at least some sense of stability. It is a familiar prairie story of perseverance in a harsh land.

Morag's ancestors came to Canada from Sutherland, possibly during the Highland Clearances, although nobody knows for sure, "and started the farm when probably nothing was here except buffalo grass and Indians." Through the power of words, she relives the tales of her ancestors who lived a long time ago in a country far away. Morag listens to stories of a battle on the moor and its tragic consequences. After the spirit of the clans were broken, many of the people scattered across the countryside, she is told, and some of them made their way west and settled in Manitoba, where the descendants of these Gunns, MacLeods, Camerons and Duncans made a new life on the prairies.

She obsesses about lost languages, the forgotten words of Gaelic, unknown to her and her generation. "Yet it seemed a bad thing to have lost a language," she muses "the lost languages, forever lurking somewhere inside the ventricles of the hearts of those who had lost them." Later, she admits, in a letter to a friend, that she feels compelled to visit Scotland, "to Sutherland, where my people came from. What do I hope to learn there? Don't ask me. But it haunts me, I guess, and maybe I'll have to go." The myths from Sutherland that she grew up listening to are her reality, but the land that spawned them is not her land "except a long long way back." The land where she was born—Manitoba—is now her land. And so Morag Gunn, the character, writes a novel about the original Scots settlers of the Red River in Manitoba, of the sea journey from Scotland to Hudson Bay, of the brutal winter spent in Churchill, and of the long arduous walk to York Factory in the spring. "Look ahead into the past," she concludes, "and back into the future, until the silence."

The Margaret Laurence House is located in her hometown of Neepawa, Manitoba.

"Letter from America." A pop song written and performed by the Scottish duo the Proclaimers, the identical twin brothers Craig and Charlie Reid (b. 1962); the song appears on their debut album *This Is the Story* (1987). As the title indicates, the song is a commentary on Scotland's long history of emigration, and the economic troubles that led many, either by choice or by force, to emigrate to the United States and Canada. It makes explicit references to not only economically depressed towns (Bathgate, Irvine, Linwood, Methil) but also to Clearance sites (Lochaber, Sutherland, Skye). Significantly, the sleeve artwork for the 12-inch single consists of a colour image of Nicol's *Lochaber No More* painting superimposed onto a black and white photograph of the interior of the Gartcosh Steel Works, in North Lanarkshire, after it closed in 1986. The lyrics also seem to make mention of the voyage of the *Hector*, the emigrant ship that left Loch Broom in 1773 en route to Nova Scotia ("I've looked at the ocean / tried hard to imagine / The way you felt the day you sailed / from Wester Ross to Nova Scotia").

Lever, William (Lord Leverhulme) (1851-1925). English industrialist and politician, born in Bolton; best known as establishing the soap company, Lever Brothers, with his younger brother James in 1885. During the First World War he bought the Isle of Lewis. He was one of the numerous utopian entrepreneurs who tried, usually unsuccessfully, to transform the Hebrides into a capitalist dream. His goal was to turn Stornoway, the largest town on the island, into one of the greatest fishing and fish-processing centres in Britain. He established a chain of 400 retail fish shops, called MacFisheries Ltd. After failing in Lewis, he turned his attention to Harris, with the idea of establishing a port at Obbe, which he renamed Leverburgh. But that also proved a failure. After he sold Lewis in 1923, he donated most of the island to the people of Lewis and the Stornoway Trust.

Lewis, Isle of. In the early 19th century the Isle of Lewis was mired in poverty. The owner, the Earl of Seaforth, tried various development ideas, including kelp, distilling and commercial fishing enterprises, but they failed to produce any real economic benefits. The inevitable clearances followed: in the late 1820s more than 100 families were removed while coastal communities at Loch Roag were cleared in 1836, the people removed and put on a ship to America. The parishes of Barvas and Lochs as well as Stornoway, the largest town, were especially impoverished. By 1838, notes Richards, Seaforth helped with assisted-emigration to Canada: 15 families, or 70 people, were given passage when their land was converted into sheep walks. In that year alone, writes Richards, it was estimated that some 85 per cent of the island was "in a desperate state, in part because their rents had been doubled...." But even as the people were suffering the Seaforth Estates was teetering on the verge of bankruptcy.

In 1846 James Matheson bought the island. In 1828 he had founded Jardine Matheson and Co., the successful tea and opium merchants, where he made his fortune. He retired from the business in 1843 and bought property after property in the Highlands, including Lewis. But the Great Highland Famine of the 1840s continued to lead to mass emigration and removals. Large areas of land were subsequently set aside not only for sheep farming but also deer stalking. As the famine years passed, Matheson began a rigorous policy of population reduction, mainly through a combination of removals and emigration. Richards refers to a mass exodus from Lewis to Québec and Ontario in the early to mid 1850s. Between 1851 and 1855 Matheson sent more than 2,000 people away to Canada at the cost of some £10,000. He offered relatively generous terms to the tenants, but there was a catch: those who refused to emigrate and fell into arrears were evicted anyway. In this way, entire villages were cleared. The choice whether to emigrate or face the risk of eviction was a difficult and anxiety-inducing decision.

Lewis Settlement. Refers to families from Lewis who settled in Bruce County, Ontario, in 1851. The families received financial assistance from their landlord, Sir James Matheson, but if they had remained behind they would have faced eviction anyway; they had very little choice. Most of the emigrants, about 500 people or 109 families, went to the Eastern Townships in Lower Canada (Québec), before settling in Goderich in Bruce County in the summer of 1852 where they were joined by 18 more families from Lewis.

The Canadian musician, Angus Macleod, released *The Silent Ones: A Legacy of the Highland Clearances* in 2000, a recording that tells the story of Ontario's Lewis Settlement in Bruce County.

Livingston, William (Uilleam MacDhunlèibhe) (1808-1870). Poet born in Kilarrow, near Bowmore, Islay. A tailor by profession, he worked mainly in Glasgow and Greenock. Largely self-taught, Livingstone was an advocate for Gaelic language and culture. He wrote long epic poems as well as shorter pieces. The latter were bitter attacks against the Clearances and their consequences.

Loch, James (1780-1855). Scottish economist; born near Edinburgh; Commissioner of the Sutherland estates and creator of the Policy of Improvement that led to the Highland Clearances. Its goal was to remove the indigenous Highland population from the interior in order to resettle them on the coast where they could grow food or fish or, failing that, emigrate. His philosophy can best be summed up by his belief that the "slothful must remove or starve as man was not born to be idle, but to gain his bread by the sweat of his brow." During the Sutherland Clearances, which he supervised, between 1811 and 1820, some 15,000 crofters were removed from the interior to coastal communities.

Lochaber. In 1801, clearances took place on the estates of the Locheils of Lochaber. Initially the people who were evicted moved to Fort William, but many more, fearful of additional clearances, emigrated in 1802 and 1803. The clan chief evicted his clanfolk from Loch Arkaig to Loch Leven. Specifically, in 1802, the Lochiel tacksman Archibald McMillan, brought with him about 500 people from the Glengarry and Lochiel estates to Upper Canada (Ontario). McMillan chartered three ships, the *Helen* of Irvine, the *Jean* of Irvine, and the *Friends of John Saltcoats* (other passengers sailed on the *Neptune* from Loch Nevis). These emigrants came to be known as the Lochaber emigrants. Several historians have written specifically about them, including Marianne McLean and Lucille H. Campey and especially Rae Fleming.

Lockhart-Ross, Sir John of Balnagowan (1721-1790). In 1762, Lockhart-Ross introduced black-faced Linton sheep on his Balnagowan estate in northern Scotland. He and others like him quickly learned, however, that it was the white-faced and sturdier Cheviots that were better suited for the harsh climate of the Highlands. They also quickly came to the conclusion that, to take full advantage of any economic opportunities that might arise and for the sheep to prosper, the ranges where they grazed had to be cleared of people.

long memory. Among the strongest characteristics of the Highland psyche is a long memory. History is not something that happened long ago but rather something that is very much a part of the living tradition: stories and songs have long been handed down through the generations, from parent to child. Eric Richards has commented on the remarkable collective memory of Scots not only in Scotland but also throughout the larger Scottish diaspora. "The persistent anger" directed toward the Clearances, he notes, "is fuelled by a continuous sense of betrayal, and is remarkable for its stamina."

Lord Selkirk Association of Rupert's Land. Formed and incorporated in 1908 to honour Thomas Douglas, the Fifth Earl of Selkirk, and to commemorate the 100th anniversary of the Selkirk Settlers who arrived at the Red River on October 27, 1812, in what is now Winnipeg.

Lost Cause, The. A literary and cultural movement in the American South after the fall of the Confederacy to the larger forces of the Union Army. The term first appeared as the title of Edward A. Pollard's book, *The Lost Cause: A New Southern History of the War of the Confederates*, published just a year after the war ended, in 1866. Pollard, an editor at the *Richmond Examiner*, justified the Southern secession from the union as a just and noble cause. The tenents that he advocated included the particularly strong Southern virtues of chivalry, nobility and bravery; a defence of states' rights; and a belief that slavery was a benign institution.

Like the Highlands, the American South on the eve of the Civil War was a pre-modern and pre-industrial society. General Robert E. Lee, the Confederate general and icon of the Lost Cause, was the prototypical Southern gentleman. The devastating loss by the Confederate Army at the Battle of Gettysburg in 1863, specifically the infantry assault ordered by Lee against Maj. Gen. George G. Meade's forces that came to be known as Pickett's Charge, came to epitomize the futility of the Southern cause. The name came from Maj. Gen. George Pickett, one of three Confederate generals, who led the assault. Pickett's Charge was both a psychological and physical blow to the Confederate army with massive casualties and injuries.

In the years following the the end of the war, several Lost Cause periodicals emerged, including the *Southern Opinion*, a weekly Richmond newspaper, and the *Confederate Veteran*. During the 20th century, the Lost Cause was reflected in books and films (both the 1936 novel and 1939 film adaptation of Margaret Mitchell's *Gone with the Wind*) and, more controversially, in Thomas Dixon's 1905 novel *The Clansman* and pioneer filmmaker D. W. Griffith's seminal film adaptation of it, *Birth of a Nation*, in 1915. In both the book and the film, the Ku Klux Klan are depicted as noble defenders of Southern culture and tradition.

The Lost Cause romanticized the Old South of the Confederate era, pining for a Confederate past where the ugliness of slavery is either presented in the most idyllic of terms possible or ignored completely. Further, the Lost Cause maintained that secession, not slavery, caused the outbreak of war and celebrated the gallantry of the Southern soldier. Gen. Lee himself was cast as an almost Christ-like figure in Southern iconography.

The Southern American states also lay legitimate claim to a rich Scots cultural inheritance. Like their Canadian counterparts, Southern writers found much to emulate in the writing of Burns and Scott. Scott's novels were particularly influential throughout the South, especially during the pre-Civil War era at the height of romanticism that is often associated with the period. Plantations were named after Scott's novels and place names that appeared in his works cropped up throughout the South. Ironically, the desire in the South to reclaim a Scottish past, which meant almost exclusively a Highland past, increased as the Gaelic ethnicity of the area was declining. Southern writers, for example, adapted Scott's plot points to create their own version of an idyllic romanticized South, populated by heroic warriors and chivalrous gentlemen. Indeed, one can argue that the Old South owes more to, or at least as much as, Sir Walter Scott and tartanism than any continuity of strong cultural ties. Even so, strong cultural links exist between the American South and Scotland: the Southern general and the Highland clansman, the gentleman planter and the Highland chief, the false image of the bonny Highland laddie and the nostalgic figure of the singing country cowboy.

Many fiction writers in the South who wrote historical romances were influenced by Scott, as well as by James Fenimore Cooper and Washington Irving, including Nathaniel Beverley Tucker, William Alexander Caruthers, John Esten Cooke, Augusta Evans Wilson, Caroline Lee Hentz and, especially, John Pendleton Kennedy. In novels such as *Swallow Barn* (1832), Kennedy, the Baltimore politician and writer, composed fictional sketches that helped establish what has been called the plantation novel, with its depiction of a mythic genteel past. Kennedy in particular emulated the works of Sir Walter Scott, substituting the plantations of the antebellum South for Scott's castles and mansions and evoking a lost world of aristocracy and chivalry. The Old South became imbued with this wistful image as an idyllic Garden of Eden that existed only in the rich Southern literary imagination.

Michael Newton refers to a "sensibility of defeat" that permeates much of Southern literature, especially William Faulkner's portrayals of the post-Civil War South (Faulkner himself was of Scots descent). This literature did not reflect a resurgence of Scottish influence in the contemporary South; rather, on the contrary, Newton contends, it simply served the cultural needs of the region. The strong Southern sense of place and feeling of being different, of a connection to a land most have never seen and indeed which many had emigrated from nine or more generations ago, endured in the South for very complex reasons.

In some profound way, Southerners share a common psychological heredity with Scotland. A strong streak of fatalism runs through much of Southern culture. Like the Scots, they have acquired an outsider status within their own country, and look in from the outside. Henry Shapiro refers to the "otherness" quality in Appalachian culture, which he compares with a similar feeling in Scotland, especially in Highland Scotland.

The South of the Lost Cause, then, has much in common with the Scotland of the Lost Cause. At some level, the defeat of Bonnie Prince Charlie at Culloden in April 1746 and the surrender of Robert E. Lee to Abraham Lincoln at the Appomattox Courthouse in 1865 are opposite sides of the same coin. The wistful quality of Southern literature and the haunting quality of much North American Scots literature share a common source: a lament for what might have been. It is this "what if" aspect of both Southern and Scottish life that continues to linger. In this vein, a Confederate Memorial Tartan now exists and, as Tom Devine observes, it is not unusual to see tartan dress and Confederate uniforms worn simultaneously at Scottish gatherings in what Devine calls "a kind of Bonnie Prince Charlie meets Robert E. Lee lost-cause combo, yet another confirmation that heritage has less to do with history than with the realisation of emotions in response to an imagined past."

Lovat, Lord (Simon Fraser) (ca. 1667-1747). Jacobite and chief of Clan Fraser, born in Tomich in Ross-shire. An enigmatic and paradoxical figure, in 1699, he succeeded his father as 12th Lord Lovat. Three years later, in 1702, he fled to France but returned to Scotland a year later as a Jacobite, or supporter of the Stuart kingship. In 1715, however, during the Jacobite Rising, he switched allegiances, taking the government's side. For this he received a full pardon. Subsequently, during the 1745 Jacobite Rising he sent his son and clan members to fight for the Young Pretender, Charles Edward Stuart, while, paradoxically, maintaining his loyalty to the government. He escaped after the Battle of Culloden but was captured by government forces and taken to London for trial, convicted of treason, and executed on Tower Hill, reportedly the last man in Britain to be publicly beheaded.

Lowland Clearances. Less well known than the Highland Clearances, the Lowland Clearances involved the clearing of cottars from the land some 100 years before their Highland counterparts, causing widespread rural depopulation.

By the late 17th century extensive sheep farms had been established in the Lowlands, replacing the abandoned farm towns. Numerous lairds—Sir David Dunbar at Baldoon near Wigtown being perhaps among the most prominent—let their estates to commercial tenants, a practice which reached its climax in the 1720s. Thus, according to Tom Devine, the arable lands were cleared and "enclosed" by dykes.

Previously, the Lowlands had consisted of dozens of settlements called fermtouns, where people lived and worked communally, farming the runrig strips and herded their animals on the common land. When landowners in the mid-18th century began to collectivize their estates, the people were replaced by sheep; the fermtouns essentially disappeared. Like the Highlands years later, cottages were pulled down and the poorest residents of rural society—the subtenants and the cottars—moved into the new villages that were being built at the edges of the big estates or were eventually swallowed up by the towns and cities of central Scotland.

The cottar system had allocated small portions of land in return for services. But since cottars made up to one-half of the families in some areas of Lowland Scotland, their removal from the land was significant. Subsequently, landlessness became widespread. The scale and speed of the transformation in the Lowlands might have contrasted sharply with the slow process of change during the Highland Clearances, but the impact was still considerable. By the 1830s, contends Devine, the agricultural system had changed so much that Scottish farming, once criticized for its backwardness, was now being praised for its efficiency.

Enclosure changed the face of the Scottish Lowlands. Scattered patterns of strips of land were now gathered into individual fields that were separated by the now-familiar use of hedges, ditches and dykes. Farmers too were able to get better yields from oats, barley and wheat. Most Lowland farms turned to the rotation system of farming. Multiple tenancies, once the norm, were now virtually eliminated. And yet ruins were common sights, just as in the Highlands.

Thus, from roughly 1760 to 1830, thousands of people from Berwickshire to Buchan, Solway to Shetland, Aberdeenshire to Orkney, were forced from the land, abandoning hundreds of settlements. Whether called the Lowland Clearances or the Highland Clearances, some historians prefer they they be called by the more inclusive Scottish Clearances. It is important to point out then that during the early 18th century both Lowlanders and Highlanders lived a rural lifestyle and worked the same system of subsistence farming, the runrig system.

By the 19th century, however, conditions had changed. Farming in the Lowlands was now primarily for commercial purposes, the connection between people and the land had been severed. Inhabitants lived in planned villages which housed the surplus labour that had been forced out because of the changes in the agricultural system. The subsequent overflow led to the growth of towns and later the great urban cities of Central Scotland. According to Aitchison and Cassell, Scotland "experienced the fastest urban growth in Western Europe in the last two decades of the 18th and the first two decades of the 19th century."

Significant, indeed profound, differences did exist between the Lowland Clearances and the Highland Clearances. Unlike the Highland Clearances, which took a long time, the Lowland equivalent was of relatively short duration and in piecemeal fashion. Devine has called this "clearance by stealth." Another difference between the Highland and the Lowland Clearances was the overall lack of opportunity north of the Highland line; that is, with little or no industry, there were few jobs for the people who were evicted.

Like the Highland Clearances, resistance was sporadic. In 1724 the tenants and cottars in Southwest Scotland revolted. In Galloway, groups of men and women travelled throughout the area tearing down dykes erected by the landowners. Sometimes cattle were injured or even killed. As in the Highlands, the Church of Scotland clergy sided with the landowners, warning the people of "the sinfulness and danger" of their behaviour. The lairds told the levellers, as they were called, that the stone walls were built not to divide the estate but to protect the land from the road. In truth, the landlords erected the stone dykes to enclose their grazing pasture and to prevent the animals from wandering off. The old-fashioned runrig system that was prevalent in the fermtouns essentially was an impediment to what Aitchison and Cassell refer to as the "expansionist visions of the landlords." In other words, the inhabitants of the fermtouns were in the way, and like their Highland cousins decades later, they were removed from the land.

The lairds continued with the enclosures and landlords encouraged tenants to adopt new and improved farming systems. Those who did not were either removed or they left on their own accord. Many chose to emigrate. On the other hand, and unlike the Highland Clearances, one of the most significant consequences of the Levellers revolt had a positive outcome: oftentimes the owners made sure that those who were cleared had somewhere to go and had an alternative way to make a living. This does not mean that there were no more disturburances. Undoubtedly, the protests continued, but not to the extent of the Galloway incidents.

The displaced inhabitants of the Lowland Clearances had choices, unlike in the Highlands. Many of those who were removed ended up in planned villages. These planned villages were built between the early 18th and mid-19th century. Of course, planned villages were not confined to the Lowlands. They were very much a part of the Highland Clearances, including many towns along the coasts of Caithness, Sutherland; along the Cromarty Firth, including Helmsdale; Thurso;

Inveraray; and villages on Islay. In the central Highlands they include Crieff, Tomintoul and Grantown on Spey. Others were planned fishing villages such as Burghead as well as the interior villages of Keith and Huntly. The great engineer Thomas Telford designed two planned villages, Ullapool in the West Highlands and Pulteneytown at Wick in Caithness. William Adam designed Fochabers and helped build Inveraray. Among the most famous planned villages is New Lanark south of Glasgow.

In addition, the differences between what occurred during the Lowland Clearances and the Highland Clearances is a matter of degree and numbers. Unlike the Highland Clearances, with the Lowland Clearances there has been no comparable trauma on the collective psyche; there is no comparable Lowland Clearances mythology. Another difference is that the landmark crofting legislation of 1886 did not go any further than Argyll and Inverness-shire, nor did it apply to Aberdeenshire, Morayshire, Perthshire or the Isle of Arran.

The end result of the Lowland Clearances was the radical transformation of rural lands in the second half of the 18th century. Between the 1760s and the 1820s the Scottish countryside fundamentally, and irrevocably, changed. If, as Devine estimates, in the 18th century only one Scot in eight lived in a town and made a living by cultivating the land or working in such rural industries as spinning, weaving, fishing and mining, by the end of the century, by 1790, the fermtouns for all intents and purposes ceased to exist altogether. What's more, the removal of the cottars created a new social order "in which only a tiny minority of the population had rights to land," notes Devine.

However, the devastation wrought by the Lowland Clearances should not be dismissed or trivialized. Given the larger population, more people were affected by the Clearances in the Lowlands. Thus, becoming landless "...was much more significant for larger numbers of people in lowland society than it was in the Gaeltachd," notes Devine. Devine further points out that the hill country of southern Lanarkshire witnessed scenes of depopulation "which are usually regarded as more reminiscent of the Highland glens...."

Lowlanders' attitude toward Highlanders during the Clearances. During the height of the Clearances, Lowland Scots' attitudes toward Highlanders was at its nadir. In the pages of many Lowlander newspapers, ranging from the *Scotsman* to the *Fifeshire Journal*, were numerous examples of contempt, even hatred. Correspondents referred to the Gaels in almost shocking terms, as an "inferior race," for example, but also as a "dirty race," "perverse" and "degraded." Highlanders were denounced in Lowland newspapers as lazy and indolent, as a people not deserving of charity or relief. During the Highland Famine, an editorial in the *Fifeshire Journal* stated the paper's position in the bluntest of terms. "Let those who will not work starve—their doom is just and righteous, and for the benefit of society." In sum, increasingly the Highlanders were being dismissed as a "surplus" and "useless" population. The attitude was simple: the more of them who leave Britain—forcibly or voluntarily—the better. Emigration, it was deemed, was the only real solution for the intractable Highland problem. "the Scottish Gaels were just as alien or foreign a people to the Scottish Lowlanders as some Asian or other far away, and presumably, inferior, people."

During the 1840s and up to the 1870s Britain underwent a remarkable economic transformation; during the first half of the 19th century the population as a whole doubled. The golden age of farming and the rage for "improvements" went hand in hand with this. For many complicated reasons, the Highlands were being left behind.

Loyalists. American colonists who remained loyal to the British Crown during the American Revolutionary War. At the time they were often called Tories, Royalists, or the King's Men. On the opposite side were the Rebels, or Patriots, those who supported the revolution. When the Americans defeated the British, approximately 20 per cent of the Loyalists fled to other parts of the British Empire, in Britain or, especially, to British North America, especially Ontario, New Brunswick, Nova Scotia and Québec, where they received the sobriquet of United Empire Loyalists. Most were given land or cash as a reward for their loyalty. The highest numbers of Scots loyalists were Highlanders from New York, North Carolina, Maryland and Virginia. In fact, according to Wallace Brown, more loyalists were born in Scotland than any other country.

Loyalty was a powerful concept to the Highlander. Even some thirty years after Culloden, many, although not all, remained loyal to the Crown. Some historians, like I. C. C. Graham, attribute their loyalty to being the logical extension of the tenant-landlord relationship and their unquestioned obedience to the chief. Others emphasize that loyalties were mostly based on clan ties, upon clan kinship. Thus, if a tacksman, and it was the tacksman after all who often led his clansmen overseas, was also a member of one's clan, that would lead naturally to feelings of loyalty. Devine points out that the Highlanders were recent emigrants who had benefited greatly from generous land grants provided by the British government. Others had served in the British army between the crucial pre-Revolutionary years of 1756 and 1763. What's more, the Highlanders were essentially conservative in nature. "Wanting to replace George II or George III with Charles Edward Stuart was not at all the same as wanting to do away with monarchs altogether," notes James Hunter.

In Virginia, Loyalists were referred to as the "Scotch party." Thomas Jefferson was so incensed by the Scottish loyalist tendencies toward the Crown that he reportedly included an insult against the Scots in his first draft of the Declaration of Independence. Fortunately, a Scot, John Witherspoon, the minister and president of Princeton College (later Princeton University), persuaded him to remove the slight. Meanwhile, in neighbouring Georgia, the legislature passed an act prohibiting the immigration of Scots into the state.

M

Mac Mhaighstir, Alasdair (Alexander MacDonald) (ca. 1695-ca. 1770). Undoubtedly the most famous of the 18th-century Gaelic poets (Flora MacDonald was his first cousin). His collection of poems, *Ais-eiridh na Sean Chanoin Albannaich* (The Resurrection of the Ancient Scottish Tongue) was among the first secular printed work to appear in the Gaelic language. He wrote poems in praise of the Gaelic, nature poems and, most famously, incitement poems advocating the Jacobite Risings. His best known poem is probably "Birlinn Chlann Raghnaill" (The Galley of Clan Ranald), which was published in 1751.

MacAulay, Donald (Dòmhnall MacAmhlaigh) (b. 1930). Born in Bernera, Lewis; graduate of Aberdeen and Cambridge universities; taught at Edinburgh, Dublin, and Aberdeen universities; was Head of the Celtic Department at Aberdeen University and is an influential figure in the modern renaissance of Gaelic poetry. A city-based exile, his poetry has been described as unpretentious and uncompromising but also quite and subtle. As a city-based exile from the Gàidhealthachd, MacAulay's themes include community and the individual, identity and the importance of place. Among his Clearances-related poetry are "Old Woman" and "Landmark."

MacCaig, Norman (1910-1996). Poet, born in Edinburgh, and educated at the Royal High School and the University of Edinburgh, where he read classics. A primary school teacher by profession, he was often considered among the finest Scottish poets of his generation. Upon retiring from teaching, he lectured in English studies at Stirling University from 1970 to 1979. He was the son of a Hebridean mother, who was born in Scalpay, Harris. He wrote about his island roots in "Return to Scalpay." Among his major works include *Riding Lights* (1955), *A Man in My Position* (1969) and *Collected Poems* (1990). One poem in particular, "A Man in Assynt," addresses the land rights issue by asking a question: "Who possesses this landscape?— / The man who bought it or / I who am possessed by it?"

MacCallum, Rev. Donald (1849-1929). Born in Craignish, Argyll; Church of Scotland minister and among the most prominent Presbyterian clergy to support the crofters during the land agitation movements. Over the years he was minister at Morvern, Arisaig and South Morar, Waternish on Skye, Heylipol on Tiree, and Lochs on Lewis. He was imprisoned in Skye for inciting violence and class hatred but released without going to trial.

MacCodrum, John (1693-1779). Gaelic poet, born in North Uist, who was known for his entertaining and often quite humorous songs. As a devout Jacobite, he was appointed as the bard to Sir James Macdonald of Sleat, Skye, in 1763. Among his best-known works is "Oran do na fogarraich" (Song to the Fugitives), an early example of criticism of clan chiefs, which comments on the high rents imposed on the people of North Uist and which subsequently led to massive emigration by the clansmen as well as the tacksmen. MacCodrum was one of the last of the professional Gaelic songmakers.

MacColla, Alasdair (d. 1647). Considered one of the greatest of the Highland warriors; commanded Highland and Irish forces under Montrose in 1644-1645.

MacColla, Fionn (Tom Macdonald) (1906-1975). Born in Montrose; author of *And the Cock Crew* (1945), a major Clearance novel that criticized Calvinism and the role it played in the Clearances. The title takes its name from the gospel story of Peter, who betrayed Christ.

MacDiarmid, Hugh (Christopher Murray Grieve) (1892-1978). Poet and pioneer of the Scottish literary renaissance. Born in Langholm, Dumfries-shire, and educated at Langholm Academy, MacDiarmid was a teacher at Broughton Higher Grade School in Edinburgh before turning to journalism. After serving with the Royal Army Medical Corps during the First World War, he married and settled in Montrose, where he practised journalism and became involved in local government as a town councillor. He also edited several anthologies of contemporary Scottish writing, including *Northern Numbers* (1920-1922) and *The Scottish Chapbook* (1922-1923). Although he wrote mostly in Scots, he was far from being parochial. Indeed, he reinvigorated the Scots tradition by, like Robert Burns, drawing his vocabulary from various regions and periods of Scottish history. His best known works include *Sangschaw* (1925), *Penny Wheep* (1926), and especially his undisputed masterpiece, *A Drunk Man Looks at the Thistle* (1926). He was also a founder-member of the Scottish National Party as well as an off again, on again member of the Communist Party. In addition, he was a great friend and admirer of Sorley Maclean and a fierce advocate of the Gaelic literary renaissance of the 20th century.

MacDonald, Allan "the Ridge" (1794-1868). Bard from Lochaber emigrated to Cape Breton in 1816 and went to Mabou Ridge before moving to South River, Antigonish County, Nova Scotia, in 1847. He is the cousin of John "the Hunter" MacDonald. Unlike his cousin, Allan the Ridge defended his adopted homeland.

Macdonald, Calum (b. 1953). Percussionist and co-songwriter for the Gaelic rock band Runrig; born in North Uist. Calum and his older brother Rory formed Runrig on Skye in 1973. Calum usually writes the lyrics, Rory the melody. Since former lead singer Donnie Munro left the band in 1997, Rory has taken lead vocal duties on the Gaelic songs (Bruce Guthro, who replaced Munro, usually sings the English songs, but, it is important to point out, not exclusively). Macdonald previously attended Jordanhill College and worked as a physical education teacher until Runrig turned professional.

See also Bruce Guthro; Rory Macdonald; Donnie Munro; Runrig

Macdonald, D. R. Canadian author, born in Cape Breton; his great grandfathers were among the early Highland Scot settlers. In his best known work, *Cape Breton Road*, he revisits the emigrant journey, only this time he tells the story of a young man, Innis Corbett, down on his luck who returns to Cape Breton after getting into a series of petty skirmishes with the law in Boston. It is a nice twist of fate: a descendent of Highlanders who were evicted from their ancestral home centuries before is now returning to the land that those evicted Highlanders originally settled.

In *Cape Breton Road* the dual ties of memory and blood—blood memory—loom large. Born in Cape Breton, Innis Corbett emigrates with his parents when still a young boy to Boston, the Boston States, as Massachusetts was called by Cape Bretoners. Innis is raised by his mother when his father is killed in a car accident. He falls in with a rough crowd and, ultimately, is deported back to Cape Breton for a series of minor crimes—car thefts mostly—and smoking pot. By the late 1970s, Innis is living with his bachelor uncle on the island of his youth. "Who do you belong to?" That is the question that haunts Corbett and is a major theme throughout Macdonald's work.

In "Eyestone," the title story in Macdonald's collection of the same name, the road is once again reversed as Royce leaves Boston to reinvent himself in his ancestral homeland of Cape Breton, which in turn his ancestors from Scotland had fled to so many centuries earlier. As in the work of other Canadian authors such as Margaret Laurence and Alistair MacLeod, Macdonald's characters feel that a part of them is missing. The passing of each generation leaves behind less and less of nothing, both culturally and linguistically. In "Poplars," in the same volume, one character laments that "So many of those words are going unspoken, and words die, too, like anything that lives." In stories such as "Green Grow the Rashes, O," Macdonald captures the elusive beauty of the language, as one modern-day emigrant Gael looks back at her younger self on the island of Harris:

> Certain feelings had no shape in English, and sometimes she whispered them to herself.... The sands of Harris.... Those strange and lovely summers, so distant now—brief, with emotions wild as the weather, days whose light stretched long into evening and you went to bed in a blue dusk.

MacDonald, Dan R. (1911-1976). Fiddler of Eigg extraction; born in Judique, Nova Scotia.

Macdonald, Flora (1722-1790). The ultimate Jacobite heroine, born in South Uist. At the age of 13, she was adopted by Lady Clanranald, wife of the clan chief. After the Battle of Culloden she helped Bonnie Prince Charlie (Charles Edward Stuart) escape, disguised as her maid "Betty Burke," from Benbecula to Portree, Skye. Subsequently, she was arrested and held in the Tower of London for one year. Upon her release (1750), she married Allan Macdonald, the son of Macdonald of Kingsburgh in Skye. It was here, in 1773, where she famously entertained Dr. Samuel Johnson and James Boswell during their Hebridean visit. The following year she and her husband emigrated to North Carolina. During the American Revolution, Allan Macdonald became a brigadier-general, fighting for the British Crown; his sons also served in the British Army.

Initially the couple went to Cross Creek, possibly to the intersection of Green and Bow Streets in modern-day Fayetteville (a market marks the spot) before moving to Mount Pleasant (now known as Cameron's Hill), some 20 miles further on. Flora's half-sister, Annabella, and her husband, Alexander MacDonald, were already there.

A historical marker indicates the spot:

> FLORA MacDONALD
> Scottish heroine, spent the winter of 1774-1775, at Mount Pleasant, the home of her half-sister Annabella MacDonald, which stood 400 yds. S.W.

Allan Macdonald fought at the Battle of Moore's Creek Bridge in February 1776. Another marker, placed by the Cumberland County Historical Society on Cool Spring Street in Fayetteville, reads:

FLORA MACDONALD
Near this spot the Scottish heroine bade farewell to her husband, ALLAN MACDONALD OF KINGSBURGH, and his troops during the march-out of the Highlanders to the Battle of Moore's Creek Bridge, February 1776

Allan Macdonald was captured nine days later and spent nearly two years in prison, first in Halifax and later in Philadelphia, and he and his wife's property was forfeited. He was paroled in exchange for an American prisoner in New York. Flora returned to Britain in October 1779, followed by her husband five years later. They spent their last years on Skye, where Flora died on March 4, 1790; Allan died two years later on September 20, 1792.

MacDonald, James Roderick (Jamie). Raised in North Carolina, his ancestors arrived in North Carolina in 1802 from the Isle of Skye. He obtained his PhD in Scottish Studies at the University of Edinburgh in 1993 (his thesis was on "Cultural Retention and Adaptation among the Highland Scots of Carolina"). A fluent Gaelic speaker, he was instrumental in the founding of the United States Mòd, the North Carolina Mòd, and the Grandfather Mountain Gaelic Song Week. He taught in the Department of Celtic Studies at St. Francis Xavier University in Antigonish, Nova Scotia. He was also the first American to compete and win a prize in the Gold Medal competition at the National Mòd in Scotland for solo Gaelic singing. Eagle-eyed observers know that he appeared in the Grampian television documentary *The Blood Is Strong*.

MacDonald, John "the Hunter" (1795-1853). Born in the Braes of Lochaber, he sailed from Tobermory on the *Janet* and landed at what is now Port Hawkesbury, Cape Breton, in 1834. His cousin is Allan "the Ridge" MacDonald. After a difficult first winter, he settled at Mabou Ridge. But he never became fully satisfied with life in the New World; he yearned for the Highlands. His poems reflect his disillusionment, especially in "Oran Do Dh'America" (Song for America), in which he laments the homeland and heritage that he left behind ("the friendly, hospitable land, / and my beloved kinsmen"). He detested the weather ("the land of snows") and looked unfavourably toward his new neighbours ("rowdy and boastful").

Macdonald of Sleat, Lord (Godfrey William Wentworth). Fourth Baron of the Isles. He authorized the clearing of his people from North Uist and Skye.

MacDonald, Michael (Micheil Mór MacDhòmhnaill) (ca. 1745-1815). Poet, a native of South Uist; immigrated to Prince Edward Island in 1772 with the Glenaladale pioneers before settling on the western shore of Cape Breton in Judique. Three years later he wrote "Fair Is the Place," considered the oldest existing Gaelic song in Cape Breton. Unlike some of his contemporaries, MacDonald chose to concentrate on positive aspects of pioneer life in the New World.

Macdonald, Rory (b. 1949-). Born in Dornoch; bass guitarist, vocalist and co-songwriter for the Gaelic rock band Runrig.
See also Bruce Guthro; Calum Macdonald; Donnie Munro; Runrig

Macdonell, Alasdair Ranaldson of Glengarry (1773-1828). In 1788, he became the 15th Chief of Clan Macdonell of Glengarry. He was educated at Oxford and inherited huge estates from Glengarry in the Great Glen to Knoydart; he was a model for Fergus MacIvor in Scott's *Waverley* novels. Macdonell cleared his people from Glengarry. A haughty and flamboyant man, his behaviour was so egregious—he evicted small tenants who refused to enlist in his military endeavours—it prompted Robert Burns to compose his satirical poem "Address of Beelzebub." He died in an accident in 1828 while stepping off a steamer in the Caledonian Canal.

Macdonell considered himself to be the last true Highland chief. He played the role to the hilt. He always wore the traditional dress and seldom travelled without his retinue of armed servants and piper. He was a member of the Highland Society and the Celtic Society of Edinburgh. When King George IV made his famous visit to Edinburgh, Macdonell made sure his presence was known. He continued the evictions that his mother initiated to make way for sheep, which led many of his clan to emigrate to another Glengarry, in Upper Canada (Ontario).

Macdonell, Bishop Alexander (1762-1840). Born Glen Urquhart, Inchlaggan, Scotland; the first Roman Catholic bishop of Kingston, Upper Canada (Ontario). When his fellow clansmen were evicted from Glengarry, Father Macdonell went with them to Glasgow and later formed the Glengarry Fencibles; he became the first Catholic chaplain in the British Army. When the regiment was disbanded, Rev. Macdonell petitioned the government to grant the soldiers a tract of land in Canada; in 1804, 64,750 ha (160,000 acres) were set aside in what is now Glengarry County, Ontario.

During the War of 1812 between the United States and Britain, he raised another regiment, the Glengarry Light Infantry Fencibles. Three years later he became the first Roman Catholic bishop at St. Raphael's Church, in Ontario.

MacDougall, Allan (Ailean Dùghallach) (ca. 1750-1828). Born in Glencoe, Ailean Dall ("Blind Allan") was the poet to Alasdair Ranaldson MacDonell of Glengarry. MacDougall composed panegyric and satiric verse, including a lament at Glengarry's funeral. He also wrote bitter attacks on the Lowland shepherds who he blamed for the depopulation of the Highlands during the Clearances era.

Macfarlane, Murdo (1901-1982). Known as the Melbost Bard, Macfarlane was a published poet and advocate for Scottish Gaelic, especially during the 1970s. Born and brought up in Melbost, Isle of Lewis, he was taught Latin, English and French but received no education in Gaelic, his mother tongue. He spent some time working for Lord Leverhulme on various schemes but eventually left to travel to North America in the 1920s and spent many years in Manitoba. Dissatisfied, he returned to Scotland in 1932, and served in the military during the Second World War. His best-known song is "Cànan Nan Gàidheal" (The Language of the Gael), the title track of Catherine-Ann MacPhee's 1987 recording of the same name. His work has inspired other contemporary Gaelic musicians, including the Gaelic bands Capercaillie and Runrig.

MacInnes, John (b. 1930). Born in Uig, Lewis, but raised as a child on Raasay where he attended primary school; educated at Portree Secondary School in Skye; studied English at the University of Edinburgh where he met the piper and singer Calum Johnston and the singer Flora MacNeil, two influential figures in his life. At Edinburgh he specialized in Old and Middle English as well as Old Norse. Among his professors at Edinburgh (he enrolled in the Department of Celtic Studies) were K. H. Jackson and the Reverend William Matheson. In 1958 he was appointed to a Junior Research Fellowship in the School of Scottish Studies and then as a tutor in Old and Middle English there, a post he held until 1963. He was a senior lecturer at the university from which he retired in 1993.

MacInnes has written countless essays, reviews and journal articles on wide ranging issues affecting Gaelic Scotland, including "The Choral Tradition in Scottish Gaelic Song," "The Oral Tradition in Scottish Gaelic Poetry," "The Seer in Gaelic Tradition," "The Panegyric Code in Gaelic Poetry and its Historical Background," "Gaelic Poetry in the Nineteenth Century," "Language, Metre and Diction in the Poetry of Sorley Maclean" and "Gaelic Song and Dance."

Macintyre, Duncan Bàn (Donnchadh Bàn Mac-an-t-Saoir) (1724-1812). Poet; born in Glenorchy, Argyll. He spent a good part of his life as a forester and gamekeeper in Glen Etive, Ben Doran and Glen

Lochay, and served in the Argyll regiment during the 1745 Rising. In 1766 he moved to Edinburgh where he was employed in the Edinburgh City Guard from 1766 to 1793. From 1793 to 1799 he served in the Breadalbane Fencibles. He began publishing his poetry in 1768. He is best known for his nature poems. His masterpiece, "In Praise of Ben Dorain" is a *paean* to nature as it follows the movement of the deer and the lines of the landscape. He was prescient in his own way. As early as the late 18th century he already saw and commented on the popularity of sheep farming that was leading to the depopulation of the Highlands.

He is buried in Greyfriars Churchyard in Edinburgh.

Maciver, Donald (Dòmhnall MacIomhair) (1857-1935). Born in Uig, Lewis, he composed "An Ataireachd Ard" (The Surge of the Sea), considered an enduring Gaelic masterpiece about change and the transience of life. His song has been recorded numerous times, most notably by Catherine-Ann MacPhee on *Cànan nan Gàidheal*, Runrig on *Heartland* and Capercaillie on the soundtrack to the television documentary *The Blood Is Strong*.

Mackenzie, Alexander (1838-1898). Scottish historian, author, magazine editor and journalist; born in Gairloch. In 1869 he settled in Inverness, where he later became an editor and publisher of the *Celtic Magazine*. Mackenzie wrote several clan histories but he is best remembered today for his *The History of the Highland Clearances* (1883), the first significant work on the Clearances and which no less than John Prebble has called "an indignant, impassioned and uncompromising indictment of Highland landlords and the diaspora of a people."

Mackenzie, Sir George Steuart of Coul (1780-1848). A mineralogist by trade, he was the author of *A General View of Ross and Cromarty* as well as a staunch advocate of the Clearances and sheep farming. Mackenzie drew up the influential *Report for the Board of Agriculture: General View of the Agriculture of Ross and Cromarty* in 1813.

MacKenzie, Hugh F. (1895-1971). Born in Christmas Island, Cape Breton; piper, violinist, Gaelic instructor and radio broadcaster. He was one of the founders of the Gaelic Society of Cape Breton.

Mackie, J. D. (1887-1978). Historian born in Edinburgh and educated at Middlesborough High School and Jesus College, Oxford. He was appointed lecturer in modern history and head of the department of modern history at St. Andrews University in 1908, where he introduced Scottish history into the curriculum and where he remained until 1926 before being appointed as Professor of Modern History at London University. During the First World War he served with the Argyll and Sutherland Highlanders. He became Professor of Scottish History and Literature at the University of Glasgow from 1930 to 1957. His most popular work was the well-received *A History of Scotland*, first published in 1964.

MacKinnon, Jonathan (1869-1944). Born in Whycocomagh, Cape Breton; of Skye descent; editor of the Sydney, Nova Scotia-based *Mac-Talla* (Echo), the world's longest-running Gaelic-only weekly (1892-1901) and later biweekly (1901-1904). *Mac-Talla* published current events on the Gaelic-speaking world as well as poetry and traditional stories, often Clearances-related.

MacLachlan, John (1804-1874). Of Rahoy, Ardnamurchan; trained as a doctor at Glasgow University; composed numerous love songs and several poems on the Clearances, including "Dìreadh a-mach ri Beinn Shianta" (Climbing up toward Ben Shiant).

Maclean, Dougie (b. 1954). Singer, songwriter and multi-instrumentalist; born in Perthshire. He was a fiddler and guitarist with the Tannahill Weavers in the late 1970s and in the 1980s briefly with Silly Wizard, before forging out on his own as a solo artist. A composer of gentle songs (and tunes), he boasts a lovely, reassuring voice. His recordings include *Craigie Dhu* (1983); *Fiddle* (1984); *Singing Land* (1986); *Real Estate* (1988); *Whitewash* (1990); *Indigenous* (1991); *Riof* (1997); *Marching Mystery* (1994), whose title track is inspired by the Lewis chess pieces; *Who Am I* (2001); *Inside the Thunder* (2005) and *Resolution* (2011). His most famous composition is the wistful "Caledonia." In 1992, "The Gael," a haunting tune from his album *The Search* (1990), a collection of instrumental music commissioned for the opening of the Official Loch Ness Monster Exhibition, was used as the main theme for Michael Mann's film set during the French and Indian War, *The Last of the Mohicans* (1992). Since 2005, Maclean has organized and performed in the Perthshire Amber Festival, a ten-day music festival based in Dunkeld, Scotland. His themes include community, heritage and the importance of the land in the Gaelic tradition. His philosophy is best summed up in the composition, "Solid Rock": "You cannot own the land / the land owns you," a sentiment that shares much with Native American attitudes toward land ownership and which Maclean tacitly acknowledges in his work.

MacLean, John (Bàrd Thighearna Cholla) (1787-1848). Author of "The Gloomy Forest." A native of Tiree, he was a shoemaker by trade and was given the honorific title of Bard to the Laird of Coll; hence, he is also known as the Bard MacLean. Cut from the same mould as the ancient bards of the Gaelic tradition, MacLean was considered the greatest of the Gaelic bards to immigrate to North America. He emigrated in 1819 to Barney's River, Pictou County, Nova Scotia, then moved to Glenbard, Antigonish County, in 1830. He published an anthology of songs—including his own—in 1818. Initially, he reacted negatively to emigrant life—he especially disliked the cold climate and the endless trees—but over the years his attitude gradually softened. The trees of Nova Scotia were the subject of what many scholars consider the greatest of all Scots emigrant songs, "A' Choille Ghraumach" (The Gloomy Forest). Maclean writes about the cultural shock that he felt in the so-called New World, living in the wilderness on Barney's River. Above all, he misses the "jovial company" that he left back home.

He is buried in Glenbard Cemetery, a pilgrimage stop for local residents and visitors alike.

Maclean, Sorley (Somhairle MacGill-Eain) (1911-1996). Born in Raasay; attended Raasay Primary School and Portree Secondary School (now Portree High School); graduated from the University of Edinburgh; schoolmaster in Edinburgh and later in Plockton, Ross-shire. He offered a Gaelic perspective of history in his poetry. Maclean had deep roots in the Western Isles: his father, Malcolm Maclean, was a tailor from Raasay, his mother, a Nicolson from Skye.

Maclean's influences were wide ranging. He learned many of the great Gaelic songs from his grandmother, Mary Matheson. Her people had moved to Skye from Lochalsh on the mainland in the 18th century after being cleared in Glas-na-Muclach by the Earl of Seaforth. His aunt Peggy was also "full of old songs." Other influences included the Gaelic poet William Ross and Mary MacPherson, the great Skye agitator and songwriter as well as the radical tradition of the Land League movement generally. Early literary influences included 17th-century metaphysical poets and the Romantic poets, specifically Donne, Wordsworth, Shelley and Blake but also the classical Greek and Roman poets and his contemporaries, such as Yeats, Eliot, Pound and, in Scotland, Hugh MacDiarmid, especially MacDiarmid's "A Drunk Man Looks at the Thistle."

The turning point in Maclean's life was the outbreak of the Spanish Civil War and the defeat of fascism in Spain; he had a lifelong hatred of fascism. In 1937 he took a teaching post at Tobermory High School on Mull, where he taught from January to December 1938. His time on Mull was a "traumatic experience"; the widespread clearances that took place there in the 19th century made it a "heart-breaking place" for someone named Maclean, the best known of Mull surnames. He found its physical beauty different from that of Skye and "with the terrible imprint of the Clearances on it" it was "almost unbearable for a Gael." He wrote numerous important poems here, including "A Highland Woman."

In early 1939 he moved from Mull to Edinburgh, teaching English at Boroughmuir High School. Living in Polworth, he attended weekly gathering of poets at the Abbotsford Bar in Rose Street. That same year he began working on one of his major poems, "An Cuilithionn" (The Cuillin). Conceived as a very long poem, it commented on the human condition, from Skye to Europe to the outer world. See more on this poem below.

In September 1940, he entered the Signal Corps, based at Catterick Camp in Yorkshire before being sent in December 1941 to Egypt, where, from late 1941 to early 1943, he was on active service with the Royal Horse Artillery. He was badly wounded at the Battle of El Alamein in November 1942, when a land mine exploded near him. He spent the next nine months recuperating in various hospitals, lastly at Raigmore Hospital in Inverness.

In 1943 he returned to Edinburgh to resume teaching at Boroughmuir. The following year met Renee Cameron of Inverness. They married two years later. During his time in Edinburgh he wrote his best-known poem, "Hallaig" which was composed during 1952 to 1953 and first appeared in *Gairm* in 1954. In 1947 he was promoted to Principal Teacher of English at Boroughmuir. He returned to the Highlands in 1956 as Headmaster of Plockton Secondary School, where he remained until he retired in 1972. After his retirement he and his wife moved to his great grandmother's house at Peinnachorrain in Braes, Skye.

In 1970, *Four Points of a Saltire* was published, which consisted of the poetry of Maclean but also George Campbell Hay, William Neill and Stuart MacGregor; it was considered an important milestone in Gaelic poetry. The following year Iain Crichton Smith's English translation of *Dain do Eimhir* as *Poems to Eimhir* made Maclean's work available to a non-Gaelic speaking readership. In 1977, he published *Reothairt is Contraigh* by Canongate; his own selection of his poetry from 1932 to 1972 with several new poems. From 1973 to 1975, he was Creative Writer in Residence at Edinburgh University; and from 1975 to 1976 he was Filidh (poet-in-residence) at the Gaelic College on Skye, Sabhal Mòr Ostaig.

It was always Maclean's intent to be an international poet who just happened to write in Gaelic—to write Gaelic poetry of international significance. In 1939 he began work on a major poem, "The Cuillin," a very long poem, an ambitious poem, about the Clearances, exile, exploitation but also a meditation on the human condition—rooted in a specific place, beginning with the history of Skye to the West Highlands to Europe and the rest of the world. MacDiarmid's "A Drunk Man Looks at the Thistle" was a major inspiration for this poem, but he never finished it.

Another of Maclean's Highland poems, "Highland Woman" describes a woman, she of the "bent, poor, wretched head" with the "load" of fruit on her back, the sweat streaming down her brow and cheek. She is no longer young: the "twenty autumns" that have have gone by and a life of "unremitting toil" have all taken their collective toll on her, both physically and spiritually.

Some of his best known and most critically acclaimed poems are set on Raasay. "Hallaig" is a haunting poem about loss, and the passage of time. Employing symbolist imagery and metaphor, it is memory made palpable. The Irish poet Seamus Heaney has called it a "shimmer of the transcendent." It makes allusions to the Clearances, from Screapadal to Suishnish, to people who have vanished ("In Screapadal of my people / where Norman and Big Hector were"). The poem places him firmly as part of the larger Gaelic bardic tradition. He eulogizes the memory of the dead, the Macleans and the Macleods, and "where every single generation is gone" even as he celebrates its physical beauty, the "mild moss" and "the steep slopes" as the sun goes down on Dun Caan. Similarly, in "The Woods of Raasay," amid the "bracken and birch" he recalls the "music of laughter"—yet with graveyards on each slope of the hillside.

Maclean's work has inspired various contempory musicians, from the Gaelic rock band Runrig to the classical and jazz composer Alasdair Nicolson. He remains an iconic figure, a literary giant, both in the Gaelic world and on the larger worldwide poetry stage.

He died on November 24, 1996, at Raigmore Hospital in Inverness at the age of 85 after a short illness.

Maclean, Will (b. 1941). One of the leading artists in Scotland; Emeritus Professor of Visual Arts at the University of Dundee; an artist of social realism and surrealist images. The Clearances are one of the central themes of his work. He was born and raised in Inverness, the son of a harbour master. His father, John Maclean, was a living link to the Gaelic world (though the younger Maclean is not a Gaelic speaker); family members on his mother's side were cleared from Coigach and his maternal great grand aunt defied Sheriff William Ivory at the Battle of the Braes on Skye. He trained for the merchant navy at the HMS Conway, and spent two years at sea. He attended evening classes at Edinburgh College of Art before enrolling in Gray's School of Art in Aberdeen.

Maclean uses collage, assemblage and found objects. Some critics have compared his work to the box constructions of the American artist Joseph Cornell, who used the technique of assemblage or bricolage, made from found objects in a novel way to create something entirely new. Maclean's work offers a decidedly Highland perspective on the world—an unsentimental one. Its themes are many, including childhood loss intertwined with the passing of Gaelic culture, time, memory, dispossession, the vanishing of a culture and the destruction of a way of life. The dark side of progress is a constant and enduring theme.

Three Fires, Achnahaird (1975) presents a dark view of Achiltibuie, a coastal village located 16 km (10 miles) northwest of Ullapool—curing of fish and hides ... skull of an animal—all suggest a macabre landscape and evoke an overall haunting quality. Technically, Achnahaird is a Bronze Age site but it might as well be a Clearance site. In *Memories of a Northern Childhood* (1977) Maclean uses a clay pipe and fishing gear to recreate the archaeology and memory of his childhood.

Highlands and Clearances themes are evident and indeed prominent throughout his work. *Two Sights of the Sea* (1982) features a clever intertwining of the ocean and the Gaelic tradition of second sight. The consequences of the Clearances are clearly seen in *I didn't go willingly, I went sadly* (1983), which is also the title of a poem by Murdo Macfarlane of Lewis about domestic service girls who had to leave their homeland to find work. The centre of the piece is a photograph of the girls. In *Quarantine Passage/Grosse-Île* (1994) he recalls the Highland emigrants who passed Grosse Île, the emigration centre in Québec, Canada, from 1832 to 1932, along with the more famous Irish famine victims.

Highland themes continue in *Welcome to South Uist* (1981), a pencil drawing; *Skye Fisherman: In Memoriam* (1989), a memorial to his uncle, William Reid; *View of Raasay from Ashaig* (1985), a pen and wash sketch; and *Memorial for a Clearance Village* (1974).

Archibald Geikie's account of the eviction of Suisnish inspired Maclean's *Beach Allegory* (1973), an elegiac portrait consisting of a fire burning on a makeshift altar against a deserted landscape, said to be that of Boreraig, another Clearance village on Skye. Maclean has also fashioned highly intricate pencil drawings with Highland Clearance themes, including *Memorial to the Glendale Martyrs* (1983).

Maclean's work has been commissioned by various organizations. In 1986 he created an etching, *The Melancholy of Departure*, for the exhibition on the Clearances, *As an Fhearann/From the Land*, at An Lanntair in Stornoway. His work also appears on the cover of the Gaelic rock band Runrig's recording, *Mara* (1990): *Fisherman with Coalfish* is a combination of painting with resin and zinc and collage. In November 2006 he collaborated with Arthur Watson on the *Crannghal* sculpture.

Installed at Sabhal Mòr Ostaig, the Gaelic college on Skye, it was inspired by the vessel that brought Columba to Scotland.

The Emigrant Ship (1992) is a major work inspired by the Glencalvie Clearances as well as homage to William McTaggart's painting of the same name. It incorporates the "wicked generation" words etched on the diamond pattern of the glass window of Croick Church at Glencalvie with the graffiti image of an emigrant ship that he found scratched on the wall of a deserted school house in a cleared settlement on the Isle of Mull. It is a powerful image that evokes the pain and uncertainty of clearances and emigration but also the loss of land and culture.

Sorley Maclean's poetry has also been a major influence on Maclean's work. *Sabbath of the Dead* (1978) was inspired by Maclean's poem "Hallaig," taking its title from a line in Maclean's poem. Like the poem, Will Maclean's work is a lament for a land now devoid of people, in its images of the hills of Raasay as seen from across the water, a piece of driftwood and a crab's claw stretching toward the sky, a palpable sense of absence but also anger and anguish. *Inner Sound* consists of a boarded up window of a deserted croft; through the window one can see the image of a submarine, linking the Clearances with militarism. The boarded-up window makes references to other specific lines from Sorley Maclean's "Hallaig": "The window is nailed and boarded / through which I saw the West."

Among other important works is a set of ten coloured etchings commissioned by Charles Booth-Clibborn, *A Night of Islands* (1991). One of the most significant etchings illustrates Derick Thomson's poem, "Strathnaver": Under a dark and starry sky are the horns of a sheep in a creel (a basket that holds fish) and the smoking timbers from a destroyed cottage, symbolizing the horrors of the Strathnaver Clearances.

More recent works have land rights as their theme as part of a remarkable series of memorial cairns on the Isle of Lewis that commemorate key events in the struggle for crofting rights. Using traditional Scottish building materials, from brochs to black houses, and undertaken with the assistance of the stonemason James Crawford, the first cairn, Pairc Cairn (1994), located at Lochs on the southern part of Lewis at Balallan, opened in 1994 to commemorate the Pairc Deer Raid of November 1887. The cairn is in the shape of an open, broch-like circular tower. The second cairn, at Griais (1996), commemorates the confrontation at the farm raid of Griais and Coll between Lord Leverhulme and the locals. It appears in the form of a pillar representing Lord Leverhulme set between two rounded forms that emerge from the earth, that is, the people. The third cairn is at Aignish (1996) and commemorates a farm raid at Aignish in 1888—the most violent confrontation of the crofter's war—in memory of the men and women of Point who raided the farm at Aignish and were sent to prison.

MacLeish, Archibald (1892-1982). Considered by many to be the quintessential American poet, MacLeish was the son of a Glasgow Scot with Highland blood. A Pulitzer-prize winning poet and man of letters, his work addressed universal truth—the fear of loss and the fleeting passage of time—even as quite a few of his poems touch on Scottish themes.

MacLeish grew up in a mansion, in Glencoe, Illinois, on Lake Michigan, which his father, Andrew MacLeish, named after an old Scots ballad, "Craigie Lea." He was a very reserved man: "My father came from a very old country in the north and far away," MacLeish once recalled, "and he belonged to an old strange race, the race older than any other. He did not talk of his country, but he sang bits of songs with words he said no one could understand anymore."

"Hebrides" is an elegiac poem about the emigration of the children of Gaels ("all gone off / over the water") and of the elderly couple left behind who presumably will never see their offspring again. Dedicated to "my Gaelic son," "The Thrush in the Gaelic Islands" comments on the Clearances as MacLeish remembers the stories that his Glasgow-born father, Andrew, told him.

"Years ago in the highlands, the Hebrides / landlords cleared the land for sheep." The images are often striking: that of a man who walked by empty crofts from Northbay in Barra "clear to the far side" while dogs ran in and out of the now-deserted dwellings.

In the spring of 1969, MacLeish accompanied his son, Kenneth, to the Isle of Barra for a *National Geographic* article. The younger MacLeish wrote the article while the elder wrote a short poem for the occasion.

MacLeish died on April 20, 1982, a few weeks short of his 90th birthday.

MacLennan, Hugh (1907-1990). Born in Glace Bay, Nova Scotia; author and professor of English at McGill University (one of his students at McGill was the Canadian singer-songwriter and poet Leonard Cohen).

In *Two Solitudes*, Hugh MacLennan refers to "a Scottish kind of sternness, a Scottish melancholy that finds pleasure only in sad ideas," while in *Each Man's Son* (1951), he describes a "passionate loyalty" that the displaced Highlanders now feel for their adopted home. His character Daniel Ainslie is one of those who stayed behind in Cape Breton, and possesses a feeling just as fierce and committed as the original settlers articulated generations ago.

So for several generations the Highlanders remained here untouched, long enough for them to transfer to Cape Breton, the same passionate loyalty their ancestors had felt for the hills of home. It was long enough for them to love the island as a man loves a woman, unreasonably, for her faults no less than for her virtues. Each man's son was driven by the daemon of his own hope and imagination—by this energy or by his fear—to unknown destinations. For those who stayed behind, the beast continued to growl behind the unlocked door.

In his fine essay, "Scotchman's Return," MacLennan explains this loyalty in personal terms. His father, a third-generation Canadian, had never seen the Highlands before he visited them while on leave during the First World War. "He never needed to go there to understand whence he came or what he was.... All the perplexity and doggedness of the race was in him, its loneliness, tenderness, and affection...."

Like his father, MacLennan's characters live in two worlds—the present of their Canadian home and the past of their Scottish ancestors. "But we can't escape ourselves forever," MacLennan once wrote, "and more of ourselves than we choose to admit is the accumulated weight of our ancestors." In one of the most poignant passages in Scots-Canadian literature, he tries to explain this peculiarly Canadian connection to the Scottish past and in particular to the vestigial harm done by the legacy of the Highland Clearances.

> Above the sixtieth parallel in Canada you feel that nobody but God has ever been there before you, but in a deserted Highland glen you feel that everyone who ever mattered is dead and gone.

MacLennan once said he belonged "to the last Canadian generation raised with a Highland nostalgia...." He asks, "Am I wrong or is it true that it is only now, after so many years of not knowing who we were or wanted to be, that we Canadians of Scotch descent are truly at home in the northern half of North America?"

In MacLennan's *Barometer Rising*, one of the first novels set in Halifax, the main characters—John Macrae, Big Alex Mackenzie and Angus Murray—all come to the Nova Scotia mainland from Cape Breton. Since the first language of all three is Gaelic, Cape Breton is viewed as being linguistically and culturally different from the rest of Canada, as if it belongs to another country and century altogether.

MacLennan is considered the first major English-speaking writer in Canada to attempt to depict Canada's national character even as some critics have criticized his work as being outdated and his portrayal of characters too stereotypical. Along with Robertson Davies, he was considered among the finest essayists in 20th-century Canadian literature.

MacLeod, Alistair (b. 1936). Born in North Battleford, Saskatchewan, but raised in Cape Breton, MacLeod has published sparingly—only a handful of story collections and one novel—yet he is among the most highly respected writers in the English-speaking world. While hardly a household name, except perhaps in his native Canada, he continues to earn accolades for his stellar body of work. His stories earned him a place in the Modern Library's 200 greatest English writers since 1950. MacLeod's terse yet evocative prose captures the dual nature of the emigrant experience and the familial ties that remain, even generations removed. His themes are on memory and remembrance; elegy and loss; continuity and disruption, rootedness and exile. Both of his grandparents were native Gaelic speakers.

As a young man MacLeod worked at various occupations—as a logger, miner and fisherman—to finance his education. He attended the Nova Scotia Teachers College, St. Francis Xavier University and the University of New Brunswick before receiving his PhD from the University of Notre Dame. He taught creative writing at the University of Indiana and for many years taught at the University of Windsor, where he was a professor of English and from where he retired in 2000. He has published two collections of short stories, *The Lost Salt Gift of Blood* in 1976 and *As Birds Bring Forth the Sun and Other Stories* in 1986, which were gathered into one volume, *Island*, in 2000, along with two additional stories, the title story and "Clearances." His first and only novel, *No Great Mischief*, was published in 1999.

No Great Mischief evokes one of the most seminal events in Canadian history: the Battle of the Plains of Abraham. MacLeod's version takes place at a uranium mine in northern Ontario as a clan of Cape Breton Highlanders fight a drunken battle with a group of French-Canadian miners, which leads ultimately to the death of their leader, Fern Picard, and the conviction on second-degree murder charges of Calum MacDonald, the brother of the novel's narrator. In the original battle, the French general, Montcalm, fell while fighting the 78th Fraser Highlanders at Québec under the leadership of General James Wolfe. But Wolfe is no leader to the descendents of those Highlanders. Instead, the narrator's maternal grandfather complains that Wolfe "was just using them against the French." After all, it was Wolfe who, in a letter to a friend, dismissed them with the cynical comment, "No great mischief if they fall." They were, in other words, expendable.

Picard is murdered by a descendent of the Highland regiment; the MacDonald clan in the novel are also descended from another Calum MacDonald, a survivor of the Battle of Culloden. The clan emigrated from Moidart to Cape Breton generations ago. *No Great Mischief* is an immigrant tale of permanent displacement.

The past is astonishingly real in MacLeod's work; there is a palpable connection to history. In a conversation between the two MacDonald brothers, Alexander, a dentist, says to Calum, a former miner, "We are probably what we are because of the 1745 rebellion in Scotland. We are, ourselves, directly or indirectly the children of Culloden Moor, and what happened in its aftermath."

MacLeod is an observer of a specific location: Cape Breton, Nova Scotia. He is a storyteller but also a subtle teller of tales. He relates his stories in a gentle self-effacing voice that echoes the uncertainty of his characters and the fragility of the landscape itself. Significantly, he writes in the present tense. As Joyce Carol Oates observes, "The voice varies from story to story but it is recognizably the same voice...." He is a witness to the history of his own people.

MacLeod refers at one point to the Gaelic language as a "beautiful prison," a language that unites the clan, unites his family, and yet cuts them off from the rest of the world. A question appears in his work—"Where do you come from?"—that can be answered simply as, "I am from [fill I the blanks]," or it can be answered with a bit more complexity, "Yes, but I am of the old country too." That in a nutshell describes the work of Alistair MacLeod because the connections that his characters feel to their ancestral homeland—Scotland—is strong and pervasive. But it also means something else, something more tangible. Scotland is not just a place far away where the characters in his fiction came from a long time ago. It is also very much a part of them in the present even though they might never have actually set foot in the country of their ancestors. MacLeod's characters are, in every sense of the phrase, haunted by ancestors.

MacLeod's characters look at this far away Scotland with a sense of exile, a certain longing, a looking back that can and does last for generations. They live in two worlds—the Canada of today, the Scotland of yesterday—but both are very much a part of their inherent makeup. Grandparents, in his work, are carriers of culture. In MacLeod's stories the past is ever present, through history and story, through myth and song; these are influences that last many lifetimes.

It would be no stretch to refer to MacLeod as one of the children of the Clearances, and certainly he is a child of the worldwide Scottish diaspora. The writer John Sutherland in the pages of the *New York Times* once described as the Clearances as "ethnic cleansing, early 19th-century style. Ancient anger smolders," he writes, "like the glow of a peat fire, at the heart of these stories. A more complex anger, one senses, is directed inward. The author is himself one of those sons who deserted the 'physical life' of his people." The message here is that MacLeod is perhaps the last generation that intimately knows the past, that feels the past in his bones.

Many of MacLeod's protagonists live in perpetual exile. In "The Return," Alex, a ten-year-old boy from Montréal, returns with his parents to his father's home in Cape Breton. "Some of the people around us are talking in a language that I know is Gaelic although I do not understand it...," he admits. Many of the earliest recollections of MacLeod's characters are the memories of another place—that is, someone else's memories. One of the characters has cut himself off from his Nova Scotian mining family to please his middle-class Montréal wife, but he still thinks of Cape Breton as home. Ten years pass since his marriage when he finally visits his parents, but by then they feel alienated from him. They no longer have much in common except blood and heritage and apparently that isn't enough. "The Boat" is narrated by a professor who teaches at a Midwestern university but reminisces about growing up in Nova Scotia:

> The houses and their people, like those of the neighbouring towns and villages, were the result of Ireland's discontent and Scotland's Highland Clearances and America's War of Independence.

At its core "The Boat" is about the essential unknowability of people whom we think we *should* know: family members, in this case. The narrator is the teenage son of Cape Breton fisher people, descendants of the Irish who emigrated to Canada and the Scots who fled the Highland Clearances. The boat of the title is a small vessel called the *Jenny Lynn*, named after the boy's mother.

The boy's father is addicted to reading but the mother hasn't read a book since high school when "she read Ivanhoe and considered it a colossal waste of time." While her son discusses the water imagery of Tennyson at school, his father and uncle fish in their ancestral grounds. The main tension is the opposing choices made by father and son regarding their life's work: fishing vs. teaching and writing—that is, physical labour vs. the life of the mind. Like many native Cape Bretoners, the boy eventually leaves the island. We already know he is a teacher at a Midwestern university—a teacher, not surprisingly, of literature. He decides to leave after his father drowns. The body is found shredded by fish and gulls, a shocking and disturbing image.

Sometimes, MacLeod seems to be saying, all that remains of a life are the memories of ghostly voices and old photographs. MacLeod's people "carry certain things within" them—things that they do not always know about or fully understand "and sometimes it is hard to stamp out what you can't see." Instead, they recall stories that memorialize the past, that commemorate tribal connections. The same tales are told over and over again, but each time with just enough difference to make them meaningful to the listener and meaningful in turn for the narrator who, with each telling, comes to better understand his past and himself. The voice of the oral tradition is always on hand, ready to be retrieved.

MacLeod's characters possess a yearning and understanding of bleak and forlorn landscapes, as well as an appreciation of sacrifice and hardship and a feeling of sadness toward those who have lived an easier life (read: shallow), free from the strife of earlier and presumably hardier generations. They are in perpetual exile, these people—in exile from Scotland, the original homeland, and quite often from Cape Breton, the "adopted" homeland—and in exile even from themselves.

In "The Road to Rankin's Point," a young man, age 26, comes home to his grandmother on Cape Breton to die, to learn how to face death. We don't learn the exact details of his condition, only that his time is limited and that he is a descendant of the MacCrimmons of Skye. Bagpipers to Clan MacDonald, the MacCrimmons have the gift of music and the gift—curse?—of foreseeing their own deaths.

The grandmother plays the music of her time just as her grandchildren dance to the music of their time, many miles away in the nightclubs and strip joints of Toronto and Las Vegas.

> My grandmother gets up and goes for her violin which hangs on a peg inside her bedroom door. It is a very old violin and came from the Scotland of her ancestors, from the crumbled foundations that now dot and haunt Lochaber's shores.

She plays two Gaelic airs, "My Heart Is Broken since Thy Departure" and "Never More Shall I Return or MacCrimmon's Lament." The grandson writes about the message his grandfather had written on the rafters of the barn, "We are the children of our own despair, of Skye and Rum and Barra and Tiree." He does not know why he wrote it but wonders, "what is the significance of ancestral islands long left and never seen? Blown over now by Atlantic winds and touched by scudding foam." His grandmother in turn asks him, "What is to become of us?" after she learns of his pending death. The past is never far from the minds of those who populate the present. In "Second Spring," the narrator describes a narrow dirt road that was "apparently the original path followed by the first settlers in the 1770s when they walked along the shore on their way to their new lands."

Another constant theme is exile. MacLeod's own people left one island—the island of Eigg in the Hebrides—for another—Cape Breton—in the 1790s. In "The Closing Down of Summer," the collapse of coal mining in the Maritimes has led to the displacement of Cape Bretoners. This is a different kind of exile from that suffered by those whose poverty forced them to seek work in the factories and domestic service jobs in the Boston States, as Cape Bretoners called Massachusetts or New England. Here, though, it is the skill of the miners that takes them from Cape Breton to the mines of South Africa and South America.

The same themes appear over and over again in MacLeod's work: preservation, timelessness, the passage of time along with an intertwined history of family and the love of a particular place. One of his stories, "Island," has personal and linguistic survival as its theme. It is a study of isolation that also touches on myth. MacLeod uses patterns of repetition and return, characters that are indicative of the great ballads, of oral narratives. Elements of fantasy and even a touch of the ghost story also figure in it. What is imagined and what is real?

In "Island" a woman is asked by the authorities to leave the lighthouse after many decades of service. She is told to live "somewhere else"—a request that is as devastating to her as it was to the Clearance Highlanders evicted from their Scottish homelands so many years before. "After they had gone she walked the length and width of the island. She repeated all the place names, many of them in Gaelic, and marvelled that the places would remain but the names would vanish. 'Who would know?' she wondered....' 'Who will remember?'"

Some stories explicitly refer to the Clearances. In "Clearances" the main character lives in the same house that his grandfather built. Gaelic was the language of his parents and ancestors and it was his earliest language. During the Second World War he visited the Highlands, and as he journeyed farther north and west he became "aware of the soft sounds of Gaelic around him," aware of the sounds being different yet similar.

"You are from Canada?" asked a shepherd that the narrator meets on his Scottish journey. But more specifically he asks, "You are from the Clearances?" After many generations, the memories linger. Back home in Canada, he "would look across the ocean, imagining he could see the point of Ardnamurchan and beyond. Sometimes he would try to explain the Highland landscape to his father and his wife, though never mentioning his experiences in the trenches." It is an unusual situation that MacLeod presents here, where the son describes to the father the landscape of their ancestors.

> He looked toward the sea; somewhere out there, miles beyond his vision, he imagined the point of Ardnamurchan and the land which lay beyond. He was at the edge of one continent, he thought, facing the inevitable edge of another. He saw himself as a man in a historical documentary, probably, he thought, filmed in black and white.

In "The Tuning of Perfection" we meet Archibald, the 78-year-old descendant of an immigrant who has "come to be regarded as the 'last of the authentic old-time Gaelic singers' and is still remembered as 'the man from Skye'." Twenty years before the story opens, Archibald had been the topic of interviews and articles in such pieces as "Cape Breton Singer: The Last of His Kind." The story begins by making a direct reference to the Clearances, "the violence he had left in Scotland." And later on we are introduced to a different kind of clearance—the sweeping away of the memory of Gaelic by Archibald's descendants. There is a clearance of traditional commitment, of loyalty and responsibility.

In *No Great Mischief*, MacLeod's first, and, thus far, only novel, Alexander Macdonald is not sure which memories are real and which memories belong to other people's stories. The past and the present become blurred in his mind. The characters in the novel are often overwhelmed by the transience of life and the very real possibility of facing an uncertain future; instead, they talk mainly of the distant past and of faraway places. Indeed, they even "remember" events of a place they had never experienced, a Scotland they had never seen.

We learn that Alexander Macdonald's great-great-great-grandfather came from Moidart to the New World in 1779. They already had friends and relatives in the Cape Fear River area of North Carolina, all of whom fought in the Revolutionary War: "At night they sang Gaelic songs to one another across the mountain meadows where they would fight on the following day." Like many of MacLeod's characters, Macdonald relays this information in a matter-of-fact manner, with no sentimentality attached. The memories of dead ancestors flit in and out of his mind during the ordinary routines of the day.

More than one writer has commented on MacLeod's writing style as being redolent of the vocal rhythms of the Highlands even as his voice also indicates a touch of the Gaelic.

In October 2012, the Vancouver Writers Fest commissioned MacLeod to write a short story, to celebrate the Fest's 25th anniversary. Entitled "Remembrance," it's set in Cape Breton. A limited edition chapbook of the story was published.

Macleod, Angus. Canadian musician and a direct descendant of Lewis immigrants. Macleod studied folklore at Memorial University in St. John's, Newfoundland. In 2000 he released *The Silent Ones: A Legacy of the Highland Clearances*, which consists of eight songs and four instrumentals, and tells the story of the Lewis settlers evicted in 1851. The record features bagpipes, fiddle, whistle, mandolin and hammered dulcimer along with lead vocals by Sarah Buckingham and the use of narration and spoken word, the latter mostly in Gaelic.

The CD traces their history from the days of the Great Highland Famine, the evictions and their migration. The middle section chronicles their hardships in the Canadian backwoods. The final section brings us to the present day and the gradual erosion of Gaelic culture in western Ontario.

Between 1851 and 1855, more than 2,000 Lewis residents came to Ontario as part of the landowner James Matheson's scheme to settle them in the New World because of overpopulation and the potato famine. Many of these arrivals went to the Eastern Townships of Québec, where a sizable number of Lewis folk had already settled. But an equally sizable number went to Ontario, many of whom found work building the Great Western Railway in Hamilton. When Crown land became available in 1852, 109 families journeyed to the town of Goderich where they boarded boats that took them to their new homes in the woods.

The crofters settled together in an area of Bruce County, Ontario, maintaining their language and culture well into the 20th century. The CD was recorded at Macleod's recording studio located on a plot of land that was originally settled by his great grandfather, also named Angus Macleod.

See also Lewis, Isle of

Macleod, Calum (1911-1988). Crofter, seaman, lighthouse keeper and writer, Calum Macleod is best known for the road on Raasay that bears his name. Born in Glasgow, Calum Macleod was the son of Donald Macleod of Arnish, Raasay, and Julia Gillies of Fladda. The elder Macleod worked as a merchant seaman in Glasgow at the time of his son's birth. At the outbreak of the First World War, Macleod moved back to the croft in northern Raasay with his mother where he spent the rest of his childhood while his father continued to serve in the merchant navy.

In the mid-1930s Macleod was an assistant postman on Raasay and later became the island's sole postman, travelling on foot, covering an area of twelve miles in one day, in all weather. In 1950 he purchased his grandfather's house at South Arnish until eventually becoming a lighthouse keeper on the nearby island of Rona.

After many years of asking the government to build a road at the northern end of Raasay, to no avail, Macleod decided he would do it himself. Using Thomas Aitken's 440-page manual *Road Making and Maintenance: A Practical Treatise for Engineers, Surveyors, and Others*, which be bought for half a crown (about two pounds in today's money) as a guide, he began to work on what was not much more than an old narrow footpath. Over a decade or so from roughly 1964 to 1974 (the actual dates are difficult to pin down precisely), he constructed a 2.8 km (1¾ mile) road between the ruins of Brochel Castle and the township of Arnish. A number of years later, the road was surfaced by the local council. It consisted of a single track road with some 20 passing places.

By the time the road was completed, in 1982, Macleod and his wife, Alexandrina, were the last inhabitants in Arnish.

Macleod built the road with his own hands using a homemade wooden wheelbarrow, picks, axes, shovels, sledgehammers, spades and a crowbar. He cleared the land, laid the foundations, blasted rockfaces (with the assistance of the Department of Agriculture and Fisheries for Scotland) and erected culverts. While the work was remarkable enough in itself, what is even more remarkable is that he did it in his spare time: after labouring on his croft and working part time at the lighthouse on Rona.

Macleod was the great-grandson of Charles Macleod, a crofter and fisherman who testified before members of the Royal Commission of Inquiry into the Condition of Crofters and Cottars in the Highlands and Islands in 1883. In 1925 he won a Gold Medal in a Gaelic essay competition organized by the Celtic Society of New York. (The society's annual awards were open to overseas entrants.) Later in life, he contributed regularly to the Gaelic quarterly magazine *Gairm* and wrote a long essay entitled "Fàsachadh An-Iochdmhor Ratharsair" ("The Cruel Clearance of Raasay"), which in 1982 won the joint first prize in the Gaelic Books Council's competition; it was later published in book form, posthumously, in 2007 with a short biography provided by his daughter, Julia Allan. In 1983 he was awarded the British Empire Medal for his decades of "community service" to the post office and to the Northern Lighthouse Board.

By the time Macleod finished the road, he was a famous man. Journalists and television crews made their way to the croft on Raasay to interview him. He appeared on the BBC Radio Four program *It Takes All Sorts*, in the BBC television documentary *The Island that Nearly Made It*, and in the Grampian television documentary *The Blood Is Strong*. He even kept up a correspondence with families of the Clearance diaspora, descendents of people cleared from Raasay in the 1850s who had emigrated to Australia, New Zealand, South Africa, the United States and Canada.

Macleod died at the age of 76 on January 26, 1988, while working on his croft. His body, slumped over in his wheelbarrow, was found by his wife; Coll, his loyal white collie, was by his side.

In August 1990 a cairn built in his memory by Donald John Graham was unveiled on a hill above the ruins of Brochel Castle. A plaque on the cairn appears in both Gaelic and English:

RATHAD CHALUIM
RE IOMADH BLIADHNA B'E SEO AM FRITH-RATHAD
GU ARNAIS
1 ¾ MILE CHAIDH A LEUDACHADH AGUS A'

DHEASACHADH
GU RATHAD
MOR LE IONADAN LEIG SEACHAD GU IRE
TEARRAIDH LE
CALUM MACLEOID, B.E.M.
(1911-1988)
ARNAIS MU DHEAS
SHAOTHRAICH E NA AONAR AGUS CHUIR ECRIOCH
AIR AN OBAIR AN CHEANN DEICH BLIADHNA

CALUM'S ROAD
THIS FORMER FOOTPATH TO ARNISH—A DISTANCE
OF 1 ¾ MILES—
WAS WIDENED TO A SINGLE TRACK ROAD WITH
PASSING PLACES AND PREPARED FOR SURFACING BY
MALCOM MACLEOD, B.E.M.
(1911-1988)
SOUTH ARNISH
HE ACCOMPLISHED THIS WORK SINGLE-HANDEDLY
OVER A PERIOD OF TEN YEARS.

Macleod's stubborn and quixotic task has been commemorated in numerous other ways, too. The Scots band Capercaillie composed a tune, "Calum's Road" (it is featured in *The Blood Is Strong*). In his honour the Gaelic rock band, Runrig, wrote a song, "Wall of China / One Man," that appears on their album *The Stamping Ground*. The play, *Calum's Road*, based on the book of the same name by Roger Hutchinson, toured Scotland in the autumn of 2011.

See also Raasay

Macleod, Dennis. An entrepreneur originally from Easter Ross who led a campaign to erect a Clearances memorial and study centre in Helmsdale. In September 2003, plans for the monument were abandoned because of costs. Instead, in its place emerged a more modest proposal: a statue that would commemorate the Clearances and the Scots diaspora. The statue, *The Emigrants*, is in Helmsdale, while a replica statue, called *Exiles*, is in Winnipeg.

The Clearances are personal to Dennis Macleod—his ancestors were among those cleared from Kildonan. In the late 1950s he worked at Dounreay as a radio chemist on the development of nuclear submarines before making his fortune by exploring and operating mineral mines in Africa.

The purpose of the memorial is to ensure that what happened will not be forgotten. In his travel memoir, *In Waiting*, Michael Russell commented on Macleod's Clearances project, thinking it important because it would remind Scotland and the outside world "that a society that thinks only of economic progress—only of the fashionable theories of the moment—can inflict terrible wrongs on innocent people even when they are kind-hearted and well intended; indeed, especially so."

Macleod, Donald (1814-1860). Donald Macleod, the author of the incendiary Clearances memoir *Gloomy Memories*, was a relentless foe of the governmental policies that led to the Clearances. Even today, he is considered a deeply polarizing figure—agitator to some, hero to others. Although he also wrote about the Durness riots of 1840 and 1841, it is his account of the Strathnaver Clearances for which he is best known. Along with Donald Ross, Macleod was the first journalist to write about the Clearances who was actually a native Gael. As one of the best-known Clearance pamphleteers and a propagandist for his people, Macleod wrote in a forceful and descriptive style, using highly emotional—some would say inflammatory—language. His work was reprinted in Alexander Mackenzie's *History of the Highland Clearances* in 1883; his account of the infamous Sutherland Clearances was serialized in 1840 in the *Edinburgh Weekly Chronicle* before appearing as the *History of Destitution in Sutherlandshire* in 1841.

Born toward the end of the 18th century in the township of Rosal in Strathnaver, Sutherland, Macleod was the son of a farmer and stonemason who grew up during the height of the Clearances when family after family was being evicted from their homes. Macleod's own background is rather sketchy. John Prebble has described him as a "deeply religious man, though fiercely anti-clerical...." In 1818 he married the daughter of a "well-known and highly esteemed" man from the parish of Farr. He served his apprenticeship as a stonemason under his father, William Macleod.

Macleod saw firsthand the effect that the governmental policies had on the Highland landscape. He was a witness, in 1814, when the infamous Patrick Sellar, the sheep farmer and factor (manager) who was charged with committing a series of atrocities that made his name notorious in Highland history, pulling down and burning William Chisholm's house in Strathnaver, where his nearly one-hundred-years-old, bed-ridden mother-in-law, Margaret Mackay, lay. When Macleod told Sellar that the old woman was too ill to move, he reportedly uttered, "Damn her, the old witch. She has lived too long. Let her burn!" Consequently, the house was set on fire and she was carried out and placed in an adjacent shed. Macleod burned his own hands while trying to help the woman. Her daughter, Janet Mackay, dragged her mother from the shed just as Sellar ordered that it also be burned. "God receive my soul!" the old woman reportedly cried. "What fire is this about me?"

She died less than five days later. Macleod also reported in his work that some men wandered off into the woods in a daze, on the verge of insanity, before succumbing to the elements.

Two years later, in 1816, when Sellar was brought to trial in Inverness under the charge of culpable homicide, Macleod somehow was listed as a witness—for the defence. Macleod never did take the witness stand—one can only wonder what he would have said—but some Clearance scholars, including Douglas MacGowan, believe that the intent on Sellar's part would have been an effort to destroy Macleod on the stand. After all, Sellar referred to Macleod's reports in the Edinburgh press as nothing less than "villainous libels."

In the meantime, the Clearances continued. In October 1830, eight men evicted Macleod's wife and children from their house in Sutherland while Macleod was working in Caithness; their furniture was thrown out and the doors and windows of the house nailed shut. During the night his wife went in search of her husband, admonishing the children to stay within the small space she fortified outside the house by using the furniture as a kind of protection. They found each other a day later but the children, led by the eldest child, a very brave seven-year-old, had chosen to do their own separate search, eventually finding shelter at a great-aunt's house. The eldest, according to Macleod, carried the infant on his back while the other two children held on to his kilt "and in this way," writes Macleod, they travelled in darkness, "through rough and smooth, bog and mire...." The family was evicted again, a year or so later. This latest crisis proved too much for Mrs. Macleod, essentially reducing her to a kind of madness. But even after the family had moved to Edinburgh, Macleod continued his correspondence with his contacts up north.

After the Strathnaver Clearances, Macleod worked for a time in Wick and even as far south as Edinburgh while his wife and children remained in Sutherland. Between 1840 and 1841 the *Edinburgh Weekly Chronicle* published twenty-one of Macleod's devastating letters as "History of the Destitution of Sutherlandshire" that would eventually become *Gloomy Memories*—making him famous. Clearances historian Eric Richards has called *Gloomy Memories* "a crucial" but "contentious" document, "an impassioned and vituperative account," but not, he believes, "by any measure, a careful telling of the story."

In 1841 the first edition of *Gloomy Memories*, a reprint of his letters to the *Edinburgh Weekly Chronicle*, was published. A second edition was published in Greenock in 1856 and an expanded third edition in Toronto in 1857. The later editions of the memoir's full title leaves little doubt about Macleod's point of view and, indeed, indicates the depth of his anger: *Gloomy Memories in the Highlands of Scotland versus Mrs. Harriet Beecher Stowe's Sunny Memories in (England) a Foreign Land: Or a Faithful Picture of the Extirpation of the Celtic Race from the Highlands of Scotland.*

The later editions of *Gloomy Memories* were published partly as a vigorous response to the American writer Harriet Beecher Stowe's *Sunny Memories*, a two-volume journal of her European tour released in 1857. The success of her anti-slavery novel *Uncle Tom's Cabin* had made Stowe one of the most famous women in the Western world. Consequently, in 1853, the Duchess of Sutherland invited Stowe to visit her at Dunrobin Castle. Stowe was familiar with Macleod's anti-government pamphlets and in *Sunny Memories* she essentially called Macleod a liar, insisting that his account of the Clearances were "ridiculous stories."

What's more, Macleod was appalled by the government's emigration scheme following the publication of the MacNeill Report in 1851, which provided assistance to landlords intent on helping people to emigrate. Macleod believed the scheme did little but promote further depopulation.

Macleod's enemies, of which he had many, called him a fanatic. Eric Richards has written that Macleod "frequently employed hyperbole for passionate emphasis...." Others condemned him as a crank and "a troublesome and turbulent character." There is no denying that he was a passionate man, but in his heart he felt he was a journalist—he turned the craft of journalism into a calling—even though it would take many years for his words to appear in print. He believed that his fellow Gaels were being "exterminated" either by famine or by forced emigration.

By 1857, Macleod had immigrated to Canada—James Campbell has described him as an unsuccessful bookseller—and was living somewhere in Woodstock County, Ontario. He died three years later. It remains uncertain where or how he died.

Macleod is memorialized by a cairn located on the B873 roadside opposite the River Naver across from the Rosal site. The plaque reads:

IN MEMORY OF
DONALD MACLEOD
STONEMASON
WHO WITNESSED THE
DESTRUCTION OF ROSSAL
IN 1814 AND WROTE
'GLOOMY MEMORIES'

See also Patrick Sellar; Harriet Beecher Stowe

MacLeod, Donald of Gleanies. Sheriff-Deputy of the County of Ross, he suppressed the sheep riots of 1792 and 1820 and was an apologist for the landlords. An advocate of the improvements, he maintained that sheep farming—and thus the Clearances—ultimately benefited everyone.

MacLeod, Mary (Màiri nighean Alasdair Ruaidh) (ca. 1615-ca. 1707 [poss. -1705]). Gaelic poet, born in Rodel, Harris. She came to Dunvegan, Skye, as a nurse where she wrote many Gaelic songs, only 16 of which survive. Her songs were often composed in honour of the MacLeods and other great clan families such as the Mackenzies of Applecross. Her praise poetry, breaking from classical metres, is notable for its uniqueness since it was composed in a less structured and thus more spontaneous manner.

MacLeod, Murdo (Murchadh MacLeòid) (1837-1914). Born in Leurbost, Lewis; temperance agent and evangelist based in Glasgow; best known as a composer of hymns.

MacLeod, Neil (Niall MacLeòid) (1843-1913). Native of Glendale, Skye; born into a musical family (his father published a booklet of songs in 1811). He composed popular poetry, including "The Skye Crofters."

MacNeacail, Aonghas (b. 1942). Writer, poet and songwriter, born in Uig, Skye. Derick Thomson has said that he belongs to the so-called third wave of modern Gaelic poets. He has held several writer-in-residence posts. He composes poetry in both Gaelic and English and he is strongly influenced by Scottish folk music, Gaelic psalm singing and the pibroch. In an essay, "Rage against the Dying," he passionately and eloquently has written about the difficulty of being a Gaelic writer in the modern world.

MacNeacail has also collaborated with numerous musicians on various projects, including on several compositions with the Scots folk band Capercaillie: "Breisleach/Delirium," "Oran/Song" and "Am Fear Allabain/The Wanderer." In 1990 he wrote an instrumental piece inspired by Sorley Maclean's "Hallaig" for organ. In 1993, he again turned to Maclean, writing a solo vocal with ensemble or orchestra on Maclean's "The Woods of Raasay." In 1998, with the Glasgow composer William Sweeney, Paragon Ensemble commissioned him to write *An Turus*, the first full-length opera in Gaelic inspired by the medieval tale of Diarmid and Grainne. In 1999, also with Sweeney, he co-wrote "Na thàinig anns a church ud/All that came in that one coracle," a song to open the new campus at Sabhal Mòr Ostaig, the Gaelic University, on the Isle of Skye.

Among his other works include "Gleann Calbhaidh Ban/Glencalvie Bare," with Dee Isaacs, a song for a glass installation exhibition of the

Dingwall-born Sue Jane Taylor's Drover Cycle at An Tuireann Gallery in Portree in 1999; the five-part radio drama, *Driven West*, about Scots on the 19th-century Cherokee Trail of Tears for BBC Radio Scotland in 1993; and *Ceol Mòr/The Big Music*, a documentary on the band Runrig for Scottish Television in 1992.

MacPhee, Catherine-Anne (b. 1959). Gaelic singer; born on the Isle of Barra and grew up in the village of Eoligarry. At the age of 17 she joined the Scottish Gaelic repertory theatre, Fir Chlis (Northern Lights), the first of its kind in Scotland, and later joined John McGrath's 7:84 Theatre Company. She is best known though as an exquisite interpreter of traditional and contemporary Gaelic songs. Her first record *Cànan Nan Gàidheal* (The Language of the Gael) (1987) consists of mostly traditional Gaelic songs as well as several contemporary Gaelic songs such as the title cut by Murdo Macfarlane and Runrig's "Cearcall A'Chuain" (The Ocean Cycle) and Donald Maciver's "An Ataireachd Ard" (The Surge of the Sea). Her second record, *Chi Mi'n Geamradh* (I See Winter) (1991) features the Runrig title track as well as a Gaelic spinning song, several waulking songs and a Gaelic song by Hugh F. MacKenzie from Grand Narrows, Cape Breton, "Bu Deonach Leam Tilleadh" (I Would Willingly Return). From a Clearances perspective, her most important recording is *Catherine-Ann MacPhee Sings Màiri Mhòr* (1994), the soundtrack to the 1993 biographical BBC TV film about Màiri Mhór, which starred Alyxis Daly as the great songwriter-agitator. MacPhee is Màiri Mhór's greatest interpreter, her vocals capturing beautifully the anger but also the pride and affection MacPherson felt toward her native Skye even as she evokes the visionary glow of a lost Golden Age. There is also a pervasive sadness in her songs, a poignancy as well as a preoccupation of the fate of the Gael.

Her most recent album, *Sùil Air Ais* (Looking Back), was released in 2004. MacPhee emigrated to Ottawa, Ontario, in 2001.

MacPherson, John (the Glendale Martyr) (1845?-1924). Born in Glendale, Skye; crofter spokesperson; campaigned during the Land Agitation movement; was the leader of a group of crofters that defied orders forbidding grazing of cattle on the Waterstein farm in 1883 and that demanded the return of the common grazing ground that they believed had been taken from them during the Clearances. Due to the uproar, the government sent officials to Skye to look into the matter. Five crofters, including MacPherson, agreed to go to court in a token trial on principle. They served a two-month sentence in Calton Jail, Edinburgh, and earned the sobriquet of the Glendale Martyrs. Their action is commemorated by a memorial near Glendale, Skye, seven miles west of Dunvegan on the B884 road. Consequently, the Napier

Commission was established to investigate the crofters' grievances, which resulted in the historic *Crofters Act* of 1886. In July 2010, a homecoming of the Glendale diaspora took place at the site.

MacPherson's exploits inspired the Gaelic rock band Runrig to write "Recovery," the title track of their album of the same name which explored the social history of the Gael.

MacPherson, Mary (Màiri Nic a'Phearsain) (Màiri Mhór nan Òran / Big Mary of the Songs) (1821-1898). Poet-agitator born Mary MacDonald in Skeabost, on the Isle of Skye. Her father, John MacDonald, was a crofter on Skeabost; her mother, Flora MacInnes, was the daughter of Neil MacInnes, a crofter, in Uig, also on Skye.

She married Isaac MacPherson, a shoemaker and chimney sweep, in 1847. Two years earlier she had moved to Inverness. In 1872 she was sentenced to 40 days in prison for allegedly stealing clothes from her employer's wardrobe (a charge that she vehemently denied). By all accounts, it was an unjust conviction and imprisonment. It was her imprisonment that, she said, "brought [her] poetry into being." She worked in Glasgow as a nurse before retiring to Skye in 1882.

MacPherson's poetry is about not only her personal troubles, but also the suffering of her fellow Gaels, especially as a result of the Clearances. Nine thousand lines of her poetry were transcribed from recitation by John Whyte and published in 1891 in a collection edited by Alexander MacBain. Her many poems include "When I Was Young" in which she fondly reminiscences about the site of a ruined homestead near Flodigarry in the northern end of Skye that reminds her of better days when "happy youngsters would have song and dancing." In a direct reference to the Clearances she laments the absence of the "light-hearted youngsters who are now evicted." Another, "The Island of the Mist," is a *paean* to her beloved Skye even as she reflects on the "thousands who have been banished." She declares that the Gaels should remember to stand up for their rights and "hold" the banner high for

> ...the wheel will surely turn for you
> by the strength and power of fists;
> your cattle will yet have to pasture,
> and each farmer live in style,
> and the English will be banished
> from the green-clad Misty Isle.
>
> ...
>
> the humiliation that I endured
> was what gave my poetry life.

Years later, other Gaels from Skye would write similar lyrics about the need to remember and cherish their Gaelic heritage, even going so far as to use similar imagery. In "Cum 'Ur N'aire" (Stay Aware), the Gaelic rock band Runrig encourages Gaels to never forget where they came from and that to remember their culture as being "unique" and "precious." Similarly, "An Cuibhle Mòr" (The Big Wheel), also by Runrig, is both literal (about the travelling life of musicians) and allegorical (about the journey of life itself). "This is the big wheel," they write, "Turning our youth to old age."

MacRae, Donald (1851-1924). Also known as the "The Alness Martyr." A native of Plockton and a schoolmaster, MacRae played a leading role in the land agitation movements in Easter Ross and in Lewis.

MacRae, John (Iain mac Mhurchaidh). Circa mid-18th century Loyalist poet during the American Revolution. He immigrated from Kintail to North Carolina in 1774 and was captured in February 1776 at the Battle of Moore's Creek Bridge.

Mac-Talla (The Echo). Based in Cape Breton, the short-lived *Mac-Talla* was the first all-Gaelic periodical published in North America. It began in May 1892 and stopped publishing in 1904.

Malthus, Thomas Robert (1766-1834). Born in Surrey; English scholar, influential in political economy and demography, who argued that poverty was the result of uncontrolled reproduction. He became known for his theories about population fluctuation, especially in his six-volume work, *An Essay on the Principle of Population*, published from 1798 to 1826, in which he observed that population is typically controlled by outbreaks of famine and disease. His theories were influential in economic, political and social circles in the 18th century, especially among the Improvers in Britain. Thinkers along the lines of Charles Darwin would use Malthus's theories as foundations for his idea of natural selection.

To apply his theories to a Highland perspective, he believed that the only way for evictions to be truly effective would be for the houses to be utterly demolished so that the evicted tenants could not return; otherwise, notes Richards, "they would simply be reoccupied by newly reproducing paupers." In this way too emigration could have a positive effect on the state in two ways: by creating markets for British industry abroad while reducing the surplus, and therefore unnecessary, population at home. His impact was wide ranging and spanned many decades, from Charles Darwin and Karl Marx to John Maynard Keynes and Mao Zedong. Clearly, his theories were instrumental in the shaping of the Improvement and emigration policy schemes of the Clearances era.

Marx, Karl (1818-1883). German philosopher, economist, sociologist, historian, journalist and revolutionary socialist. Marx's ideas played a significant role in the development of the socialist movement. Among his best known books are *The Communist Manifesto* (1848) and *Capital* (1867-1894). He often worked closely with his friend and fellow revolutionary socialist, Friedrich Engels. In May 1849, Marx moved to London, where he would remain for the rest of his life, a year after the publication of Robert Somers's *Letters from the Highlands*, which played a major influence on his thinking. Thus, from a Highland perspective, his work is important for another reason: he wrote on racial inequality and the exploitation of the working class by the capitalist structure. Marx quoted from Somers's work in Volume II of *Capital*. In the Highlands, Marx observed, the "clearing of estates" proceeded in a systematic fashion and on a very large scale. The Clearances, he wrote, quoting Somers,

> is pursued ... as an agricultural necessity, just as trees and bushwood are cleared from the wastes of America and Australia; and the operation goes on in a quiet, business-like way, that neither excites the remorse of the perpetrators, nor attracts the sympathy of the public.

Marx commented too on clearances involving deer forests, which he referred to as a second Clearance. He contended that by clearing both sheep and people, the Highlands were little more than aristocratic playgrounds.

Matheson, Sir James (1796-1878). Born in Lairg, Sutherland, attended Edinburgh's Royal High School and the University of Edinburgh; proprietor of Lewis, who made his fortune with Jardine, Matheson and Co., one of the most successful merchants in China. In 1844, Matheson purchased the Isle of Lewis from Lady Stewart MacKenzie of Seaforth. He was considered a benevolent and quite generous proprietor, whereas he built Lews castle and began an ambitious improvements projects that included the building of piers, harbours, roads and bridges. He increased his programs during the Highland Potato Famine and by 1850 had reportedly spent £329,000 of his own money on the island. Consequently, he was rewarded in 1851 with a baronetcy. He was a Member of Parliament (MP) for Ashburton from 1843 to 1852 and for Ross and Cromarty from 1852 to 1868. After his death, his wife erected a memorial to him in the grounds of Lews Castle. Between 1851 and 1855, he assisted 1,771 people to emigrate.

McCulloch, Horatio (1806-1867). Landscape painter of some renown; born in Glasgow; he was influenced by his fellow artist John Knox. In 1838 he was elected to the Royal Scottish Academy. He is best known for his romantic landscapes of the Highlands such as *Glencoe* (1864), which depicts the Highlands in all its wild grandeur. *My Heart's in the Highlands* (1860), originally titled *The Emigrant's Dream of His Highland Home*, evokes the memory of the Clearances from an emigrant's misty perspective. Probably the most common, and striking, aspect of McCulloch's work is the absence of people in his Highland landscapes.

McCulloch trained in the studio of Glasgow landscape painter John Knox (1778-1845) for about one year and at first earned his living as a decorative painter. He moved to Edinburgh in 1825 and began painting in the tradition of Alexander Nasmyth, often said to be the father of Scottish landscape painting. McCulloch regularly went on sketching tours of the West Highlands during the summer, completing the sketches back in his studio. Other times, though, his paintings could gestate for many years, such as was the case for *Glencoe*. Either way, his romantic images of the Highlands as wild—and empty—came to epitomize the iconic view of the Highlands. Among his other works on the Highlands include *The Entrance to Glencoe from Rannoch Moor* (1846), *The Cuillins from Ord* (1854), *Loch Lomond* (1861), *Loch Katrine* (1866) and *Loch Maree Ross-shire* (1866).

McDonald, Father Allan (1859-1905). Born in Fort William, he was a poet, parish priest and collector of Gaelic songs, stories and legends, who built the church of St. Michael on the island of Eriskay. He died prematurely at the age of 46.

McDonald, Ellice Jr. A former stockbroker from Wilmington, Delaware; helped create the Clan Donald Centre on the Isle of Skye and is a trustee of the Clan Donald Lands. He established the Clan Donald Trust, bought about 8,000 ha (nearly 20,000 acres) back of traditional clan lands and helped to restore Armadale Castle, the ancient stronghold of Clan Donald. He was also High Commissioner of Clan Donald USA from 1976 to 1983. In addition, he is founder and trustee of several major foundations, including the Glencoe Foundation, the Clan Donald Foundation, the Ellice and Rosa McDonald Foundation (formerly the Invergarry Foundation) and the Gurkha Welfare Trust Foundation USA.

McDonald, Steve (b. 1950). New Zealand singer-songwriter who in 2000 released a recording, *Highland Farewell*, that chronicles the Clearances in music. Like other projects of this sort, the lyrics offer a simplified and even romanticized portrait of the Clearances. Still,

McDonald's anger seems sincere as he references rack-renting, Croick church and the Glencalvie Clearances, the Rev. Norman MacLeod and Badbea. Significantly, the album's cover art consists of Thomas Faed's painting *Oh Why I Left My Hame.*

McGrath, John (1935-2002). Writer, director and filmmaker; born in Birkenhead, Cheshire. Described as being a combination of Germany's Bertolt Brecht and Italy's Dario Fo, McGrath was widely regarded as one of the most influential figures in 20th-century British theatre on both sides of the border and used the techniques commonly associated with epic theatre. McGrath did his National Service stint before reading English at St. John's College, Oxford, and then turning to television.

In 1971, along with his wife Elizabeth MacLennan and her brother David MacLennan, he co-founded the 7:84 Theatre Company. Two years later the company divided into Scottish and English divisions with McGrath remaining artistic director of both branches. McGrath wanted a theatre company that had a relevancy to contemporary audiences and that would offer a socialist perspective. The company was started "more or less," he said, "on the spur of the moment, as a lot of these things happen...."

The 7:84 Company took its name from a statistic that had appeared in an issue of *The Economist* that 7 per cent of the population of Britain owned 84 percent of the wealth. McGrath wanted to attract a non-theatre-going audience to his productions but he especially wanted to write and produce theatre about the daily life of the working class.

His best-known play, *The Cheviot, the Stag and the Black Black Oil*, revolves around class and politics in the history of the Highlands as well as global capitalism from the Clearances to the discovery of oil in the North Sea. Its intent was to raise awareness and to entertain while educating. McGrath used the ceilidh form in the Gaelic tradition that included local stories and local music. The play evoked a deep cultural memory. *Cheviot* toured for six weeks in the Highlands and Islands, stopping at village halls, dance halls, community centres and schools. The original cast included Alex Norton, Bill Paterson, John Bett, Dolina MacLennan and fiddler Allan Ross, among others. A rousing success in Scotland, it was considered one of the most successful radical theatre pieces in British theatrical history. The cast researched, performed and played their own parts. It remains an iconic play in the cultural history of the Highlands and indeed of Scotland generally.

McGrath resigned from the 7:84 Theatre in 1988. But he continued to write and direct Scottish-themed plays. The ambitious epic *Border Warfare* (1989) examines the historical relationship between Scotland and England and the development of Scottish national identity from the Dark Ages to the present day. *John Brown's Body* (1990), named after the famous shipyard in Glasgow, is about the evolution of the Scottish working class. *The Last of the MacEachans* (1996), set in the modern-day Highlands, offers a commentary on identity, migration and displacement.

His other works include the play *There Is a Happy Land*, a television drama based on that play was broadcast on Channel 4. *There Is a Happy Land* also played in Cape Breton when the Canadian Popular Theatre Alliance invited the 7:84 Theatre Company to attend the Alliance's biennial festival.

McGrath also wrote *Màiri Mhór: The Woman from Skye*, a play which featured the songs of Màiri Mhór nan Oran as sung by Catherine-Ann MacPhee. The play toured four weeks in Scotland: a week in the Western Isles and on Skye and Inverness, a week in Aberdeen, and a week in Edinburgh and Glasgow. He produced and wrote the screenplay for the film *Màiri Mhór* (1994). In 1992 Wildcat commissioned McGrath to adapt Neil Gunn's *The Silver Darlings* which also toured throughout Scotland.

During his long career, McGrath wrote more than 60 plays, including several other Highland plays, including *Random Happenings in the Hebrides* (1970), set in the Hebrides between 1964 and 1970. In 1982 he founded Freeway Films, where he produced *The Dressmaker* (1985), *Carrington* (1995) and *Aberdeen* (2002). He received Lifetime Achievement Awards from BAFTA, in 1993, and the Writers' Guild of Great Britain, in 1997, as well as honourary doctorates from the University of Stirling and the University of London.

McLean, Allan Campbell (1922-1989). Novelist; born on Walney Island, Barrow-in-Furness, Cumbria. During the Second World War he joined the Royal Air Force (RAF), serving in the Mediterranean and North Africa. *The Year of the Stranger* is set on Skye. His great-grandfather, Allan McLean, left his croft on Mull for a tenement in Glasgow. McLean's father worked at the John Brown shipyard in Clydebank before leaving to work in Barrow-in-Furness, England. When McLean returned to the Highlands, and in particular to Skye, he told Derek Cooper that he was the first member of his family "to return to the Highlands in three generations."

McLeod, Rev. Norman (1780-1866). Clergyman and schoolmaster born at Stoer Point, Assynt; a Presbyterian minister and one of the founding fathers of New Zealand, McLeod persuaded his Gaelic-speaking followers to emigrate with him to Pictou, Nova Scotia, in 1817, before settling at St. Ann's, in Cape Breton, in 1820. He remained there until 1851 but, dissatisfied, he persuaded his followers to go with him again, this time to Australia. After travelling the globe over a remarkable 40-year period, McLeod and his Normanites, as they were sometimes called, finally settled in Waipu on the North Island of New Zealand.

McLeod underwent a religious conversion as a young man. He enrolled at the University of Aberdeen in 1807 and graduated in 1812, before studying for the ministry at the University of Edinburgh. He drew large crowds with his preaching, often antagonizing the established church. He taught at schools, first in Assynt and then in Ullapool, at a time when widespread Clearances were taking place in the area. A fiery preacher with messianic zeal, he encouraged his followers to return to the principles of Knox and Calvin. His supporters were enterprising people and knew in Clearances-era Scotland they would have no chance of owning their own piece of land, so when McLeod suggested they emigrate to the New World with him, they agreed.

In July 1817 McLeod set sail for Pictou on the *Frances Ann* with more than 400 men, women and children. Later he accepted a call from a Highland Scots settlement in Ohio (it is unclear exactly where in Ohio), built a boat which his critics pejoratively called the Ark (while referring to McLeod as Noah) and with his followers made their way to America. Enroute to Ohio they stopped at St. Ann's in Cape Breton. Some reports indicated that they might have encountered a storm which blew them off course while others suggest that they liked the community so much that they decided to stay. Either way, at St. Ann's he served the role of preacher, teacher and magistrate while his community of Normanites grew and flourished. In 1827 he was ordained Presbyterian minister by the Presbytery of Geneva in Upstate New York.

In 1847 a disastrous potato blight caused massive crop failure in Cape Breton. The potato failure and a shortage of suitable farmland for his people led McLeod to consider leaving. Late in 1848, McLeod received a letter from his son, who was in Australia, encouraging his father to emigrate there. In 1851, the *Margaret*, with 130 (some sources say 140) followers aboard, including McLeod and his family arrived in Adelaide. A second ship, the *Highland Lass*, left in 1852. With the gold rush in full force and a lack of land in Australia available for his party, McLeod wrote to George Gray, the governor of New Zealand, about the possibility of obtaining land for all of his Nova Scotia migrants. They purchased a schooner, the *Gazelle*. In September 1853, the group arrived on New Zealand's North Island and settled around the Waipu River.

Four more ships followed: the 217-ton brig *Gertrude* in 1856; the 107-ton *Spray* in 1857; the 224-ton *Breadalbane* in 1858; and the 336-ton *Ellen Lewis* in 1860. More than 800 people altogether made the journey (although some sources say the number was closer to 1,000).

McLeod selected nearly 27,000 ha (66,000 acres) in Northland, about 160 km (100 miles) north of Auckland, in a settlement called

Waipu (pronounced why-poo) where he established a Gaelic-speaking community. Although Waipu was the main settlement area for the Nova Scotia pioneers, other communities sprouted up at Leigh, Kauri and Whangarei Heads.

McLeod's property in St. Ann's was developed into the Gaelic College of Celtic Arts and Crafts. A granite millstone memorial to McLeod stands at the head of St. Ann's Harbour, in Gaelic and English. The English inscription reads:

> Rev. Norman McLeod
> 1780-1866
> As clergyman, schoolmaster and magistrate he moulded the character of this community for a generation. Born at Stoer Point, Assynt, Scotland, he emigrated to Pictou in 1817, led his band of Scots to St. Ann's in 1820 and remained here until 1851, when he again led his followers first to Australia and finally to New Zealand.

A memorial to McLeod was erected in Clachtoll, near Lochinver, Scotland. Yet another memorial is in Waipu, a pillar that has carved on its six sides the names of the ships that brought the Scots to the other side of the world. The House of Memories (also known as the Waipu Museum), a small regional history museum, opened in 1953 to commemorate McLeod and his followers as well as to document the history and to house the photographs and genealogical information of the Nova Scotia migration. In 2002, the Waipu Heritage Trail was established. The Trail consists of 16 sites, including the House of Memories Museum which contains the records of the migrants, and the Waipu Cemetery.

McPhee, John (b. 1931). American writer and consummate journalist of Scottish descent who is widely considered among the pioneers of creative nonfiction. McPhee won the Pulitzer Prize in General Nonfiction in 1999 for *Annals of the Former World*. Since 1974, McPhee has been the Ferris Professor of Journalism at Princeton University. Born in Princeton, New Jersey, he was educated at Princeton High School and Princeton and Cambridge universities. He began writing for *Time* magazine, which led to his work at the *New Yorker*, beginning in 1965, where he remains today. Many of his books were originally written for the magazine.

McPhee is the great-grandson of Scottish emigrants from the Isle of Colonsay. In 1967 he spent the spring on the island of his ancestors, which he wrote about in *The Crofter and the Laird* (1970). According to McPhee, he is the descendant of Clearance Highlanders although some of his forebears were part of the migration from the Highlands to the

Lowlands where they settled in Renfrewshire. Other members of the McPhee family went elsewhere, to Australia, Canada or the United States. In the 1860s, his great-grandfather immigrated to the States to work in the coal mines of the Mahoning Valley in Ohio, from whom sprang about 130 descendants who scattered across the American continent, including, says McPhee, railroad engineers and conductors, firemen, steelworkers, teachers, football coaches, a police officer, doctors, lawyers and janitors. McPhee's grandfather, Angus, worked in a steelmill. The family line has produced several writers: McPhee, of course, as well as two of his daughters, Jenny and Martha.

McQueen, Alexander (1969-2010). The controversial fashion designer born in London of Scottish ancestry; his paternal grandparents were from Skye. McQueen often used fabric to comment on historical and cultural aspects of Britain. Known for his superb craftsmanship, he would use such objects as shells, lacemaking, metalworking, embroidery and even antlers made of resin. McQueen was considered one of the most inventive fashion designers of the late 20th and early 21st centuries.

McQueen used his original tartan design as well as the traditional McQueen tartan to refer to his own Scottish heritage and to Scotland's often violent past and volatile relationship with England. His work used the powerful significance of tartan, its potent symbolism, as shorthand for clans and warfare.

In his seminal *Highland Rape*, his 1995-1996 collection, which received strong criticism at the time, featured models wearing torn and quite revealing garments that was almost brutal in nature. The collection, which helped to establish his reputation as the *enfant terrible* of British fashion, referred to the Jacobite Rising generally and the Clearances specifically. Many critics thought, wrongly, that he was advocating violence against women. By "rape," McQueen later explained, he was referring to what he thought as the rape of Scotland by England, especially during the Clearances era. For the Highland Rape show the runway was smothered in heather and bracken. Many of the McQueen tartan outfits recalled 19th-century tight-fitting shapes: tartan-trimmed jackets with breasts partially exposed, sort of like a Harlequin romance cover meets Flora Macdonald.

The theme of the Widows of Culloden collection in 2006-2007, was the Jacobite Rising that ended on the blood-soaked fields of Culloden Moor in 1746. Models (including the supermodel Kate Moss) wore traditional Scottish dress, from the belted plaid *fèileadh mòr* to the short, tailored kilt of the *fèileadh beag*. As fashion writer Jonathan Faiers points out, through his models McQueen traces the ways in which the traditional dress of the Highlands became commodified and, ultimately, Anglicized as a mere fashion statement, devoid of its complicated historical past. Thus, in the same collection, whether Victorian ball gowns, suits, dresses, or skinny trousers, all appear in McQueen tartan. McQueen himself described the collection as "romantic but melancholic and austere...."

McQueen committed suicide in February 2010 in London. His ashes were scattered on the Isle of Skye.

McTaggart, William (1835-1910). Painter, born on the family croft in Kintyre, Argyll, educated in Campbeltown. In 1852, McTaggart entered the Trustees' Academy, where he studied under Robert Scott Lauder, known as the most renowned landscape painter of his time. McTaggart's work commented on the modern Highlands especially in his remarkable series of emigration painting, which rejected the romanticism of the early Scottish landscape painters, such as Horatio McCulloch, in favour of a more modernist, and realist, approach. Alexander Moffat has called McTaggart Scotland's first great modern painter.

A social realist, McTaggart was a Gaelic speaker himself who came from a fishing and crofting family. His love of the sea and a childhood spent on the Mull of Kintyre are clearly expressed in his work. The emigrants series of portraits began as landscapes. Little by little he added details, including the figures that seem to be overwhelmed by the grandeur of nature. McTaggart revolutonized the practice of painting in Scotland by employing the Scottish equivalent of open-air painting made popular by Monet and other French Impressionists in France. But unlike the mild climate in France, McTaggart had to deal with the vagaries of the wild and often stormy Highland weather. It was not unusual for him to use ropes and the assistance of his son to anchor the easel.

His paintings offer meditations on the Gàidhealtachd and what it means to be a Gael and are often inspired by his own childhood memories of the Clearances. He painted three major works on Scottish emigration from the west coast of Scotland to the New World, including *Crofter Emigrants Leaving the Hebrides* (1891) and *The Sailing of the Emigrant Ship* (1895), the latter considered his masterpiece that offered profound reflections on the effect of emigration on Kintyre. Many emigrants had left from Carrdale in Argyllshire, including his own sister, Barbara.

One of his major works, *The Storm* (1890), captures the ferocity of nature but also the fragility of people caught in the middle of it, as a small fishing community launches a rescue boat in order to assist a fishing boat in trouble. Another storm-tossed painting is the *Coming of St. Columba* (1895), which depicts the Celtic saint arriving in Kintyre in the 6th century, before his more famous arrival on the tiny island of Iona.

Meek, Donald (b. 1949). Born Tiree; noted Gaelic scholar; lecturer in Celtic and Scottish studies, University of Edinburgh, from 1979 until his recent retirement. Meek became the first Professor of Celtic at the University of Aberdeen in 1993. Previously he had been assistant editor of the *Historical Dictionary of Scottish Gaelic* at Glasgow University (1973-1979) and Lecturer, Senior Lecturer and Reader in Celtic at Edinburgh University (1979-1992). Among his works include a volume on the life and songs of Mary MacPherson (1977). *Tuath Is Tighearna* (Tenants and Landlords) (1995) is the first anthology of Gaelic poetry on the Clearances and the Land Agitation movement and he edited *Caran an t-Saoghail / The Wiles of the World* (2003), an anthology of 19th-century Gaelic verse.

Miller, Hugh (1802-1856). Born in Cromarty of a Lowland father and a Highland mother. Miller always thought of himself as a Lowlander and yet he was among the most sympathetic of Lowland writers toward the Gael. A stonemason by trade, he was also a geologist, naturalist and writer and the editor of the pro-Gael newspaper, *Witness*.

An enigmatic and, ultimately, tragic figure—he committed suicide on Christmas Eve 1856—Miller had many interests, from folklore and poetry to science and religion. He first wrote about the Clearances in his book *The Cruise of the Betsey* (1845). Originally written for the *Witness*, it was later published in book form. Accompanied by a friend—a Free Church minister—Miller toured the Hebrides in 1844 and 1845. He wrote with candor and sympathy on what he witnessed: the terrible poverty of the people, their squalid living conditions, and their "shrivelled frames worn out by famine."

He referred to the Clearances as "extermination" and "bad policy" and devoted many pages in the *Witness* to covering the Clearances and to destitution in the Highlands generally. The real causes of the Clearances, he believed, were clear. They included competition for land among the larger farmers, the "uncomplaining character" of the inhabitants, their fear of God and, presumably, sense of fatalism and the "almost intractable difficulties" of many of the landlords. Miller, in the pages of the *Witness*, proposed a series of remedies, which included security of land tenure, challenging the rights of the landlords in court and, especially, the abolition of the laws of entail and primogeniture.

Hugh Miller's Cottage, the only thatched cottage in Cromarty, is located on Church Street in the village and is a museum run by the National Trust for Scotland.

Mitchell, Joseph (1803-1883). A civil engineer; born in Forres, Morayshire, and educated at Inverness and Aberdeen; witnessed firsthand and wrote about the Clearances in his memoir, published in two volumes, *Reminiscences* (1883-1884), in which he adamantly condemned the landlords.

Moffat, Alexander (b. 1943). Scottish portrait painter. In 1978 he painted a rather iconic portrait of Sorley Maclean. Two years later he created an allegorical painting entitled *Poets' Pub*, a group portrait of Scottish writers gathered around the central figure of Hugh MacDiarmid. The writers are Sorley Maclean, Norman MacCaig, Iain Crichton Smith, George Mackay Brown, Sydney Goodsir Smith, Edwin Morgan, Robert Garioch and Alan Bold.

Muir, Edwin (1887-1959). Orcadian poet and novelist, born in Deerness. In 1901 when his father lost his farm, the family moved to Glasgow when Muir was fourteen, a devastating experience for Muir. Within a few years his father, mother and two brothers died. In 1950 he was appointed Warden of Newbattle Abbey College, a college for working-class men, in Midlothian, near Edinburgh, where he met fellow Orcadian poet, George Mackay Brown. In 1955 he was made Norton Professor of English at Harvard University. He returned to Britain in 1956 but died in 1959 at Swaffham Prior, Cambridge.

In 1935, Muir travelled from the Lowlands to the Highlands and wrote about it in *Scottish Journey*, now considered a modern travel classic. As an Orcadian, he had always felt removed from Scotland—("I'm not Scotch," he said, "I'm an Orkneyman, a good Scandinavian, and my country is Norway, or Denmark, or Iceland, or some place like that.") —and it is this sense of detachment that comes through in *Scottish Journey* as he drives through areas of Scotland with extremely high levels of unemployment. Well aware of Scottish history, Muir conceived his book as being a second Scottish Clearance, comparable but different from the Highland Clearances, "a silent clearance ... a clearance not of human beings, but of what they depend upon for life."

In the chapter simply called "The Highlands," he offers remarkable insight, and sympathy, toward the plight of the Clearance Highlanders, equating the Age of Improvement with the Industrial Revolution. "They were robbed of their life by exactly the same process which built Glasgow," he writes, and then adds that anyone who wishes to understand this process that depopulated the Highlands should read Neil Gunn's Clearances novel, *Butcher's Broom*. What's more, he suggests that the destruction of Highland life took place in three phases: 1) the slaughter that took place after the defeat at Culloden, 2) the Clearances themselves and 3) the time that he was writing about—and which he felt was symbolized by—the slaughtered animals that disfigure the walls of Highland hotels. For this "disastrous phase" he puts the brunt of the blame on Sir Walter Scott and Queen Victoria since "Scott sent the tourist wandering over the Highland hills, and Queen Victoria built Balmoral." The result of these two acts was to turn the Highlands into a "huge game preserve" where inhabitants become trespassers in their own land.

More than sixty years later, Michael W. Russell, now a Member of the Scottish Parliament for Argyll and Bute and the Cabinet Secretary for Education and Lifelong Learning under First Minister Alex Salmond, followed in Muir's footsteps in the equally compelling travel memoir, *In Waiting: Travels in the Shadow of Edwin Muir*. Like Muir, Russell comments on the Clearances on his Highland journey: "their bitter memory may not be on everyone's lips, but their sad effect remains in most hearts" since its living legacy is pervasive not only in its piles of stones but also in its lack of people. To Russell the lesson of the Clearances is that change—when it must happen, and of course change is an unavoidable trait of the human condition—should be done with a modicum of humanity.

Muisel (Strathmore). Ruined village that was the boyhood home of the Gaelic poet Rob Donn (1715-1778). He is buried in the cemetery at Balnakeil in Durness.

Mulock, Thomas Anglo-Irish journalist and Baptist minister, fierce defender of the Highlander and advocate of the oppressed even though he spent most of his life outwith Scotland. He did not arrive in Scotland until 1849, when he was sixty years old. He condemned landlords, writers and government officials alike, including Thomas Carlyle, Disraeli and Prince Albert.

He studied at Oxford, attended the bar and opened a law firm in Liverpool. He left England for a time, giving lectures in Geneva and Paris before returning to enter a Baptist ministry and then founded a chapel in Stoke-on-Trent. He returned to Liverpool to write for the *Morning Chronicle*.

Although Mulock spent all of two years in Scotland he quickly earned a reputation as a crusading journalist. He wrote about the Clearances in the *Inverness Advertiser* and the *Northern Ensign*, including coverage of the North Uist evictions on the estate of Lord Macdonald. At one point he compared the eviction of the Gaels with the expulsion of Jews from Spain and the Huguenots from France. What's more, he refused to accept overpopulation as the reason for emigration. "What the people really require," he insisted, "is *land*." The problem was not that there were too many people, but that the holdings were too small and the rents too high. To Mulock, the truly "useless" part of the population was not the cottars but the landed aristocracy. It would be better to remove them from their palaces, pointing out to his readers that many in fact were absentee landlords who were exploiting the land, and the Highlanders on it, to support their luxurious lifestyles down south.

In December 1849, Mulock took over as editor of the *Advertiser* after the sudden death of its editor, James MacCosh. Mulock was editor for four months before leaving the struggling paper to work for a new publication, the *Northern Ensign*. He stayed fifteen months there, continuing his criticism of landlords and their policies. How would the landlords like it, he asked, if they were to be transported "against [their] Scottish will from Torrisdale to Toronto?"

Yet less than two years later, by April 1851, Mulock had changed his mind and was encouraging the Gaels to emigrate after all. Frustrated by the lack of progress, he seemed to conclude that since in all likelihood the people would not be given the land they needed to prosper it was time to go. There was no other option. It was a sudden about-face by one of the most outspoken activists of the Clearances era.

Munro, Donnie (b. 1953). Born in Uig, Isle of Skye; former lead singer of the Gaelic rock band Runrig and now director of development and the arts at Sabhal Mòr Ostaig, the Gaelic university on Skye. He was educated at Portree Primary and High School before attending Gray's School of Art in Aberdeen, and he earned a postgraduate degree in teaching at Moray House in Edinburgh. He became a member of Runrig in 1974 although he did not turn professional until 1982. Munro shared vocal duties with Rory Macdonald, but to many he was the voice and iconic front man of the band. He left in 1997 to pursue a career in politics even as he continued to make solo records, including *Heart of America*, in collaboration with Blair Douglas (a former member of Runrig) and Richard Macintyre. In 1991 he was elected as Rector of the University of Edinburgh, a position he held until 1994, and was elected as the first rector of the University of the Highlands and Islands (UHI) Millennium Institute in 1998. During the 1997 General Election he ran for the British Parliamentary seat for Ross, Skye and Inverness West but lost to Charles Kennedy. He ran again in 1999 for a seat in the Scottish Parliament for the same area but lost again, this time to John Farquhar Munro.

In 1996 he gave the prestigious Sabhal Mòr Lecture, at Sabhal Mòr Ostaig, an annual event. In a wide-ranging talk, Munro commented on the myth of the Highlands, the legacy of the Clearances, the future of crofting and the success of the Assynt Crofters' Trust while evoking the names of Màiri Mhòr MacPherson (to whom he referred as the Skye Bard of the Land League) to the Lewis Bard Murdo Macfarlane to Sorley Maclean.

> The history of the Highlands is one inextricably linked with the manipulation of two of its greatest assets, people and land. The utterly indefensible exploitation of land which began with the destruction of the old order through the removal of people already impoverished by their circumstances, the implementation of large sheep farms taking control of the best of the land and the subsequent conversion, due to monetary incentives, to the large deer forests and estates which have become synonymous with the Highlands and Islands.

Murdoch, John (1818-1903). Born Ardclach, Nairn, but brought up in Islay, Murdoch was an outside "agitator," as he was called. Murdoch had spent some time in Ireland as an Inland Revenue officer in Dublin where he also became involved in Irish politics and the Irish land reform struggle there. After he retired he settled in Inverness and founded the *Highlander* newspaper (1873-1881) promoting the crofters' cause.

N

Nairne, Lady Carolina (née Oliphant) (1766-1845). Songwriter; born in Gask, Perthshire; the daughter of a Jacobite laird. She wrote songs under the pseudonym Mrs. Bogan of Bogan, which were published in *The Scottish Minstrel* (1821-1824) and posthumously as *Lays from Strathearn*. Her most famous songs include the lament for Bonnie Prince Charlie, "Will ye no' come back again," "The Land o' the Leal," "Caller Herrin" and "The Auld Hoose," many of which became standard fare for the mid-20th-century folk revival.

Napier, Lord (Francis Napier, 10th Lord Napier and 1st Baron Ettrick) (1819-1898). Diplomat and colonial administrator, born at Thirlestane Castle in Selkirkshire. Napier served as the British Minister to the United States (1857-1859), Netherlands (1859-1860), Russia (1861-1864) and Prussia 1864-1866), and as the Governor of Madras from 1866 to 1872. From a Highland perspective, he is best known for being the chairman of the historic Napier Commission.

Napier Commission. Officially the Royal Commission of Inquiry into the Condition of Crofters and Cottars in the Highlands and Islands. It was appointed in 1883 with Francis Napier (10th Lord Napier) acting as chairman under the Liberal government of William Gladstone and was assembled to inquire into the conditions of the crofters in seven counties: Argyll, Inverness-shire, Ross and Cromarty, Sutherland, Caithness, Orkney and Shetland. Members of the Commission travelled throughout the Highlands and Islands interrogating witnesses. Altogether it held meetings in 61 places; 775 people gave evidence. Most of the crofters spoke only Gaelic. A. D. Cameron in his invaluable history of the commission notes that "every word they said" was translated and, "if necessary, written down in shorthand" and given to Neill and Co. on Old Fishmarket, in the High Street along Edinburgh's Royal Mile "to be printed for presentation to Parliament and sale to the public on 28th April, 1884." In addition to the actual Report and an additional 500 pages of written evidence, the Commission printed 3,375 pages of oral answers to 46,750 questions. All meetings were open to the public and were meant to be as transparent as 19th-century society allowed. All in all, it was a remarkable social document of a place and time.

Each community selected a spokesperson and was encouraged to speak freely without fear of reprisals. Angus Stewart of Braes, Skye, specifically asked for assurance that he would not be evicted by the landlord or the factor for being frank. Witnesses included factors but also merchants, fish curers, headmasters, physicians, ministers and priests. Although the Commission's namesake, Lord Napier, served as the head, other prominent members included some of the wealthiest landowners in Britain. The five members were Charles Fraser-Mackintosh, MP for Inverness; Donald Cameron of Lochiel, Conservative MP for Inverness-shire; Sir Kenneth Mackenzie of Gairloch; Alexander Nicolson from Skye, who was sheriff of Kirkcudbright; and Donald MacKinnon, professor of Celtic at the University of Edinburgh.

The meetings took place in the following times and locations:

1883

Skye
8 May, Ollach Schoolhouse, Braes
9 May, Snizort Free Church, Skeabost
10 May, Schoolhouse, Uig
11 May, Schoolhouse, Stenscholl
14 May, Schoolhouse, Stein, Waternish
15 May, Church, Dunvegan
16 May, Free Church, Broadford
17 May, Schoolhouse, Isle Ornsay
18 May, Free Church, Bracadale
19 and 21 May, Free Church, Glendale
22 May, Torran Schoolhouse, Raasay
23-24 May, Courthouse, Portree

Barra, Benbecula and North and South Uist
26 May, Schoolhouse, Castlebay, Barra
28 May, Inn, Lochboisdale, South Uist
29 May, Torlum School Room, Benbecula
30 May, Free Church, Locheport, North Uist

Harris and Lewis
31 May, Schoolhouse, Obbe, Harris
2 June, Free Church, St. Kilda
4 June, Free Church, Meavaig, Harris
5 June, School, Breasclete, Lewis

6 June, Free Church, Barvas, Lewis
7 June, Schoolhouse, Lionel, Lewis
8-9 and 11 June, Drill Hall, Stornoway, Lewis
12 June, Church, Keose, Lewis
13 June, Free Church, Tarbert, Harris

Shetland
13 and 19 July, Court House, Lerwick
14 July, Church, Mid Yell
16 July, Reading Room, Baltasound
17 July, Northmavine Church, Hillswick
18 July, near Schoolhouse, Foula

Orkney
20 July, Drill Hill and Church, Sanday
21 July, Schoolhouse, Harray and Schoolhouse, Birsay
23 July, Court House, Kirkwall

Sutherland
24-25 July, Farr Free Church, Bettyhill
26 July, Free Church, Kinlochbervie
27 July, Church, Lochinver
6 October, Free Church, Helmsdale
8 October, Free Church, Golspie
9 October, Drill Hall, Bonar Bridge

Ross
30 July, Free Church, Ullapool
31 July, Church, Poolewe
1 August, Church, Shieldaig
2 August, Church, Balmacara
3 August, Church, Glenshiel
10 October, Free Church, Dingwall

Inverness
4 August, Church, Glenelg
6 August, Arisaig
11-13 October, Town Hall, Inverness
15-16 October, Court House, Kingussie

Lowlands
19-20 October, Court House, Glasgow
22 and 24 October, Court of Justiciary, Edinburgh
26 December, Public Hall, Tarbert, Loch Fyne

Argyll
7 August, Kirkapoll Church, Tiree
8 August, Bunessan Church, Mull
10 August, Temperance Hall, Tobermory
11 August, Church, Lochaline
13 August, Baptist Church, Lismore

Caithness
4 October, Free Church, Lybster

Unshackled, the crofters spoke on many things, about their methods of farming and fishing, on seasonal work, on familial relationships, on the ubiquitous poverty engulfing them but also on the lack of proper roads and fertile soil and, of course, on the Clearances and their aftermath.

The Report made several conclusions: for tenants whose holdings had rental values of more than £6 per year Napier proposed security of tenure on a 30-year lease; for tenants whose holdings were below £6, he recommended voluntary assisted emigration.

The Napier Commission Report was far from being the last word on the crofters' conditions. To say that they were a disappointment on many levels is an understatement. But it was a beginning and the Commission's recommendations laid the groundwork for future legislation and stopped the evictions and the worst kind of rack renting, but it did not give the land back to the people. It did not end the struggle for land reform. Several years later, in 1886, Parliament passed the *Crofters' Holdings Act* (Scotland).

Native Americans. Among the greatest ironies of the Clearances was that many displaced Highland Scots in turn displaced Aboriginals from their land when they immigrated to new worlds. When Europeans first arrived in America, the indigenous population ranged from three to seven million people. But, between warfare among the various tribes and Americans settlers, as well as diseases introduced by the Europeans, the population dropped considerably. By 1900, the indigenous population had fallen to a paltry 300,000 by some estimates; most were by then living on reservations. During the last century or so the population has slowly inched up. According to the 1990 U.S. census, nearly two million now live across that country.

What Aboriginals and Gaels have in common of course is the issue of land dispossession. The former were confined to land unwanted by Europeans, otherwise known as reservations, by means of treaties or legislation. These reservations, which are held in trust for the various tribes by the federal government, are all that remains of the vast lands and resources that sustained the continent's first peoples.

A character in John McGrath's anti-capitalist, Clearance play, *The Cheviot, the Stag and the Black Black Oil*, compares the removed Gaels with Native Americans in the U.S.: "the Red Indians were reduced to the same state as our fathers after Culloden—defeated, hunted, treated like the scum of the earth, their culture polluted and torn out with slow deliberation and their land no longer their own." This statement echoes the famous statement, perhaps apocryphal, by U.S. Gen. Philip Sheridan, "The only good Indian is a dead Indian," and recalls too both the Sand Creek Massacre of 1864 in Colorado—when more than 150 Native Americans, predominantly women, children and the elderly, were killed by the Union Army—and the Wounded Knee Massacre of 1890 in South Dakota when the Seventh Cavalry slaughtered 250 Sioux people.

Highlanders often empathized with Native Americans. Historian James Hunter, in *Glencoe and the Indians*, makes direct reference to the parallels between Scotland's clans and the Native peoples of the New World. The Gaelic rock band Runrig has attempted to create "a tribal feel," as Rory Macdonald once wrote, in such songs as "Our Earth Was Once Green" from *The Cutter & the Clan* (the album cover itself uses a Native American-like symbol in its design), finding common purpose in the identification with place, the significance of genealogical names and the importance of maintaining continuity with the past. The popular singer-songwriter Dougie Maclean also finds thematic parallels between Native American traditions and Highland traditions, as expressed in his music, especially in his earlier work. A link can also be made between the depiction of the Gael in art and that of the Native American. In Thomas Faed's *The Last of the Clan*, for example, the Highlanders are portrayed as noble victims of modernity much like the images of Native Americans in the paintings of the American artist Charles Russell (1864-1926) or the sculptor of James Earle Fraser.

Perhaps yet another parallel between Native Americans and the Gaels can be drawn with the uniquely 19th-century American spirit of Manifest Destiny—that is, the prophetic belief that Americans were destined to settle the entire American continent. Similar to the Improvers whose theories led to the Highland Clearances, the politicians who avidly promoted Manifest Destiny justified removing Native Americans from their ancestral lands in order to make room not for sheep, as in the Highlands, but for white, European settlers, many of them, ironically, of Highland (and Lowland) Scots descent. Whether in the Highlands or in the United States, the law was used to justify expulsion and, indirectly, exile; thus, in effect, the laws of both countries created a population of refugees. The lyrics of the great American troubadour, Woody Guthrie (himself of Scots descent), perhaps best capture the essence of the refugee problem from a 20th-century Dust Bowl perspective that could just as easily apply to the Clearance Highlander and the Native American:

Rich man took my home and drove me from my door
And I ain't got no home in this world anymore

See also Runrig

Neat, Timothy (b. 1943). Filmmaker; director of the film *Hallaig*; born and raised in Cornwall. He completed a Fine Art degree at the University of Leeds and moved to Scotland in 1968. From 1973 to 1988, he lectured in the History of Art at Duncan of Jordanstone College of Art and Design in Dundee. During his time there, he became the founder-editor of a fine-art periodical called *Seer*. He also took over management of the Scottish Sculpture Trust, supervising the funding and erection of the Hugh MacDiarmid Memorial Sculpture in Langholm (1985), among other projects.

In addition, he has made a number of independent films and documentaries on Scottish, and specifically Highland, themes, including *The Summer Walkers* (1976) and *Hallaig* (1984). In 1991 he was employed as a documentary consultant for Scottish Television and during his time there, he wrote the libretto of an opera, *Mackintosh*, in collaboration with the American composer Russell Currie.

Neat is also the author of numerous books, including *When I Was Young: Voices from Lost Communities in Scotland* (2000); a two-volume work, *The Voice of the Bard: Living Poets and Ancient Tradition in the Highlands and Islands of Scotland* (2002); and a two-volume biography of the Scottish poet and songwriter, Hamish Henderson (2009).

New Lanark. Located in the valley of the River Clyde near the town of Lanark, New Lanark was a utopian community town founded by David Dale (1739-1806) in 1786 and managed and later partly owned by Dale's son-in-law, the Welsh social reformer and utopian socialist Robert Owen (1771-1858). Dale, a Scots merchant, recruited large numbers of Highlanders into his cotton mills at New Lanark by placing advertisements in local newspapers. He even contacted Highland ministers, asking them to persuade members of their congregation who were contemplating emigration to reconsider and come down south to New Lanark. Most of the workers who came to New Lanark in the late 1780s hailed from southern Argyll, Perthshire and Inverness, and as far north as Sutherland and Caithness. They included some of the earliest victims of the Clearances. Dale offered these Highlanders an additional incentive: accommodation. He had built housing that could handle up to 200 families and called one street in the village Caithness Row.

Today New Lanark is a UNESCO World Heritage Site.

newspaper coverage. The two largest Scottish newspapers, the Edinburgh-based *Scotsman* and the *Glasgow Herald*, held mostly negative views of the Highlanders and their plight, as did, to a lesser degree, the *Inverness Courier*. As Fenyö points out, circulation of these three newspapers alone doubled that of the three pro-Highlander newspapers, the *Witness*, the *Inverness Advertiser* and the *North British Daily Mail*. Smaller papers such as the *Perth Constitutional* and the *Fifeshire Journal*, expressed even more negative views, Fenyö going so far as to call them not only contemptuous but verging on "sheer hatred with openly racialist tones." Either way, newspaper coverage of the Clearances, and/or the Highland question, appeared in mostly every issue of the major publications during the peak years of the Clearances.

Nicol, John Watson (1856-1926). Born in Edinburgh, Nicol is best known for his Clearances painting *Lochaber No More* (1883) in which two emigrants, a Highland couple and their loyal dog, give a wistful backward look at Scotland as their ship prepares to leave for the New World. The husband, a shepherd, wears an anxious expression, his right hand covering his mouth. The wife, surrounded by their worldly possessions, sits on their trunk, one arm and her head resting on another object, her face averted away from the spectator's view. The painting, a portrait of despair, has appeared numerous times on book covers and it was even modified and updated by the Proclaimers on the 12-inch single of their 1987 emigration song "Letter from America." Surely it is no accident that Nicol's painting shares the same title as that of a popular Jacobite lament written in the form of the pibroch.

Lochaber No More is a visual elegy. Like Thomas Faed's equally evocative *The Last of the Clan*, Nicol's *Lochaber No More* is one of the most iconic visual images of not only the Scottish emigrant experience generally but of the Highland Clearances specifically.

Nicolson, Alasdair (b. 1961). Composer and artistic director of the St. Magnus International Festival in Orkney, Nicolson was born in Inverness and raised on the Isle of Skye and the Black Isle. He studied at Edinburgh University. In 2012 Nicolson became the artistic director of the Bath International Music Festival. One of his compositions, *The Tree of Strings*, won the IBM Young Composer's Prize in 1993. Another of his works, *Crann nan teud*, which refers to the Gaelic phrase for the Celtic harp, the clarsach, was inspired by the works of Sorley Maclean.

In 2002 the Scottish Chamber Orchestra and Highland Festival commissioned Nicolson to write *The Blue Rampart*, which toured the Highlands. Nicolson also wrote the opera *Sgathach* with a libretto in Scots Gaelic by Aonghas MacNeacail, which had its premiere at the Highland Festival in 1997.

No Great Mischief (novel). The highly acclaimed first and thus far only novel by the Canadian author Alistair MacLeod. The Canadian playwright David S. Young (b. 1946) adapted it for the Toronto-based Tarragon Theatre (2004).
See also Alistair MacLeod

Noble, Sir Iain (1935-2010). Born in Berlin, the son of a British diplomat and a Norwegian mother. Noble, a self-taught Gaelic speaker, was one of the founders of Sabhal Mòr Ostaig, the Gaelic College on Skye. He attended Eton and University College, Oxford. The Nobles have been landowners in Dunbartonshire and Argyllshire since the 15th century, often with careers in the military or in business, and Noble began his own career by establishing a merchant bank, Noble Grossart, in Edinburgh in 1969. When he was bought out, he used the proceeds to buy part of the MacDonald Estates on Skye, and subsequently developed many business interests on Skye and elsewhere, including Hotel Eilean Iarmain and the whisky company Pràban na Linne which produces a vatted malt whisky called Poit Dhubh ("Black Pot"). An entrepreneur and idealist—a rare combination—Noble was directly responsible for the introduction of the first Gaelic road signs in Scotland.

North Carolina. The first record of Scots in North Carolina dates back to 1732 when three Scots—James Innes, Hugh Campbell and William Forbes—received land grants on the Cape Fear River. Between 1732 and 1775, some 700 emigrants with Highland names received land grants. Most of these came from Islay, Jura, Kintyre and other parts of the Argyll peninsula.

The first large group of Scots to settle in Cumberland County came in 1739. They departed Argyllshire on the vessel *Thistle* on June 6, 1739, and arrived in lower Cape Fear in September. They then journeyed up the river and settled on land given to them by North Carolina's royal governor, Gabriel Johnston, himself a Scot.

This group settled mostly in a district in the upper Cape Fear region known as the Bluff, about four miles south of the Lower Little River. Communities also formed around the South Black River, Big Raft Swamp, Drowning Creek and Lower Cape Fear. Most settled in what is now Cumberland County, named after, ironically, the Duke of Cumberland—otherwise known as "the Butcher" or "Stinking Billy" to Highlanders—the same general who defeated the Jacobite army at Culloden in 1746.

In 1740 Governor Johnston, in an effort to encourage emigration by "foreign protestants," granted tax-exempt land to the settlers. There were so many Scots in the Cape Fear Valley by this time that the area soon earned the sobriquet of "Little Scotland."

The centre of the little Highland settlement was the area near Rockfish Creek and Cross Creek. Highlanders arriving in North Carolina usually disembarked either at Brunswick or Wilmington. In the 1760s the settlement was given the name of Campbellton and chosen as the county seat of Cumberland County. The Campbellton charter included the thriving community of Cross Creek. In 1778, the county court was moved from Campbellton to Cross Creek. It assumed a new name, too, Fayetteville, in honour of the Marquis de Lafayette, the French hero of the Revolutionary War.

In 1758 the first Presbyterian congregation, Bluff Church, was established. Its minister was the Reverend Hugh Campbell. Another Presbyterian church with Scottish origins, the Long Street Presbyterian Church, was established in 1766 along Yadkin Road. The first minister to serve the Highlanders was Hugh McAden, who did not have the Gaelic. Finally, in October 1758, the Rev. James Campbell, a native of Argyllshire who was living in Pennsylvania, came to the Cape. Under Campbell, the emigrants established several churches, including Barbecue Church and Long Street Church. Barbecue Church still exists and is North Carolina's oldest Presbyterian congregation, but instead of the original log cabin it is housed in a modern red brick building.

In general, the emigrants who came to North Carolina were from the northern regions of mainland Scotland: Argyllshire but also Ross, Sutherland, Inverness-shire, Strathglass, Glenmoriston, Glengarry and Glen Urquhart as well as the Hebridean islands of Skye, North and South Uist, Lewis, Arran, Jura, Gigha and Islay. In late 1767 Highlanders from Jura landed at Brunswick, and settled on vacant lands in Cumberland and Mecklenburgh counties.

Generally speaking, the first great wave of Highland emigration to North Carolina was not because of poverty but rather due to changed circumstances in their native land. "It was hope, not fear or obedience, that prompted the migration," concluded Duane Meyer.

Scottish Heritage USA is based in North Carolina. Founded in 1965, the organization works with the National Trust for Scotland to sponsor the exchange of ideas, people and information between Scotland and the United States.

See also Cape Fear; failed 1884 emigration to North Carolina

North Uist Clearances. Numerous clearances took place here in the 1810s and continued sporadically until at least 1850. The most notorious occurred at Sollas in 1849 but subsequent evictions also occurred over the following decades. As late as 1895, for example, in Lochmaddy there was a famous photograph taken from a residence near the Old Court House. The photograph, which has appeared in numerous Clearances publications, depicts a mother and her family of four, bundled up against the cold. The children look straight at the camera; the mother, a protective arm around the youngest, closes her eyes, perhaps too weary to face the trauma ahead. Off to the side, an older child, a teen, buries her nose in a handkerchief. In the foreground a bowler-hatted man (perhaps the factor?) sits at a table, writing something down on a piece of paper, presumably the eviction notice. It is a powerful reminder of the human tragedy of the Clearances.

And even well into the 20th century agitation continued in one form or another on the island. Rob Gibson reports that a successful land raid took place in 1952 at Balelone Farm; the landlord was the Norfolk-based Lt. Col. Cator.

See also Sollas, North Uist

Northern Association of Gentlemen and Farmers, Breeders of Sheep. A protection agency established in 1798 by farmers in Inverness, Argyll, Perth, and Ross for preventing the theft of sheep from their farms. Throughout the Highlands there were sporadic instances of sheep stealing.

Northern Ensign. One of two Highland newspapers, the other being the *Inverness Advertiser*, that was "dedicated to the Highlands." Established in 1850, the weekly was based in Wick. Its reporters included Thomas Mulock, Donald Ross and Donald Macleod.

notice of removal. The first step to eviction. For an example, see the appendix.

O

On the Origin of Species (1859). The famous and indeed revolutionary book by Charles Darwin had an impact on the Clearances in subtle but profound ways. Darwinian-like ideas had been circulating in Britain since at least the 1840s, inspired at various times by the work of Thomas Robert Malthus, Jeremy Bentham, Herbert Spencer and others. Such phrases as "the survival of the fittest"—coined by Spencer, not Darwin—and "struggle for survival" had been inculcated into the brains of not only economists but also sociologists and politicians. By the time Darwin's book was published, it was no longer a novel idea but rather something that people could readily accept and even embrace as the way of the world. These ideas were certainly being applied during the Clearances era on many levels.

Orkney. Unlike the Highlands, the Clearances when they did occur in Orkney were not as severe because of the old Norse feudal system of land tenure that offered a measure of protection from sudden eviction. Even so, in 1886 the landlord General Burroughs evicted a crofter, James Leonard, from Rousay, after he had given evidence to the Napier Commission. The single largest eviction from the islands also occurred on Rousay when in 1845 George William Traill, the uncle of General Burroughs, cleared 200 people from Quandal.

Otago. A region located on the South Island of New Zealand founded by Scottish settlers in the 1840s. In March 1848 the two emigrant ships arrived from Greenock, the *John Wickliffe* and the *Philip Laing*, led by William Cargill, a veteran of the Peninsular War. Dunedin (the Gaelic name for Edinburgh) is the second largest city on the South Island and the major city of the Otago region. Although the city and region are Lowland in origin, the University of Otago, which is located in Dunedin, does offer a Scottish Studies program through the Centre for Irish and Scottish Studies. Several courses at the university, such as "Scottish History since 1688," have examined the Highland Clearances and their impact on New Zealand.

other Clearance sites. It is impossible to list every place where Clearances took place. The following attempt lists some of the other places associated with the Clearances, along with the date:

- **Baddoch.** A particularly early example of a clearance, the Baddoch, Perthshire clearance occurred in 1733.
- **Balmoral**, Perthshire. Converted to sheep in 1833 and then to deer in 1848.
- **Balnagowan**, Sutherland. In 1790 the Balnagowan estate of Sir Charles Ross was converted to sheep farms. As Eric Richards notes, some of the evicted remained on the Sutherland estate as squatters and sub-tenants.
- **Blair Atholl**, Aberdeenshire. Numerous Clearances occurred here, in 1770-1772 and again in 1777-1779.
- **Campbeltown.** Near the Mull of Kintyre, the uplands of the peninsula was largely converted into a sheepwalk in the late 18th century with mixed farming.
- **Cape Wrath**, Sutherland. Between 1807 to 1820, when Lord Reay evicted 5,000-10,000.
- **Coigach**, Ross-shire. Cleared in 1852-1853 to make way for deer forests.
- **Coll, Isle of.** During the Highland potato famine, between 1846 and 1853, MacLean of Coll evicted 92 families from the island. Many moved to Australia, Canada and South Africa.
- **Dunmaglass**, Inverness-shire. Site of a former township; the last of the MacGillivray chiefs, John William XIII, sold Dunmaglass to Col. Sopper, an Englishman, in 1890. After becoming involved in a conflict with a tenant, Sopper evicted that tenant, and others who objected to such behaviour. Subsequently, their homes were demolished and stones from the crumbled houses were piled to form a huge heap. "This mound of stones," suggests Rob Gibson, "is a dramatic reminder of the finality of such Clearances."
- **Farr and Lairg**, Sutherland. In 1807, 70 families were cleared from here.
- **Fort William**, Inverness-shire. Clearances took place during numerous episodes, particulary from 1784-1787 and from 1789-1792.
- **Glen Dee**, Aberdeenshire. Cleared for deer in 1829.
- **Glenelchaig**, Ross-shire. In the first decade of the 19th century, Duncan Mor Macrae, the factor for the Seaforth estate, instituted clearances in Kintail.
- **Glen Ey**, Aberdeenshire. Nine families were evicted ca. 1830 to make way for deer.

- **Glen Clunie**, Aberdeenshire. Cleared for sheep and later converted into a deer forest in 1884.
- **Glen Lui**, Aberdeenshire. One of the earliest examples of the Clearances. Lord Grange evicted his tenants to make way for deer rather than sheep as early as 1726.
- **Glen More, Isle of Mull.** Cleared ca. 1830.
- **Glen Quoich**, Perthshire. In 1785, some 500 people were evicted from Glen Quoich and set sail for Canada aboard the emigrant ship *MacDonald*.
- **Glen Tanar**, Perthshire. Cleared in 1855-1858 for deer.
- **Leckhelm**, Ross-shire. In 1879 the Aberdeen paper manufacturer Alexander George Pirie (1836-1904) bought the Leckhelm estate near Loch Broom and then removed the tenantry to turn the land into a sporting estate; specifically he introduced cricket to the area, which Richards calls "the ultimate symbol of cultural imperialism from the south."
- **Letterfearn**, Inverness-shire. Fifty families were cleared in the first decade of the 19th century.
- **Lorgill**, Skye. Site of a cleared township. In May 1830 ten families were given a month's notice to leave.
- **Moidart**, Inverness-shire. In 1851 numerous crofters emigrated to Canada from Loch Shiel estates. In the 1840s Lord Cranstoun cleared many townships around the Sound of Arisaig; Kinloid, a mile north of Arisaig, cleared in 1853.
- **Morvern**, Argyll. Cleared many times in the 18th century, including 1758-1764, 1765-1769, 1771-1774, 1776-1783, 1785-1787, 1789 and 1791-1792.
- **Muck, Isle of**. MacLean of Coll offered assistance for up to 150 people to emigrate but many of the people preferred to stay, instead putting up makeshift huts in the township of Keil by the harbour.
- **Muie**, Sutherland. Cleared in 1882.
- **Mull, Isle of**. Dervaig was cleared in 1857 and Treshnish in 1862 while Mishnish (near Tobermory) was converted to sheep farms in 1842.
- **Rannoch**, Argyll. Clearances took place in 1824 and again in the 1850s and 1860s.
- **Rogart**, Sutherland. Clearances took place in 1819 and 1820.
- **Rothiemurchas**, Speyside. Cleared of sheep for grouse-shooting in 1827 and then deer in 1843.
- **Shetland**. Numerous sites were cleared in Shetland, including Tingwall in the 1850s, Unst in 1867 and Queendale in 1874. In North Yell entire villages were cleared around this time period.
- **Shiaba**. This township on the Isle of Mull was cleared in 1847 by the Duke of Argyll; the people went to Canada.

- **Strath Oykel**, Sutherland. Clearances took place in 1800.
- **Strathrusdale**, Ross-shire. Clearance occurred in 1792.
- **Upper Deeside**, Aberdeenshire. Gradually cleared from 1780 to 1815.
- **West Greenyards**, Sutherland. Cleared in 1854.

Outer Hebrides. Also known as the Western Isles, consists of six islands: Barra, South Uist, Benbecula, North Uist, Harris and Lewis, and the smaller islands of Vatersay, Eriskay, Scalpay and Bernera. The islands have different religious heritages also divided largely along geographic lines. The islands of Barra and South Uist are Roman Catholic while Benbecula is both Catholic and Protestant. Largely Protestant North Uist is mostly the Church of Scotland, but Harris is divided between the Church of Scotland and the Free Presbyterian Church whereas the strongest denomination on Lewis is the staunchly conservative Free Church of Scotland.

P

Pairc Deer Raid. Occurred on November 22, 1887; involved poor cottars from the parish of Lochs, Lewis, who raided the Pairc deer forest which then was on lease to Joseph Arthur Platt. The mastermind behind the plan was Donald MacRae, a schoolmaster from Balallan. The crofters spent a total of three days in the forest and killed, according to some estimates, as many as 200 deer. The cottars said they raided the forest because they were starving. Six men were arrested and brought to trial at the High Court in Edinburgh on January 16-17, 1888; they were acquitted.

Passenger Vessels Act (1803). Ostensibly passed for humanitarian reasons but in fact temporarily delayed emigration and thus allowed time for the various schemes of the Improvers to take hold. Specifically, the *Act* stipulated daily requirements of beef, bread, oatmeal, molasses and water to each passenger, and additional space allocations, and led, ultimately, to a significant increase in fares.

Pelican Lake Settlers. *See* crofter colonies.

Pennant, Thomas (1726-1798). Naturalist and antiquary born in Whitford, Wales. For our purposes, he is important because of his highly influential travel writing on Scotland. Pennant was considered the best travel writer of his day. In 1769 he made his first tour of Scotland (he went on a second tour in 1772). Accompanied by a small party, he embarked on an eight-week journey to the Hebrides. The voyage was considered the most thorough exploration of the region up to that time. His *Tour of Scotland* was published in 1771, two years before James Boswell and Samuel Johnson's more famous journey. Pennant, like Johnson, made the observation that the ancient customs were fast disappearing. But Pennant, unlike Johnson, admired the rough Highland scenery, finding the "naked" mountains to be "awefully magnificent." He did not romanticize the Highlanders themselves. To Pennant, the Highlanders were indolent. He differed from Johnson in another way.

Unlike Johnson, Pennant believed their indolence was a natural trait, and that they were content with what they had. Even so, he was critical of the landowners and their policies of rent raising that too often led to mass emigration. Emigration, he felt, was bad for the state and a result of poor management.

"People's Clearance." A phrase used by Canadian historian J. M. Bumsted to describe the phase of what he considered voluntary emigration from roughly the 1740s to the end of the Napoleonic War. Other historians, specifically Marianne McLean, disagree with his conclusion that the emigration was voluntary, insisting that, on the contrary, it was at least partly motivated by conditions back in Scotland, including the ravaging effects of the Clearances.

Perthshire. The Central Highland region of Perthshire has seen its share of Clearances, as early as the 1750s when the Duke of Argyll made great changes. Loch Tayside and Glen Quaich were cleared before the mid-19th century. Glen Quaich was cleared of 55 of its 60 families so that the Breadalbane Campbells could make way for sheep farming. The area by Tummel Bridge near Loch Rannoch was cleared by the trustees of the Forfeited Estates in the 1750s before "being returned to the Robertsons of Struan." The Forfeited Estates administration protected to some extent the Black Wood of Rannoch with its ancient native pines, from the ravages of over-grazing by sheep and deer. In Glen Tilt was emptied in 1784 to create a pleasure park for the Duke of Atholl.

Pictou, Nova Scotia. Known as the Birthplace of New Scotland, the town of Pictou was the destination for the ship *Hector*, which arrived on September 15, 1773. A replica of the Hector was built and now is the focal point of the Hector Heritage Quay. The Hector Festival, which celebrates the arrival of the *Hector*, takes place every August. The Rev. Norman McLeod emigrated to Pictou from Scotland before settling with his parishioners at St. Ann's on Cape Breton Island and then sailing to Waipu in New Zealand (*see* McLeod, Rev. Norman). In 1812, Hector Maclean, the 23rd Chief of Clan Maclean, emigrated to Pictou from the Morvern peninsula in Lochaber with 500 people, virtually the entire population of the region.

Pinkerton, John (1758-1826). Historian and antiquary, born in Edinburgh, believed in the the racial inferiority of the Celtic race in general and of the Highlanders specifically. In his *Dissertation on the Origin and Progress of the Scythians or Goths* (1787), he referred to the Celts as the aborigines of Europe—uncivilized and savage. He expanded his theory two years later in 1789 with *An Enquiry into the History of Scotland*. In it he mentioned physical and moral characterizations that he believed proved the inferiority status of the Gael, contrasting them unfavourably to Lowlanders. According to his observations, Lowlanders are "tall and large, with fair complexions, and often with flaxen, yellow, and red hair, and blue eyes." The Highlanders, on the other hand, are "generally diminutive" with "brown complexions and almost always with black curled hair and dark eyes." Thus, the Lowlanders are, by nature, "'industrious" and "sensible" whereas the Highlanders are "indolent" and "strangers to industry."

The second half of the 18th century saw the rise of not only anthropology but also such bogus sciences as phrenology and physiognomy, studies that were concerned with the classification of races.

poetry of the Clearances. Changes wrought by the Clearances were reflected in the poetry of the era, particularly during the 19th century. Among the themes the poems tackled were the arrival of the ubiquitous sheep, the loss of the indigenous population, the disappearance of traditional customs and rituals and an overall feeling of decline as communities headed toward inexorable collapse. Sometimes poets blamed Lowland entrepreneurs or were outraged by the non-Gaelic speaking shepherds, the foreign hordes who invaded their once idyllic landscapes. These same poets lamented not only the loss of a population—the empty glens of literature and art—but also the loss of rich Gaelic pastimes such as shinty, storytelling, music and song—that no longer exist.

A pre-Clearance Gaelic poet Duncan Bàn Macintyre (1724-1812) saw something ominous in the coming of the sheep and offered a prophecy of sorts: some day only sheep and shepherds would dominate the Highlands; there would be no peasantry or houses or Gaelic customs. As it turns out, Macintyre was himself cleared, in 1766, from Glenorchy. Like most of the early Gaelic poets, he set his lyrics to a known melody.

Contrary to popular perception, though, Donald Meek maintains that pre-1874 Clearance poems do attack the landlords and factors. They quite often not only display anger but also reveal a strong desire for revenge. Meek describes these types of poems as "strong, verbal weapons." The anonymous "Oran air Fear a bha a' Fuadachadh nan Gàidheal" (Song to One Who is Evicting Highlanders), for example, is very explict in its anger. The narrator envisions the day when the factor or landlord (it is unclear which one) will be "buried in cow dung, nettles will grow on his grave, and people will clap their hands and rejoice at his funeral." More gentle (initially at least), but just as powerful, is "A' Direadh a-mach ri Beinn Shianta" (Climbing up toward Beinn-Shiant) by John MacLachlan, which comments on the desolation caused by the landlords before condemning their greed and damning them to hell.

Indeed, some poetry expressed a very deep resentment toward the landlords, their own clan chiefs who evicted them from the land. It is important to note that many of the Gaelic nature poems describe the pre-Clearance Highlands as being idyllic, a Garden-of-Eden-like place. The great 20th-century Gaelic poet Sorley Maclean referred to these poems, and others like them, as exhibiting a deep longing, a "romantic nostalgia" for a hopelessly gone past, rather than a realistic examination of change. Others agreed that the Clearances, and before them the defeat at Culloden, had a detrimental effect not only on the morale of the Gael but also on the poetry of the Gael. "The poetry that was inspired by the infamies of Culloden and the Clearances could not be other than gloomy," notes W. J. Watson.

The composers of these poems often blame the sheep or Lowlanders or Englishmen rather than the chiefs—rather than their own kin—for the evictions. As Thomas McKean observes, the Gaels' self-esteem was at a historic low during the 18th century; thus, it was hardly surprising that most of the people most of the time did not rebel against their own kin (see the "resistance" entry for exceptions) or toward a system that taught them that authority was always right "and beyond the question of ordinary folk." These attitudes were often reflected in the poetry of the era.

And yet the Clearances prompted numerous Gaelic poets to rage against the depopulation of the Highlands. One poet in particular, William Livingstone (1808-1870), would write about the beauty of his native Islay but then end with a bitter attack against the conditions that led to the absence of people there. In a similar vein John Smith (1848-1881) in "Song for Sportsmen" attacked the Scots themselves for allowing the land and their heritage to fall into the hands of strangers and outsiders, sportsmen and industrialists.

The poet and activist Ewen Robertson (1842-1895) was the son of a crofter. He grew up in Tongue, Sutherland. He left home ca. 1860 to work in the Greenock shipyards. Eventually he moved to England before returning to Scotland to participate in the Highland Land League. He went on to represent the residents of Tongue at hearings of the Napier Commission. In his poetry, he isn't afraid to name names.

Another 19th-century poet, Donald Maciver (1857?-1953), was a school master born in Uig, on Lewis. During his own lifetime, he witnessed the depopulation of his township. "The Surge of the Sea," which has become a modern Gaelic classic, has come to symbolize permanence in a changing world. Sorley Maclean once said that the song crystallizes "the idea of human desolation and a mournful sound in nature, a mood of universal sadness, a sense of the transience of the world...." For Gaels, the sea was both highway and barrier, a source of nourishment and danger.

Although there are Clearance poems that offer vigorous attacks on the landlords, much of Clearance poetry is retrospective. The common motifs include a sense of desolation and loss. "There is in Clearance poetry," wrote Maclean, "a tendency to a vague generalised regret without a definiteness even of indictment, a common failure to face the real cause...." He considers this one of the intellectual failings of 19th-century Gaelic poetry: the real cause being not the fault of Lowlanders or Englishmen or even the factors—but of the chiefs themselves.

The crofter resistance movement of the 1880s announced a change in the attitudes and directions expressed in the poems. Undoubtedly the most famous of the 19th-century Clearance poets was Mary MacPherson, or Màiri Mhór nan Òran, Big Mary of the Songs, as she was commonly known.

Mary MacPherson was the poet of the Land League, and above all a poet of the people, a poet of *her* people. Although she often romanticizes the pre-Clearance period, especially in such poems as "When I Was Young," she nevertheless was a composer of radical Gaelic songs. She allied herself with the land agitators, and she sang at crofter rallies. She was, in other words, a protest singer.

Big Mary did not begin to write poetry until she was more than 50 years old. In 1848 she left Skye to marry Isaac MacPherson, a shoemaker from Skye who was living at the time in Inverness. By the time he died in 1871, she had four children to support and was working for an English army officer named Captain Turner. Turner's wife wrongfully accused her of stealing clothes from the household, but the arrest had political overtones. Her late husband had been active in trade unionism. What's more, the trial in Inverness was conducted in English even though she had only the Gaelic. Jailed for 42 days, she never forgot the humiliation she experienced. It was in an Inverness prison that she began to write songs: with her first song, "I Am Tired of English Speakers," she wrote about injustice, first her own, and then others'.

Màiri Mhór left Inverness and went to Glasgow, where she trained as a nurse, earning a diploma in obstetrics, before returning to Skye in 1882 and becoming involved in the land reform movement. She attended crofters' gatherings throughout Skye and recited or sang her poems. Her songs were circulated widely by the people. Alas, she blamed the English speakers almost exclusively rather than the real villains: the indigenous Highland aristocracy. She spent her last days in Skeabost. She never did learn to write but instead dictated some 9,000 lines of poetry to John Whyte of Glasgow who transcribed them and published them in 1891 in an anthology, *Poems and Songs of Mary MacPherson*, edited by Alexander MacBain.

Thus, when Màiri Mhór started writing her songs, in the late 19th century, attitudes in the Highlands were changing—after nearly a century of upheaval and eviction after eviction. By this time, the press in both the Lowlands and in England (including the *Times*) had written about the Clearances, bringing the subject finally to the attention of the average person who couldn't believe that such things were taking place in Britain. Questions were being asked in Parliament. And then, bit by bit, little by little, the people themselves began to fight back in places like Lewis, Glendale in Skye, and especially Braes, also in Skye, which ended in 1882 at the Battle of the Braes. Significantly, Sorley Maclean refers to the Battle of the Braes as the end of the Clearance period and the beginning of the crofter resistance movement.

Other Land Agitation poets include Lachlan Livingstone of Mull, Neil MacLeod of Skye, John Smith of Lewis and Murdo MacLeod, also of Lewis. Sometimes a poet commented directly on specific events that affected the crofting community, such as John MacRae's "Oran air Bill nan Croitearan" (Song on the Crofters' Bill) in which the poet criticizes the inadequacies of the *Crofters' Bill* of 1886.

A form of poetry unique to the Gael is the *brosnachadh*, which is steeped in the Gaelic heroic tradition. These poems recall the exploits of the traditional Gaelic warriors of the Golden Age and are reflected in the Land Agitation poems of Livingstone, Smith and MacLeod but also the exhortatory poems of MacPherson. Yet another type of Gaelic poem is the *moladh*. These are initially praise poems celebrating Gaelic heroes, but in the 1870s and 1880s the focus shifts away from clan chiefs and toward members of the community, the people themselves and their leaders. The Rev. Donald MacCallum is commemorated in several poems for his role in the Pairc Deer Raid of 1887 on Lewis.

Another example of Clearance poetry is the Clearance satires such as Calum Campbell MacPhail's 1880s poem, "Aoir na Bairlinn" (Satire on the Eviction Notice). Most prominent of the Clearance satire poems, though, probably belongs to the so-called Ivory Cycle, prompted by the behaviour in the 1880s of Sheriff William Ivory, of Inverness-shire, who achieved a form of notoriety for his efforts to collect arrears in Skye in late 1886. Mary MacPherson perhaps wrote among the most pungent of retorts in "Oran Cumha an Ibhirich" (Elegy-Song on Ivory), a mock elegy. Upon hearing about Ivory's alleged death by drowning in a body of water on the moors, the poet sees his funeral as a time for rejoicing and celebration. During the years of the Crofters' War, some of the more astute politicians, their ears close to the ground, were very much aware of the political clout of the poets. At least one politician, Charles Fraser-Mackintosh, even took Mary MacPherson along with him when he was campaigning. Fraser-Mackintosh later became a member of the Napier Commission.

There are also notable examples of Clearance elegies. John MacLean's "Manitoba" was written about a group of MacLeans who emigrated from Balephuil, Tiree, to Manitoba in 1878 and captures the sorrow felt by those left behind at the departure of emigrants who are now gone and who had contributed so much to the life of the community. Another elegy, "'Venus' nan Gàidheal" (The "Venus" of the Gaels), describes the voyage of an emigrant ship carrying inhabitants of Islay from Port Ellen to Canada in 1862, which concentrates on the death of some of the passengers when the ship encounters stormy weather. What makes the poem remarkable, contends Donald Meek, is its "hard-headed realism." Upon reflection, the narrator decides to cross the ocean to "the land of the trees," as Nova Scotia was called. "Not all Gaelic poets spent their time bemoaning their fate and condemning the supposed perpetrators of their misery," offers Meek.

The Clearance poetry of the 20th century continues along this more aggressive path. Iain Crichton Smith, who wrote a novel of the Clearances, *Consider the Lilies*, and a Clearances play which he set in Hell, offers a particularly harsh denunciation of Patrick Sellar, the notorious factor, in his poem, "The Clearances."

"Strathnaver" by Derick Thomson is one of the most powerful of the 20th-century Clearance poems. Written from the perspective of a Clearance victim, Thomson describes what happened. The protagonist watches helplessly as the rafters of his father's house burn under "a blue-black sky." That was the year, the narrator recalls, when the authorities "hauled the old woman out on to the dung-heap" though she had "no place in which to lay her head." The heather that now blooms on the slopes of Strathnaver and Kildonan hides the wounds of Patrick Sellar, but not the memories.

The most acclaimed Gaelic poet of the modern era is Sorley Maclean (1911-1996). After his retirement as headmaster of Plockton High School, Maclean moved to Skye, and lived on the croft of his great-grandfather, in Braes—Angus Stewart had been the first witness to testify before the Napier Commission. His poems are often based on traditional Gaelic meters and styles. In addition to the poetry of such Gaelic poets as William Ross and Mary MacPherson, he was also influenced by the 17th-century metaphysical poets, the Romantic and Symbolist poets, as well as Yeats, Pound and Eliot.

Among his best-known poems, "The Woods of Raasay," is very much in this symbolist style; it is a celebratory poem about the forests of his native land that goes from descriptions in the style of Gaelic praise poems to a complex meditation on love and idealism but also death as he recalls the "music of laughter," yet with graveyards on each slope of the hillside. The poetry emerges as a reflection of his own painful family history. All four sides of Maclean's family were evicted from one

Raasay township after another. Dozens of families that were evicted from Raasay emigrated to Prince Edward Island or Australia. Three and a half miles north of Hallaig is Screapadal. In 1841, 17 families lived there. Like Hallaig, it is now in ruins.

His masterpiece remains "Hallaig," a poem that uses symbolist imagery and metaphor and yet is still part of the Gaelic bardic tradition. First published in 1954, it is also homage to a long-deserted township on Raasay where his ancestors once lived before it was cleared to make room for a sheep farm in the 1850s. In the poem, the trees are transformed into girls. It begins with a one-line epigraph ("Time, the deer, is in the wood of Hallaig") and concludes with the symbolic death of Time. "Hallaig" is a survival poem, the survival of memory. It is a haunting poem about time and loss made palpable, and it captures the essence of the Clearances. If not for the Clearances, the people and their descendents who once lived there would still be there. Instead there are only ghosts, and words written down of what once was. In the poem he references particular Clearance sites, Screapadal "of my people / where Norman and Big Hector were" and Suishnish, another site of brutal Clearances, where he recalls another time, perhaps before the Clearances, when the inhabitants enjoyed happier times, "each one young and light-stepping, without the heartbreak of the tale."

Among the best of the younger Gaelic poets whose work is influenced by the Clearances is Angus Peter Campbell, who was born and brought up on South Uist. He attended secondary school in Oban, where his English teacher was Iain Crichton Smith. Campbell received degrees in history and politics from the University of Edinburgh. The writer in residence at the time that he was attending was Sorley Maclean.

In one of his most powerful poems, "Human Rights," Campbell evokes other tragedies from around the world—"Auschwitz, Strathnaver, Africa"—thereby equating the Clearances with the Holocaust, or at least placing it on the same plain (he later references Dachau and Belsen) before mentioning the evictors by name: "...in Uist John Gordon of Cluny was the landlord, / in Lewis the opium-king Matheson." He compares powerful people, landowners such as "...the Duchess of Sutherland" with ordinary Highlanders Donald John MacAskill, Iain MacIsaac, Neil Campbell. "The graveyards are full."

In "Do Unto Others," he refers to one of the most famous of Clearance sites, Croick Church, in Glencalvie: "The pathetic graveyard at Croick / and hear you saying that it served them right / for being a wicked generation."

Here Campbell makes mention of the ministers who preached to the people that their sufferings were a sign from God, that God was punishing them for their sins, that they were indeed members of the

Wicked Generation. It was something they took to heart, even etching those words on the church's windowpane. In "The Highlands," he brings the story of the Clearances, the story of the Highlands, full circle, proclaiming that the braes of Glenelg and the mountains in Kintail and Skye are "like shrouds covering the dead ... flung over so much horror" and much like Maclean's "heartbreak of the tale," the ghosts still hover, the memories still linger for, as Campbell so poignantly notes, "the world is not empty without reason."

Most of the poets who write or have written about the Clearances are Gaels but occasionally they come from outwith Scotland. In September 1977 the American poet Richard Hugo and his family lived for several months on Skye. The result was the poetry collection *The Right Madness on Skye*. He dedicated "The Braes," about the Battle of the Braes, to Sorley and Renee Maclean. Even he had not known about the incident; he could have very easily driven past it: "I'd drive unaware Celt blood flows / even now in the grass, the result of violent gesture / against the injustice of seizure." He writes about the resistance put up by the crofters, the men and women, who eventually "won ... in London." And in words reminiscent of Iain Crichton Smith damning Patrick Sellar to hell, Hugo puts a curse on another Clearance villain, Balligall (spelled "Ballingall" in the poem), Lord Macdonald's factor on Skye who removed the people from Suishnish and Boreraig in 1853. "Roast, roast in the fires of hell," Hugo writes. But it was here in Braes, he suggests, "where the poor woke up a nation."

In "The Clearances," Hugo visualizes the landlords callously or at least unthinkingly making their decisions to evict over a cup of tea; the wave of a glove and a nod of the head and it was done. He imagines too what it must have been like for the Clearance Highlanders on the day of departure, on their last look at Skye. "Think of their fear," he says. And then he asks a remarkable question: "When you can't read, not even a map, where does home end and Tasmania start?"

popular music of the Clearances. During the past few decades numerous songs have been written about or inspired by the Clearances, especially in the folk, folk-rock and rock genres. But classical composers, such as Sally Beamish or William Sweeney, either have addressed the topic directly or commented on aspects of Highland history and culture affected by the Clearances. Beamish, for example, wrote *The Singing*, a concerto for accordion and orchestra that evokes the tragedy of the Clearances, creating bagpipe effects (without actually using a bagpipe) and Gaelic text.

In recent years, several musicians have recorded Clearance tribute albums: the Canadian Angus Macleod in *The Silent Ones: A Legacy of the Highland Clearances*, about the Clearances of 1851 from Lewis and the subsequent migration of 109 families to Bruce County, Ontario; and *Highland Farewell* by Steve McDonald, a New Zealander, and the grandson of Clearance Highlanders.

In the folk vein, Andy M. Stewart, the lead singer of the now defunct folk group Silly Wizard, has written and recorded several Clearances songs. The Gaelic rock band Runrig has probably written more about the Clearances, and its legacy, than any other contemporary group. (*See* Runrig)

Numerous Scots musicians have been influenced by the work of the iconic Gaelic poet Sorley Maclean. They have either set his poems to music (Maclean's love poem "The Blue Rampart" by Capercaillie), or they actually name check him in their own songs (Runrig's "Nightfall on Marsco"). Martyn Bennett (1971-2005) set "Hallaig" to music.

The following is a brief—by no means comprehensive—sampling of modern recordings that feature songs or music that is about or was somehow inspired by or is in some way redolent of the Highland Clearances.

- Bennett, Martyn. *Bothy Culture* (Rykodisc, 1997). An ingenious fusion of traditional Gaelic.
- Capercaillie. *The Blood Is Strong* (Survival Records, 1995). Contains six extra tracks from the television programs *Highlanders* and *A Prince among Islands*.
- Capercaillie. *Delirium* (Green Linnet, 1991). Includes "Waiting for the Wheel to Turn," "Cape Breton Song," "You Will Rise Again" and "Servant to the Slave." Two years later, in 1993, Capercaillie released *Secret People*, which contains the song "Four Stone Walls" with its direct reference to the Clearances ("It's an order for eviction.")
- *Catherine-Ann MacPhee Sings Mairi Mhor* (Greentrax, 1994). Soundtrack from the TV production *Màiri Mhór*.
- Ceilidh Ménage. *Plaids & Bandanas: Song Links from Scots Drovers to Wild West Cowboys* (Blue Banana Music, 1999), Rob Gibson and company's thrilling collection of songs and airs of drovers and cowboys that connect Celtic Scotland with the American West.
- Cowboy Celtic. *Gunsmoke, Whisky & Heather* (Centerfire Music, 2006).
- *Na Fògarraich. Songs of the Scottish Highlanders in the United States* (Saorsa Media, 2001), scholar Michael Newton's ambitious and impressive CD of Gaelic songs, including several with strong Clearances content such as "On the Desolation of the Scottish Highlands," "From Uist to North Carolina," "I'm Tired of This Exile" and "We Will Go to America."

- Paul Mounsey. *Nahoo Two* (Iona, 1997). Like his fellow Scot Martyn Bennett, Mounsey excels in sampling sounds from around the world, mixing and reconceptualizing them to create exquisite and wildly weird soundscapes that evoke not only Gaelic melodies and songs but also Brazilian, Middle Eastern and Native American music. The tune "Another Clearance" contains samples of Gaelic singing taken from music from the Western Isles while the majestic sweep of "Red River" (intentionally or not) recalls the long journey of the emigrants from Kildonan to the Red River Valley of Manitoba.
- Runrig. *Proterra* (Ridge Records, 2003). Includes "Empty Glens."
- Runrig. *Recovery* (Ridge Records, 1981). Includes the title cut.
- Stewart, Andy M., Phil Cunningham and Manus Lunny. *Fire in the Glen* (Shanachie, 1989). Includes "Treorachadh/I Mourn for the Highlands" and the title track.
- David Wilkie and Cowboy Celtic, featuring Denise Withnell. *The Drover Road* (Shanachie, 2001).

Prebble, John (1915-2001). Popular historian of the Clearances; born in Middlesex, England, but grew up in Sutherland (Saskatoon), Saskatchewan, Canada, in a predominantly Scottish township before returning to England. He became a journalist in 1934 and served during the Second World War with the Royal Artillery.

Prebble introduced and popularized the history of the Highland Clearances to generations of readers. In his foreword to his groundbreaking book, *The Highland Clearances* (1963), he wrote, "This book is the story of how the Highlanders were deserted and then betrayed. It concerns itself with people, how sheep were preferred to them, and how bayonet, truncheon and fire were used to drive them from their homes." Although some historians, such as Gordon Donaldson, dismissed the book as "utter rubbish," the vast majority of historians and independent scholars tend to agree with Prebble's conclusions.

The *Clearances* book was part of Prebble's so-called *Fire and Sword* trilogy which chronicled the fall of the clan system. Other works in the trilogy are *Culloden* (1962) and *Glencoe* (1966). But Prebble wrote other works with a Scottish theme (both Highland and Lowland), including *Darien: The Scottish Dream of Empire* (1968); *The Lion in the North: A Personal View of Scotland's History* (1973); *Mutiny: Highland Regiments in Revolt, 1743-1804* (1975); *John Prebble's Scotland* (1984); and *The King's Jaunt: George IV in Scotland* (1988).

primary sources on the Clearances. For examples, see the appendix.

Prince Edward Island. Often called the most Scottish province in Canada (nearly 40 per cent of residents claim Scottish ancestry). In 1772, John MacDonald, the laird of Glenaladale, brought 250 of his followers to an 8,000 ha (20,000 acre) estate on Prince Edward Island. In 1803, Thomas Douglas, the Earl of Selkirk, brought an additional 800 Highlanders with him to PEI from Argyll, Ross-shire, Skye and the Uists. The emigrants sailed on the *Polly*, the *Dykes* and the *Oughton*. Many of the emigrants settled in the area known as Belfast. In 2003, this event, known as the Crossing, or An Tarsainn, was commemorated on PEI, Skye and Raasay in honour of the 200th anniversary of the journey. The activities in Portree were particulary memorable: a performance of Angus Peter Campbell's play '*Siúcar nan Craobh* (Sugar from Trees). In addition, former Runrig members Donnie Munro and Blair Douglas performed a rendition of the band's emigration song, "Dance Called America." On PEI, Lord Selkirk Park, located in the community of Eldon, is named in honour of Selkirk's emigrants.

Protestant work ethic. The mid-19th century, when the Clearances were at their height, was also the era of the Improvers. Ordinary people became obsessed with the idea of improving themselves and, thus, by extension, society at large. It is this pervasive ethos that quite often led to rampant anti-Highland prejudice. The message in the popular press and in the literature of the day, as well as in government policies, essentially promoted what came to be known as the three "selves": self-reliance, self-discipline and self-control. This attitude helped create a negative attitude toward the poor in general and the Highlander in particular. Poverty and indolence were thus irrevocably intertwined and, thus, generally speaking, the Highlander was regarded with contempt.

Purser, John (b. 1942). Composer, poet, playwright and broadcaster. Born in Glasgow, Purser studied at the Royal Scottish Academy of Music. From 1985 to 1987 he was manager of the Scottish Music Information Centre. His compositions include numerous works for orchestra, choral music and songs, chamber music and sonatas. He is the author of several radio plays, including *Carver* (1991) as well as the author of the monumental *Scotland's Music*, the companion to his BBC radio series of the same name. The book was first published in 1992 before appearing in an expanded edition in 2007.

R

Raasay. A small island off the west coast of the Isle of Skye. After the Jacobite Rising of 1745, Macleod of Raasay, the owner, lost his estate, fell into ruin, and left for Australia. In 1843, the island was sold to George Rainy, who evicted more than 100 people and shipped them to Australia. His ownership was short-lived, however; in 1876, Henry Wood assumed control, and ran the island as a sporting estate. Before the outbreak of the First World War, the Wood family put Raasay up for sale. It was bought by the Scottish Rural Workers Approved Society and then taken into public ownership by the Board of Agriculture for Scotland. A memorial cairn to the Raasay Clearances is located near the headland of Rudha na' Leac. Sorley Maclean's poem "Hallaig" is reproduced on the cairn.

See also "Hallaig"; Raasay House

Raasay House. Located near Inverarish on the Isle of Raasay, where James Boswell and Samuel Johnson stayed on their famous tour of the Hebrides in 1773. While staying on the island, Boswell danced "a Highland dance" on the top of Dun Caan (or Dùn Cana), the highest hill on the island ("where we sat down, ate cold mutton and bread and cheese and drank brandy and punch").

In 1961 the Department of Agriculture offered Raasay House (including the kennels, gardener's house, boathouse, an old fort, the mansion house of Borrodale and an additional 4.25 ha (10.5 acres) of land to the highest bidder. Dr. Green bid a lowly £4,000 and was able to get everything. The enigmatic Dr. Green was a doctor from Surrey; the local media gave him the sobriquet of "Dr. No" for his penchant of giving a negative response to any improvement suggested on the island. The writer Derek Cooper has called him "a seaside Howard Hughes." Stubborn and frequently in defiance of public opinion, he also had run-ins with Inland Revenue commissioners. He tried to keep Raasay "unspoilt" but the public apparently had little admiration for him.

In 1981, a former army major, Rod Stewart Liddon, set up the Scottish Adventure School Trust, a training centre for unemployed young people, at the House, which by this time had fallen into a derelict state. In 1984, three former staff members (Roddy MacDonald, Tekela Koek and Lyn Rowe) of the Trust became the founding directors of Raasay Outdoor Centre. In 2008, Raasay House was purchased by the Community Council. On January 18, 2009, a fire virtually destroyed Raasay House, by then an outdoor adventure centre. At the time of writing, there were plans to reopen in April 2013.

Rachmanism. Refers to the exploitation and intimidation of tenants by unscrupulous landlords. It is named after Peter Rachman (1919-1962), a London landlord in the Notting Hill neighbourhood in the 1950s and 1960s, who subdivided large properties into smaller flats. In order to maximize his income, he reportedly removed the mostly white tenants who had a form of rent control and replaced them with West Indian immigrants and subsequently raised their rent. The new immigrant tenants had no or little protection under the law. The *Rent Act* of 1965 provided security to tenants. Rachman's often devious, predatory and generally unsavoury practices led some 20th-century critics of the Clearances to use his name in this context.

racism. During the peak of the Clearances, in the mid-19th century, race became an issue. In fact, race became the determining factor which helped determine which people were "useless" or even expendable among the less productive members of society. Perhaps an editorial in the Scotsman best summed up the attitude at the time; "On one side of the Firth of Clyde, you find the county of Ayr, teeming with industry and plenty, and on the other, the county of Arygle, rotting in idleness and famine." As the theory went, the inferior Celtic race was doomed to failure and, preferably, extinction. Like a cancer in the body, the sickly Celtic inhabitants of Britain had to be removed for the benefit of the greater society. To non-Gaels like Patrick Sellar (to cite one notorious example) the Highlanders were barbarians who spoke a barbaric tongue, and degenerates whom he compared to the "aborigines of America" and, by implication, they had no legal right to their lands. Or as Aitchison and Cassell write, "In Manitoba, the Dakotas or Australia, possession bassed on unwritten community memory had no force against the title deeds of white settlers."

rack-renting. The practice of landlords' raising the rent beyond the amount that crofters were able to pay; an inflated rent.

Raeburn, Henry (1756-1823). Considered one of the great portraitists of the Scottish Enlightenment (another is Allan Ramsay). Raeburn began his career as an apprentice goldsmith in Edinburgh and took lessons from the famous painter Alexander Runciman. Although not otherwise formally trained, he had a natural talent and earned a reputation of being a painter of great vision who captured the personality and immediacy of his subjects. His best-known Highland portraits are of the fiddler Niel Gow (1793) and especially of Colonel Alasdair Macdonell of Glengarry (1811), the controversial Highland chief who forced many of his tenants to emigrate to Canada. As Murdo Macdonald notes, however, Raeburn's attitude toward Glengarry is ambivalent, not celebratory. According to Macdonald, Raeburn has taken "the established tradition of full-length portraits in Highland dress and remade it in the light of the failed Jacobite project." Hence, maintains Macdonald, "[t]he conceptual shift is from tartan as something to wear to tartan as something to dress up in." Another portrait by Raeburn, of Sir John Sinclair of Ulbster (ca. 1795), president of the Board of Agriculture, depicts his subject as a formidable figure in traditional Highland dress. Raeburn's portraits are known for their immediacy and their ability to capture the character, the essence, of his subjects.

Rainy, George from Edinburgh; owner of Raasay. Rainy made his fortune in sugar plantations. Rainy cleared the entire population of twelve townships, or ninety-four families, to Australia from Raasay between 1852 and 1854 turning the land into a sheep and sporting estate. Those who refused to leave Scotland were banished to the nearby island of Rona.

Rent Day. Traditionally held annually on Whitsunday (the seventh day after Easter) when the laird received his rent, either in kind or in money.

Report to the Board of Supervision in Scotland (1851). Emigration, the report concluded, was the only solution to the Highland problem. There were too many people and not enough jobs. What's more, the population could not be made self-sufficient unless a "portion" was removed by a systematic and assisted emigration. In some parishes, the report determined, more than half of the inhabitants would probably need to emigrate. The report led to the passage of the Emigration Advances Act, which provided loans to landowners to help them with the emigration from their estates. The report and Sir John MacNeill, chairman of the Board of Supervision of the Scottish Poor Law, played important roles in the creation of the Highland and Island Emigration Society.

resistance. The general consensus is that there wasn't much resistance during the Highland Clearances, that the Highlanders en masse accepted their fate meekly and passively. This assumption is not entirely accurate. Indeed, there were instances of sporadic resistance to the Clearances at numerous times over the decades. Tom Devine refers to the myth of passivity. As evidence he points to more than 50 acts of defiance that occurred between 1780 and 1855. Resistance occurred at Kildonan in 1813, Glencalvie in 1843, Sollas in 1849 and Coigach in 1852. Women in particular were oftentimes more involved than men, sticks and stones being their most common weapons of choice. One of the earliest rebellions occurred in 1792 at Easter Ross when people of several districts gathered together and attempted to drive out the flock of sheep that threatened their way of life.

The greatest single collective act of defiance, according to Devine, was the breakaway of the Free Church in 1843 from the established Church of Scotland; the Disruption, as it was called, was not only a political movement but also an attack on landlordism, as congregations in the crofting region opposed unpopular ministers appointed by landowners.

On the other hand, truly sustained resistance (as opposed to, say, intermittent acts of rebellion) did not seriously begin until the 1880s when the worst days of the Clearances were in the past. For many crofters the chief source of inspiration was Michael Davitt's Land League in Ireland. Founded in 1879, the Land League was a form of agrarian rebellion. Two years later, in 1881, Parliament had passed the *Irish Land Act* granting to the Irish a security of tenure and making possible the "fixing" of fair rents. Inspired by the Irish Land League, the Highlanders formed their own political organization, the Highland Land Law Reform Association, which formed its own Crofters' Party. During the Crofters' War and Land Agitation movement of the 1880s and later, rebellion took the form of rent strikes and land raids. Food riots occurred at places such as Avoch, Banff, Burghead, Evanton, Invergordon, Inverness, Macduff and Wick.

For most of the Clearances era, however, the people did not resist the evictions. The reasons for their passivity are varied and complex. But chief among them include the belief of Presbyterian ministers that the evictions were the will of God. They, in turn, warned their congregations not to resist for fear of certain damnation. Another problem was the lack of any organized and sustained leadership within the crofting communities. In addition, fewer roads in the Highlands and Islands made communication difficult since the population often lived in acute isolation from one another.

In truth, the fear of being evicted "hung like the Sword of Damocles," as Eric Richards so evocatively put it, causing many Highlanders to adopt a severe posture of deference to the landlords almost comparable to slaves in the American South during the Civil War. To put it modern terms, the Highlanders suffered a form of post-traumatic stress, always on edge, uncertain about their future.

Still another problem was the very real fear of transportation to the colonies, including the penal colony of Botany Bay in Australia, especially in post-Culloden Scotland. The 19th-century traditional Scottish ballad "Jamie Raeburn" is about just that: a baker in Glasgow who was sent to the colonies for an unspecified transgression. In the song, the eponymous protagonist laments his fate, ostracized from family and friends for a crime he did not commit.

Here is a partial list of places where resistance occurred:

- Aignish, Lewis, 1888
- Balchladdich, Assynt, 1839
- Braes, Skye, 1882
- Coigach, Ross-shire, 1852
- Durness, Sutherland, 1841
- Glendale, Skye, 1883
- Greenyards, Sutherland, 1845
- Gruids, Sutherland, 1821
- Kildonan, Sutherland, 1813
- Sollas, North Uist, 1849

Rhymer, Thomas the (Tómas Reumair). A historical figure who lived in the early 14th century; also known as Thomas of Erceldoune or True Thomas, because it was said he could never tell a lie. He was a 13th-century poet and prophet and the protagonist of the famous eponymous Scottish ballad (Child ballad #37, "Thomas Rhymer"). He prophesied that the Gaels would one day assume their rightful place in Scotland again, an allusion, some thought, to the Jacobite Risings of 1715 and 1745. He also made mention of sheep grazing on Highland land ("the jaw-bone of the sheep would put the plough on the hen-roost"), which later generations of Highland poets (and indeed non-poets) believed referred to the Clearances. Among his other predictions were the death of the Scottish king Alexander III, the defeat of King James IV at the Battle of Flodden and the Union of the Crowns between Scotland and England in 1707. The Child ballad attributes his clairvoyance to the time he spent in Elfland, typically seven years, according to custom. He may also be the source of "Tam Lin," another supernatural Scottish Border ballad (Child ballad #39).

Richards, Eric. Emeritus Professor of History at Flinders University in Adelaide, Australia, and a specialist in the history of Australia, British and internal migration. Richards's magisterial volumes on the Highland Clearances are classics in the field. He is a member of the Gaelic Society of Inverness and the winner of the Book Award of the Scottish Arts Council in 1982 and the Scottish History Book of the Year in 1999.

rigs. Ridges.

ring-net fishing. Traditional method of fishing by setting a line of nets in a circle; evolved on the west coast of Scotland after the Clearances as a direct response of the forcible movement of farming people to fishing villages. Neil Gunn's novel *The Silver Darlings* is about such people. The Highland painter Will Maclean's work also makes reference to this very Highland method of fishing.

Robertson, Ewen (1842-1895). Nineteenth-century bard of the Clearances. A granite pillar was erected in his honour about 2.5 km (1.5 miles) south of the old road from Tongue. His most famous song is "Mo mhollachd aig na caoraich mhor" (My curse upon the big sheep), which condemns the Duke and Duchess of Sutherland as well as Patrick Sellar in the harshest of language. The son of a crofter, Robertson grew up in Tongue, Sutherland, and was active in the Highland Land League. He also represented the people of Tongue at the Napier Commission hearings.

Rodger, Willie (b. 1930). Printmaker and painter; born in Kirkintilloch; trained at Glasgow School of Art; art teacher for many years at Lenzie Academy and Clydebank High School. Rodger concentrates on relief process printmaking but he has also done work in pen and ink and oil. Among his works is "Clearances," a simple woodcut portraying a father and mother accompanied by their young daughter after being evicted from their home, presumably with all of their worldly belongings. The father carries twigs over his right shoulder, the mother a basket, and the young girl a forlorn doll followed by two barking dogs.

romanticizing the Highlands. Even as the Highlanders were being cleared, there was a trend in public opinion, both in Scotland and England, romanticizing the Highlands as the land of mountains and lochs populated by a noble people. Basically, the Highlander became the British equivalent of the noble savage archetype made famous by Jean-Jacques Rousseau, who populated an imaginary landscape of grandeur and magnificence. Paintings by such artists as Horatio McCulloch, Peter Graham, Thomas Faed and others depicted a sublime landscape of moody mountains and pristine lochs. Significantly, what was missing was the Highlander him- or herself; the land was absent of human habitation altogether. The message was subtle but clear: the emptier, the better. The Gael was perceived as a doomed race, and hence all the better as a subject for romanticization—the Highlander became a romantic hero safely ensconced in a distant past. Like the Native Americans of North America, once-feared Highlanders became idealized figures in literature and art even as their language and culture were being destroyed by a systemic policy of institutionalized anglicization.

roots tourism. Also called ancestral tourism; an activity made by people of Scots descent—typically, but not exclusively, from the United States, Canada, Australia or New Zealand—who visit Scotland, and the Highlands and Islands in particular, to search for and visit sites—historic and personal—associated with their ancestors. Tourism is of course one of Scotland's premier industries and has been for many years, at least since Sir Walter Scott wrote his Waverley novels, which motivated his readers to see the places that he wrote about with their own eyes. Tourism in the Highlands and Islands accounts for 15 per cent of employment and about 20 per cent of the region's gross domestic product. Indeed, the Scottish Tourist Board continues to market Scotland as a land existing outside of time, as a land apart, emphasizing the rugged and barren (read: empty) beauty of the Highlands. Significantly, about 70 per cent of these so-called roots tourists visit the Highlands, even though their ancestors might have hailed from the Lowlands. According to this mindset, to be truly Scottish (of a Scotland that matters) one must be a Highlander.

In the 20th century nothing quite exemplified Scotland to the outside world so much as Mel Gibson's wildly popular film *Braveheart* (1995). Paul Basu references a 1997 Stirling Council and Forth Valley study which reported that 39 per cent of those surveyed acknowledged that the film influenced their decision to visit Scotland. Indeed, the city of Stirling and surrounding area was aggressively promoted as being "The Land of Braveheart" and "Braveheart Country." Other films such as *Rob Roy* (1995), about the "Highland Robin Hood," and more recently the Pixar animated film *Brave* (2012), have also positively affected Scottish tourism figures. Once again, the reflection of Scotland that these films seek to project is a Highland image.

Rosal deserted township. Name derived from the Norse, "hrassa vall" (horse fields). Rosal is one of the largest townships in Strathnaver, Sutherland, that was cleared, in 1814 and again four years later. At the time, the village housed about 13 families. During the 1960s the site was excavated and surveyed in 1962 under the direction of Horace Fairhurst. Some 70 recognizable structures were uncovered during the excavations, including longhouses, barns, outhouses and corn-drying kilns; the artifacts are now in the Strathnaver Museum. The Forestry Commission maintains a series of interpretive panels that describe daily life in the village before the Clearances.

Directly across from the Rosal site and on the opposite bank of the River Naver is a plaque in honour of Donald Macleod, the stonemason,

Clearances historian and author of the seminal *Gloomy Memories*. Also in the area is a monument to the 93rd Sutherland Highlanders. The regiment served with distinction throughout the British Empire but most famously during the Crimean War in 1854 when the *Times of London* correspondent William Russell described the unit as a "thin red streak tipped with a line of steel" which became popularized as the "Thin Red Line"; today it generally refers to a military formation that is thinly deployed.

Ross, Donald [n.d.]. Glasgow lawyer who wrote about the evictions in Strathcarron, Sutherland, and the destitution in Knoydart, Inverness-shire; from Ross-shire, probably Dornoch. Ross is best known for his accounts of the Knoydart evictions and the Greenyards, Sutherland, "massacre." He was a tireless campaigner for the Gael, an investigative journalist before the term was even used. His work primarily appeared in the *North British Daily Mail* and the *Inverness Advertiser*. He argued that there would be plenty of land for the people if it were managed properly and if people were taught "the necessary skills." The problem was not the indolence of the people, he insisted, as much as the lack of tenure, aggravated by the constant threat of eviction.

After Thomas Mulock left the *Ensign*, Ross became one of its most prolific, and passionate, writers on the Clearances. Unlike Mulock, who had grown pessimistic about the fate of the Highlanders and even recommended emigration as the only option, Ross remained hopeful that their situation could be improved, for a time at least, until he too agreed with Mulock, giving up hope that any real change, either from the landlords or the government, was forthcoming.

Ross did not, however, stop writing about the Clearances. On the contrary, his career entered an entirely new phase: that of a journalist who, rather than campaigning for change, would simply write about what he witnessed with his own eyes. Consequently, his reporting in such work as *The Glengarry Evictions and The Russians of Ross-shire, on the evictions in Knoydart and Greenyards* emphasized the brutality of the evictions and contained graphic descriptions of the beatings that the Highland women were subjected to after they put up some resistance to the removals. Using the phrase "savage butchery," he went on to describe how the officers used their batons to break the backs and smash in the skulls of "defenceless women":

> The men who can hold up their heads, and brag that they were maimed, and bruised, and levelled to the ground, with their sticks, so many females in half-an-hour [*sic*], are a disgrace to a civilised and Christian country.

Despite his obvious knowledge and clear passion on the subject, Ross never questioned the rights of the landlords to evict the people, just the way they went about it.

Rum, Isle of. In 1826 Rum was cleared of its 400 people by Maclean of Coll; they emigrated to Cape Breton. In 1957, the island became a Nature Reserve. The island was cleared of its inhabitants—some 400 people—to make way for one sheep farmer and 8,000 sheep.

runrig. A communal approach to farming and a form of subsistence farming that existed in pre-Improvement Scotland in both the Highlands and Lowlands; a primitive and essentially wasteful type of agriculture that was vulnerable to climate and disease. It was the predominant form of agriculture in Highland Scotland from the 16th century and would even endure in places into the 20th century.

Runrig. Had its origins as a Scottish country-dance band, a ceilidh band; in the mid-1960s called the Skyevers although the band didn't actually form until 1973. Two brothers from Skye (but originally from North Uist), Rory Macdonald, his younger brother Calum Macdonald and an accordionist friend from Skye, Blair Douglas, all met in Glasgow, as part of the so-called expatriate Gaelic mafia. They called themselves the Run-Rig Dance Band. Wearing purple shirts, black trousers and bowties, they played their first official ceilidh gig at Glasgow's Kelvin Hall. Donnie Munro, also from Skye, was enrolled at Gray's School of Art in Aberdeen but saw the band perform at home in Skye in the summer of 1973 at the local village hall. Shortly thereafter, he was asked to join the band.

The band has never thought of themselves as Celtic revivalists or Gaelic-language activists. Their music is organic; that is, they create music that comes out of their own Gaelic traditions and experiences. And yet by no means are they provincial or parochial. On the contrary, their influences are wide ranging, from Elvis Presley and the Beatles to Led Zeppelin and Fairport Convention to Highland authors (Neil Gunn), poets (Sorley Maclean) and historians (James Hunter, John MacInnes).

Runrig's early albums, including *Play Gaelic* (1978) and *Recovery* (1982), were largely folk and acoustic based before they moved on to explore a broader and more expansive rock sound. Many of their most successful songs are anthemic in theme and arrangement. Prior to signing a recording contract with Chrysalis Records in 1988, all of their records were released on their own Ridge Records label and they have since returned to that arrangement.

Other members of the band include or have included Malcolm Jones (b. 1959), Iain Bayne (b. 1960) and Brian Hurren (b. 1980). Bruce

Guthro (b. 1961), who replaced Donnie Munro when he left the band, is the current lead vocalist. Other former band members have included Blair Douglas, Robert Macdonald, Campbell Gunn, Richard Cherns and Peter Wishart.

The band's music is steeped in the history and culture of the Gael; many of their songs are in Gaelic (of the 115 songs listed in their songbook, 40 are in Gaelic). The lyrics reflect their Christian faith (although not to the point of being preachy or off-putting) and many of their songs have a hymnal quality. Their themes are ancestry and heritage, remembrance, land rights, exile and emigration. The sea is a recurring motif. One album in particular, *Recovery*, is nothing less than the social history of the Gael in musical form. "Their popularity in Scotland," writes Aonghas MacNeacail in the foreword to *Flower of the West: The Runrig Songbook*, "has done much to change attitudes to Gaelic: where once the language belonged out there, among the hicks ... its recognition is now widely seen as an essential element in defining what it means to be Scottish."

Their studio albums are *Play Gaelic* (1978), which consists of entirely Gaelic songs; *Highland Connection* (1979); *Recovery* (1981); *Heartland* (1985); *The Cutter and the Clan* (1987), which was their first recording on a major label; *Searchlight* (1989); *The Big Wheel* (1991); *Amazing Things* (1993); *Mara* (1995); *In Search of Angels* (1999), their first album with Bruce Guthro as lead singer; *The Stamping Ground* (2001); *Proterra* (2003), with Paul Mounsey; and *Everything You See* (2007).

Runrig has often sung about the Clearances, whether indirectly or specifically, as well as commented on the Highland experience or exhibited Gaelic influences:

- "Abhainn An T-Sluaigh" (The Crowded River) from *The Big Wheel*: influenced by Gaelic psalm singing and an example of Gaelic "soul" music;
- "An Toll Dubh" (The Dungeon) from *Recovery*: the band's attempt to emulate the waulking of the tweed, the traditional Gaelic custom where newly woven cloth is soaked in urine and then bounded around a wooden table by a collection of women. Rather than doing it the old way, though, they chose a less romantic solution: old telegraph poles;
- "An Ubhal As Àirde" (The Highest Apple) from *The Cutter and the Clan*: a modern-day Gaelic psalm and the first Gaelic song to make it into the U.K. Top-20;
- "Canada" from *Amazing Things*: a song set on the Canadian prairies but inspired by the pathos of emigration;
- "Cearcal A' Chuain" (The Ocean Cycle) from *Highland Connection*: a hymn-like ode to the sea and life itself, it has become a modern-day Gaelic standard;

- "Cum 'Ur N'aire" (Stay Aware) from *Play Gaelic*: a warning not to forget one's heritage;
- "The Cutter" from *The Cutter and the Clan:* a heartfelt tale of the modern-day pains of emigration and the ties that bind inspired by the real-life figure of Johnny Morrison, a lorry driver from Lochmaddy, North Uist, who emigrated to Canada but returned every year to cut his mother's peat;
- "Dá Míle Bliadhna" (Two Thousand Years) from *In Search of Angels*: a *paean* to lost history, and the often painful legacy of being a Gael;
- "Dance Called America" from *Heartland:* the title and image is taken from Boswell's *Journal of a Tour to the Hebrides* at Ostaig on the Isle of Skye in October 1773, in which the Highland aristocracy at the time told the Scotsman about a dance called America that mimicked the 18th-century emigration epidemic ("the epidemical fury of emigration") but the Macdonald brothers also make specific reference to the Clearances in their mentioning of the landlords (the "peasant trials"), the "Improvers" and the clergy who did next to nothing to prevent it ("the praying men of God / Who stood and watched it all go on"). The phrase is also the title of James Hunter's book, *A Dance Called America: The Scottish Highlands, the United States, and Canada*, published in 1994;
- "Empty Glens" from *Proterra:* a Clearance song that makes subtle reference to two 1960s folk-protest classics, Dylan's "Blowin' in the Wind" and Pete Seeger's "Where Have All the Flowers Gone?";
- "Fichead Bliadhna" (Twenty Years) from *Highland Connection*: a scathing critique of an education system that ignored Highland, and specifically, Gaelic history;
- "Flower of the West" from *The Big Wheel*: steeped in Hebridean imagery and influenced by Neil Gunn's *Highland River*;
- "Fuaim A' Bhlàir" (The Noise of Battle) from *Recovery*: the martial beat and the *puirt-a-beul-* (mouth music-) influenced chorus accompany the lyrics that recall the time when the Gaels were the primary foot soldiers of the British Empire, from France and Germany to Spain and Italy to the "plains of Canada";
- "The Old Boys" from *Recovery*: homage to Col. Jock Macdonald of Viewfield, Portree, but also a lament to the loss of an older way of life accompanied by, and appropriately so, the sound of the pipes;
- "Recovery" from *Recovery*: originally called "After the Clearings" (the same line appears in the lyrics); the inspiration for the title track came from *The Making of the Crofting Community* by James Hunter, which Calum Macdonald had been reading, as well as the centenary of the *1886 Crofting Act*; it is a song that looks at the tragedy of the past (with reference to John MacPherson, the Glendale Martyr) and nods toward a brighter future;

- "Rocket to the Moon" from *The Cutter and the Clan*: a rousing song about emigration—specifically the Selkirk Settlers in Winnipeg—written on a scrap of paper while the songwriter was riding in a bus in Manitoba;
- "Saints of the Soil" from *The Greatest Flame*: celebrates the community buyout of the Assynt crofters;
- "Siol Ghoraidh" (The Genealogy of Goraidh) from *Searchlight*: a tribal calling out of names;
- "Skye" from *Heartland*: homage to the band's island home with a touch of mouth music thrown in for good measure;
- "The Summer Walkers" from *The Stamping Ground*: inspired by Timothy Neat's book of the same name and referring to the travelling people (some call them gypsies), and among the great bearers of folk tradition;
- "'S Tu Mo Leannan / Nightfall on Marsco" from *Recovery*: a nod to one of the band's major inspirations, Sorley Maclean;
- "Tir A' Mhurain" (Land of the Maram Grass) from *Searchlight:* a song of welcome to the Gaelic world, its landscape and its language as well as a celebration of survival.

See also Bruce Guthro; Calum Macdonald; Rory Macdonald; Donnie Munro

S

Sabhal Mòr Ostaig. In 1973 the late Sir Iain Noble, a merchant banker and Gaelic learner, established Sabhal Mòr Ostaig, the Gaelic College, on Skye's Sleat peninsula on former MacDonald estate sites. By creating the college, he hoped to reverse the "brain drain" that historically affected the area. Housed in a converted farm steading, it started on a humble scale with short courses, summer schools and night classes in Gaelic and the Gaelic culture. In 1998, its new Columba Campus, Àrainn Chaluim Chille, opened, its lighthouse-like tower inspired by the Iron Age brochs scattered throughout the north and west of Scotland. In 2002, the college opened a satellite Gaelic centre on Islay, the Columba Centre, or Ionad Chaluim Chille Ile. The Fàs building has graphics, film and broadcasting studios, houses artists-in-residences and even has a daycare centre. In addition, the Fàs building houses Cànan, a Gaelic multimedia company and Sealladh, a film company. In 2010, the Skye campus had 75 full-time students, 111 part-time students, 182 distance learners and 755 people attending short courses. It offers four degree courses in Gaelic and Gaelic culture, media and traditional music and has initiated working partnerships with the University of Aberdeen and the Royal Scottish Academy of Music and Drama in Glasgow.

Sage, Rev. Alexander (1753-1824). Minister of Kildonan, in Sutherland, from 1787 to 1824, during the height of the Clearances.

Sage, Rev. Donald (1789-1869). Born Kildonan, Sutherland; son of Alexander Sage; minister at Achness during the last of the Strathnaver Clearances. He wrote *Memorabilia Domestica* (1889), an important eyewitness account of the Strathnaver Clearances.

Scott, Sir Walter (1771-1832). Novelist and poet, born in Edinburgh. Scott witnessed a Clearance when he accompanied his father, who was a Writer to the Signet, as a child. (Under Scots law, a Writer to the Signet is a judicial officer who prepares warrants and writs or, in English and American parlance, roughly, an attorney at law.) The Clearance witnessed involved a family named MacLaren in the "romantic scenery" of

Loch Katrine, as Scott recalled. When the party arrived at the scene, though, the house was already empty. They stayed at the dwelling overnight and even had some of the food that had been left behind. The MacLarens, as it turned out, went to America. "I sincerely hope they prospered," Scott offered.

The influence of Scott in romanticizing the Highlander and the Highlands cannot be overestimated. It was he who orchestrated the visit of George IV to Edinburgh in 1822. What's more, Scott was popular in the Americas, especially in the southern American states. As Michael Newton has observed, "His imaginative repackaging of Highland heritage inspired people to give [Scottish names that appeared in his works to] their pets, their children, their homes, and their plantations."

Scottish Centre for Diaspora Studies (SCDS). Under the direction of Tom Devine, the Centre was established in 2008 with an endowment of £1 million from Alan Macfarlane, an Edinburgh fund manager, and his family; it is believed to be the largest single private donation ever made for historical research in the U.K. The Centre is housed at the University of Edinburgh within the University's School of History, Classics and Archaeology. Its purpose is to reassess Scotland's influence on the world stage and in particular to examine how Scots influenced societies and cultures abroad—not just in Australia, New Zealand, Canada and the United States, but also in such areas as Sweden, Poland, France and Asia. SCDS organizes conferences, symposia, seminars, workshops and public events on the topic of the Scots diaspora. Another purpose of the Centre is to develop a critical mass of doctoral students in the history of the various Scottish diasporas from medieval times to the present with particular emphasis on their nature, origins and impact at home and abroad. The Scottish government has funded various postdoctoral fellowships in the Centre. In October 2012, the Scottish government awarded the Centre £37,000 to support a two-day conference during the Year of Homecoming (July 2014) under the title "The Global Migrations of the Scottish People: Issues, Debates and Controversies."

Scottish Centre for Island Studies (SCIS). An inter-disciplinary approach to learning that falls under the aegis of the Faculty of Business and Creative Industries, at the University of the West of Scotland. The SCIS sponsors or co-sponsors numerous events. In 2011, along with Sabhal Mòr Ostaig, it sponsored Ainmeil Thar Cheudan: A Centenary Celebration of Sorley MacLean (1911-2011).

Scottish Crofting Federation (SCF). Based in the Kyle of Lochalsh, SCF is an independent non-governmental organization. It is the only member-led organization dedicated to crofting and is the largest association of small-scale food producers in the U.K. The purpose of SCF is to safeguard and promote the rights, livelihoods and culture of crofters and the crofting communities.

Scottish diaspora. Until recently such a phrase was considered by scholars to be an oxymoron. According to the literature, there was no such thing as a Scottish diaspora per se. Paul Basu, however, makes a strong case for its existence. Using R. Cohen's set of characteristics, Basu bases his conclusion on numerous factors, including (1) the dispersal of people from the homeland, often in a traumatic way; (2) the popularity of several overseas destinations, specifically British North America (now Canada), Australia, New Zealand, the United States and South Africa; (3) a collective memory and myth about the homeland, including an idealization of the ancestral home; (4) an ethnic group consciousness over a particular period of time based on a strong sense of distinctiveness. Significantly, the idea of Scotland, the Scotland of the diasporic imagination, is Highland Scotland, not Lowland Scotland. It is the land of mountain and sea, kilt and tartan. It is not, to emphasise a point, urban Scotland or the radical Clydeside Scotland. Whether in Nova Scotia or North Carolina or New South Wales, the identity that is embraced by the overseas Scots communities is also a Highland identity.

Generally speaking, the Scots assimiliated quickly and easily. With a few exceptions—Cape Breton in Nova Scotia, Glengarry County in Ontario, Winnipeg in Manitoba, perhaps Cape Fear in North Carolina and Waipu in New Zealand—there is no definable Scottish community identity aside from the fondness for Burns suppers and participation in Highland games. In other words, there are not many truly hyphenated Scots, and nowhere was integration more rapid than in the United States even though well over one million Scots settled in the U.S. between 1815 and 1914. "This is a startling feat of amnesia," Aitchison and Cassell conclude. "American Scots, one of the most successful of all the immigrant nationalities, soon had little reason to think about Scotland except in terms of a comfortable nostalgia." The truth is, most Americans of Scots ancestry paid no particular heed to Scotland. They might express an admiration for the country and wish it well, but on a day-to-day basis, Scotland as a country barely entered their mind. They did not become involved in Scottish politics. It is probably fair to say that you could ask almost any American Scot who is the head of the Scottish government; in all likelihood you will be met with a blank stare or the scratch of the head. As Aitchison and Cassell point out, the Scotland that the vast majority of diasporic Scots typically are interested in is the Scotland of old, not the Scotland of the future, nor even the Scotland of the present.

Even so, some 30 million people around the world claim some kind of Scottish ancestry. How many of that number is of Highland background is hard to say, but the Scottish diaspora is a subject that increasingly has been studied by scholars throughout the world, including Celeste Ray, Michael Newton, Jenni Calder, Jim Hewitson, Billy Kay, James Hunter, Tom Devine, Lucille Campey and Duncan Sim, among others.

Selkirk, Lord Thomas Douglas (1771-1820). Fifth Earl of Selkirk; founded the Red River Settlement in Canada in 1811, where many of the Kildonan people emigrated, and he was a great defender of emigration for the betterment of the people. Selkirk believed that the establishment of Scottish settlements in Canada—that is, relocating Scots to British North America—was a solution to the perennial "Highland problem." Born at Saint Mary's Isle, Kirkcudbrightshire, Scotland, Selkirk attended the University of Edinburgh, studying to become a lawyer.

He brought dozens of families from the dispossessed Highlanders with the intent of transforming the Red River area into a farming colony. In addition to Red River, he also purchased land and settled crofters in Belfast, Prince Edward Island (1803) and in Baldoon, in Upper Canada (Ontario), in 1804.

See also Selkirk Settlers

Selkirk Settlers. The origins of Winnipeg (Manitoba, Canada) began with the arrival of 23 Highlanders from Kildonan in Sutherland in August 1812, the first permanent settlement in what was to become Winnipeg.

In 1811 Selkirk purchased stock in the Hudson's Bay Company (HBC) and was granted the territory of an area called Assiniboia, which consisted of more than 300,000 square kilometers (116,000 square miles) in fur-trading country. He planned to develop an agricultural colony but complicating the transaction was a rival fur company, the North West Company that was opposed to the colony in Rupert's Land, as it was called. Selkirk thought he had a good case since his claim from the HBC charter of 1670 granted a monopoly in Rupert's Land.

Selkirk selected Miles Macdonell as governor of the new settlement. Macdonell's party sailed, on the *Edward and Ann* from Stornoway in July 1811. The ship landed at York Factory on the Churchill River on September 24, too late to make the inland voyage to Assiniboia. Instead they wintered along the Nelson River. On August 30, 1812, they travelled 700 miles to the site of their new colony, situated near the fork of the Red and Assiniboine Rivers. They settled on the west side of the Red River, north of what is now known as Winnipeg's Point Douglas.

A second group of colonists sailed on the *Prince of Wales* in June 1813, leaving from Stromness. Of this second group, most were from Kildonan and Helmsdale in Sutherland. They had offered to pay more rent to the landlords in order to stay, but were rebuffed; they chose exile to the Red River Colony instead, paying Selkirk the passage money of £10 per head for 40 ha (100 acres) of land at 5 shillings per acre along with one year's provisions. The second group endured a rough passage on an overcrowded ship—typhus broke out and there were several deaths. The party arrived at Fort Churchill on the Churchill River instead of York Factory where accommodation and supplies were waiting. Weak with fever and lacking proper clothing and supplies, several died at a makeshift camp. In early April, 31 men and 20 women led by Archibald McDonald left York Factory on snowshoes, hauling supplies on sleds. They reached York Factory in three weeks. The rest of the party arrived at Red River on August 25, 1814, more than a year after leaving Orkney.

Macdonell was concerned about the scarcity of food at the settlement. In January 1814 he placed an embargo on export of pemmicam from Assiniboia. Pemmicam was made from buffalo meat, a staple food of the fur trade. North Westers refused to obey the embargo, attacked the colony and burned the buildings. The remaining settlers fled to the Jack River, near Norway House under the protection of Chief Peguis. In August they were rescued by Colin Robertson, Selkirk's recruiter. The group then returned to the colony where John McLeod of the HBC and a settler by the name of Hugh McLean and several others built Fort Douglas, the colony's new headquarters.

A third party, mostly from Kildonan, sailed on July 17, 1815, on the *Hadlow*, arriving at Red River on November 3 the same year under Robert Semple, the new governor of the colony. Lord Selkirk was still in Canada seeking government aid for the defence of the Red River settlers, but was unsuccessful. What's more, the North Westers refused to recognize the HBC's charter rights, culminating in a conflict between the North Westers and the HBC by spring 1816. Under the orders of the North West Company, Captain Cuthbert Grant rode toward Fort Douglas, accompanied by 70 men covered in full war paint. Indians had warned Semple of the party but he chose to try to negotiate and went on foot with about 20 men for a meeting where angry words were exchanged. Outnumbered, Semple and his men were slaughtered in what has come to be known as the Battle of Seven Oaks. With the aid of Peguis, Macdonell's troops retook Fort Douglas. Once again, the settlers returned.

In June 1817, Lord Selkirk reached the Forks, where he stayed for four months. He organized plans for the settlement to be called Kildonan. The settlers were promised a Gaelic-speaking minister.

Selkirk left the settlement for the last time in September 1817 and returned to England in November 1818. Exhausted and suffering from ill-health, he died on April 8, 1820, in Pau, France, of consumption.

In 1821 the HBC and the North West Company merged. Kildonan eventually grew and its name was changed to Winnipeg, the capital and largest city in Manitoba.

See also Selkirk Settlers Monument; Winnipeg, Manitoba

Selkirk Settlers Monument (*Exiles*). A full-scale bronze replica of *The Emigrants* statue in Helmsdale. Dedication ceremonies took place in September 2008 in Winnipeg, a few yards from the spot on the Red River where the first Scots settlers arrived in 1812. Many of them were from Kildonan in Sutherland. The replica was commissioned by the St. Andrew's Society of Winnipeg and co-sponsored by John Webster and Dennis Macleod, directors of Clearances Centre Ltd.

See also Helmsdale; Winnipeg

Sellar, Patrick (1780-1851). Born in Moray; advocate and later sheep farmer and factor to the 1st Duke of Sutherland. Sellar ordered countless evictions during the Highland Clearances and personally ordered some of the most egregious evictions himself.

As the largest sheep farmer in Scotland, Sellar had a reputation for being both harsh and greedy. He personally supervised the notorious evictions at Rosal village (ironically, Sellar's grandfather was evicted from Morayshire during the Lowland Clearances). Because of his actions at Rosal, he was put on trial in Inverness in April 1816, on the charge of culpable homicide (manslaughter) for the murder of two people, including an old woman. A jury composed of his peers found him not guilty.

Although Sellar died a wealthy man in 1851 at the age of 70, he must surely be remembered, certainly in the Highlands and throughout the Highland diaspora, as one of the most hated men in Scottish history.

Fictional versions of Sellar appear in several works, including Neil Gunn's novel *Butcher's Broom* (1934), Kathleen Fidler's children's story, *The Desperate Journey* (1964) and Iain Crichton Smith's *Consider the Lilies* (1968). Several scathing poems have been written about him, including Smith's bitter "The Clearances." In the traditional poem, "Satire on Patrick Sellar," he is described as having a "grey head like a seal" while his "lower abdomen resembles that of a male ass." The character of Sellar also appears in John McGrath's incendiary play *The Cheviot, the Stag and the Black Black Oil*.

Sellar is buried at Elgin Cathedral.

See also Donald Macleod; Rosal; Strathnaver

sept. Subdivision or branch of a clan.

Seven Men of Knoydart. Refers to the seven men who unsuccessfully staged the last "land raid" on British soil. In 1948, seven ex-servicemen claimed their right to the land on the farms of Scottas and Kilchoan, by Inverie, from the pro-Nazi owner, Lord Brocket. In 1991 the Knoydart Land Raid Commemoration Committee erected a cairn at Inverie in honour of the Seven Men of Knoydart.

Shaw, Margaret Fay (1903-2004). A pioneering collector of Scottish Gaelic song and folklore and photographer, Shaw was born in Glenshaw, Pennsylvania, USA, of partial Scots and English heritage. (Her great-great grandfather, John Shaw, had emigrated from Scotland to Philadelphia in 1782.) Orphaned as a teenager, she was sent to stay with a distant cousin in Helensburgh, outside of Glasgow, and spent a year at St. Bride's School there. At a recital in Helensburgh, she heard Gaelic songs for the first time—from none other than the famous collector Marjory Kennedy-Fraser. It was a life-changing experience. She later returned to the United States, but before long went back to Scotland, arriving on the island of South Uist in 1929 and cycling her way through the Hebrides before choosing to settle on South Uist. "Of all the islands I'd visited," she wrote, "there was something about South Uist that just won me; it was like falling in love; it was the island that I wanted to go back to." She lived for six years on the island with two sisters in a small cottage.

In 1934 she met the folklorist John Lorne Campbell. They married a year later. In 1938 the couple bought the island of Canna. Many years later, in 1981, they bequeathed it to the National Trust for Scotland. Shaw continued to live on the island, at Canna House, even after Campbell died in 1996.

Her most important work is *Folksongs and Folklore of South Uist* (1955), which is considered a classic in its field. Her autobiography, *From the Alleghenies to the Hebrides,* is a delightful and evocative portrait of island life. Like George Washington Wilson, Werner Kissling, Paul Strand, Gus Wylie, Murdo MacLeod and others, her black and white photography captures the immediacy of island life and the lifestyles of the crofters that she chronicled so lovingly, whether a pipe-smoking middle-aged islander making heather rope or two young girls in home-made Halloween masks.

Shaw's love of the Hebrides was deep and enduring, and it was reciprocated; it is where she is buried.

See also John Lorne Campbell; Werner Kissling; Paul Strand; George Washington Wilson

Sheep Clearances. Another term for the Highland Clearances.

Shetland. Clearances occurred throughout Sheltand, including Unst and Yell. Perhaps the worst instances though took place on the island of Fetlar in 1822 and again in 1870 when the Nicolsons of Brough cleared the entire west side of the island.

shielings. Between June and August, families went up into the hills' high pastures for grazing cattle in the summer and lived in small huts called "shielings" in order to allow the cattle new grass to feed on after the long, dark winter. Livestock were also taken into the hills during summer when scarce arable land was needed for crops. Time spent at the shielings was not all work, though. It was promised that there would be plenty of time for fun and socializing—young people used the shielings as an opportunity for courting, for example. The shieling system disappeared with the introduction of sheep farming.

shinty. A very old game—thought to predate Christianity—played primarily in the Highlands but also in areas with large Highland populations. It is similar to the Irish game of hurling although it has its own rules and regulations. From a North American perspective it is probably most similar to field hockey or ice hockey, although, again, there are significant differences. Scottish immigrants in Nova Scotia have referred to it as "shinny." The fast-moving game is played with a stick (called a *caman*), traditionally made of hickory, ash or birch tree, and a leather ball. The rules of the game are governed by the Camanachd Association.

There is a close link between shinty and Gaelic identity. In Gaelic poetry its absence has been evoked to symbolize negative social change: the depopulation of the glens means fewer people available to play the game. Poets ranging from William Livingston to Mary MacPherson (Big Mary of the Songs) have placed the game in the context of the Clearances and emigration. Typically, shinty was played on New Year's Day throughout the Highlands and Islands. In "The Glasgow Shinty Match" ("Camanachd Ghlaschu"), MacPherson celebrates the game's being played by exiled Highlanders in Glasgow. When the match ended, the players would walk over to Hope Street—specifically, to the rooms of the Glasgow Highland Association, writes MacPherson, with "a piper ahead of them." Runrig has referred to shinty in several songs: the word "caman" appears on "Recovery" ("See the young men late in the glen / All with camans in hand"), in "Pride of the Summer" ("the camans swing without warning") and especially "Clash of the Ash," which celebrates the amateur status of the sport ("We don't play for fame, we don't play for cash"). The song appears on their 2007 release

Everything You See. The album jacket features a shinty player, caman in hand and in a full swing.

Sinclair, Reverend Dr. Alexander Maclean (1840-1923). Presbyterian minister, author, self-educated Gaelic scholar and educator; born in Glenbard, Nova Scotia. In May 1888, Sinclair became the pastor of a church in Belfast, PEI, where descendants of many of the Selkirk Settlers of 1803 still kept the Gaelic language and traditions alive. Throughout the following decade and into the early years of the 20th century, while attending to his congregation, Sinclair published numerous collections of Gaelic poetry and a number of genealogical studies. These include *Comhchruinneachadh Ghlinn-a-Bhaird: the Glenbard Collection of Gaelic Poetry* (1890); *The Gaelic Bards from 1411 to 1715* (1890); *The Gaelic Bards from 1715 to 1765* (1892); *Orain le Iain Lom Mac-Dhomhnaill: Poems by John Lom MacDonald* (1895); *The Gaelic Bards from 1775 to 1825* (1896); *Na Bàird Leathanach: The Maclean Bards* (1898-1900); and *The Gaelic Bards from 1825 to 1875* (1904).

Sinclair also contributed important articles to the *Transactions of the Gaelic Society of Inverness* in Scotland, the *Celtic Review* and the *Celtic Monthly*. Between 1907 to 1914, he lectured on Gaelic language and literature at St. Francis Xavier College in Antigonish and at Dalhousie University in Halifax.

Sinclair, Sir John of Ulbster (1754-1835). As the first, and highly influential, president of the Board of Agriculture and one of the most prominent of the so-called Improvers, Sinclair brought improved methods of agriculture and stock-breeding to northern Scotland, but he also brought the Great Cheviot Sheep, which would change the landscape and history of Scotland. Sinclair trumpeted the superior quality and higher value of Cheviot wool. He sponsored and organized—and wrote the introduction to—the *Statistical Account of Scotland* in 1799, a pioneering work of statistics, which was published in 21 volumes (1791-1799). Despite being a Highlander himself, Sinclair was more critical than his English counterparts, calling his fellow Gaels not only indolent but also savage. In fact, barbarism, he suggested, seemed to be their natural state.

> Content to live in activity and idleness, without even the necessaries of life, they would rather starve in the midst of profusion than apply themselves to industry and labour.... They would rather cringe to their landlord and their laird to obtain the crumbs that fall from his table than attempt to get a decent and comfortable livelihood, by cultivating the land entrusted to their care, or applying themselves to any trade....

Sinclair was a great advocate of the new agricultural methods that were sweeping the country in the late 18th century. Consequently, large tracts of land on his Caithness estate were let out to tenants that Sinclair brought in to keep these new breeds of Cheviot sheep. Ultimately, this meant that the tenants who were already there were given smaller plots of land elsewhere, often in environmentally hostile coasting areas. At the same time, he believed that sheep and people could co-exist. In his own Caithness, for example, he maintained that sheep farming could be introduced and the rental value of the properties be increased without removing the people.

de Sismondi, Jean Charles Léonard (1773-1842). Born in Geneva, a Swiss economist who criticized the land ownership rights in Britain, among the first serious critic of industrialization and the negative consequences of laissez-faire capitalism. De Sismondi compared British property laws unfavourably to Swiss property laws. "The law has given the Swiss peasant the guarantee of perpetual ownership," he wrote, "while in the British Empire it has given this same guarantee to the Scottish Lord, and left the peasant in insecurity. Let anyone compare the two countries and judge the two systems." His theories influenced two other critics of the Clearances, the stonemason turned journalist Hugh Miller and Karl Marx.

Skene, W. F. (William Forbes) (1809-1892). Historian, born in Inverie, Knoydart, Inverness-shire; educated at the Royal High School in Edinburgh as well as in Frankfurt and Aberdeen. Graduated in law and practised as a lawyer in Edinburgh. His major works include *The Highlanders of Scotland* (1837) and the massive *Celtic Scotland; a History of Ancient Alba* (3 vols., 1876-1880).

Skye Museum of Island Life. Located two miles south of Duntulm, Skye, on the western shore of the Trotternish peninsula. Consisting of a group of seven thatched cottages and old smithy, it represents island life in a crofting township at the end of the 19th century. Nearby, along a footpath, is Kilmuir Cemetery, where Flora Macdonald lies beneath an enormous Celtic cross not far from where she landed with Bonnie Prince Charlie who was disguised as her Irish maid "Betty Burke."

Smith, Adam (1723-1790). Scottish philosopher and economist born in Kirkcaldy and one of the major figures of the Scottish Enlightenment. Smith exerted a profound influence on the Highlands albeit indirectly; although possessing little first-hand knowledge of the region, his economic theories, especially his advocacy of lassiez-faire capitalism, affected the thinking of the Improvers. He referred to the Highlands as a backwater of feudalism whose only cure for ingrained poverty was the proper division of labour.

Smith, Iain Crichton (Mac a' Ghobhainn) (1928-1998). Poet and novelist, born in Glasgow but raised on the Isle of Lewis, he was educated at the Nicolson Institute, Stornoway, and was a graduate of Aberdeen University. In addition to being a writer he was also a teacher in Clydebank, Dumbarton and Oban, where he retired in 1977. His first collection of poems, *The Long River*, was published in 1955, followed five years later by the highly praised *Burn Is Aran*. Themes of exile, homecoming, eviction and identity are common in his work, particulary in such poems as "Going Home," "Two Songs for a New Ceilidh," "Culloden and After" and "The Exiles." But his best-known work is undoubtedly the short novel *Consider the Lilies* (1968). Written from the point of view of an elderly woman evicted from her croft by the notorious factor, Patrick Sellar, it is a powerful indictment of the Clearances. Another of Smith's poems, "The Clearances," also condemns Sellar. Employing the collective voice of all victims of the Clearances, Smith wishes nothing less than to see Sellar burning in hell in the same way that he torched the thatched roofs of the Clearance Highlanders so that his "hot ears slowly learn" what it was like. Smith's work also reflects his disdain for dogma and most forms of authority, especially blind obedience.

Soillse. Established in 2009, Soillse ("enlightenment") is a national network for Gaelic research with connections to various academic centres, including Sabhal Mòr Ostaig. Among its purposes is to influence government policy on Gaelic education and language.

Sollas Clearances, North Uist. One of the most infamous Clearances took place at Sollas in North Uist in the late 1840s. Hundreds of people left Lord Macdonald's North Uist estate in 1849, and sailed to Québec. His evictions at Sollas caused great controversy. Significantly, it was also one of the few—but certainly not only—times where the people put up resistance.

At the time of the first attempt at eviction, in August 1849, Sollas had some 600 souls. The land was under trust—that is, administered by the agents of trustees. The owner Lord Macdonald wanted to remove virtually the entire population from the estate and ship them off to Canada. But the people refused to go. Some of the more outspoken people even warned officers of "instant death" should they try to remove them from their homes. After the first attempt failed, the officers tried again, only to be met by a flurry of stones and other projectiles. The virulence of the resistance convinced the authorities to allow the people to stay until the following spring but only if they, ultimately, agreed to emigrate.

Authorities were not about to give up entirely. They returned with a contingent of nearly forty constables from Inverness and still the people refused to budge, asking at the very least that they be allowed to stay on until the "next season." Refusing to compromise, the authorities then proceeded with the ugly business of clearing people off the land, throwing the furniture out of their modest dwellings and evicting weeping mothers, often with babies in their arms. As the evictions continued, a crowd gathered, which soon grew from about 50 to some 100 residents, mostly women but also a few men and boys, some armed with large stones.

And yet, despite the severity of the situation, many if not most of the mainstream press continued to support the landlords. The editorial in the *Scotsman* opined: "That the removal of the cottars in the Western Highlands will generally be a benefit to the land, and through that to the country at large, is, we fear, *indisputable*." On the other hand, the *Inverness Courier* turned a more sympathetic, if paternalistic, approach, protesting against the "extensive and systematic expatriation of the people." Instead, the *Courier* suggested that rather than forcing the people to emigrate perhaps it would be better to try to improve their condition at home. Finally, faced by the devastation caused by the Highland potato famine, hundreds of North Uist inhabitants accepted assisted passage in ships to Canada and Australia in 1850 and 1852.

See also North Uist; resistance

Somers, Robert (1822-1891). As editor of the *North British Daily Mail* between 1849 and 1859, Somers was a crusading critic who wrote about the Clearances. Prior to assuming the editorship of the *Daily Mail*, Somers was for a brief time editor of the Edinburgh-based *Scottish Herald* until it merged with the Hugh Miller's *Witness* when Somers became an assistant under Miller. In 1847 Somers joined the Glasgow-based *Daily Mail* and was sent to the Highlands as a "special commissioner." During that autumn he wrote one of the most comprehensive—if romanticized—critiques of the Clearances in a series of 27 letters published in 1848, along with an additional 4 letters, as *Letters from the Highlands*.

Somers's letters recommended often radical proposals for the Highland solution even as he sometimes expressed patronizing views toward the people. He called the Improvement policy then running rampant in the country "barbarous," as well as a "heartless extirpation" of a people. He also appeared alarmed at the "gigantic scale" of the operations as deer began increasingly to supplant the once ubiquitous sheep. The crofters, he claimed, were no better than serfs; they were, in fact, slaves. Sheep walks and deer forests, according to Somers, were a waste of land and labour not to mention a squandering of precious natural resources. As remedies, he suggested the passage of a liberal and effectual poor law and legislation that would not only protect the unemployed but virtually guarantee a right to work. "Liberty to work is a natural right," he insisted. Moreover, he recommended abolishing the archaic Scots feudal law of entail and encouraged a greater and better means of education. The solution to the Highland problem, claimed Somers, lay with the redistribution of the soil—that is, taking back the land from the sheep farms and the deer forests and giving it back to the people—radical ideas for their time.

Southey, Robert (1774-1843). English poet, one of the so-called Lake Poets, was born in Bristol and served as Poet Laureate of Great Britain for 30 years from 1813 until his death in 1843. Although his fame has been long eclipsed by that of his contemporaries and friends William Wordsworth and Samuel Taylor Coleridge, Southey's verse still enjoys some popularity.

In 1819, through a mutual friend, Southey met the premier civil engineer in Britain, Thomas Telford, and struck up a friendship. From mid-August to early October 1819, Southey accompanied Telford on an extensive tour of the latter's engineering projects in the Scottish Highlands, keeping a diary of his observations along the way. The report was published in 1929 as *Journal of a Tour in Scotland in 1819*. Southey was shocked by the destruction of the old Highland society even as he expressed dismay at the squalid living conditions that he witnessed. But he was especially sickened by the behaviour of the landlords.

Spencer, Herbert (1820-1903). Born in Derby; philosopher, sociologist and political theorist. Spencer had a major influence on Charles Darwin—he wrote about evolution before Darwin—and it was he, not Darwin, who coined the famous phrase "survival of the fittest," in *Principles of Biology* (1864), after reading Darwin's *On the Origin of Species*. Spencer applied evolutionary ideas to modern society and is sometimes called a Social Darwinist, applying the survival of the fittest to society in general. Spencer's theories thus appealed to the Improvers and to the Adam Smith-type laissez faire economists who believed in free markets and resisted outside interference with natural law, even if it led to starvation and eviction.

squatters. The lowest class in Highland society, the squatters had no rights.

Statutes of Iona (1609). Passed by the Scots Parliament which required the chiefs to educate their sons in Lowland schools; consequently, by the early 19th century the Gaelic aristocracy was already heavily anglicized, the sons of gentlemen were educated in English. (Prior to the statues, the upper classes had been educated in classical Gaelic.)

Stewart, Andy M. (b. 1952). Former lead vocalist and instrumentalist of the popular Scots folk group Silly Wizard; especially known for his beautiful renditions of traditional Scottish songs as well as his original compositions in the traditional style; born in Perthshire. Silly Wizard formed in 1972 and disbanded in 1988. Stewart wrote several songs about the Highland Clearances, specifically "The Highland Clearances" for the band's *So Many Partings* (1990); "I Mourn for the Highlands" and the title song appear on his 1991 recording with Phil Cunningham and Manus Lunny, *Fire in the Glen*. Stewart set the music to "I Mourn for the Highlands" to a Gaelic song, "The Dispersal of the Gaels," written in 1898 by the prolific Gaelic writer Henry Whyte (1852–1913)—a romanticized portrait of the Clearances that depicts the Highlanders as essentially passive if "gallant and brave" while condemning the landlords as "tyrants" who "brought desolation," replacing men with sheep and deer.

The covers of both albums depict the worst images of the Clearances and are reminiscent of the contemporary illustrations of evictions: *Fire in the Glen* shows a Highland couple walking away from their ruined cottage as flames shoot from the roof; their loyal dog trails behind; *So Many Partings* portrays a wizened Highland couple standing outside their smouldering croft, their only belongings a creel wrapped around the woman's upper body, while the man carries a walking stick, a basket and sleeping gear.

Stewart, Gen. David of Garth (1772-1829). Soldier and historian; born in Perthshire. Stewart served at various times with the 42nd, 77th and 78th Highlanders and with the 90th Perthshire Light Infantry. In 1794 he served in the West Indies campaign and later saw action during the Napoleonic Wars in Eygpt and on the Peninsula. Promoted to the position of major-general, in 1829 he was appointed governor general of St. Lucia but died shortly after his arrival. He is best known as the author of *Sketches of the Character, Manner and Present State of the Highlanders of Scotland* (1822), considered the first reliable history of the Scottish regiments and the clan system.

Stowe, Harriet Beecher (1811-1896). Born in Litchfield, Connecticut; the daughter of the outspoken and popular preacher Lyman Beecher. Stowe was an American abolitionist during the Civil War. Although she wrote more than twenty books, her best known is the wildly popular—and highly influential—anti-slavery novel *Uncle Tom's Cabin*. The book inspired the abolitionist movement in the North even as it inflamed the residents of the South. John Prebble has called the book sentimental and melodramatic but even he could not deny its impact, ranking it "with the Bible, the Koran, and *Das Kapital* in its profound effect on human emotions and actions."

When Harriet Beecher Stowe (whom Prebble describes rather uncharitably as a "dumpy" woman) toured Britain in 1853 she was one of the most famous women in the world, even for a time a bigger name than, notes Prebble, Dickens or Thackeray. The second Duchess of Sutherland invited her to spend a few days at Dunrobin Castle in the Highlands. Stowe made a second visit to Britain in 1856, staying at Inveraray Castle and gathering "notes on the Clearances."

In 1857 she published a journal of her visit which she optimistically called *Sunny Memories of Foreign Lands*. Among other things, it was a defence of the Duchess of Sutherland and the Improvement policy that led to the Clearances. When Donald Ross, the Glasgow lawyer and muckraker, had sent her some of Donald Macleod's pamphlets on Sutherland that described the tenants who had been turned out of their homes and their cottages set on fire so they would not be able to return, Stowe still refused to believe that her friend the Duchess would do anything to harm her people. She referred to negative stories about Patrick Sellar as scandalous, especially in light of the fact, she pointed out, that he had been exonerated by a jury of his peers. And as for the Duchess, she dismissed the criticism of her as "ridiculous" and "excessively absurd," concluding that "if there had been the least shadow of a foundation for any such accusations, I certainly should have heard it."

Donald Macleod had his own response but his memories were less "sunny." His book, *Gloomy Memories*, was published in 1857.

Strand, Paul (1890-1976). Iconic American photographer and filmmaker who along with other giants of the profession helped turn photography into a 20th-century art form. Influenced by Ansel Adams and Edward Hopper, he studied under Lewis Hine at the Ethical Culture Fieldston School and often used the camera as a tool for social reform.

As a Communist during the Cold War, Strand chose to travel to South Uist at a time when it had been announced the previous year that the island would be the base for a rocket testing range in order to test NATO's first nuclear missile (the site was never built). In 1954, Strand and his wife Hazel spent three months on South Uist and Benbecula photographing fishermen and crofters and their wife and children. He had as his guide Dr. Alasdair Maclean, the brother of Sorley Maclean. Strand once said that he liked to photograph "people who have strength and dignity in their faces; whatever life has done to them, it hasn't destroyed them. I gravitate toward people like that." The portraits that appeared in the finished book, *Tir a'Mhurain: Outer Hebrides*, offer evocative and powerful images of a lost time. In the mid-1950s South Uist, everyone spoke Gaelic and the women sang the old Gaelic songs.

Long out of print (it was originally published in 1962 in Leipzig in the former communist East Germany), *Tir a'Mhurain* (Gaelic for "the land of bent grass") was re-released in a new edition (in 2005) by Aperture, consisting of 105 duotone black and white photographs. In 1983 the Paul Strand Archive was bequeathed to Aperture, a non-profit foundation and publisher of fine art photography.

Strathaird Clearances, Skye. Some of the tenants on the farms owned by MacAlister were in arrears and unable to pay. In 1850, the tenants on four farms, or 477 people, were given writs of removal. They refused to emigrate.

Strathconon Clearances. Located in Easter Ross, the Strathconon estate belonged to the Balfour family, the same family as future prime minister Arthur James Balfour. The Clearances in the area, though, date as far back as 1803 when James Hogg reported during his tour of the Highlands that sheep farms were being created in the area. The people who were cleared in the 1840s from Strathconon were not in arrears; rather they were evicted to make way for two sheep farmers, one from Moray and the other a local. Some of the displaced went to neighbouring estates; others went to the Black Isle. According to Alexander Mackenzie, some 500 people were removed from their ancestral lands. Like the famous and widely covered Glencalvie Clearances, the Strathconon Clearances received extensive coverage. The *Inverness Courier*, for example, sent a reporter to cover the flittings.

Strathglass Clearances, 1801. Cleared by William Chisholm and his wife Elizabeth Macdonell; within a year, the tenants were in Nova Scotia, or on their way there. Notes Edwin Muir:

> Then, with the chieftain dead and his heir studying at Cambridge, the removal of tenants was continued by his wife. She was a MacDonnell of Glengarry.... The son then returned to the north and completed the clearances so thoroughly that within a decade of their commencement, about 10,000 clansfolk were removed from the strath and the only Chisholms remaining were said to be the chiefs themselves.

Two years later, four ships carried 500 people from Strathglass. It was during these years that more than 5,000 people, according to Richards, were driven from the glens. Indeed, many people emigrated from Fort William, Isle Martin and Knoydart during these times.

Strathmore Clearances, Sutherland. Cleared in 1819; some 100 people were forced on emigrant ships from nearby Loch Eriboll for Ontario.

Unfortunately, their ship sunk on the journey over during a winter storm, and all on board perished.

Strathnaver Clearances. Among the most notorious of the Clearances; occurred in three phases. The first, which began in 1807, led to the creation of the great sheep farms, stretching from the shore of Loch Naver to near Lairg as well as the lands around Letterbeg. During the second phase, the farm let to Patrick Sellar was cleared between 1814 and 1816. The third occurred from 1819 to 1822 when farms of Langdale which were also let to Sellar. Further Clearances and reorganization of sheep farms took place after the purchase of the Reay and Bighouse estates by the Sutherland family. But Clearances also occurred after the three main phases had ended. Between 1839 and 1841, for example, a fish merchant, James Anderson, cleared 32 families from various farms in the area.

Other townships in Strathnaver that were cleared include Achanlochy, some one and a half miles south of Naver Bridge on a minor road to Skelpick and Dunviden, an additional two miles south; Achadh an Eas on the east side of Loch Naver; Grumbeg on the west side of the loch; and Grummore, also on the west side of the loch. Foundations of houses are evident throughout the area.

Between 1807 and 1821, some 10,000 people were removed from Strathnaver and elsewhere on the vast Sutherland estate. Many were relocated onto marginal land on the coast in villages such as Bettyhill. Main areas of resettlement were around Scourie, around Durness, and on the coasts of Tongue and Farr. In order to make ends meet many of the Highlanders were forced to do jobs they were not well suited for, including fishing and kelp-gathering. In 1814, factors ordered the tenants out of their homes. All possessions were burned. Women, the elderly and children stood outside as all their worldly belongings were destroyed. To make sure the inhabitants didn't return burnt dwellings were levelled so that the sheep that were to replace them could graze. When the kelp industry collapsed following the end of the Napoleonic Wars, many chose emigration to the New World. Furthermore, potato crop failures in 1836 and again in 1846 led to additional emigration.

One of the largest townships to be cleared was Rosal (see separate entry).

See also Rosal village; Patrick Sellar; Strathnaver Museum

Strathnaver Museum. Surrounded by a graveyard and housed in the former St. Columba's Parish Church in the small fishing village of Bettyhill, about 19 km (12 miles) north of Syre and 48 km (30 miles) west of Thurso, the locally run museum features period models and artifacts. In the church graveyard is a Pictish cross, ca. 800 AD.

Built ca. 1700, the building was renovated in 1975 and opened the following year. Through graphics, artifacts and models, the museum tells the story of the Strathnaver Clearances, including an exhibit on the Clearance village of Rosal and a small model of Achanlochy. One of the rooms is dedicated to Clan Mackay (Mackay is still the most common surname in the area).
See also Strathnaver

Strathnaver Trail. A Clearances trail mapped with introduction and site notes written by Jim A. Johnson, published by the Highland Council and funded by the Heritage Lottery Fund, the Highland Council, Caithness and Sutherland Enterprise, Scottish Natural Heritage and Entrust. In all it lists 16 sites, including the following:

- Grummore settlement which was cleared in the early 19th century for sheep farming;
- Grumbeg burial ground, settlement and chambered cairn; a pre-Clearances settlement. Among the ruins are the remains of a 4,400- to 6,000-year-old chambered tomb;
- *Gloomy Memories*' memorial to the author and stonemason, Donald Macleod;
- Syre and Syre Church; a corrugated iron church and Patrick Sellar's former house;
- Rosal settlement, souterrain and hut circles; Rosal was once of the largest of the approximately 50 pre-Clearances townships of Strathnaver;
- 93rd Sutherland Highlanders, a monument, originally located at Syre, commemorating the raising of the famous Highland regiment;
- Achanlochy settlement, an early pre-Clearances township;
- Farr Church (Strathnaver Museum) and Farr Stone: St. Columba's Church, now the Strathnaver Museum, was built in 1774 on the site of an older church from at least ca. 1223 while the Farr Stone is an 8th-century Christianized Pictish stone.

Strathnaver Trilogy. *See* fiction of the Clearances

Strathspey. Numerous Clearances took place in Strathspey: Glen Banchor was cleared of seven families to make way for sheep while Glen Feshie was let as a deer forest in 1812. Glen Avon (pronounced "A'an") was cleared to make way for deer in 1838 and again in 1841. At the foot of the Cairngorms, Glenmore was cleared in 1827 by the Duke of Gordon to make way for grouse shooting, followed by deer forests (1843). In addition, he built the original Glenmore Lodge. The Glenmore people, says Rob Gibson, were removed to the village of Boat of Garten. In 1923 the Gordon family sold the estate to the Forestry Commission.

Stuart, Charles Edward (1720-1788). The famous Bonnie Prince Charlie of romantic myth; in reality, a rather pathetic figure, the straw man of Highland history—hardly the stuff of legends. Commonly known as Bonnie Prince Charlie or The Young Pretender, he was the second Jacobite pretender to the thrones of England, Scotland and Ireland. This claim was as the eldest son of James Francis Edward Stuart, the son of King James VII (James II of England). Charles is perhaps best known as the leader of the failed Jacobite Rising of 1745, in an attempt to restore the Stuart monarchy to the British throne, which ended in defeat at the Battle of Culloden, effectively ending forever the Jacobite cause and—correlated by popular sentiment if not historical fact—the beginning of the end of traditional Highland culture. Charles's chase through the Highlands of Scotland after the uprising has turned him into the romanticized figure of later years that, after the immediate threat had subsided, could safely appear on shortbread tins.

In 1688, King James II of England and VII of Scotland was deposed for political and religious reasons and replaced on the throne by his daughter Mary and her Protestant husband, William of Orange (the King Billy of legend). Those who disagreed with the deposing of the Stuart monarch and felt that the Stuarts were the true and only heirs to the English, and later, British throne, were called Jacobites (Jacobus being the Latin for James). Thus, the Jacobite Risings began in 1690 when Bonnie Dundee (John Graham of Claverhouse, Viscount Dundee, 1648-1689, nicknamed "Bonnie Dundee") tried to regain the throne for King James. In 1715 King James's son, James, otherwise known as the Pretender, made another attempt, and once again in 1719. The most famous Jacobite attempt to regain the British throne for the Stuarts was the 1745 Rising of Charles Edward Stuart (Bonnie Prince Charlie).

The prince arrived in Scotland in 1745 to claim the British throne for his father, on the French ship *du Teillay* with only the Seven Men of Moidart at his side and little other support. News of the prince's arrival at Loch nan Uamh was kept secret while he persuaded the local chiefs to support a military campaign. On August 11, 1745, Charlie crossed the loch and went to Kinlochmoidart, where he stayed until 17 August. From there he eventually travelled up Loch Shiel to stay at Glenaladale before arriving at Glenfinnan by rowboat. On August 19 at 5 pm, he raised the standard. Initially, the Jacobite army could boast of some rather remarkable victories—including one that went as far south as Derby in the English Midlands—before ultimately retreating back north to Scotland.

The 1745 campaign, which had begun with such promise, ended with a devastating defeat at Culloden Moor on April 16, 1746. With no support from the French, as expected, and government troops searching the countryside and patrolling the shorelines, Charles decided to hide out in the Hebrides. With the assistance of Flora Macdonald, he sailed out on April 26. After several months on the run, he returned to the mainland, finding shelter in a series of caves, before leaving Scotland forever at midnight on September 19, 1746.

Charles Edward Stuart died in Rome, a dissipated and pathetic figure, on January 31, 1788.

Suishnish, Skye. The prominent geologist Sir Alexander Geikie witnessed firsthand the Suishnish Clearances of 1854. Will Maclean's *Beach Allegory* (1973) was inspired by it, as was Sorley Maclean's long (and unfinished) poem *The Cuillin* (1938). Suishnish is important for another reason: it was among the last of the major Clearance episodes. It was also one of the few times where a death was directly attributable to the Clearances: after being evicted a man returned to his ruin of a home and died from exposure to the cold and snow. Like Strathnaver, Suishnish was a particularly cruel clearance. Some of the people who were evicted were quite elderly: some were older than 80 and at least one was 90. Richards cites the case of a partly bedridden 96-year-old woman who, after being removed from her dwelling, remained homeless for several weeks.

Suishnish is notable for yet another reason: resistance. Although relatively minor in effort, three of the so-called offenders were brought to trial and charged with obstruction of justice.

Sutherland. A vast country in the Northern Highlands. John Macleod has called Sutherland "one of the saddest places in Scotland" since most of its population was evicted during the most notorious of the Clearances. The worst of the Sutherland Clearances took place roughly between 1807 and 1821, unmatched in both scale and organization. Factors of the Countess of Sutherland and her husband Lord Stafford removed between 6,000 and 10,000 people to the coast says Tom Devine in what was "the most remarkable example of social engineering undertaken in early nineteenth-century Britain."

Sweeney, William (b. 1950). Glasgow-born composer whose work is strongly influenced by Scottish folk music, especially the Gaelic tradition. Among his Gaelic-inspired works is *An Turus*, an opera based on the medieval tale of Diarmid and Grainne (1997)—and in fact the first full-length opera in Gaelic—and "An Coilltean Ratharsair" (The Woods of Raasay) (1993), a song based on Sorley Maclean's poem. In the 1980s, he composed for acapella voices "Salm an Fhearainn" (Psalm of the Land), which was inspired by Gaelic psalm singing.

T

tack. A lease or verbal leasing agreement. Titles to the lands were for the most part the exclusive property of tribal Highland chiefs, who carved out what were called tacks, or tenancies, from the land and then distributed them to their relatives. The tacksmen, as they were called, granted sub-tenancies in return for rent and other services.

tacksmen. Large tenants or large leaseholders who sublet land to the lower members of Highland society. Tacksmen served as tenants-in-chief during peacetime and clan officers during war; tacksmen sublet to their tenancy and then usually sublet again and again until, by the time it reached the lowest rung on the social ladder, the cottar, the land offered bare subsistence.

As elite members of Scottish society tacksmen acted as factors or estate managers under a laird. They sublet their own land to subtenants who did most of the work. During the Age of Improvement which, in the 1770s, introduced better farming methods, their role in Highland society was becoming increasingly obsolete. When they themselves faced higher rents, many chose to emigrate. Consequently, many promoted group emigration, encouraging large numbers, sometimes entire communities, to emigrate with them en masse to the New World.

Their decline, points out Tom Devine, "was one of the clearest signs of the death knell of the old Gaelic society." They were replaced by other members of the middle class, largely sheep farmers from the south and cattle ranchers.

Telford, Thomas (1757-1834). Civil engineer, architect and stonemason born at Glendinning, in Eskdale, Dumfries-shire; the son of a shepherd. Telford was a noted road-, bridge- and canal-builder. In 1823, an Act of Parliament provided for the building of up to 40 or so churches and manses in communities without any church buildings; hence the use of the term "parliamentary church." The government commissioned Telford to develop a design that was affordable and simple. Ultimately, 32 of his churchs were built in the Highlands and Islands, including, most famously, the Croick Church, site of the infamous Glencalvie Clearances.

Thomson, Derick S. (Ruaraidh MacThòmais) (1921-2012). Poet; born in Stornoway; was the most influential and important voice in Gaelic poetry during the second half of the 20th century. Thomson grew up in Pabail (Bayble), home of another great Gaelic poet, Iain Crichton Smith (Iain Mac a' Ghobhainn).

He was educated at the Nicolson Institute in Stornoway and at the universities of Aberdeen, Cambridge and North Wales. He served in the Royal Air Force (RAF) during the Second World War and taught at the universities of Edinburgh, Aberdeen and Glasgow, where he became Professor of Celtic in 1963, from which he retired in 1991. In 1952 he founded the Gaelic language quarterly *Gairm* and was instrumental in establishing the Gaelic Books Council in 1968, serving as its chairman from 1968 to 1991. He was also president of the Scottish Gaelic Texts Society, a former member of Scottish Arts Council and the first recipient of the Ossian Prize, in 1974.

He published numerous collections of poetry including *Creachadh na Clàrsaich* (Plundering of the Harp/Clarsach), which shared the Scottish Book of the Year Award in 1983. Among his notable works is *An Introduction to Gaelic Poetry*, which was first published in 1974; he also edited the invaluable *Companion to Gaelic Scotland* in 1983. His publications include an English-Gaelic dictionary that appeared in 1981 and was for many years considered the most important reference book of its kind.

A master of free verse, Thomson's themes were many, including fond memories of growing up on Lewis, his faith, heritage and especially the emotions associated with the Clearances. His powerful Clearance poem, "Strathnaver," takes as its title one of the most brutal of Clearance memories, evoking the travesties of Patrick Sellar. By calling him—and others of his kind—out by name he makes real those who did the unthinkable; that is, he denounces a man who put an old woman "out on to the dung-heap" in order, he notes with great sarcasm, to "demonstrate how knowledgeable they were in Scripture." It remains one of the most magnificent of the contemporary Clearance poems.

Thomson died in Glasgow at the age of 90.

Timespan Heritage Centre. Located on Dunrobin Street, in the Highland town of Helmsdale; a local history museum whose purpose is to record and display local history and life. In 2011 the museum introduced a Highland Clearances 200th Anniversary Project called Museum without Walls. It was established in honour of the 200th anniversary of the instigation of large-scale clearances of the Strath of Kildonan (in

1813, a party of more than 80 people left Kildonan and emigrated to the Red River Settlement, which would later become Winnipeg). The museum uses digital technology on its interpreted Clearances Trail in the Strath of Kildonan, a software application (app) for smart phones and tablets. App users can access the information or they can go to Kildonan itself. Visitors can download the app in Timespan or hire an iPod. The Trail consists of ten locations from Helmsdale and *The Emigrants* monument to the area around nearby Kinbrace and the local cemetery. In addition, the Trail features wooden waymarkers.

Tiree. Between 1846 and 1852, 93 tenants and their families were cleared by the Duke of Argyll; many emigrated to Bruce and Grey counties in Ontario. At the turn of the 20th century, the Crofters' Commission and the Congested District Board ordered a number of large amalgamated farms to be restored as crofts.

Tobar an Dualchais / Kist–o-Riches. An online oral archive consisting of 11,500 hours of recorded songs, tunes and folklore in Gaelic, Scots and English culled from the archives of the School of Scottish Studies in Edinburgh, the National Trust for Scotland's Canna Collection and BBC Scotland.

Tolbooth Steeple. Inverness. Located at Church and Bridge Streets, the building was erected in 1791 and housed the old courthouse and town jail. It was here, in 1816, that a jury acquitted Patrick Sellar of culpable homicide (manslaughter) for his part in the Strathnaver Clearances two years earlier. Highland Heritage, an education trust, sponsored the raising of a plaque in 1993 on the Church Street side of the steeple. The plaque ends with the Gaelic words, "*Se fìrinn is ceartas a sheasas*" (It is truth and justice that will endure).

townships. Scotland once had thousands of "townships," small farming communities where groups of families worked together. Two hundred and fifty years ago, the world began to change. The townships were replaced by modern farms, crofting and large estates. A few townships remained, but most of these had gone by 1900. Auchindrain was the last to survive, until 1963.

Auchindrain is a nationally significant township because with its random scatter of vernacular buildings it retains, to a far greater extent than anywhere else, the character and feel of a township from before the start of agricultural improvement in the late 18th century, a time when most of Scotland's rural population lived in these types of communities.

transhumance. As practised in the Highlands; refers to moving livestock to the hill pastures during the summer months to take advantage of the land's grazing potential.

Trevelyan, Sir Charles (1807-1886). British civil servant; born in Taunton, Somerset; Assistant-Secretary to the Treasury. He administered Irish relief works during the infamous Irish Famine of the 1840s as well as relief during the Highland Potato Famine of 1846. He also served as chairman of the Highlands and Islands Emigration Society, and chairman of the Society's London Committee, and supervised relief operations of the Central Board for Highland Relief in Scotland. During the height of the Irish Famine, Trevelyan famously wrote that the famine was a "mechanism for reducing surplus population," a view apparently influenced by the theories of English economist Thomas Malthus. He applied this theory too to the Highland situation, seeking a "final settlement" for the so-called Highland problem. One of his "solutions" involved transporting a "surplus" population of some 30,000-40,000 people to Australia. Ideally, it would be for the benefit of the country, he believed, if the idle Highlanders were replaced by industrious Germans, "an orderly, moral, industrious and frugal people, less foreign to us than the Irish or Scotch Celt...." In Trevelyan's way of thinking, the Highlands were not really overpopulated, they were just saturated, as Fenyö notes, by the *"wrong kind of people."* *The Scotsman* also agreed with Trevelyan's "solution." Collective emigration, the paper maintained, would remove "a diseased and damaged part of our population. It is a relief to the rest of the population to be rid of this part." Tom Devine makes the disturbing point that from a modern standpoint this approach "might be described as a strategy of ethnic cleansing."

U

Uig Clearances (Lewis). In 1796, 358 summons of removal were issued by Francis Humberston Mackenzie for the entire parish of Uig in Lewis, turning it into a sheep farm. Many of the people who left Lewis in the latter half of the 18th century went to what they called the Cold Country (Canada), to work in the fur trade for the Hudson's Bay Company. Throughout the 19th century a succession of landlords evicted their tenants to make way for sheep. Between 1780 and 1813, some 500 summons of removals were issued, rising to 2,300 between 1818 to 1832. In 1793, for example, the entire parish of Uig was let as a sheep farm. Uig, thus, became a parish of deserted townships. One of the landlords, James Matheson, offered to pay passage of his destitute tenants to Canada and some 1,700 or so accepted, with most of them settling in the "gloomy forests" of Nova Scotia, Prince Edward Island, Québec and Ontario.

Ullapool Museum. Located at 7-8 West Argyll Street, in the West Highland town of Ullapool. A natural and social history museum that is housed in a former Church of Scotland building designed by the engineer Thomas Telford. The museum has a model of the *Hector*, the vessel that brought Scottish emigrants to Pictou, Nova Scotia, in 1773, and letters from descendants now living outwith Scotland. Exhibits examine the earliest settlers of the area, the evolution of the clan system, the Highland Clearances and the development of the fishing industry.

Ulva. A small island off the west coast of Mull where 350 people out of a population of 500 were evicted between 1847 and 1849 by the proprietor F. W. Clarke.

V

Valtos. Crofters of Valtos on Skye were notable because they were the first crofters in Skye who refused to pay increased rents for their crofts.

Vatersay raiders Vatersay is the westernmost permanently inhabited island in Scotland. For years the men from Barra had appealed to the owner, Lady Cathcart, for crofts on Vatersay which at the time was run as a single farm and inhabited only by a farmer and his workforce. Lady Cathcart, who lived in a castle in Aberdeenshire, refused the requests. In 1908, close to starvation, ten men from Barra and Mingulay chose to take matters into their own hands. They were imprisoned in Edinburgh for refusing to leave Vatersay, the island that they had raided (or invaded) and where they had erected makeshift huts and planted potatoes without the permission of the landlord. They were charged with breach of interdict (or injunction) and contempt of court.

Their arrest caused such an uproar throughout Scotland that two years later the government agreed to buy Vatersay and repopulate it with descendants of people who had been cleared from the island when the notorious Gordon of Cluny owned it.

Since 1991 it has been linked by a causeway to the Isle of Barra. The island is also known for a ceilidh band, the Vatersay Boys; the band members are great-grandsons of Vatersay raiders, Duncan Campbell and Donald MacIntyre. A darker side of Vatersay was portrayed in the 1986 BBC production, *Flight from Vatersay*, about a bored and disillusioned young man who migrates to Glasgow in search of a better life and a brighter future.

village bards (*bàird bhaile*). Local poets who composed songs, both serious and satirical, for informal house visits or visiting sessions. The village bard was an important figure in the Gaelic oral tradition for centuries and even up to the Second World War. Although unpaid for their efforts, they were considered the spokesmen or spokeswomen for their communities and wielded considerable power on public opinion.

The roots of the unpaid village bards date back to the professional bards, an exclusively male profession. However, several women performed the functions of the bards. They included Sìleas na Ceapaich (Julia MacDonald of Keppoch) and Màiri nighean (Mary MacLeod). Either way, the professional male songmakers were employed by chiefs and composed primarily eulogies, elegies and various other praise poems.

As the clan chiefs became more and more anglicized, they turned their interests to maintaining their expensive lifestyles in Edinburgh and London. Because their tenants were no longer needed militarily and were systemically cleared from the land to make way for more profitable sheep, and later deer, the clan chiefs consequently no longer needed the services of professional bards.

W

Wade, George (1673-1748). British Army officer who held Highland command from 1726-1737. Wade built roads and bridges from Dunkeld to Inverness and down the Great Glen. In 1715 he was appointed to disarm the clans after the Jacobite Rising. In 1724 he recommended the recruitment of Highlanders under Gaelic-speaking officers, but he is best known for the so-called Wade roads and bridges. He directed the construction of more than 390 km (240 miles) of roads and more than 30 bridges. Wade's military roads linked the garrisons at Ruthven, Fort George, Fort Augustus and Fort William.

During the Jacobite Rising of 1745, Wade was appointed Commander-in-chief but, unable to combat the Jacobite forces that at one point had advanced as far south as Derby, he was replaced by the infamous Duke of Cumberland who defeated the Jacobite army at Culloden Moor in April 1746.

Wade is buried at Westminister Abbey.

Waipu (New Zealand). Centre of a significant Presbyterian settlement led by Rev. Norman McLeod, a Presbyterian minister who led his people from the Highlands of Scotland to Waipu on the New Zealand's North Island after spending many years at St. Ann's, Cape Breton, Nova Scotia. Five shiploads containing more than 800 settlers (some sources say as many as 1200) arrived at Waipu in the 1850s.

See also Rev. Norman McLeod

Watson, Doc (Arthel Watson) (1923-2012). American singer and folk guitar virtuoso and founder of Merlefest, an annual gathering of folk musicians in North Wilkesboro, North Carolina, named in honour of his son, also a musician, who died at age 36 in a tractor accident on the family farm in 1985. Blind because of an eye infection before his first birthday, Watson is one of the few examples of a Clearances diasporic musician who has documented reports of his family flight from Scotland to escape the Clearances. His great-great-grandfather settled in the northwestern corner of North Carolina which reportedly reminded him of the Highlands. In what could be perceived as the emotional equivalent of an American version of the Clearances, the musician made reference to "outsiders" who were taking over his beloved community when the writer Nicholas Dawidoff visited Watson in the hamlet of Deep Gap in the late 1990s. They bulldozed acres of old hardwood forests in the area and replaced them with upscale housing developments and plantations. But when Watson was growing up in the region, it consisted of no more than a few hundred farmers and "woodsmen" without electricity in small ramshackle wooden houses. Watson shared a bed with two of his brothers.

He was a popular figure during the folk revival of the 1960s, playing in Greenwich Village coffeehouses and on the college circuit alike.

Watson was a master of traditional styles of American roots music, from folk to bluegrass to gospel, a genre which became known as Americana. He drew on bluegrass flat-picking guitar techniques but performed in his own idiosyncratic style. His style influenced generations of young musicians, especially during the 1960s. Indeed, he is credited with single-handedly increasing the use of acoustic flat-picking and fingerpicking on the guitar. His flat-picking style, according to folklorist Ralph Rinzler, had no precedent in country music history. Watson died after undergoing abdominal surgery in a Winston-Salem, North Carolina, hospital.

Weber, Max (1864-1920). German sociologist and political economist best known for coining the phrase "Protestant work ethic" and author of the seminal *The Protestant Ethic and the Spirit of Capitalism* (1904). Weber influenced social theory, social research and sociology itself for generations. The concept of the Protestant ethic emphasizes diligence and frugality in that the moral benefit of hard work is a reflection of a person's good moral character. Although Weber's book was published after the heyday of the Clearances, its legacy was felt during the early decades of the 20th century in the lingering negative attitudes held by non-Gaels toward Gaels, who believed that Highlanders were at heart lazy and lacking in virtue.

West Highland Free Press. Newspaper that began publication in April 1972 in Kyleakin by Brian Wilson, who originally hailed from Dunoon. While at Dundee he had spent a summer working on a newspaper based on the Isle of Arran."[T]he idea of an island paper stayed with me." After graduating from University of Dundee (where he edited the school newspaper), Wilson enrolled at the Centre for Journalism Studies at Cardiff. Wilson and three fellow graduates—Jim Innes, Jim Wilkie and Dave Scott—started the *West Highland Free Press* when two sisters—a retiree and a schoolteacher—in Kyleakin offered them office and accommodation space. From the start, Wilson made his position clear: his goal was to establish a truly community newspaper "representing and respecting the aspirations, interests and beliefs of the people we ask to buy it." His targets were also quite clear. He sought to upset the status quo and attack, when necessary and appropriate, the moneyed and landowner class. The Gaelic slogan on its masthead ("*An Tir, an Canan 'sna Daoine*"—the Land, the Language, the People) sums up its ethos. Its regular columnists and contributors include writer and poet Angus Peter Campbell, who writes a weekly Gaelic column; founding editor Brian Wilson; and journalist and author Roger Hutchinson.

Now employee-owned, the paper continues as the fourth estate watchdog.

West Highland Museum, Cameron Square, Fort William. Established in 1922, the purpose of the museum is to record, preserve and display items of interest to the West Highlands. Special emphasis is placed on the Jacobite Risings of the 18th century. Among items of note are bagpipes recovered from Culloden and a 19th-century Scottish harp. Less dubious is the so-called secret portrait of Bonnie Prince Charlie, which, when polished, reveals the perfect likeness of the fugitive prince.

whiteness. In the 19th century several ethnic groups were not considered "white," including Jews, Italians, Irish and Slavs. Lowland Scots typically identified themselves with the Anglo-Saxon English, and thus maintained their distance from the Scottish Gaels. There is evidence that English and Lowland Scots colonists in the 18th century did not consider Gaels to be white. James Oglethorpe, for example, the leader of the Georgia settlement, separated the Highlanders from other whites.

Wilkie, David (1785-1841). Painter; born in Cults, Fife; the son of a parish minister. In 1799 he studied at the Trustrees' Academy in Edinburgh. He emulated the Dutch style of the Old Masters in such works as *The Penny Wedding* (1818) and *The Preaching of John Knox before the Lords of Congregation, 10 June 1559* (1882). His historical paintings were Scottish in theme and manner. *Blind Fiddler* (1806), for example, evokes an idyllic Highland setting even as it offers an example of Highland poverty, albeit with great sympathy and attention to detail.

From a Highland perspective, the most important of his paintings is probably *Distraining for Rent* (1815). "Distraint" refers to the seizure of property in order to receive payment of rent. Consequently, during the act of distraining, the "distrainor" seizes the personal property of another person without prior court approval. In the painting a farmer and his family, unable to pay the rent, must confront the reality of eviction. Even as the farmer's neighbours protest, the bailiff fills out an inventory of contents, ignoring the emotional turmoil surrounding him. Given that many of his patrons were aristocrats Wilkie took great artistic risk with this painting. Indeed many patrons reacted negatively toward his work.

Wilson, George Washington (1823-1893). Pioneering Scottish photographer who established a successful business that mass-produced photographic prints. A native of Aberdeen, he earned a reputation as one of Scotland's premier photographers. His clients included Queen Victoria and Prince Albert (he documented the building of Balmoral Castle from 1854 to 1855). More than 40,000 of Wilson's photographic plates exist today; most of them are housed at the University of Aberdeen. Wilson printed his images onto a 21-cm (3.25-inch) square glass plate; his staff members hand-coloured each work and sold the images to the lantern slide companies that proliferated in the 1880s. In the role of Photographer Royal for Scotland, Wilson made several visits to the Highlands and Islands.

Wilson took some now classic images of the Highlands during the Clearances era.

Winnipeg, Manitoba. Founded by Highland Scots from Kildonan in Sutherland at beginning of the 19th century; included those from the last great wave of Highland emigration in the 1920s. In the summer of 1813, more than 100 people, who were evicted from their homes in and around the vicinity of the Highland town of Helmsdale, left Sutherland for the Red River in Manitoba on the Canadian prairie. Because they arrived so late in the season they were forced to winter by Hudson Bay. By 1814 they reached their destination at the intersection of the Red and Assiniboine rivers in what would become the modern city of Winnipeg.

In June 2008 a statue commemorating the thousands of Scots who were evicted during the Clearances was unveiled in Winnipeg. Called *The Exiles*, the statue is the first of its kind outwith Scotland. The statue is a replica of *The Emigrants* statue that First Minister Alex Salmond unveiled in Helmsdale. *Exiles* is a ten foot high bronze statue depicting a family of four as they leave Scotland and look ahead to a presumably brighter future. It is located close to the Red River where the Earl of Selkirk settled Clearance Highlanders.

Witness. Anti-Clearance newspaper. Under the editorship of Hugh Miller, the *Witness* had the third highest circulation in Scotland, after the *Glasgow Herald* and the *Scotsman*.

Wylie, Gus (b. 1935). Although born in Lowestoft, Suffolk, Wylie spent a considerable part of his childhood in rural Scotland after being evacuated there during the Second World War. He studied fine art at the Royal College of Art. He was a professor of photography at the Rochester Institute of Technology in New York and has also taught in Florence and at the Royal College of Art. His black and white photography of the Hebrides has earned him acclaim as one of the best modern photographers of the Western Isles and places him in the tradition of Werner Kissling and Margaret Fay Shaw, among others.

His photographic books on the Hebrides include *Hebridean Light* (2003) and *The Hebrideans* (2005).

Y

Year of the Sheep (Bliadhna Nan Caorach) (1792). Refers to a climactic moment in Highland history but is more often evoked for the mass resistance to the introduction of the four-footed creatures. Prior to the insurrection there occurred sporadic outbursts. The roots of the insurrection itself, as it was called, originated in protest against the increasing number of sheep in the years up to 1792.

Open insurrection occurred during the summer of 1792. Sometimes called the Ross-shire Insurrection, it started at Kildermorie, on the estate of Sir Hector Munro of Novar. He had leased a large portion of his land to two brothers, Captain Allan Cameron and Alexander Cameron, of Lochaber. They had replaced the original small tenants. When the Cameron brothers brought their own sheep into the area, the few tenants who remained—and who were grazing their own cattle on the heights of Strathrusdale, just south of Kildermorie—were not pleased. Nor were the brothers content with the situation. They impounded, or "poinded," the cattle and demanded payment before they would release them; in other words, they demanded ransom. The Strathrusdale people refused to pay the fines. What's more, they asked the people of a neighbouring Ardross estate if they would help rescue their cattle. They agreed, and were led by Alexander Wallace, otherwise known as "Big Wallace." All told, some fifty men assembled. The cattle were freed and returned to Strathrusdale.

Humiliated, the Camerons lodged a complaint—a precognition—that is, an investigation prior to formal legal action. In late July 1792, witnesses to the precognition on their way to give evidence at Alness were blocked. Stoked by their success, the Strathrusdale people became even bolder. They announced an ambitious plan to retrieve all of the sheep in the counties of Ross and Sutherland in order to drive them across the Beauly River at churches in Alness, Urquhart, Resolis and Kincardine. The plan: people were told to gather at Strathyokel on July 31. The tenants also had demands: a reduction of rents, an increased availability of arable land and an end to the enclosure of common pastures.

About 200 people gathered on July 31, to drive the sheep down south. It took about eight days to finish the exercise. In the meantime, the local authorities got together their own group. Ultimately, twelve people were arrested. The Strathrusdale ringleaders were brought to trial in Inverness in September 1792, and charged with riot, assault and battery—they were found not guilty. However, during the second trial involving the farmers who opposed the sheep walks, seven men were arrested and found guilty and received varied sentences which ranged from fines and imprisonments to seven years' "transportation" to being banished from Scotland for life.

The insurrection made its mark, creating anxiety not only in Edinburgh but as far south as London. It has since entered the Highland folk memory.

York boats. The principal mode of transportation in North America by members of the Hudson's Bay Company (HBC). Modelled on Orcadian fishing vessels, which in turn were descendants of Viking longships, they were able to traverse the vast continent's rivers and lakes.

York Factory, Manitoba. A settlement and factory, or trading post, of the Hudson's Bay Company (HBC), located about 190 km (120 miles) southeast of Churchill. From 1821 to 1873 it was the headquarters of the Northern Department of the HBC. It was designated a National Historic Site of Canada in 1936.

Young, William (1764-1842). First Commissioner and later the chief factor under James Loch for the Stafford estates responsible for some of the early evictions in Sutherland. He later became a wealthy sheep farmer.

Z

Zorra. Township in Oxford County, Upper Canada (Ontario), settled by emigrants from Sutherland, who had initially settled in Pictou before moving farther west. With worsening conditions in Sutherland, there was a subsequent exodus from the parishes of Farr and Rogart who joined the settlement during the early 1840s. Even more emigrants came during the era of the Highland Famine.

Appendix

There is a wealth of primary material on and about the Clearances. The following are some examples, consisting of primary documents, comments, reporting and song lyrics on the Clearances. With a few exceptions, I have chosen to let the words speak for themselves.

Factor Patrick Sellar

The crimes of which Mr Sellar stands accused, are,—
1. Wilful fire-raising; by having set on fire, and reduced to ashes a poor man's whole premisses, including dwelling-house, barn, kiln, and sheep cot, attended with most aggravated circumstances of cruelty, *if not murder!!!*
2. Throwing down and demolishing a *mill*, also a capital crime.
3. Setting fire to and burning the tenant's heath pasture, before the legal term of removal.
4. Throwing down and demolishing houses, whereby the lives of sundry *aged* and *bed-ridden* persons were endangered, if not *actually lost!*
5. Throwing down and demolishing barns, kilns, sheep cots, &c. to the great hurt and prejudice of the owners.
6. Innumerable other charges of lesser importance swell the list.

I subjoin a copy of Mr Cranstoun's last letter to me upon this subject, for your Lordship's information, and have the honour to be, &c.

    (Signed) ROBr. McKID.
Robert MacKid, sheriff-substitute of Sutherland, brought Patrick Sellar to trial.

Very much of the destitution and poverty now existing is the result of reckless, improvident and early marriages entered into without the slightest forethought of future consequences.
    —*George Rainy, owner of Raasay*

I have seen the people reduced to such poverty that they were obliged to feed themselves upon dulse [sea lettuce flakes] from the shore.... I see them now reduced to such a hard condition that I can compare them to nothing but the lepers at the gates of Samaria—death before them and death behind them.
—*Donald Martin, crofter, Tolsta, Lewis, giving evidence to the Napier Commission*

I found Flora Robertson or Matheson, a widow, aged ninety-six years, at Suishnish, in the parish of Strath, Isle of Skye, suffering from the infirmities of old age, and only allowed by the parish the sum of two shillings and sixpence per month. Anything more wretched than the appearance of this old woman I never yet witnessed. Her bed, a pallet of straw and some pieces of old blanket, was on the bare floor. Her appearance, as she lay on this collection of straw and rags, with a thin threadbare dirty blanket over her, was enough to have excited pity [*sic*] in any breast. Her face and arms had the colour of lead—she was evidently starving. She was evicted by the Inspector of the Poor for the parish of Strath in September last, when the rest of the people of Suishnish were turned out. The Inspector showed her no mercy. He then acted as a ground-officer for Lord Macdonald, and assisted by a few similar characters with himself, he carried out that shameful clearance in Suishnish and Boreraig, without regard to age or sex.... After the poor old woman was ejected from her son's house, she was assisted to a neighbouring sheep-cot by two of her grandchildren—Peggy, aged eight years and "Willie," aged eleven years. These poor children helped the old creature up the brae—sometimes they tried to carry her; but their strength was not equal to the task, and they had to just help her as she crawled on her hands and feet.
—*Donald Ross, eyewitness account of the Suishnish Clearances, 1853*

...it was the most wretched spectacle to see these poor people march out of the glen in a body, with two or three carts filled with children, many of them mere infants, and other carts containing their bedding....
—Times *reporter, on the Glencalvie Clearances, 22 October 1845*

In one case it was found necessary to remove the women out of the house by force.... One of them threw herself upon the ground and fell into hysterics uttering the most doleful sounds ... another put up a petition to the sheriff that they would leave the roof over her house ... and the third made an attack with a stick on an officer.... The following year the district was completely and mercilessly cleared of all its remaining

inhabitants numbering six hundred and three souls.
—*Report on the Sollas, North Uist Clearances in the* Inverness Courier, *1849*

Why should we emigrate? There is plenty of waste land around us; for what is an extensive deer-forest in the heart of the most fertile part of our land but waste land?
—*Donald Macdonald, Back of Keppoch*

The land is our birthright, even as the air, the light of the sun and the water belong to us as our birthright.
—*Rev. Donald MacCallum*

[I]t is the wish to [sic] the people that their grievances should be remedied, in order to put a stop to the system of oppression and slavery under which they are labouring at present.
—*Alexander Morrison, Stornoway, giving evidence to the Napier Commission*

The history of the Highland Clearances is a black page in the account with private ownership in land and if it were to form a precedent—if there could be a precedent for wrong-doing; if the sins of the fathers ought to be visited upon the children—we should have an excuse for more drastic legislation than any which the wildest reformer has ever proposed.
—*Joseph Chamberlain, Inverness, September 19, 1885*

...if the present land laws exist much longer the whole population will be paupers except the ministers, factors and landlords.
—*John MacPherson, Glendale, in the* North British Daily Mail, *May 14, 1886*

It was well known to many, if it was somewhat difficult to prove, that professional agitators preceded the Commission and instructed the poorer classes what to say.
—*The Duke of Argyll*

It would be as easy to stop the Atlantic Ocean as to stop the present agitation until justice has been done to the people.
—*John MacPherson, the Glendale Martyr*

The principal thing we complain of is our poverty. The smallness of our holdings and the poor quality of the land is what has caused our

poverty, and the way in which the poor crofters are huddled together, and the best part of the land devoted to deer forests and big farms.
—*Angus Stewart, crofter's son, to Napier Commission; the Gaelic poet Sorley Maclean was his descendant*

Surrounded by sheep farms on every side of us, we have no place for sheep or a horse. Whenever we speak about a horse we will be advertised as lazy. Will you say "lazy man" to a people who carry 200 to 400 creels full of sea-weed every spring time to spread on the arable land?
—*Alexander Nicolson, of Digg, on Staffin Island, on accusations of laziness, to Napier Commission*

I had many relatives among those who were sent away [from Sollas] to America. Several reached America but very few are alive today. We heard that some are well off and some are not. None of those who were evicted ever came back.
—*John Morrison, of North Uist, to Napier Commission*

What good can we get out of deer? The sheep are bad enough. They were the cause of the people being expelled from their places, but still they are better than deer. We can get no use of the deer, whereas if we can afford to buy a sheep, it will at all events provide us with clothes. As for the deer, we are not allowed to kill or eat them. The sheep need shepherds and there is some work connected with sheep for us in the way of smearing and shearing. But deer require no herd, and they can leap the fences and eat our crops. I don't know any work in connection with the deer except some gillies, perhaps.
—*Murdoch Kerr of Achmelvich, crofter's son, to Napier Commission*

[w]e passed through a straggling group of cottages on the hill-side, one of which, the most dilapidated and smallest of the number, the minister entered, to visit a poor old woman, who had been bed-ridden for ten years. Scarce ever before had I seen so miserable a hovel.... The little hole in the wall had formed the poor creature's only communication with the face of the external world for ten weary years. ...What perhaps first struck the eye was the strange flatness of the bed-clothes, considering that a human body lay below: there seemed scarce bulk enough under them for a human skeleton. The light of the opening fell on the corpse-like features of the woman,—sallow, sharp, bearing at once the stamp of disease and of famine; and yet it was evident, notwithstanding, that they had once been agreeable....
—*Hugh Miller, in Eigg, 1845, from* The Cruise of the Betsey *(1857)*

As to those ridiculous stories about the Duchess of Sutherland, which have found their way into many of the prints in America, one has only to be here, moving in society, to see how excessively absurd they are ... the Howard family, to which the duchess belongs, is one which has always been on the side of popular rights and popular reform. Everywhere that I have moved through Scotland and England I have heard her kindness of heart, her affability of manner, and her attention to the feelings of others spoken of as marked characteristics.

Imagine, then, what people must think when they find in respectable American prints the absurd story of her turning her tenants out into the snow, and ordering the cottages to be set on fire over their heads because they would not go out.

Harriet Beecher Stowe, from Sunny Memories of Foreign Lands, Letter XVII *(1854)*

~

Donald Macleod's response to Harriet Beecher Stowe:
I agree with you that the Duchess of Sutherland is a beautiful accomplished lady, who would shudder at the idea of taking a faggot or a burning torch in her hand, to set fire to the cottages of her tenants.... Yet it was done in their name, under their authority, to their knowledge, and with their sanction....

I think, Madam, had you the opportunity of seeing the scenes which I, and hundreds more, have seen ... the ferocious appearance of the infamous gang who constituted the burning party, covered over face and hands with soot and ashes of the burning houses, cemented by torch grease and their own sweat, kept continually drunk or half drunk while at work; and to observe the hellish amusements some of them would get up for themselves.... When they would set fire to a house, they would watch any of the domestic animals making their escape from the flames, such as dogs, cats, hens, or any poultry, these were caught and thrown back to the flames; grand sport for demons in human form.

—*Donald Macleod, from* Gloomy Memories in the Highlands of Scotland *(1857)*

~

Donald Meek indicates that no version of the following blistering poem survives in Scotland. Rather it apparently was brought over with the emigrants to Prince Edward Island. Ian Grimble contends that it was written soon after Sellar's trial, and acquittal, for culpable homicide in Inverness in 1816 although, as Grimble notes, it was not published until

1889 in *The Glenbard Collection of Gaelic Poetry*. The incident in the poem refers to the eviction of William Chisholm at Rosal in Strathnaver by Sellar. Chisholm's mother-in-law, Margaret Mackay, was still in the house when the fire was set. She reportedly died five days later in an outhouse. "Roy" refers to the land surveyor who accompanied Sellar while "Young" is William Young, Sellar's comrade in arms, a successful corn dealer and later the chief factor under James Loch for the Stafford estates. Meek theorizes that "Simpson" was a sailor.

Satire on Patrick Sellar (English translation)
By Donald Baillie

I saw a dream,
and I would not mind seeing it again;
if I were to see it while awake,
it would make me merry all day.

A big fire was ready
and Roy was right in its middle,
Young was incarcerated,
and there was iron about Sellar's bones.

Sellar is in Culmailly,
left there like a wolf,
catching and oppressing
everything that comes within his range.

His nose is like an iron plough-share
or tooth of the long-beaked porpose;
he has a grey head like a seal
and his lower abdomen resembles that of a male ass.

His long neck is like that of the crane,
and his face has no appearance of gentleness;
his long, sharp-shinned legs
resemble ropes of large sea-tangle.

What a pity that you were not in prison
for years, existing on bread and water,
with a hard shackle of iron,
strong and immovable, about your thigh.

If I could get at you on an open field,
with people tying you down,
I would pull with my fists
three inches [of flesh] out of your lungs.

You yourself and your party
went up to the braes of Rosal,
and you set fire to your brother's house,
so that it burned to ashes.

When death comes upon you,
you will not be placed in the ground,
but your dung-like carcase will be spread
lie [yes] manure on a field's surface.

Sellar and Roy
were guided by the Devil,
when they commanded that the compass
and the chain be set to [measure] the land.

The Simpson man behaved like a dog
as befitted the nature of a seaman.
wearing a blue jacket from a shop
and trousers of thin cloth.

It was the black packet of the oil
that brought them to this land,
but they will yet be seen drowned
[and thrown up] on seaweed on the Banff shore.

   —From Donald S. Meek, ed., Tuath is Tighearna: Tenants and Landlords *(1995)*

~

One of the most explicit of 19th-century Clearance poems, Anne Lorne Gillies reports that the tune to which Robertson set the poem was originally composed in honour of Rev. Patrick MacDonald of Strathnaver. Gillies calls Robertson's poem a "masterpiece of hatred and contempt." Once again, Patrick Sellar is here as well as the First Duke of Sutherland and the Duchess of Sutherland.

MacKay Country (Sutherland) (English translation)
By Ewen Robertson

My curse upon the great sheep!
Where now are the children of the kindly folk
who parted from me when I was young,
before Sutherland became a desert?

Appendix

Sixty years have passed
since I left Sutherland.
Where are all my beloved young men
and the girls that were so pretty?

Sellar, you are in your grave—
the wailing of widows in your ears;
the destruction you wrought upon the people
up until last year—have you had your fill of it?

First Duke of Sutherland, with your deceit,
and your consorting with the Lowlanders,
you deserve to be in Hell—
I'd rather consort with Judas.

Duchess of Sutherland, where are you now?
Where are your silk gowns?
Did they save you from the hatred and fury
which today permeates the press?>

My curse upon the great sheep!
Where now are the children of the kindly folk
who parted from me when I was young
before Sutherland became a desert?

 —*From* Songs of Gaelic Scotland *by Anne Lorne Gillies (2006, pp. 267-68).*

~

The following is partial sample of a writ of removal.

A Writ of Removal
SUMMONS OF REMOVAL
Major Charles Robertson of Kindeace
vs
Donald Macleod, Esquire & Others

1846
Allan MacIntyre
Sheriff Clerk
Call per John Mackenzie
Summons of Removing
Major Charles Robertson of Kindeace
against
Donald Macleod, Esq., residing at Kingsburgh, Isle of Skye.
David Ross, Snr., alias Greishich, residing at urlar of Glencalvie
David Ross, alias Greischich, residing at urlar of Glencalvie
Alexander Ross, alias Greischich, residing at urlar of Glencalvie.

...the said Defenders ought and should be declared and ordained by Decree and Sentence of me or my Substitute.

To flit and Remove themselves, Bairns, Family, servants, subtenants, cottars and dependants, Cattle, Goods and gear, forth and from possession of the said Subjects ... and to leave the same void, redd and patent, at the respective terms of Removal above specified, that the Pursuer or others in his name may then enter thereto and peaceably possess, occupy and enjoy the same in time coming. And
In the event of their opposing this action to make payment to the pursuer of the sum of Ten pounds Sterling, or such other Sum as shall be modified at the Expenses of Process, besides the Expense of Extracting and Recording the Decree to follow thereon.

All in terms of ... and the laws and daily practice of Scotland, used and observed in the like cases in all points as if alleged. MY WILL IS HEREFORE. I commend you that on sight hereof, ye pass and lawfully Summon, warn and charge the Said Defenders personally, or at their dwelling places, to appear before me or my Substitute within the ordinary Court place at Tain....
Allan MacIntyre,
Sheriff Clerk Depute.

—*From John Prebble,* The Highland Clearances *(1963), pp. 310-13.*

Appendix

(Above) Croick Church window (background) courtesy of the author. Photo of the etching: ("Glencalvie people the wicked generation") courtesy of David Kratz, www.northernsights.net.

(Overleaf) (detail) James Kirkwood. 1804. By permission. National Library of Scotland [NLS shelfmark: EMS.s.74].

References

Adam, Margaret I. "Highland Emigration of 1783-1803." *Scottish Geographical Magazine*, May 1934.

———. "The Highland Emigration of 1770." *Scottish Historical Review* 16 (July 1919): 281-93.

———. "The Causes of the Highland Emigrations of 1783-1803." *Scottish Historical Review* 17 (January 1920): 73-89.

———. "The Eighteenth Century Highland Landlords and the Poverty Problem." *Scottish Historical Review* 19 (1922).

Adams, Ian and Meredyth Somerville. *Cargoes of Despair and Hope: Scottish Emigration to North America 1603-1803*. Edinburgh: John Donald, 1993.

Aitchison, Peter and Andrew Cassell. *The Lowland Clearances: Scotland's Silent Revolution 1760-1830*. Edinburgh: Birlinn, 2012.

Albini, Joseph L. and Jeffrey Scott McIllwain. *Deconstructing Organized Crime: An Historical and Theoretical Study*. Jefferson, NC: McFarland and Company, 2012.

Alvarez, Lizette. "Land Reforms in Scotland Give Big Estates the Jitters: Tenants Are Getting Broader Rights to Buy." *New York Times*, February 23, 2003.

Andrews, Evangeline W., ed. *Journal of a Lady of Quality: Being the Narrative of a Journey from Scotland to the West Indies, North Carolina and Portugal in the Years 1774 to 1776*. New Haven, CT: Yale University Press, 1939.

Ascherson, Neal. *Stone Voices: The Search for Scotland*. London: Granta Books, 2002.

Aspinwall, Bernard. *Portable Utopia: Glasgow and the United States 1820-1920*. Aberdeen: Aberdeen University Press, 1984.

Atkinson, Tom. *The Empty Lands*. Edinburgh: Luath Press, 1986.

Bailey, Patrick. *Orkney*. Newton Abbot, U.K.: Pevensey Press, 1995.

Bailyn, Bernard. *The Peopling of British North America: An Introduction*. New York: Vintage, 1988.

———. *Voyagers to the West: A Passage in the Peopling of America on the Eve of the Revolution*. New York: Vintage, 1988.

Baldacchino, Godfrey, ed. *Island Songs: A Global Repertoire*. Lanham, MD: Scarecrow Press, 2011.

Bangor-Jones, M. *The Assynt Clearances*. Dundee: Assynt Press, 1998.

Bassin, Ethel. *The Old Songs of Skye: Frances Tolmie and Her Circle*. London, 1977.

Basu, Paul. *Highland Homecomings: Genealogy and Heritage Tourism in the Scottish Diaspora*. New York: Routledge, 2007.

Bell-Fialkoff, Andrew. "A Brief History of Ethnic Cleansing." *Foreign Affairs*, Summer 1993.

Bennett, Margaret. *The Last Stronghold: Scottish Gaelic Traditions of Newfoundland*. Edinburgh: Canongate, 1989.

———. *Oatmeal and the Catechism: Scottish Gaelic Settlers in Quebec*. Montréal and Kingston: McGill-Queen's University Press, 1998.

Beresford, M. *The Lost Villages of England*. London: Lutterworth Press, 1954.

Berthoff, Rowland T. "Under the Kilt: Variations on the Scottish-American Ground." *Journal of American Ethnic History* 1, no. 2 (1982).

———. "Celtic Mist over the South." *Journal of Southern History* 52 (1986).

Black, Ronald, ed. *To the Hebrides: Samuel Johnson's Journey to the Western Islands of Scotland and James Boswell's Journal of a Tour to the Hebrides*. Edinburgh: Birlinn, 2007.

Blair, Rev. Duncan B. *Fògradh, Fàisneachd, Filidheachd / Parting, Prophecy, Poetry: Rev. Duncan B. Blair (1815-1893) in* Mac-Talla. Trans. and eds. John A. Macpherson and Michael Linkletter. Sydney, NS: Cape Breton University Press.

Blankenhorn, Virginia. "Traditional and Bogus Elements in 'MacCrimmon's Lament.'" *Scottish Studies* 22 (1978):45-67.

Blaustein, R. *The Thistle and the Briar: Historical Links and Cultural Parallels between Scotland and Appalachia*. Vol. 7 of *Contributions to Southern Appalachian Studies Series*. Jefferson, NC: McFarland, 2003.

Bolton, Andrew. *Alexander McQueen: Savage Beauty*. New York: Metropolitan Museum of Art, 2011.

Boswell, James. *The Journal of a Tour to the Hebrides*. London, 1984.

Botfield, B. *Journal of a Tour through the Highlands*. Norton Hall, U.K., 1830.

Brander, Michael. *The Scottish Highlanders and Their Regiments*. Haddington: Gleneil Press, 1996.

Brock, William. *Scotus Americanus*. Edinburgh: Edinburgh University Press, 1982.

Brooking, Tom. *Lands for the People: The Highland Clearances and the Colonisation of New Zealand: A Biography of John McKenzie*. Dunedin, New Zealand, 1996.

Brooking, Tom and J. Coleman, eds. *The Heather and the Fern: Scottish Migration and New Zealand Settlement*. Dunedin: University of Otago Press, 2003.

Brown, Ian, ed. *From Tartan to Tartanry: Scottish Culture, History, and Myth*. Edinburgh: Edinburgh University Press, 2012.

Brown, Robert and Thomas Douglas Selkirk. *Remarks on the Earl of Selkirk's Observations on the Present State of the Highlands of Scotland*. Edinburgh: Printed for John Anderson and Longman, Hurst, Rees, and Orme, 1806.

Brown, Wallace. *The Good Americans: The Loyalists in the American Revolution*. New York: William Morrow, 1969.

Bryce, George. *John Black, the Apostle of the Red River*. Toronto: W. Bigges, 1898.

Buchan, James. *Capital of the Mind: How Edinburgh Changed the World*. Edinburgh: John Murray, 2004.

Buchanan, John L. *Travels in the Western Hebrides from 1782 to 1790*. Isle of Skye, 1997.

Buchanan, Joni. *The Lewis Land Struggle*. Stornoway, U.K.: Acair, 1996.

Buie, Scott, ed. *Argyll Colony Plus: 250th Anniversary of the First Scottish Settlement in North Carolina 1739-1989*. Vol. 4, no. 3, Summer 1989.

Bumsted, J. M., ed. *The Collected Writings of Lord Selkirk, 1810–1820*. Winnipeg: Manitoba Record Society, 1988.

Bumsted, J. M. "Highland Emigration to the Island of St. John and the Scottish Catholic Church, 1769-1774." *Dalhousie Review* 58 (1978): 511-27.

———. *Lord Selkirk: A Life*. Winnipeg: University of Manitoba Press, 2008.

———. *The Peoples of Canada: A Pre-Confederation History*. Vol. 1. Toronto: Oxford University Press, 1992.

———. *The People's Clearance: Highland Emigration to British North America*. Edinburgh: Edinburgh University Press, 1982.

———. "Sir James Montgomery and Prince Edward Island, 1763-1803." *Acadiensis* 7 (1978): 76-102.

Burnett, Ray and Kathryn A. Burnett. "Scotland's Hebrides: Song and Culture, Transmission, and Transformation." In *Island Songs: A Global Repertoire*. Ed. Godfrey Baldacchino. Lanham, MD: Scarecrow Press, 2011.

Burt, Edmund. *Burt's Letters from the North of Scotland*. Ed. Andrew Simmons. Edinburgh: Birlinn, 1998.

References

Buxton, Ben. *Mingulay: An Island and Its People*. Edinburgh: Birlinn, 1995.

———. *The Vatersay Raiders*. Edinburgh: Birlinn, 2008.

Calder, Jenni. *Frontier Scots: The Scots Who Won the West*. Edinburgh: Luath Press, 2010.

———. *Scots in the USA*. Edinburgh: Luath Press, 2006.

Cameron, A. D. *Go Listen to the Crofters: The Napier Commission and Crofting a Century Ago*. Stornoway: Acair, 1986.

Cameron, E. A. *Land for the People? The British Government and the Scottish Highlands, 1880-1925*. East Linton, U.K.: Tuckwell Press, 1996.

Cameron, Elspeth. *Hugh MacLennan: A Writer's Life*. Toronto: University of Toronto Press, 1981.

Campbell, Angus Peter. *An t-Eilean/Taking a Line for a Walk through the Island of Skye*. Lochs, Isle of Lewis: Islands Book Trust, 2012.

———. "The Blood Is Strong." Booklet. London: Channel 4 Television, 1988.

———. *The Greatest Gift*. Sleat, Isle of Skye: Fountain Publishing, 1992.

———, ed. *Somhairle Dàin is Deilbh: A Celebration on the 80th Birthday of Sorley MacLean*. Stornoway: Acair, 1991.

Campbell, Douglas F. and R. A. MacLean. *Beyond the Atlantic Roar: A Study of Nova Scotia Scots*. Toronto: McClelland and Stewart, 1974.

Campbell, James. *Invisible Country: A Journey through Scotland*. London: Weidenfeld and Nicolson, 1984.

Campbell, John Francis. *Popular Tales of the West Highlands*. 2 vols. Edinburgh: Birlinn, 1994 [1860-1862].

Campbell, John Lorne. *Canna: The Story of a Hebridean Island*. Edinburgh: Canongate, 1994.

———. "Eviction at First Hand: The Clearing of Clanranald's Islands." *Scots Magazine*, January 1945.

———, ed. *Òrainn Ghàidhealach mu Bhliadhna Theàrlaich/Highland Songs of the Forty-Five*. Vol 15 of *Scottish Gaelic Texts*. Edinburgh: Scottish Gaelic Texts Society, 1983 [1933].

———, ed. *Songs Remembered in Exile: Traditional Gaelic Songs from Nova Scotia*. Aberdeen: Aberdeen University Press, 1990.

———. *A Very Civil People: Hebridean Folk, History, and Tradition*. Ed. Hugh Cheape. Edinburgh: Birlinn, 2000.

Campey, Lucille H. *After the Hector: The Scottish Pioneers of Nova Scotia and Cape Breton 1773-1852*. Toronto: Natural Heritage Books, 2004.

———. *"Fast Sailing and Copper-Bottomed": Aberdeen Sailing Ships and the Emigrant Scots They Carried to Canada*. Toronto: Natural Heritage, 2002.

———. *The Scottish Pioneers of Upper Canada, 1784-1855: Glengarry and Beyond.* Toronto: Natural Heritage Books, 2005.

———. *The Silver Chief: Lord Selkirk and the Scottish Pioneers of Belfast, Baldoon and Red River.* Toronto: Natural Heritage Books, 2003.

———. *An Unstoppable Force: The Scottish Exodus to Canada.* Toronto: Natural Heritage Books, 2008.

———. *"A Very Fine Class of Immigrants": Prince Edward Island's Scottish Pioneers, 1770-1850.* Toronto: Natural Heritage Books, 2001.

Carmichael, Alexander. *Carmina Gadelica.* 6 vols. Edinburgh: Scottish Gaelic Society Texts, 1900-1971.

Carnes-McNaughton, Linda F. and Carl R. Steen. "Fort Bragg's 1918 Genesis: Historic Communities Lost and Found." Paper presented at the SEAC 2007 Meeting, Knoxville, Tennessee.

Caudill, William Samuel. "Gone to Seek a Fortune in North Carolina: The Failed Scottish Highland Emigration of 1884." MA thesis, University of North Carolina at Chapel Hill, 2009.

Chapman, Malcolm. *The Gaelic Vision in Scottish Culture.* London: Croom Helm and Montréal and Kingston: McGill-Queen's University Press, 1978.

Cheape, Hugh. *Tartan: The Highland Habit.* Edinburgh: National Museums of Scotland, 1991.

Chisholm, C. "The Clearance of the Highland Glens." *Transactions of the Gaelic Society of Inverness.* Vol. 5 (1876-77).

Clyde, Robert. *From Rebel to Hero: The Image of the Highlander 1745–1830.* East Linton, 1995.

Connor, Ralph. *Glengarry School Days.* Toronto: McClelland and Stewart, 1990.

———. *The Man from Glengarry.* Toronto: McClelland and Stewart, 1993.

Cooper, Derek. *Hebridean Connection: A View of the Highlands and Islands.* London: Fontana/HarperCollins Publishers, 1991.

———. *The Road to Mingulay: A View of the Western Isles.* London: Futura Publications, 1989.

———. *Skye.* London: Routledge and Kegan Paul, 1970.

Coutts, Robert and Richard Stuart, eds. *The Forks and the Battle of Seven Oaks in Manitoba History.* Winnipeg: Manitoba Historical Society, 1994.

Cowan, Helen I. *British Emigration to British North America: The First Hundred Years.* Toronto: University of Toronto Press, 1961.

Craig, David. "Diary." *London Review of Books,* May 24, 2001.

———. *On the Crofters Trail: In Search of the Clearance Highlanders*. London: Jonathan Cape, 1990.

Craig, David and David Paterson. *The Glens of Silence: Landscapes of the Highland Clearances*. Foreword by James Hunter. Edinburgh: Birlinn, 2004.

Cramb, Auslan. "Who Owns Scotland?" *Scottish Life*, Spring 1997.

Creighton, Helen and Calum MacLeod, eds. *Gaelic Songs in Nova Scotia*. Ottawa, 1964.

de Crèvecoeur, J. Hector St. John. *Letters from an American Farmer* and *Sketches of Eighteenth-Century America*. Ed. Albert E. Stone. New York: Penguin, 1983 [1782 and 1925].

———. *Letters from an American Farmer and Other Essays*. Ed. Dennis D. Moore. Cambridge, MA: Belknap Press/Harvard University Press, 2013.

Crichton Smith, Iain. *Consider the Lilies*. Edinburgh: Canongate, 1987.

Crowe, Thomas Rain, Gwendal Denez and Tom Hubbard, eds. *Writing the Wind A Celtic Resurgence: The New Celtic Poetry*. Cullowhee, NC: New Native Press, 1997.

Cunningham, Rodger. *Apples on the Flood: Minority Discourse and Appalachia*. Knoxville, TN: University of Tennessee Press, 1987.

Currie, Sheldon. *The Glace Bay Miners' Museum*. Wreck Cove, NS: Breton Books, 1995.

Darroch, John. "The Scottish Highlanders Going to North Carolina." *Celtic Magazine* 1 (March 1876): 142-47.

Davidson, Hilda, ed. *The Seer in Celtic and Other Traditions*. Edinburgh: John Donald, 1989.

Davidson, Julei. "Knoydart's New Owners." *Scottish Life*, Summer 2003.

Defoe, Daniel. *A Tour through the Whole Island of Great Britain*. Ed. P. N. Furbank and W. R. Owens. Picture Research by A. J. Coulson. New Haven, CT: Yale University Press, 1991.

DeMond, Robert O. *The Loyalists in North Carolina during the Revolution*. Durham, NC: Duke University Press, 1940.

Devine, Thomas M. *Clanship to Crofters' War: The Social Transformation of the Scottish Highlands*. Manchester: Manchester University Press, 1994.

———. *Clearance and Improvement: Land, Power and People in Scotland 1700-1900*. Edinburgh: John Donald, 2006.

———. *To the Ends of the Earth: Scotland's Global Diaspora*. London: Allen Lane/Penguin Books, 2011.

———. *The Transformation of Rural Scotland*. Edinburgh: Edinburgh University Press, 1994.

Devine, Thomas M. and W. J. Orr. *The Great Highland Famine: Hunger, Emigration, and the Scottish Highlanders in the Nineteenth Century*. Edinburgh: John Donald, 1988.

Dobson, David. *Scottish Emigration to Colonial America, 1607-1785*. Athens, GA: University of Georgia Press, 1994.

Dodgshon, Robert A. *From Chiefs to Landlords*. Edinburgh: Edinburgh University Press, 1998.

Donaldson, Gordon. *The Scots Overseas*. London: Robert Hale, 1966.

Donaldson, William. *The Jacobite Song: Political Myth and National Identity*. Aberdeen: Aberdeen University Press, 1988.

Donnachie, Ian and George Hewitt. *Historic New Lanark: The Dale and Owen Industrial Community since 1785*. Edinburgh: Edinburgh University Press, 1993.

Dorian, Nancy C. *Language Death*. Philadelphia: University of Pennsylvania Press, 1981.

———. *The Tyranny of Tide: An Oral History of the East Sutherland Fisherfolk*. Ann Arbor, MI: Karoma, 1985.

Dressler, Camille. *Eigg: The Story of an Island*. Edinburgh: Polygon, 1998.

Dunn, Charles W. "A Gaelic Church in Boston, Massachusetts." *An Teangadóir* 4 (1957).

———. *Highland Settler: A Portrait of the Scottish Gael in Nova Scotia*. Toronto: University of Toronto Press, 1953.

———. *The Scots in North America: Past and Present* [].

"Emigration of Skye Crofters." *Scotsman*, February 6, 1884, p. 6.

"The Emigration from Skye to North Carolina." *North British Daily Mail*, July 30, 1884, p. 1.

Erickson, Charlotte J. *Invisible Immigrants: The Adaptation of English and Scottish Immigrants in Nineteenth-Century America*. Ithaca, NY: Cornell University Press, 1972.

Faiers, Jonathan. *Tartan*. Oxford: Berg Publishers, 2008.

Fairhurst, H. "Rosal: A Deserted Township in Strath Naver, Sutherland," *Proceedings of the Society of Antiquities of Scotland* 100 (1967-1968).

Farquharson, Lindsay. *General Wade's Legacy: The 18th Century Military Road System in Perthshire*. Perth: Perth and Kinross Heritage Trust, 2011.

Fenyö, Krisztina. *Contempt, Sympathy and Romance: Lowland Perceptions of the Highlands and the Clearances during the Famine Years, 1845-1855*. East Linton, U.K.: Tuckwell Press, 2000.

Ferguson, Calum. *Children of the Black House*. Foreword by Donald Meek. Edinburgh: Birlinn, 2003.

Ferguson, Lesley. *Wandering with a Camera in Scotland: The Photographs of Erskine Beveridge*. Edinburgh: Royal Commission on the Ancient and Historical Monuments of Scotland, 2009.

Ferguson, William. *The Identity of the Scottish Nation: A Historic Quest*. Edinburgh: Edinburgh University Press, 1998.

Fidler, Kathleen. *The Desperate Journey*. Edinburgh: Kelpie Books, 1984.

Finlayson, Iain. *The Scots*. New York: Oxford University Press, 1988.

Finnan, Mark. *The First Nova Scotian: The Story of Sir William Alexander and His Lost Colony of Charlesfort, Nova Scotia's First English-speaking Settlement*. Halifax: Formac Publishing Company, 1997.

Fischer, David Hackett. *Albion's Seed: Four British Folkways in America*. New York: Oxford University Press, 1989.

Fleming, Rae, ed. *The Lochaber Emigrants to Glengarry*. Toronto: Natural Heritage/Natural History, Inc., 1994.

"Flora MacDonald Homesite." In *Encyclopedia of North Carolina*. Ed. William S. Powell. Chapel Hill, NC: University of North Carolina Press, 2006.

Foote, William Henry. *Sketches of North Carolina*. New York: Robert Carter, 1846.

Fraser-Mackintosh, C. "The Depopulation of Aberarder in Badenoch." *Celtic Magazine* 11 (1877).

Fry, Michael. "Clearances? What Clearances?" *Scottish Review of Books* 1, no. 2 (2005).

———. *The Scottish Empire*. Edinburgh: Birlinn, 2002.

———. "Time to right a false picture." *Herald*, June 20, 2005.

———. *Wild Scots: Four Hundred Years of Highland History*. Edinburgh: John Murray, 2005.

Gaskell, Phillip. *Morvern Transformed*. Rev. ed. Cambridge: Cambridge University Press, 1980 [1968].

Gibson, John. *Old and New World Bagpiping*. Montréal and Kingston: McGill-Queen's University Press, 2002.

———. *Traditional Gaelic Bagpiping 1745-1945*. Montréal and Kingston: McGill-Queen's University Press, 1998.

Gibson, Rob. *Crofter Power in Easter Ross, 1884-1886*. Dingwall: Highland Heritage, 1986.

———. *The Highland Clearances Trail*. Edinburgh: Luath Press, 2006.

———. *Plaids and Bandanas: From Highland Drover to Wild West Cowboy.* Edinburgh: Luath Press, 2003.

———. "Review: Wild Scots." *Scottish Affairs* 61, Autumn 2007.

———. *Toppling the Duke.* Evanton, U.K.: Highland Heritage Books, 1996.

Gillies, Anne Lorne. *Songs of Gaelic Scotland.* Edinburgh: Birlinn, 2006.

Gillis, John R. *The Human Shore: Seacoasts in History.* Chicago: University of Chicago Press, 2012.

Gilpin, William. *Observations, Relative Chiefly to Picturesque Beauty, Made in the Year 1776, Particularly the Highlands of Scotland.* 2 vols. London: Printed for R. Blamire, 1789.

Glass, Jayne, Martin Price and Charles Warren, eds. *Lairds, Land and Sustainability: Scottish Perspectives on Upland Management.* Edinburgh: Edinburgh University Press, 2012.

Gordon, Seton. *Hebridean Memories.* Glasgow: Neil Wilson Publishing, 1995.

Goring, Rosemary, ed. *Chambers Scottish Biographical Dictionary.* Edinburgh: W. and R. Chambers, 1992.

Goring, Rosemary. *Scotland: The Autobiography.* New York: Overlook Press, 2008.

Gouriévidis, Laurence. "The Strathnaver Clearances in Modern Scottish Fiction." In *The Province of Strathnaver.* Ed. John R. Baldwin. Edinburgh: Scottish Society for Northern Studies, 2000.

Graham, Ian Charles Cargill. *Colonists from Scotland: Emigration to North America, 1707-1783.* Ithaca, NY: Cornell University Press, 1956.

Grant, Elizabeth. *Memoirs of a Highland Lady, 1797-1827.* Edinburgh: Canongate, 1991

Grant, I. F. *Everyday Life on an Old Highland Farm, 1769-1782.* London: Shepheard-Walwyn, 1981.

Gray, J. M. *Lord Selkirk of Red River.* Toronto: Macmillan, 1963.

Gray, Malcolm. *The Highland Economy 1750-1850.* Edinburgh: Oliver and Boyd, 1957.

———. *Scots on the Move: Scots Migrants, 1750-1914.* Edinburgh: Economic and Social History Society of Scotland, 1990.

Gregory, Donald. *The History of the Western Highlands and Isles of Scotland from A.D. 1493 to A.D. 1625.* London: Hamilton, Adams and Co., 1881.

Grigor, Iain Fraser. *Highland Resistance: The Radical Tradition in the Scottish North.* Edinburgh: Mainstream Publishing, 2000.

———. *Mightier than a Lord.* Stornoway: Acair, 1979.

Grimble, Ian, ed. *Alistair MacLeod: Essays on His Works*. Toronto: Guernica, 2001.

Grimble, Ian. "Emigration in the Time of Rob Donn, 1714-1778." *Scottish Studies* 7 (1963).

———. *The Scottish Islands*. Edinburgh: BBC, 1985.

———. *The Trial of Patrick Sellar*. Edinburgh: The Saltire Society, 1993.

———. *The World of Rob Donn*. Edinburgh: Edina, 1979.

Gunn, Donald. *History of Manitoba, to 1835*. Ottawa: Maclean, Roger and Co., 1880.

Gunn, Neil M. *Butcher's Broom*. London: Souvenir Press, 1977.

———. "The Tragedy of the Highland Clearances." *Radio Times*, December 10, 1954.

Halbfinger, David M. "Post-storm Cost May Force Many from Coast Life." *New York Times,* November 29, 2012.

Haldane, A. R. B. *The Drove Roads of Scotland*. Edinburgh: Birlinn, 1997.

Hamilton, Hamish. "The Women of the Glen: Some Thoughts on Highland History." In *The Celtic Consciousness*. Ed. Robert O'Driscoll. New York: George Braziller, 1982.

Hansen, M. L. *The Atlantic Migration, 1607-1860*. New York: Harper and Brothers, 1961.

Harper, Marjory. *Adventurers & Exiles: The Great Scottish Exodus*. London: Profile Books, 2003.

Harper, Marjory, ed. *Emigrant Homecomings: The Return Movement of Emigrants, 1600-2000*. Manchester: Manchester University Press, 2005.

Harper, Marjory and Michael Vance, eds. *Myth, Migration, and the Making of Memory*. The Gorsebrook Research Institute for Atlantic Canada Studies. Halifax, NS: Fernwood Publishing and Edinburgh: John Donald Publishers, 1999.

Harvey, D. C. "Scottish Immigration to Cape Breton." *Dalhousie Review* 21, no. 3 (1941).

Haswell-Smith, Hamish. *The Scottish Islands*. Edinburgh: Canongate, 2004.

Haws, Charles H. *Scots in the Old Dominion, 1685-1800*. Edinburgh: J. Dunlop, 1980.

Hedrick, Joan D. *Harriet Beecher Stowe: A Life*. New York: Oxford University Press, 1994.

Henderson, Anne M. *Kildonan on the Red*. Winnipeg: Lord Selkirk Association of Rupert's Land, 1981.

Hendry, Joy and Raymond Ross, eds. *Norman MacCaig: Critical Essays.* Edinburgh: Edinburgh University Press, 1990.

Herman, Arthur. *How the Scots Invented the Modern World: The True Story of How Western Europe's Poorest Nation Created Our World & Everything in It.* New York: Crown, 2001.

Hewitson, Jim. *Far Off in Sunlit Places: Stories of the Scots in Australia and New Zealand.* Edinburgh: Canongate, 1998.

———. *Tam Blake & Co.: The Story of the Scots in America.* Edinburgh: Canongate, 1993.

"The Highland Crofters and North Carolina." *Scotsman,* January 16, 1884, p. 4.

"Highland Crofters Emigration to North Carolina." *Scotsman,* March 1, 1884, p. 11.

"The Highland Crofters." *Wilmington Morning Star,* March 13, 1884, p. 2.

"Historian throws down gauntlet on 'Clearances myth.'" *Scotsman.com,* March 7, 2005.

Hogg, James, ed. *The Jacobite Relics of Scotland; being the Songs, Airs, and Legends of the Adherents to the House of Stuart.* 2 vols. Edinburgh, 1819-1821.

———. *A Tour in the Highlands in 1803.* Edinburgh: Edinburgh University Press, 1986.

Hook, Andrew. *From Goosecreek to Gandercleugh: Studies in Scottish-American Literary and Cultural History.* East Linton: Tuckwell Press, 1999.

Hornby, Susan. *Celts and Ceilidhs: A History of Scottish Societies on Prince Edward Island.* Charlottetown: Caledonian Club, 1981.

Houston, R. A. and W. J. Knox, eds. *The New Penguin History of Scotland.* London: Penguin, 2001.

Hugo, Richard. *The Right Madness on Skye.* New York: W. W. Norton, 1980.

Hunter, James. *The Claim of Crofting: The Scottish Highlands, 1930–1990.* Edinburgh: Mainstream Publishing, 1991.

———. *Culloden and the Last Clansman.* Edinburgh: Mainstream Publishing, 2001.

———. *A Dance Called America: The Scottish Highlands, the United States and Canada.* Edinburgh: Mainstream Publishing, 1994.

———, ed. *For the People's Cause: From the Writings of John Murdoch.* Edinburgh: Her Majesty's Stationary Office, 1986.

———. *Glencoe and the Indians.* Edinburgh: Mainstream Publishing, 1996.

———. *Last of the Free: A Millennial History of the Highlands and Islands of Scotland.* Edinburgh: Mainstream Publishing, 1999.

———. *The Making of the Crofting Community*. New ed. Edinburgh: Birlinn, 2010.

———. *On the Other Side of Sorrow: Nature and People in the Scottish Highlands*. Edinburgh: Mainstream Publishing, 1995.

———. *Scottish Exodus: Travels among a Worldwide Clan*. Edinburgh: Mainstream Publishing, 2007.

———. *Scottish Highlanders: A People and Their Place*. Edinburgh: Mainstream Publishing, 1992.

———. *Skye: The Island*. Edinburgh: Mainstream Publishing, 1986.

Hunter, Mollie. *A Pistol in Greenyards*. London: Hamilton, 1988.

Hutchinson, Roger. *Calum's Road*. Edinburgh: Birlinn, 2006.

———. *Soap Man: Lewis, Harris, and Lord Leverhulme*. Edinburgh: Birlinn, 2003.

———. *A Waxing Moon: The Modern Gaelic Revival*. Edinburgh: Mainstream Publishing, 2005.

"In the Footsteps of the Clearances: An Introduction to 18th and 19th Century Emigration from Skye and Lochalsh." Pamphlet created by Cànan, Isle of Skye, 1998.

Innes, S. A. "'They Must Worship Industry or Starve': Scottish Resistance to British Imperialism in Gunn's The Silver Darlings." *Studies in Scottish Literature* 28, no. 1 (1993).

Inverness Field Club. *Rossal: A Clearance Village in Strathnaver*. Inverness, n.d.

Jasanoff, Maya. *Liberty's Exiles: American Loyalists in the Revolutionary World*. New York: Vintage, 2011.

Johnson, Alison. *The Wicked Generation*. Belfast: Blackstaff Press, 1992.

Johnson, Samuel. *A Journey to the Western Islands of Scotland*. London: Penguin, 1984.

Johnston, Jim A. *Strathnaver Trail: The Story of a North Highland Landscape*. Inverness: Highland Council, 2003.

Johnston, Robert L. "The Deserted Homesteads of Fetlar." *Shetland Life*, 1981.

Kaplan, Wendy, ed. *Scottish Art and Design: 5,000 Years*. New York: Harry N. Abrams, 1991.

Kay, Billy. *Odyssey: Voices from Scotland's Recent Past*. Edinburgh: Polygon, 1980.

———. *The Scottish World: The Story of One Man's Journey and the Legacy of the Scottish Diaspora*. Edinburgh: Mainstream Publishing, 2006.

Kay, Peter. *A Jacobite Legacy: From Bonnie Dundee to Bonnie Prince Charlie. A Short History of the Jacobite Risings in Songs and Words.* Loughborough, U.K.: Soar Valley Music Publications, 1995.

Kelly, Douglas F. and Caroline Switzer Kelly. *Carolina Scots: An Historical and Genealogical Study of Over 100 Years of Emigration.* Dillon, SC: 1739 Publications, 1998.

Kelly, Stuart. *Scott-land: The Man Who Invented a Nation.* Edinburgh: Birlinn, 2010.

Kennedy, David. *Pioneer Days at Guelph and the County of Bruce.* Toronto: n.p., 1903.

Kennedy, Michael. *Gaelic Nova Scotia: An Economic, Cultural, and Social Impact Study.* Curatorial Report No. 97. Halifax, NS: Nova Scotia Museum, November 2002.

———. "Locaber No More: A Critical Examination of Highland Emigration Mythology." In *Myth, Migration, and the Making of Memory: Scotia and Nova Scotia, c. 1700-1990.* Ed. M. Harper and M. E. Vance. Halifax, NS: Fernwood and Edinburgh: John Donald, 1999.

Kerrigan, Catherine, ed. *An Anthology of Scottish Women Poets.* Trans. Meg Bateman. Edinburgh: Edinburgh University Press, 1991.

———. *The Immigrant Experience: Proceedings of a Conference Held at the University of Guelph-June 1989.* Guelph, ON: University of Guelph, 1992.

King, James. *The Life of Margaret Laurence.* Toronto: Knopf Canada, 1997.

Klinkenborg, Verlyn. "Doc Watson: Appreciations." *New York Times*, May 31, 2012.

Knox, John. *A Tour through the Highlands of Scotland and the Hebride Isles.* London: Printed for J. Walter, 1787.

Knox, Robert. *The Races of Men: A Philosophical Enquiry into the Influence of Race over the Destinies of Nations.* 2nd ed. London: Henry Renshaw, 1862.

Lamplighter and Storyteller: John Francis Campbell of Islay 1821-1885. Edinburgh: National Library of Scotland. Exhibition catalogue, 1985.

Landsman, Ned C., ed. *Nation and Province in the First British Empire.* Cranbury, NJ: Bucknell University Press, 2001..

Laughlan, W. F., ed. *James Hogg's Highland Tours.* Hawick, U.K.: Byways, 1981.

Lelong, O. and J. Wood. "A Township through Time: Excavation and Survey at the Deserted Settlement of Easter Raitts, Badenoch, 1995-99." In *Townships to Farmsteads: Rural Settlement Studies in Scotland, England, and Wales.* Ed. J. A. Atkinson, I. Banks and G. MacGregor. Oxford: BAR British series 293, 2000.

Lill, Wendy. *The Glace Bay Miners' Museum: A Stage Play Based on the Novel by Sheldon Currie*. Burnaby, BC: Talonbooks, 1996.

Loch, James. *An Account of the Improvements on the Estates of the Marquess of Stafford*. London: Longman, Hurst, Rees, Orme and Brown, 1820.

Lockhart, J. G. *Memoirs of the Life of Sir Walter Scott*. 7 vols. Edinburgh: Robert Cadell, 1837.

Logan, J. D. *The Pictou Poets: Treasury of Verse in Gaelic and English*. Pictou, NS: Pictou Advocate, 1923.

Lord, Steve. "The Scottish Rising to American Revolution: Flora MacDonald and the Emigration of Highland Scots." *The Highlander*, September/October 2009.

Lyle, Emily, eds. *Scottish Ballads*. Edinburgh: Canongate, 1994.

Lynch, Michael. *Scotland: A New History*. London: Pimlico, 1992.

MacAskill, John. *We Have Won the Land: The Story of the Purchase by the Assynt Crofters' Trust of the North Lochinver Estate*. Stornoway: Acair, 1999.

MacColla, Fionn. *And the Cock Crew*. Edinburgh: Canongate, 1995.

MacCulloch, J. *A Description of the Western Islands of Scotland*. 3 vols. London: Printed for A. Constable, 1819.

MacDonald, Ann-Marie. *Fall on Your Knees*. New York: Simon & Schuster, 1996.

Macdonald, C. *Moidart, Among the Clanranalds*. Edinburgh: Birlinn, 1997.

Macdonald, Calum and Rory Macdonald. *Flower of the West: The Runrig Songbook*. Aberdeen: Ridge Books, 2001.

MacDonald, C. S. "Early Highland Emigration to Nova Scotia and Prince Edward Island, 1770-1853." Nova Scotia Historical Society Collections, vol. 23 (1941).

MacDonald, Donald. *Lewis: A History of the Island*. Edinburgh: Gordon Wright, 1978.

MacDonald, D. R. *All the Men Are Sleeping: Stories*. New York: Counterpoint, 2003.

———. *Cape Breton Road*. Toronto: Doubleday Canada, 2001.

———. *Eyestone: Stories*. Wainscott, NY: Pushcart Press, 1988.

MacDonald, James Roderick. "Cultural Retention and Adaptation among the Highland Scots of Carolina." PhD dissertation, Edinburgh University, 1993.

Macdonald, Murdo. "Art and the Highlands." The Royal Scottish Academy Gillies Lecture, An Lanntair, Stornoway, April 12, 2008.

———. *Scottish Art*. London: Thames and Hudson, 2000.

Macdonald, Stuart. "Crofter Colonisation in Canada 1886-1892: The Scottish Political Background." *Northern Scotland* 7, no. 1 (1986).

MacDonell, John A. *Sketches Illustrating the Early Settlement and History of Glengarry in Canada.* Montréal: W. Foster, Brown, 1893.

MacDonell, Margaret, ed. *The Emigrant Experience: Songs of Highland Emigrants in North America.* Toronto: University of Toronto Press, 1982.

MacGillivray, Royce and Ewen Ross. *A History of Glengarry.* Belleville, ON: Mike Publishing Co., 1979.

MacGowan, Douglas, ed. *The Stonemason: Donald MacLeod's Chronicle of Scotland's Highland Clearances.* Westport, CT: Praeger, 2001.

MacInnes, Allan I. *Clanship, Commerce and the House of Stuart, 1603-1788.* East Linton: Tuckwell Press, 1996.

———. "Scottish Gaeldom: The first phase of clearance.," In *People and Society in Scotland.* Ed. T. M. Devine and R. Mitchison. Vol. 1. Edinburgh: John Donald, 1988.

MacInnes, Allan, Marjory-Ann Harper and Linda Fryer, eds. *Scotland and the Americas, c.1650-c.1939.* Edinburgh: Scottish History Society, 2002.

MacInnes, John. "The Bard through History." In *The Voice of the Bard: Living Poets and Ancient Tradition in the Highlands and Islands of Scotland,* 321-52. Ed. Timothy Neat. Edinburgh: Canongate, 1999.

———. "The Choral Tradition in Scottish Gaelic Songs." *Transactions of the Gaelic Society of Inverness* 46 (1966): 44-65.

———. "Gaelic Song and Dance." *Transactions of the Gaelic Society of Inverness* 60 (1996): 56-73.

———. "A Gaelic Song of the Sutherland Clearances." *Scottish Studies* 8 (1964): 104-106.

———. "Gleanings from Raasay Tradition." *Transactions of the Gaelic Society of Inverness* 56 (1985): 1-20.

———. "Language, Metre and Diction in the Poetry of Sorley Maclean." In *Sorley MacLean: Critical Essays,* 137-53. Ed. Raymond Ross and Joy Hendry. Edinburgh: Scottish Academic Press, 1986.

———. "MacCaig and Gaeldom." In *Norman MacCaig: Critical Essays,* 22-37. Ed. Joy Hendry and Raymond Ross. Edinburgh: Edinburgh University Press, 1990.

———. "Maclean's 'Hallaig' and 'The Tunes of His Own Mind.'" In *Sorley MacLean: Poems 1932-82.* Philadelphia: Iona Foundation, 1987.

———. "The Oral Tradition in Scottish Gaelic Poetry." *Scottish Studies* 12 (1968): 2944.

———. "The Panegyric Code in Gaelic Poetry and Its Historical Background." *Transactions of the Gaelic Society of Inverness* 50 (1978): 435-98.

———. "A Radically Traditional Voice: Sorley Maclean and the Evangelical Background." *Cencrastus* 7 (1981-1982): 14-17.

———. "The Seer in Gaelic Tradition." In *The Seer in Celtic and Other Traditions*, 10-24. Ed. Hilda Davidson. Edinburgh: John Donald, 1989.

———. "Sorley Maclean's 'Hallaig': A Note." *Calgacus* 1, no. 2 (1975): 29-32.

MacIntyre, Linden. *The Long Stretch*. Toronto: Stoddart, 1999.

MacKay, Donald. *Scotland Farewell: The People of the Hector*. Toronto: Natural Heritage, 1996.

MacKay, Iain R. "Glenalladale's Settlement, Prince Edward Island." *Scottish Gaelic Studies* 10 (1963): 17-20.

———. *The Highland Clearances*. Vol. 25. Inverness and Glasgow: An Comunn Gàidhealach, 1971.

Mackenzie, Alexander. "First Highland Emigration to Nova Scotia: Arrival of the Ship *Hector*." *Celtic Magazine* 8, 1883.

———. *The Highland Clearances*. Edinburgh: Mercat Press, 1997.

———, ed. *The Trial of Patrick Sellar*. Inverness: A. & W. Mackenzie, 1883.

Mackenzie, Osgood. *A Hundred Years in the Highlands*. London: Bles, 1972.

Mackie, J. D. *A History of Scotland*. 2nd ed. Ed. Bruce Lenman and Geoffrey Parker. London: Penguin, 1978.

MacLean, Charles. *Island on the Edge of the World: The Story of St. Kilda*. New York: Taplinger Publishing, 1972.

MacLean, Fitzroy. *Highlanders: A History of the Scottish Clans*. New York: Viking Studio Books. 1995.

MacLean, John P. *An Historical Account of the Settlement of Scotch Highlanders in America Prior to the Peace of 1783*. Cleveland: Helman-Taylor, 1900.

MacLean, Malcolm and Christopher Carrell, eds. *As an Fhearann: From the Land*. Edinburgh, Stornoway and Glasgow: Mainstream Publishing, An Lanntair, Third Eye Centre, 1986.

Maclean, Malcolm and Theo Dorgan, eds. *An Leabhar Mor: The Great Book of Gaelic*. Edinburgh: Canongate Books, 2002.

Maclean, Samuel. "The Poetry of the Clearances." *Transactions of the Gaelic Society of Inverness* 38 (1962).

Maclean, Sorley. *O Choille gu Bearradh: From Wood to Ridge: Collected Poems in Gaelic and English*. Manchester: Carcanet, 1990.

———. "Maíri Mhor nan Oran." *Calgacus*, Winter 1975.

MacLeish, Archibald. *Collected Poems, 1917-1982*. Boston, MA: Houghton Mifflin, 1985.

MacLellan, Robert. *The Isle of Arran*. Newton Abbot, U.K: David and Charles, 1968.

MacLennan, Hugh. *Each Man's Son*. 1951. Toronto: Stoddard Publishing, 1993.

MacLeod, Ada. "The Glenaladale Pioneers." *Dalhousie Review* 11 (1931-1932).

MacLeod, Alistair. *Island: Collected Stories*. Foreword by John McGahern. London: Vintage, 2002.

———. *Island: The Complete Stories*. New York: W. W. Norton, 2001.

———. *No Great Mischief*. Toronto: McClelland and Stewart, 1999.

MacLeod, Angus, ed. *The Songs of Duncan Ban MacIntyre*. Edinburgh: Oliver and Boyd for the Scottish Gaelic Texts Society, 1952.

Macleod, Calum. *Fàsachadh An-Iochdmhor Ratharsair: The Cruel Clearance of Raasay*. Clò Arnais, 2007.

Macleod, Donald. *Gloomy Memories in the Highlands of Scotland versus Mrs. Harriet Beecher Stowe's Sunny Memories in (England) a Foreign Land: Or a Faithful Picture of the Extirpation of the Celtic Race from the Highlands of Scotland*. Glasgow: A. Sinclair, 1892.

Macleod, John. *Highlanders: A History of the Gaels*. London: Sceptre, 1997.

———. *No Great Mischief If You Fall: The Highland Experience*. Edinburgh: Mainstream Publishing, 1993.

MacLeod, Norma. *Raasay: The Island and Its People*. Edinburgh: Birlinn, 2002.

MacLure, John. "How the Highlanders Took Nova Scotia" *MacLean's Magazine*, November 12, 1955.

Macmillan, Duncan. *The Art of Will Maclean: Symbols of Survival*. London and Edinburgh: Art First Contemporary Art in association with Mainstream Publishing, 1992.

MacNeil, Neil. *The Highland Heart in Nova Scotia*. New York: Charles Scribner and Sons, 1948.

MacPhail, I. M. M. *The Crofters War*. Stornoway: Acair, 1989.

MacPhee, H. "The Trail of the Emigrants." *Transactions of the Gaelic Society of Inverness* 46 (1969-1970).

MacRae, James C. "The Highland-Scotch Settlement in North Carolina." *North Carolina Booklet* 4 (February 1905).

Mahalik, David. "Music as a Living Tradition." In *The Centre of the World at the Edge of the Continent: Cultural Studies of Cape Breton Island.* Ed. C. Corbin and Judith A. Rolls. Sydney, NS: University College of Cape Breton Press, 1996.

Malthus, Thomas. *An Essay on the Principle of Population,* 1798.

Martin, Martin. *A Description of the Western Islands of Scotland circa 1695.* Edinburgh: Birlinn, 1994.

Marx, Karl. *Capital.* London, 1867.

———. "The Duchess of Sutherland and Slavery." In *Articles on Britain.* Ed. Karl Marx and Friedrich Engels. Moscow: Progress Publishers, 1971.

Matheson, William, ed. *An Clàrsair Dall: Òrain Ruaidhri Mhic Mhuirich agus a Chuid Chiùil/The Blind Harper: The Songs of Roderick Morison and His Music.* Vol. 12 of *Scottish Gaelic Text*s. Edinburgh: Scottish Gaelic Texts Society, 1970.

———. *Òrain Iain Mhic Fhearchair a Bha 'n a Bhàrd aig Sir Seamus MacDhomhnaill/The Songs of John MacCodrum: Bard to Sir James MacDonald of Sleat.* Vol. 2 of *Scottish Gaelic Texts.* Edinburgh: Scottish Gaelic Texts Society, 1938.

Mathieson, Robert. *The Survival of the Unfittest: The Highland Clearances and the End of Isolation.* Edinburgh: John Donald, 2000.

McArthur, Colin, ed. *Scotch Reels: Scotland in Cinema and Television.* London: British Film Institute, 1982.

McCrone, David, Angela Morris and Richard Kiely. *Scotland the Brand: The Making of Scottish Heritage.* Edinburgh: Edinburgh University Press, 1995.

McDonald, Forrest and E. S. McDonald. "The Ethnic Origins of the American People, 1790." *William and Mary Quarterly* 37 (April 1980).

McEwen, John. *Who Owns Scotland?* Edinburgh: Polygon, 1977.

McFarlane, Heather. *Arichonan: A Highland Clearance Recorded.* Bloomington, IN: Author House, 2004.

McGrath, John. *The Cheviot, the Stag and the Black Black Oil.* Breakish, Isle of Skye: West Highland Publishing Company, 1974.

———. *Naked Thoughts that Roam About: Reflections on Theatre 1958–2001.* Ed. Nadine Holdsworth. London: Nick Hern Books, 2002.

McIntosh, Alastair. *Soil and Soul: People versus Corporate Power.* London: Aurum Press, 2001.

———. "Wild Scots and Buffoon History." *The Land* 1 (2006).

McKay, Ian. "Tartanism triumphant: The construction of Scottishness in Nova Scotia, 1933-1954." *Acadiensis* 21, no. 2 (1992).

McKay, Neill. *A Centenary Sermon Delivered before the Presbytery of Fayetteville at Bluff Church, the 18th Day of October, 1858*. Fayetteville, NC: Presbyterian Office, 1858.

McKean, Thomas. "A Gaelic Songmaker's Response to an English-speaking Nation." *Oral Tradition* 7/1 (1992): 3-27.

McKenzie, N. R. *The Gael Fares Forth: The Romantic Story of Waipu and Sister Settlements*. Auckland: Whitcombe & Tombs Ltd., 1935.

McLean, Allan Campbell. *Ribbon of Fire*. Edinburgh: Kelpie Books, 1985.

———. *A Sound of the Trumpets*. London: Collins, 1971.

———. *The Year of the Stranger*. London: Collins, 1971.

McLean, Marianne. *The People of Glengarry: Highlanders in Transition, 17451820*. Montréal and Kingston: McGill-Queen's University Press, 1991.

McLeod, William and Meg Bateman, eds. *Duanaire na Sracaire: Songbook of the Pillagers. Anthology of Medieval Gaelic Poetry*. Trans. Meg Bateman. Edinburgh: Birlinn, 2007.

McLynn, Frank. *The Jacobites*. London: Routledge Kegan and Paul, 1988.

McPhee, John. *The Crofter and the Laird*. New York: Farrar, Straus and Giroux, 1992.

McPherson, Flora. *Watchman against the World: The Remarkable Journey of Norman McLeod & His People from Scotland to Cape Breton Island and New Zealand*. Wreck Cove, NS: Breton Books, 1993.

McPherson, Margaret. *The Battle of the Braes*. London: Collins, 1972.

McWhiney, Grady. *Cracker Culture: Celtic Ways in the Old South*. Tuscaloosa, AL: University of Alabama Press, 1988.

Meek, Donald E, ed. *Caran an t-Saoghail: The Wiles of the World*. Edinburgh: Birlinn, 2003.

———, "The Gaelic Poets of the Land Agitation." *Transactions of the Gaelic Society of Inverness* 49 (1977).

———, ed. *Màiri Mhór nan Oran*. Glasgow: Gairm, 1977.

———, ed. *Tuath Is Tighearna (Tenants and Landlords): An Anthology of Gaelic Poetry of Social and Political Protest from the Clearances to the Land Agitation (1800-1890)*. Edinburgh: Scottish Academic Press, 1995.

Meyer, Duane. *The Highland Scots of North Carolina, 1732-1776*. Chapel Hill, NC: University of North Carolina Press, 1961.

Miers, Richenda. "The Battle of the Braes." *Scottish Life*, Spring 2001.

———. "Calum's Road." *Scottish Life*, Spring 2009.

———. "Dunrobin Castle." *Scottish Life*, Winter 2004.

———. "Strathnaver's Brutal Clearances." *Scottish Life*, Winter 2008.

Miller, Hugh. *The Cruise of the* Betsey. Boston: Gould and Lincoln, 1858.

———. *Sutherland as It Was and Is, or How a Country May Be Ruined*. Edinburgh: J. Johnstone, 1843.

Mitchell, Joseph. *Reminiscences of My Life in the Highlands*. 2 vols. Newton Abbott, U.K.: David and Charles, 1971.

Mitchell, W. J. T. *Seeing through Race*. Cambridge, MA: Harvard University Press, 2012.

Mitchison, R. "The Highland Clearances." *Scottish Economic and Social History* 1 (1981).

Moffat, Alistair. *Before Scotland: The Story of Scotland before History*. London: Thames and Hudson, 2005.

———. *The Highland Clans*. London: Thames and Hudson, 2013.

Moisley, H. A. "The Deserted Hebrides." *Scottish Studies* 10 (1966): 44-68.

Moore, Christopher. *The Loyalist: Revolution Exile Settlement*. Toronto: McClelland and Stewart, 1994.

Morrison, John. *Painting the Nation: Identity and Nationalism in Scottish Painting, 1800-1920*. Edinburgh: Edinburgh University Press, 2003.

Morton, Tom. *Going Home: The Runrig Story*. Introduction by Angus Peter Campbell. Edinburgh: Mainstream Publishing, 1991.

Muir, Edwin. *Scottish Journey*. Edinburgh: Mainstream Publishing, 1979.

Muir, Richard. *The Lost Villages of Britain*. Stroud, U.K.: History Press, 2009.

Mulock, Thomas. *The Western Highlands and Islands of Scotland Socially Considered*. Edinburgh, 1850.

Munro, Donnie. *Dreams from Hard Places: Oraid Sabhal Mor Ostaig. A Lecture*. Introduction by Alistair Moffat. Glasgow: Scottish Television, n.d.

Murdoch, Alex. *British Emigration*. London: Palgrave Macmillan, 2003.

———. "Emigration from the Scottish Highlands to America in the Eighteenth Century." *British Journal of Eighteenth Century Studies* 21 (1998).

———. "A Scottish Document concerning Emigration to North Carolina in 1992." *North Carolina Historical Review* 67 (1990).

The Napier Commission. Great Britain: Royal Commission on the Crofters and Cottars in the Highlands and Islands of Scotland. *Report of Her Majesty's Commissioners of Inquiry into the Conditions of the Crofters and Cottars in the Highlands and Islands of Scotland*. Edinburgh: HMSO, 1884.

Neat, Timothy. *When I Was Young: The Islands. Voices from Lost Communities in Scotland*. Edinburgh: Birlinn, 2000.

Neat, Timothy and John MacInnes. *The Voice of the Bard: Living Poets and Ancient Tradition in the Highlands and Islands of Scotland.* Northampton, MA: Interlink, 1999.

Newman, Peter C. *Caesars of the Wilderness: The Story of the Hudson's Bay Company.* New York: Penguin, 1988.

Newton, Michael. "My Bard Is in the Highlands: Burns 2009 and a National Scottish Literature." *The Bottle Imp* 5, May 2009.

———. *Bho Chluaidh gu Calasraid/From the Clyde to Callander.* Stornoway: Acair, 2000.

———, ed. *Dùthchas nan Gàidheal: Selected Essays of John MacInnes.* Edinburgh: Birlinn, 2006.

———. "Highland Immigrant Communities in the Cape Fear Valley." *The Argyll Colony Plus*, 2003.

———. "Highland Settlers: Scottish Highland Immigrants in North America. Teaching Materials for the Study of Scottish Highland Immigrants in North America." Presented at the Highland Settlers Conference, Virginia Historical Society and University of Richmond, November 6, 2003.

———. "In Their Own Words: Gaelic Literature in North Carolina." *Scotia* 25, 2001.

———. *We're Indians Sure Enough: The Legacy of the Scottish Highlanders in the United States.* Auburn, NH: Saorsa Media, 2001.

Nicholson, Colin, ed. *Iain Crichton Smith: Critical Essays.* Edinburgh: Edinburgh University Press, 1992.

Nicholson, R. "From Ramsay's *Flora MacDonald* to Raeburn's *MacNab*: The Use of Tartan as a Symbol of Identity." *Textile History* 36, no. 2 (2005).

Nicolson, Adam. *Sea Room: An Island Life in the Hebrides.* New York: North Point Press/Farrar, Straus and Giroux, 2002.

Nicolson, James R. *Shetland.* Newton Abbot, U.K.: David and Charles, 1984.

Norton, Wayne. *Help Us to a Better Land: Crofter Colonies in the Prairie West.* Regina, SK: Canadian Plains Research Center, University of Regina, 1994.

Notestein, Wallace. *The Scot in History.* New Haven, CT: Yale University Press, 1947.

Oates, John A. *The Story of Fayetteville and the Upper Cape Fear.* Raleigh, NC: 1972.

O'Driscoll, Robert, ed. *The Celtic Consciousness.* New York: George Braziller, 1982.

Ormond, Richard. *The Monarch of the Glen: Landseer in the Highlands.* Edinburgh: National Galleries of Scotland, 2005.

Orr, Willie. *Deer Forests, Landlords, and Crofters: The Western Highlands in Victorian and Edwardian Times*. Edinburgh: John Donald, 1982.

———. *Discovering Argyll, Mull and Iona*. Edinburgh: John Donald, 1990.

O'Toole, Fintan. *White Savage: William Johnson and the Invention of America*. New York: Farrar, Straus and Giroux, 2005.

Painter, Nell Irvin. *The History of White People*. New York: W. W. Norton, 2010.

Parker, Anthony. *Scottish Highlanders in Colonial Georgia: The Recruitment, Emigration, and Settlement at Darien, 1735-1748*. Athens, GA: University of Georgia Press, 1997.

Paton, D. M. "Brought to a Wilderness: The Reverend D. MacKenzie of Farr and the Scottish Clearances." *Northern Scotland* 13 (1993).

Patterson, George. "The Coming of the *Hector*." *Dalhousie Review* 3 (1923-1924).

Payne, Michael. *The Most Respectable Place in the Territory: Everyday Life in Hudson's Bay Company Service York Factory, 1788 to 1870*. Studies in Archaeology Architecture and History. Ottawa: National Historic Parks and Sites/Canadian Parks Service/Environment Canada, 1989.

Pennant, Thomas. *A Tour in Scotland 1769*. Edinburgh: Birlinn.

———. *A Tour in Scotland and a Voyage to the Hebrides 1772*. Edinburgh, 1998.

Pennington, Bill. "The Increasing Allure of Faraway Fairways." *New York Times*, July 1, 2012.

Perman, Ray. *The Man Who Gave Away His Island: A Life of John Lorne Campbell of Canna*. Edinburgh: Birlinn, 2010.

Pitkin, R. Macbeth. "The Scots and Their Clergy." *The Highlander*, September/October 2009.

Pittock, Murray. *The Invention of Scotland: The Stuart Myth and the Scottish Identity, 1638 to the Present*. London: Routledge, 1991.

Ployen, C. *Reminiscences of a Voyage to Shetland, Orkney and Scotland in the Summer of 1839*. Lerwick, U.K.: Manson, 1894.

Powell, William S. *North Carolina: A History*. Chapel Hill, NC: University of North Carolina Press, 1988.

Prebble, John. *Culloden*. London: Penguin, 1967.

———. *Glencoe*. London: Penguin, 1968.

———. *The Highland Clearances*. London: Penguin, 1963.

———. *John Prebble's Scotland*. London: Penguin, 1996.

———. *The King's Jaunt: George IV in Scotland*. London: Collins, 1989.

———. *Mutiny: Highland Regiments in Revolt 1743-1804*. London: Penguin Books, 1977.

Purser, John. *Scotland's Music: A History of the Traditional and Classical Music of Scotland from Early Times to the Present Day*. Foreword by Stewart Conn. Edinburgh: Mainstream Publishing, 2007.

Rae, J. "The Crofter Problem." *Contemporary Review* 47 (1885).

Rankin, Effie. *As a' Bhraighe (Beyond the Braes): The Gaelic Songs of Allan the Ridge MacDonald (1794-1868)*. Sydney, NS: Cape Breton University Press, 2004.

Rankin, H. F. *The Moores Creek Bridge Campaign, 1776*. Burgaw, NC: Moores Creek Battleground Association, 1986.

Rattray, W. J. *The Scot in British North America*. 4 vols. Toronto: MacLean and Co., 1880-1894.

Ray, Celeste. *Highland Heritage: Scottish Americans in the American South*. Chapel Hill, NC: University of North Carolina Press, 2001.

Ray, Celeste, ed. *Transatlantic Scots*. Tuscaloosa, AL: University of Alabama Press, 2005.

Reid, Leonard M. *Sons of the Hector*. New Glasgow, NS: Hector Publishing, 1973.

Reid, Stanford W., ed. *The Scottish Tradition in Canada*. Toronto: McClelland and Stewart, 1976.

Richards, Eric. *Agrarian Transformation and the Evictions, 1745-1886*. Vol. 1 of *A History of the Highland Clearances*. London: Croom Helm, 1982.

———. *Britannia's Children: Emigration from England, Scotland, Wales and Ireland since 1600*. London: Hambledon and London, 2004.

———. *Debating the Highland Clearances: Debates and Documents in Scottish History*. Edinburgh: Edinburgh University Press, 2007.

———. *Destination Australia: Migration to Australia since 1901*. Sydney: University of New South Wales Press, 2008.

———. *Emigration, Protest, Reasons*. Vol. 2 of *A History of the Highland Clearances*. London: Croom Helm, 1985.

———. *From Hirta to Port Philip: The St. Kilda Emigration to Australia in 1852*. South Lochs, Isle of Lewis: Islands Book Trust, 2010.

———. *The Highland Clearances: People, Landlords and Rural Turmoil*. Edinburgh: Birlinn, 2000.

———. "The Highland Scots of South Australia." *Journal of the Historical Society of South Australia* 4 (1978).

———. "How Tame Were the Highlanders during the Clearances?" *Scottish Studies* 17 (1973).

———. *The Leviathan of Wealth*. London: Routledge and Kegan Paul, 1973.

———. "The Mind of Patrick Sellar (1780-1851)." *Scottish Studies* 15 (1971).

———. *Patrick Sellar and the Highland Clearances*. Edinburgh: Polygon, 1999.

———. "Problems on the Cromartie Estate, 1851-53." *Scottish Historical Review* 52 (1973).

———. "The Sutherland Clearances: New Evidence from Dunrobin." *Northern Scotland* 2 (1976).

Ritchie, Fiona. *The NPR Curious Listener's Guide to Celtic Music*. Foreword by Eileen Ivers. New York: Grand Central Press/Perigee, 2004.

Rixson, Denis. *The Hebridean Traveller*. Edinburgh: Birlinn, 2004.

———. *Knoydart: A History*. Edinburgh: Birlinn, 2011.

———. *The Small Isles: Canna, Rum, Eigg and Muck*. Edinburgh: Birlinn, 2001.

Robertson, J. I. *The First Highlander: Major General David Stewart of Garth*. East Linton: Tuckwell, 1998.

Robertson, P. Report on the Trial of Patrick Sellar, Esq, Factor of the Most Noble the Marquis and Marchioness of Stafford for the Crimes of Culpable Homicide, Real Injury, and Oppression before the Circuit Court of Justiciary, Held at Inverness, on Tuesday 23 April, 1816. Edinburgh, 1816.

Robinson, Neil. *To the Ends of the Earth: Norman McLeod and the Highlander Migration to Nova Scotia and New Zealand*. Auckland: HarperCollins Publishers, 1997.

Rogers, Pat, ed. *Johnson and Boswell in Scotland: A Journey to the Hebrides*. New Haven, CT: Yale University Press, 1993.

Ross, Alexander M. "Loch Laxford to the Zorras: A Sutherland Emigration to Upper Canada." *Scottish Tradition* 18 (1993).

Ross, David. *Children of the Clearances*. Illustrated by Tony O'Donnell. New Lanark, U.K.: Waverley Books, 2008.

Ross, Donald. *The Glengarry Evictions*. Glasgow: Printed by W.G. Blackie & Co., 1853.

———. *The Russians of Ross-shire or Massacre of the Rosses in Strathcarron*. Glasgow, 1854.

———. *The Scottish Highlanders: Their Present Sufferings and Future Prospects*. Glasgow, 1852.

Ross, Raymond J., and Joy Hendry, eds. *Sorley Maclean: Critical Essays*. Introduction by Seamus Heaney. Edinburgh: Scottish Academic Press, 1986.

Roy, G. Ross. "'We Are Exiles from Our Father's Land': Nineteenth-Century Scottish-Canadian Poets." In *The Immigrant Experience. Proceedings of a Conference held at the University of Guelph-June 1989*. Ed. Catherine Kerrigan. Guelph, ON: University of Guelph, 1992.

Rupert's Land to Riel: Manitoba 125 A History. Vol. 1. Winnipeg: Great Plains Publications, 1993.

Russell, Michael. *A Different Country: The Photographs of Werner Kissling*. Edinburgh: Birlinn, 2002.

———. *A Poem of Remote Lives: The Enigma of Werner Kissling*. Foreword by Gus Wylie. Glasgow: Neil Wilson Publishing, 1997.

———. *In Waiting: Travels in the Shadow of Edwin Muir*. Glasgow: Neil Wilson Publishing, 1998.

Sage, Rev. Donald. *Memorabilia Domestica, or Domestic Life in the North of Scotland*. Wick: W. Rae, 1981 [1889].

Said, Edward W. *Orientalism*. London: Routledge Kegan Paul, 1978.

Sandison, Bruce MacGregor. "The People of Helmsdale." *Scottish Life*, Winter 2006.

Sawers, June and James Sawers. *The Water Is Wide: Celtic Poems on Time, Memory, and Loss*. n.p.: Xlibris, 2009.

Sawyers, June Skinner. *Celtic Music*. New York: Da Capo Press, 2001.

———. "Croick Church and the Highland Clearances." *Keltic Fringe* 7, no. 4 (1992-1993).

———. "A Fitting Memorial to the Highland Clearances." *Keltic Fringe* 10, no. 1 (1995).

———. "A New Day Dawning: The Struggle for National Identity in Contemporary Scottish Song." *Scottish Tradition* 19 (1994).

———. *Praying with Celtic Saints, Prophets, Martyrs, and Poets*. Franklin, WI: Sheed and Ward, 2001.

———, ed. *The Road North: 300 Years of Classic Scottish Travel Writing*. Glasgow: The In Pinn/Neil Wilson Publishing, 2000.

Schaitberger, Lilian B. *Scots of McIntosh*. Darien, GA: Darien News, 1986.

Scobie, Stephen. *Taking the Gate: A Journey through Scotland*. Red Deer, AB: Red Deer College Press, 1996.

The Scots Musical Museum. Ed. James Johnson and Robert Burns. 6 vols. Edinburgh: J. Johnson, 1787-1803.

Scotsman, April 19, 1845.

Scott, Paul H., ed. *Scotland: A Concise Cultural History*. Edinburgh: Mainstream Publishing, 1993.

Scottish Parliament. *Scottish Parliament Official Report: Highland Clearances* 8, no. 7: col 700-12, September 27, 2000.

"Scotus Americanus, Information Concerning the Province of North Carolina Addressed to Emigrants from the Highlands and Western Isles of Scotland. In *Eighteenth Century [sic] Tracts Concerning North Carolina*. Ed. William K. Boyd. Raleigh, NC: Edwards & Broughton Co., 1927.

Seddon, Peter. "Clearance Drawings." *Cencrastus*, Autumn 1983.

Sellar, Thomas. *The Sutherland Evictions of 1814*. London: Longmans, Green, 1883.

Shapiro, Henry D. *Appalachia on Our Mind: The Southern Mountains and Mountaineers in the American Consciousness, 1870-1920*. Chapel Hill, NC: University of North Carolina Press, 1978.

Shaw, Margaret Fay. *From the Alleghenies to the Hebrides: An Autobiography*. Edinburgh: Canongate, 1993.

Shepperson, George. "Harriet Beecher Stowe and Scotland, 1852-53." *Scottish Historical Review* 32 (1952).

Sherwood, Roland H. *Pictou Pioneers: A Story of the First Hundred Years in the History of Pictou Town*. Hantsport, NS: Lancelot Press, 1973.

Silver, Alfred. *Red River Story*. New York: Ballatine Books, 1988.

Sim, Duncan. *American Scots: The Scottish Diaspora and the USA*. Edinburgh: Dunedin Academic Press, 2011.

Sinclair, Alexander MacLean, ed. *The Gaelic Bards from 1715 to 1765*. Charlottetown, PEI: MacTalla Publishing, 1892.

Sinclair, D. M. "Gaelic in Nova Scotia." *Dalhousie Review* 30 (1950-1951).

———. "Highland Emigration to Nova Scotia." *Dalhousie Review* 30 (1950-1951).

Sinclair, John, ed. *The Statistical Account of Scotland, 1791-1799*. Reprint. East Ardsley, U.K.: EP Publishing, 1983.

Sinclair, John C. "The Gaelic Element in North Carolina." *University of North Carolina Magazine* 10 (1860).

Sked, P. *Culloden*. Edinburgh: National Trust for Scotland, 1997.

———. *Glenfinnan*. Edinburgh: National Trust for Scotland, 1991.

Skene, W. F. *Celtic Scotland*. Edinburgh: Maclachlan and Stewart, 1880.

———. *Sketches of Highland Character*. Edinburgh: Edmonston and Douglas, 1873.

Smith, Alexander. *A Summer in Skye*. Edinburgh, 1912.

Smith, Iain Crichton. *Collected Poems*. Rev. ed. Manchester: Carcanet Press, 2011.

———. *Consider the Lilies*. London: Gollancz, 1968.

———. *Towards the Human: Selected Essays*. Loanhead: Macdonald Publishers, 1986.

Smith, Sheena. *Horatio McCulloch 1805-1867*. Glasgow Museums and Art Galleries, 1988.

Smout, T. C. *A Century of the Scottish People, 1830-1950*. New Haven, CT: Yale University Press, 1986.

———. *A History of the Scottish People, 1560-1830*. London: Collins, 1969.

Somers, Robert. *Journal of a Tour in Scotland in 1819*. London: J. Murray, 1929.

———. *Letters from the Highlands on the Famine of 1847 (1846)*. Inverness: Melvin Press, 1980.

Somhairle MacGill-eain/Sorley MacLean. Introduction by William Gillies. Exhibition catalogue. Edinburgh: National Library of Scotland, 1981.

The Songs of Duncan Ban MacIntyre 1724-1812. Ed.Angus MacLeod. Edinburgh: Published by Oliver and Boyd for the Scottish Gaelic Texts Society, 1952.

Sparling, Heather. "Cape Breton Island: Living in the Past? Gaelic Language, Song, and Competition." In *Island Songs: A Global Repertoire*. Ed. Godfrey Baldacchino. Lanham, MD: Scarecrow Press, 2011.

Stafford, Fiona. *The Sublime Savage: James Macpherson and the Poems of Ossian*. Edinburgh: Edinburgh University Press, 1988.

Stewart, David. *Sketches of the Character, Manner and Present State of the Highlanders of Scotland*. 2 vols. Edinburgh: Printed for A. Constable, 1822.

Stewart, Katharine. *Crofters and Crofting*. Glasgow: William Blackwood, 1980.

Stowe, Harriet Beecher. *Sunny Memories of Foreign Lands*. 2 vols. London, 1854.

Stuart, Kent. "The Scottish Crofter Colony, Saltcoats, 1889-1904." *Saskatchewan History* 24, no. 2 (1971).

Sullivan, Buddy. *Early Days on the Georgia Tidewater: The Story of McIntosh County and Sapelo*. Darien, GA: McIntosh County Board of Commissioners, 1992.

Szechi, Daniel. *1715: The Great Jacobite Rebellion*. New Haven, CT: Yale University Press, 2006.

Tanner, Helen Hornbeck, ed. *The Settling of North America: The Atlas of the Great Migrations into North America from the Ice Age to the Present*. New York: Macmillan, 1995.

Thomas, Clara. "'The Chariot of Ossian': Myth and Manitoba in *The Diviners*." *Journal of Canadian Studies* 13 (Fall 1978): 55-63.

———. *The Manawaka World of Margaret Laurence*. Toronto: McClelland and Stewart, 1975.

———. "Margaret, Morag, and the Scottish Ancestors. Scottish Influences on Canadian Literature: A Selection of Papers Delivered at the University of Edinburgh, May 9-12, 1991." Ed. Michael Williams. *British Journal of Canadian Studies* (1992).

Thompson, Elizabeth, ed. *The Emigrant's Guide to North America*. Toronto: Natural Heritage Books, 1998.

Thomson, Derick S., ed. *The Companion to Gaelic Scotland*. Oxford: Blackwell, 1983.

Thomson, Derick S. *An Introduction to Gaelic Poetry*. Edinburgh: Edinburgh University Press, 1989.

Thomson, William P. L. *The Little General and the Rousay Crofters: Crisis and Conflict on an Orkney Estate*. Edinburgh: John Donald, 2000.

Thornber, I. "Some Morvern Songwriters of the Nineteenth Century." *Transactions of the Gaelic Society of Inverness* 53 (1982-1984).

The Times, 20 May 1845.

The Times, 2 June 1845.

The Times, 23 August 1845.

The Times, 22 October 1846.

"To Help Scotch Crofters." *New York Times*, August 26, 1885, p. 1.

Trevor-Roper, Hugh. "The Invention of Tradition: The Highland Tradition of Scotland." In *The Invention of Tradition*. Ed. Eric Hobsbawn and T. Ranger. Cambridge: Cambridge University Press, 1983.

———. *The Invention of Scotland: Myth and History*. New Haven, CT: Yale University Press, 2009.

"Ulva Clearance Story." *Scots Magazine*, September 1984.

Vining, Elizabeth G. *Flora MacDonald: Her Life in the Highlands and America*. London: Bles, 1967.

Walker, Carol Kyros. *Breaking Away: Coleridge in Scotland*. New Haven, CT: Yale University Press, 2002.

Waterston, Elizabeth. *Rapt in Plaid: Canadian Literature and Scottish Tradition*. Toronto: University of Toronto Press, 2001.

Watson, A. and E. Allan. "De-population by Clearances and Non-enforced Emigration in the North-east Highlands." *Northern Scotland* 10 (1990).

Watson, James Carmichael, ed. *Òrain us Luinneagan le Màairi nighean Alasdair Ruaidh/Gaelic Songs of Mary MacLeod*. Vol. 9 of *Scottish Gaelic Texts*. Edinburgh: Scottish Gaelic Texts, 1934.

Watson, Roderick. *The Literature of Scotland*. London: Macmillan, 1984.

Weber, Max. *The Protestant Ethic and the Spirit of Capitalism*. London, 1930.

White, Patrick C. T., ed. *Lord Selkirk's Diary, 1803-04: A Journal of His Travels*. Toronto: Champlain Society, 1958.

Wightman, Andy. *The Poor Had No Lawyers: Who Owns Scotland (And How They Got It)*. Edinburgh: Birlinn, 2010.

Wilkie, Jim. *Metagama: A Journey from Lewis to the New World*. Edinburgh: Birlinn, 2001.

Williams, Elly. *The Leckhelm Evictions*. Ullapool: Ullapool Museum, 2003.

Williams, Scott. "The Skirl of the Bagpipes in the Carolinas: Bill Caudill Reflects on How Piping Has Shaped His Life." *Celtic Heritage*, January/February 2005.

Williams, Terry. "The Great Highland Cattle Runs." *Scottish Life*, Summer 2012.

Williamson, Theresa and Maurício Hora. "In the Name of the Future, Rio Is Destroying Its Past." *New York Times*, August 13, 2012.

Wilson, Charles and William Ferris, eds. *Encyclopedia of Southern Culture*. Chapel Hill, NC: University of North Carolina Press, 1989.

Wilton, Brian. *Tartans*. London: Aurum, 2007.

Withers, Charles W. J. *Gaelic Scotland: The Transformation of a Culture Region*. London: Routledge, 1988.

———. *Urban Highlanders: Highland-Lowland Migration and Urban Gaelic Culture*. East Linton, U.K.: Tuckwell Press, 1998.

Womack, Peter. *Improvement and Romance: Constructing the Myth of the Highlands*. Basingstoke, U.K.: Macmillan, 1989.

Wordsworth, Dorothy. *Recollections of a Tour Made in Scotland*. Introduction by Carol Kyros Walker. New Haven, CT: Yale University Press, 1997.

Wormald, Jenny, ed. *Scotland: A History*. New York: Oxford University Press, 2005.

Wronski, Richard. "Measure Would Speed State's Ability to Take Property." *Chicago Tribune*, April 10, 2012.

Yeadon, David. *Seasons on Harris: A Year in Scotland's Outer Hebrides*. Foreword by Adam Nicolson. New York: HarperCollins Publishers, 2006.

Zumkhawala-Cook, R. "The Mark of Scottish America: Heritage Identity and the Tartan Monster." *Diaspora* 14, no. 1 (2005)

Index

Note that page numbers refer to the print edition

Acair 9
Act of Union (1707) 60
Act of Proscription (1746) 9
Adam, William 139
"Address of Beelzebub" (Burns) 9, 88, 147
Admiral (ship) 9, 20
Agricultural Revolution 9
agriculture 10
Aignish (Lewis) 155-56, 217
Aird, Rev. Gustavus 10, 46, 54-56, 79, 91
Aitchison, Peter, and Andrew Cassell 9, 49, 90, 102, 138, 214, 227
Albini, Joseph L. 71
Allan, Julia 165
Alma, Battle of 20
American South 134-35
And the Cock Crew (MacColla) 10, 74, 76, 143
Anderson, James 241
Antigonish Heritage Museum 10
Ardnamurchan 11
Argyll 11-12, 18, 41, 72, 77, 120, 190, 192, 194
Argyll Colony 11, 39. *See also* Cape Fear; North Carolina
Arichonan, 12
Armadale Castle, 12
Arran 39; Arran Clearances 12-13, 127

Aros Experience 12
As an Fheareann / From the Land 13-14, 154
Ascherson, Neal 14, 30, 52, 83, 99
Asia 226
Assynt 217; Assynt Clearances 14-15
Assynt Crofters' Trust 14, 185
Assynt Foundation 15
Auchindrain 15, 247
Australia 7, 9, 12, 15-16, 19, 90, 95, 102, 125, 165, 177-78, 180, 198, 208, 213, 215, 217, 219, 226-27, 236, 248
Australian Aborigines 11, 109
Avoch 216

Badbea 17-18, 34
Baddoch 198
baile 18
Baillie, James of Dochfour 87
Balaclava, Battle of 20-21
Balchladdich (Assynt) 217
Baldoon 18-19, 228
Balmoral 198, 255
"Balmoralism" 101
Balmoral Castle 101, 110, 184, 255
Balnagowan 198
Banff 216
Bannockburn, Battle of 116
Barbecue Church 195
Barometer Rising (MacLennan) 157
Barra 19-20, 26, 37, 50, 52, 89, 101, 120, 156, 171, 188, 250
Barry, Sir Charles 63

Basu, Paul, 109, 111, 219, 227
Battle of Alma 20
Battle of Balaclava 20-21
Battle of Bannockburn 116
Battle of the Braes 21, 43, 73, 105, 109, 153-54, 206, 217
Battle of Culloden 21-22, 24, 59, 77, 97, 100, 109, 115, 117, 136, 140, 145, 158, 183, 243, 252
Battle of Falkirk 24
Battle of Gettysburg 134
Battle of Killiecrankie 22, 115
Battle of King's Mountain 22-23
Battle of Moore's Creek Bridge 23, 144-46, 173
Battle of the Plains of Abraham 23-24, 50, 79, 158
Battle of Prestonpans 24, 115
Battle of Seven Oaks 24, 229
Battle of Sheriffmuir 115
Bayne, Iain 221
Beach Allegory (Maclean) 154, 244
Beamish, Sally 24-25, 209
Beaton Institute 25
Beaton, Sister Margaret 25
Belfast (Prince Edward Island) 26, 212, 228, 233
Benbecula 19, 26, 48, 70, 89, 120, 188, 239
Ben Bragghie statue 26
Bennett, Margaret 26, 107
Bennett, Martyn 27, 94, 107, 210-11
Bentham, Jeremy 27-28, 197
Bernera Riot 28
Bett, John 176
Bettyhill 7, 28, 102
blackhouse 29
Black House Museum 29
Blackie, John Stuart 29, 128
Black, Rev. John 29, 122
Black, Ronald 93
Black Watch 79, 106-107
Black Watch (play) 107
Blair Atholl 198

Blair, Rev. Duncan Black 29-30
Bliadhna nan Caorach. *See* Year of the Sheep
The Blood Is Strong (film) 30, 35-36, 40, 103, 146
Bold, Alan 183
Boreraig (Skye) 30-31, 154, 209
Bosnia 70
"Boston States" 31, 1632
Boswell, James 31, 67, 93, 118, 145, 201, 213, 223
Braes, Battle of the. *See* Battle of the Braes
Brahan Seer 31-32
Brave (film) 219
Braveheart (film) 219
Brill, Kenny 32, 74
brochs 32
Brocket, Lord 125-26, 231
Brown, George Mackay 183
Brown, Wallace 140
Bruce County (Ontario) 132-33, 164
Bruce, James 32-33
Buckingham, Sarah 1643
Bumsted, J. M. 88, 202
Burghead 139, 216
Burke, Gregory 107
Burns, Robert 9, 88, 116, 135, 143, 147
Burt, Edmund 33
Butcher's Broom (Gunn) 74-75, 183, 230
Bute 77

Caithness 14, 34, 190, 192
Calder, Jenni 228
Caledonia (ship) 13
Caledonian Canal 34
Calgacus 58
Calgary (Isle of Mull) 34
"Calum's Road" (tune) 34-35
Calum's Road (novel and play) 35, 95, 112, 166
Cameron, Alexander 257

Index

Cameron, Allan 257
Cameron, Donald of Lochiel 188
Cameron, Hugh 35
Cameron, John of Corrychoillie 103
Campbell, Angus Peter 13, 30, 35-36, 83, 111, 208, 212, 254
Campbell, Colin 20
Campbell, Duncan 250
Campbell, Hugh 194
Campbell, Rev. Hugh 195
Campbell, James 169
Campbell, Rev. James 195
Campbell, Captain John 23
Campbell, John (factor) 72
Campbell, John Francis 37
Campbell, John Lorne 37, 231
Campbell, Robert of Glenlyon 86
Campbeltown 198
Campey, Lucille H. 18, 39, 89, 98, 133, 228
Canada 7, 9, 12, 13-14, 18-19, 23-24, 79, 87-90, 92, 95, 102, 114, 119, 121, 125, 132, 165, 180, 215, 219, 226-27, 235-36, 249
"Canadian Boat Song" (poem) 38
Canna, 38-39, 231
Cape Breton Island 39, 48, 159-63, 177, 227. *See also* Nova Scotia
Cape Breton Road (Macdonald) 144
Cape Breton University 25
Cape Fear (North Carolina) 39-40, 73, 163, 194-95, 227. *See also* Argyll Colony; North Carolina
Capercaillie 40, 103, 148-49, 166, 170, 210
Cape Wrath 198
Cargill, William 197
Carinish (North Uist) 40
Carmichael, Alexander 40-41
Carmina Gadelica (Carmichael) 40
Carnes-McNaughton, Linda F. 77
Carruthers, Robert Mackay 41
caschrom 41
Casket (newspaper) 11

Cathcart, Lady 250
Cathcart, Reginald 20
Ceilidh Ménage 104, 210
Celtic revival. *See* Highlandism
Celtic Twilight 109
Central Board of Management for Highland Relief 41
Centre for History 42
Centre for Mountain Studies 42
Chamberlain, Joseph 262
Chantrey, Francis 26, 84
Charles II 106
Cherns, Richard 222
Cheviot sheep 42, 133, 233
The Cheviot, the Stag and the Black Black Oil (play) 42-43, 92, 103, 176, 191, 230
chieftains 43
Chisholm, Donald 108
Chisholm, William 117, 240, 264
Church of Scotland 44, 63, 79
cianalas 44
clachans 44
Clan Cameron Museum 45
Clan Donald Centre 12, 45-46, 176
clan museums 46
clans 44-45
Clarke, F. W. 249
clearance (defined) 7, 46; modern examples of 47
"The Clearances" (short story) 47
Clearances studies 47, 197
Cohen, R. 227
Coigach 198, 216
Colbost Folk Museum 47
Coll 198
Colonsay 47-48
Columba Project 48
Commissioners of the Forfeited Estates 48
community buy-outs 48, 84
An Comunn Gàidhealach (Highland Association) 48
Comunn na Gàidhlig (CNAG) 48

Connor, Ralph (Dr. Charles William Gordon) 49
Consider the Lilies (Smith) 35, 49, 74-76, 207, 230, 235
Cooley, James L. 73
Cooper, Derek 177, 213
Cooper, James Fenimore, 51
Cope, John 24
Cormack, Arthur 104
Cornell, Joseph 154
Cornwallis, Lord 23
cottars 49
Countess of Sutherland (Lady Stafford, 1st Duchess of Sutherland) 121, 266
Cowboy Celtic 104, 210
Craig, David 8, 83, 111
Crawford, James 155
Crèvecoeur, J. Hector St. John de 49-51
Crieff 139
Crimean War 20, 51, 106, 220
crofter colonies 51-52
Crofter Emigrants Leaving the Hebrides (McTaggart) 182
The Crofter and the Laird (McPhee) 179
crofts 51
crofters 51
Crofters' Holdings Act (1886) 52, 85, 172, 190, 206
Crofters' Party 216
Crofters' Union 52
Crofters' War 53, 206, 216
crofting 53, 103, 129
Croick Church 44, 53-57, 59, 155, 208. *See also* Glencalvie
"The Cuillin" (Maclean) 152, 244
Culloden (film) 57-58
Culloden, Battle of. *See* Battle of Culloden
Culloden Battlefield Visitor Centre 58. *See also* Battle of Culloden
Culloden Moor Suite (jazz suite) 58-59

Culrain 59
"culture of victimization" 59
Cunningham, Phil 76-77, 211, 238

Dale, David 192-93
Daly, Alyxis 171
Darien (Georgia) 60
Darling, Frank Fraser 60
Darwin, Charles 173, 197, 237
Davies, Peter Maxwell 25, 94, 115
Davitt, Michael 105, 216
Dawidoff, Nicholas 253
The Death of General Wolfe (West) 60-61
Declaration of Independence 141
deer forests 61
Deer Park Raid. *See* Pairc Deer Raid
Deeside 61
deforcement 62
deforestation 62
Delane, John 55-56
Desperate Journey, The (Fidler) 230
Destitution Road 62
Devine, T. M. (Thomas) 8, 10, 18, 62, 72, 113, 136, 138-40, 216, 226, 228, 244-45, 248
Disarming Act (1746) 62
Disclothing Act (1748) 62
Disruption, the 55, 63, 79, 216
Distraining for Rent (Wilkie) 254
Dixon, Thomas 134
The Diviners (Laurence) 63, 130-31
Donaldson, Gordon 211
Donaldson, William 115
Donn, Rob 63, 184
Douglas, Blair 185, 212, 221
Duke of Argyll 262
Duke of Cumberland (William Augustus) 21, 24, 58-59, 77, 194-95, 252
Dunbar, Sir David 137
Dunbeath Heritage Centre 63
Dun Caan (Raasay) 93
Dunmaglass 198

Index

Dunmore, Lord 95
Dunn, Charles 95
Dunrobin Castle 63-64
Dunvegan Castle 64
Durness 217; Durness Clearances 64-65
Dust Bowl 192
dùthchas 65

Each Man's Son (MacLennan) 156
Easter Ross 173, 216
Education (Scotland) Act (1872) 66
Eigg 38, 48, 66, 161
Elgin Cathedral 66
The Emigrant Ship (Maclean) 155
emigrant ships 66-67
The Emigrants (statue) 67-68, 166, 230, 247, 255
Emigration Stone 69
enclosure movement 69-70
End of the Trail (sculpture) 78-79
Engels, Friedrich 174
England: enclosure movement in 69-70, 129
Eriskay 48, 70, 175
Eriskay: A Poem of Remote Lives (film) 70, 122-23
ethnic cleansing 8, 70-71, 83
Evanton 216
The Exiles (statue) 68, 166, 255

factors 72
Faed, John 72
Faed, Thomas 72-73, 78-79, 218
Fairhurst, Dr. Horace 74, 219
Falkirk, Battle of 24
Farr 198
Faulkner, Barry 78
Faulkner, William 51, 135-36
Fenyö, Krisztina 41, 57, 70, 83, 193
Ferguson, Patrick 23
Fergusson, Christina 117
fermtouns 10, 138-39
Ferrard, David 32, 74, 85

feu 74
Fifeshire Journal (newspaper) 193
"final solution" 111
Finlayson, Alexander 21, 73
Finlayson, Malcolm 21
Fir Chlis (Northern Lights) 171
Fire in the Glen (recording) 76-77, 238
Fleming, Rae 133
Fochabers 139
Forbes, Duncan 58
Forbes, William 194
forfeited estates 77
Fort Augustus 77
"Fort Bragg Clearances" 77-78. See also North Carolina
Fort Douglas 229
Fort George 78, 92
Fort William 78, 198
Foster, Thomas Campbell 55
France 23-24, 226
Fraser Highlanders 23, 79
Fraser, Hugh 119
Fraser, James Earle 78-79, 191
Fraser-Macintosh, Charles 79, 188, 206
Fraser, Simon 60-61
Free Church of Scotland 44, 63, 79, 91
Free Presbyterian Church 63
French and Indian War 23, 79, 119. See also Seven Years War
Fry, Michael 79-80, 98-99

Gaelic: as "language of Eden" 130
Gaelic Books Council 81
Gaelic College (Colaisde na Gàidhlig) 81
Gaelic College of Arts and Crafts 179
Gaelic Society of Cape Breton 149
Gaelic Society of London 81
Gàidhealtachd 81
Galloway 138
Galloway Levellers 138. See also Lowland Clearances

Galt, John 38
Garioch, Robert 183
Gartcosh Steel Works 131
Gartymore Land League Cairn 81

Gearrannan Blackhouse Village 81-82
Geikie, Sir Archibald 82-83, 154
genocide, 83
George II 106, 140
George III 23, 39, 140
George IV 83-84, 88, 147, 226
Georgia 141, 254
Gettysburg, Battle of 134
Gibb, Robert 20
Gibson, Henry 84, 87
Gibson, Rob 8, 11, 13, 61, 84, 103-104, 119, 196, 198, 210, 242
Gigha 11, 39, 48, 84
Gillanders, James Falconer 54-55, 72, 91
Gillespie, Thomas 84-85, 87
Gillies, Anne Lorne 117, 266
Gillis, Anna 108
Gillis, John R. 69
"Gilmartin" (song) 32, 74, 85
Gladstone, William F. 85, 128
Glasgow Argus (newspaper) 85
Glencalvie Clearances 10, 53-57, 105, 155, 216, 240, 261. *See also* Croick Church
Glen Clunie 199
Glencoe 85-86
Glencoe (McCulloch) 175
Glendale 86-87, 217
Glendale Martyrs 171. *See also* John MacPherson
Glen Dee 198
Glenelchaig 198
Glenelg 73, 87
Glen Ey 198
Glenfinnan 87
Glengarry Clearances 84-85, 87-88, 101

Glengarry County (Ontario) 49, 88-89, 147, 227
Glen Lui 199
Glen More 85, 199
Glenorchy 89
Glen Quaich 202
Glen Quoich 199
Glen Tanar 199
Glen Tilt 202
Gloomy Memories (Macleod) 49, 89, 111, 168-69, 220, 239
Gordon, Col. John of Cluny 9, 19-20, 26, 89, 250
Gordon, Seton 89-90
Gow, Niel 215
Graham, Donald John 165
Graham, I. C. C. 140
Graham, John of Claverhouse ("Bonnie Dundee"), 22, 243
Graham, Peter 218
Grand Tour 109
Grant, Alistair 115
Grant, Charles 87
Grant, Elizabeth of Rothiemurcus 90
Grantown on Spey 139
Gray, George 178
Great Britain 23-24, 52, 55-56, 97, 100, 105
Great Glen 90
Great Highland Famine 90-91, 101, 132, 164, 174, 248, 259
Greenyards 20, 91-92, 97, 113, 217
Griffith, D. W. 134
Grigor, Iain Fraser 105
Grimble, Ian 83, 264
Grosse Île 20, 92, 154
Gruids 217; Gruids Clearances 92, 97
Gunn, Campbell 221
Gunn, John 17
Gunn, Neil M. 63, 74-75, 103, 221; memorial to 92
Guthrie, Woody 192
Guthro, Bruce 92, 144, 221-22

Index

Hallaig (Raasay) 93
"Hallaig" (Maclean) 93-94, 96, 115, 152-53, 155, 170, 208, 210, 213
Hallaig: The Poetry and Landscape of Sorley Maclean (film) 94, 96, 192
Handa 94
Harris 16, 39-40, 48, 51, 120, 131, 188-89; and Harris Clearances 95
Harrower, David 35, 95, 112
Harvard University 95
Hawley, Gen. Henry 24
Heaney, Seamus 94-96, 153
Hebridean Clearances 101
The Hector (ship) 67, 96-97, 131, 202
Helmsdale 97, 121, 138, 166, 229, 246-47, 255
Hercules (ship) 16
Heritable Jurisdiction (Scotland) Act (1746) 9
Hewitson, Jim 228
Heydrich, Reinhard 111
"Hey, Johnnie Cope, Are You Awake Yet?" (song) 24, 115
Highland Clearances apology for 11; art of 72-73, 129, 131, 153-56, 176, 181-82, 193, 254-55; blame 30; children's literature on 43; crofting, as legacy of 53, 103; and deer forests 61; deniers of 79-80; end of 52-53; as ethnic cleaning 8, 70-71, 83, 160; fiction of 74-76, 103, 117, 163-64; and Holocaust 83, 111; in Jacobite songs 117; and landlords 129; legacy of 157; and long memory 134; Lowlanders' attitude, toward Highlanders during 139-40; music of 32, 74, 76-77, 103-104, 149, 163, 172, 209-11; newspaper coverage of 184-85, 186, 193, 220-21, 236, 255; phases of 101; photography of 231, 239-40, 255; planned villages 139; poetry of 142-43, 148, 153, 173-74, 203-209; reasons for 100-101; resistance to 215-17; women, role of in 55, 109. *See also* individual Clearance sites
"The Highland Clearances" (song) 57
The Highland Clearances (Prebble) 211
Highland Clearances Trail (Gibson) 103
The Highland Drover (monument) 104
Highland drovers 103; songs of 104
Highlander: figure of, as Bonny Highland Laddie 116, 135; Lowlander attitude toward 116; Otherness of 116
Highlander (newspaper) 186
Highland Farewell (McDonald) 175, 210
"The Highlander's Farewell" (song) 117
Highland Folk Museum 104
Highland and Islands Enterprise 126
Highlandism 109
Highland Land Law Reform Association 128. *See also* Highland Land League
Highland Land League 105. See also Highland Land Law Reform Association
"Highland problem" 52, 105
Highland regiments 79, 105-107
Highland River (Gunn) 74-75, 92, 223
Highlands 110; romanticizing of 218-19
Highlands and Islands Emigration Society 16, 105
Highland Society 107
Highland Society of Glasgow 107
Highland Society of London 107
Highland Village Museum 108-109

| 307 |

History of the Highland Clearances (Mackenzie) 110-11, 149, 167
Holocaust 83, 111
Holocaust effect 111
Hogg, James 38, 116-17, 240
House of Memories 179
Hudson's Bay Company (HBC) 24, 29, 228-30, 249, 258
Hugo, Richard 111-12, 209
Hunter, James 8, 48, 80, 84, 102, 112, 129, 140, 191, 221, 223, 228
Hunty 139
Hurren, Brian 221
Hutchinson, Roger 35, 112, 166, 254

I didn't go willingly, I went sadly (Maclean) 154
"improvements" 113
Improvers 28, 173, 191
"I Mourn for the Highlands" (song) 76-77
Industrial Revolution 97
Inner Sound (Maclean) 155
Innes, James 194
Innes, Jim 253
Inveraray 113, 139
Invergordon 216
Inverness 189, 193, 216, 247
Inverness Advertiser (newspaper) 57, 113, 185, 193, 220
Inverness Courier (newspaper) 41, 193, 236, 240
In Waiting: Travels in the Shadow of Edwin Muir (Russell) 184
Ireland 91, 95, 216
Irish Famine 90, 95
Irish Land Act 216
Irish Land League 216
Irving, David 80
Islay 11, 37, 39, 114, 139, 194
Isle of Arran Heritage Museum 114
Ivory, William 21, 153, 206

Jacobite Rising (1715) 45, 87, 106, 115, 136, 217
Jacobite Rising (1745) 22, 24, 45, 70, 87, 115, 136, 217, 243, 252
Jacobite Rising (Davies) 94, 115
Jacobites 21-22
Jacobite songs 115-17
James II of England 22, 87, 243. *See also* James VII of Scotland
James VII of Scotland 22, 87, 243. *See also* James II of England
"Jamie Raeburn" (song) 217
Jefferson, Thomas 141
John Muir Trust 126
Johnson, Alison 56, 117-18
Johnson, Jim A. 242
Johnson, Samuel 31, 33, 118-19, 145, 201, 213
Johnson, Sir William 119
Johnston, Gabriel 194-95
Jones, Rev. David 122
Jones, Malcolm 221
journalists: as crusaders 57
Jura 11, 39, 77, 119, 194

Kay, Billy 228
Keith 139
kelp 120, 241
Kennedy, Charles 185
Kennedy, John Pendleton 135
Kennedy-Fraser, Marjory 231
Kerr, Murdoch 263
Keynes, John Maynard 173
Kilbeg Village Project 120-21
Kildonan 121-22, 216-17, 228-30, 247, 255. *See also* Red River Colony; Winnipeg (Manitoba)
Killiecrankie, Battle of 22, 115
Kindersley, Richard 69
King's Mountain, Battle of 23
Kintyre 194
Kissling, Werner 70, 122-23, 231, 256
Knox, John 123-24, 175
Knox, Robert 124

Knoydart 97; Knoydart Clearances, 124-26
Knoydart Foundation 126
Knoydart Land Raid Commemoration Committee 126, 231
Koek, Tekela 214
Laing, Gerald 67
lairds 127
Lairg 198
Lamlash (Arran) 127
Lamond, Mary Jane 127
Land Agitation movement 21, 216
Land League movement 105, 128
land ownership 128
land reform 128-29
landlords 129
Land Reform Act (2003) 16, 129
Landscape with Tourists at Loch Katrine (Knox) 123
Landseer, Edwin 129-30
An Lanntair Gallery 13, 130
The Last of the Clan (Faed) 72-73, 78-79, 191, 193
Lauder, Robert Scott 181
Laurence, Margaret 63, 130-31, 144
Law of Entail 85
Leckhelm 199
Lee, Robert E. 134, 136
Leonard, James 196
"Letter from America" (song) 131, 193
Letterfearn 199
Leveson-Gower, George Granville (1st Duke of Sutherland) 64, 121, 266
Lever, William (Lord Leverhulme) 131-32, 155
Lewis 28, 48, 51, 73, 81, 110, 120, 131-32, 155-56, 163, 173-74, 188-89
Lewis Settlement 132-33, 163
Liddon, Rod Stewart 213
Lincoln, Abraham 136
Livingston, William 133, 204, 232

Livingstone, Lachlan 206
Lochaber 131, 133
Lochaber No More (Nicol) 72, 131, 193
Loch, James 26, 46, 133, 258, 264
Lockhart, John Gibson 38
Lockhart-Ross, Sir John of Balnagowan 133
A Lonely Life (Cameron) 35
Long Street Presbyterian Church 77, 195
Lord Selkirk Association of Rupert's Land 134
Lorgill (Skye) 199
Lost Cause 134-36
Louisiana 24
Lovat, Lord (Simon Fraser) 136
Lower Canada (Québec) 132
Lowland Clearances 70, 103, 129, 136-39
Loyalists 140-41
Luing 11
Lunny, Manus 76, 211, 238

Mac Mhaighstir, Alasdair (Alexander MacDonald) 142
MacAskill, Peter 47
MacAulay, Donald 142
MacBain, Alexander 173, 205
MacCaig, Norman 142, 183
MacCallum, Rev. Donald 143, 206, 262
MacCodrum, John 143
MacColla, Alasdair 143
MacColla, Fionn (Tom Macdonald) 10, 49, 76, 143
MacCosh, James 186
MacDiarmid, Hugh 143-44, 151, 153, 183
Macdonald, Allan 145-46
MacDonald, Allan "the Ridge" 108, 144
MacDonald, Alexander 87
MacDonald, Angus 28
Macdonald, Calum 144, 221, 223

MacDonald, Dan R. 145
Macdonald, Donald 262
Macdonald, D. R. 144-45
Macdonald, Flora 64, 145-46, 234, 244
MacDonald, James Roderick (Jamie) 146
MacDonald, Sir James of Sleat 143
MacDonald, John 212
MacDonald John "the Hunter" 108, 144, 146
MacDonald Lands Trust 120
Macdonald, Lord of Sleat (Godfrey William Wentworth) 21, 82, 184, 235
MacDonald, Michael 108, 147
Macdonald, Murdo 215
MacDonald, Rev. Patrick 266
MacDonald, Peter 21
Macdonald, Robert 222
MacDonald, Roddy 214
Macdonald, Rory 147, 185, 191, 221, 224
Macdonell, Alasdair Ranaldson of Glengarry 9, 88-89, 147, 215
Macdonell, Rev. Alexander 85
Macdonell, Bishop Alexander 147
Macdonell, Elizabeth 240
Macdonell, Josephine 125
Macdonell, Marjorie 84, 87-88
Macdonell, Miles 227-28
MacDougall, Allan 148
Macduff 216
Macfarlane, Alan 226
Macfarlane, Murdo 148, 154, 171, 186
MacGillivray, Donald 116
MacGowan, Douglas 168
MacGregor, Rob Roy 103
MacInnes, Allan 70
MacInnes, John 93, 148, 221
Macintosh, Sir Cameron 126
MacIntyre, Donald 250
Macintyre, Duncan Bàn 89, 94, 148-49, 203

Macintyre, Richard 185
Maciver, Donald 149, 171, 204
"MacKay Country" (Robertson) 266-67
Mackay, Kenneth A. 27
Mackenzie, Alexander 11, 110, 128, 149, 240
MacKenzie, A. W. R. 81
Mackenzie, Compton 37, 70
Mackenzie, Eilidh 67
Mackenzie, Sir George Steuart of Coul 149
MacKenzie, Hugh F. 149, 171
MacKenzie, John 14
Mackenzie, Sir Kenneth 188
MacKenzie, Rory Roy 108
MacKid, Robert 260
Mackie, J. D. 149-50
MacKinnon, Donald 188
MacKinnon, Jonathan 11, 150
MacLachlan, John 150, 204
Maclean, Dr. Alasdair 239
Maclean, Alexander 23
Maclean, Allan 23
Maclean, Dougie 150, 191
Maclean, Hector 202
MacLean, John 108, 150-51
Maclean, Lachlan 130
Maclean, Murdo 104
Maclean, Renee 209
Maclean, Sorley 13, 27, 35, 93-94, 96, 115, 144, 152-53, 155, 183, 193, 204-210, 213, 221, 224, 226, 244, 262
Maclean, Will 153-56, 218, 244
MacLeish, Andrew 156
MacLeish, Archibald 156
MacLeish, Kenneth 156
MacLennan, Colin 28
MacLennan, David 177
MacLennan, Dolina 177
MacLennan, Elizabeth 177
MacLennan, Hugh 156-58
MacLeod, Alistair 24, 38, 144, 158-63, 194

Macleod, Angus 133, 163-64, 209
Macleod, Calum 34-35, 95, 164-66
Macleod, Charles 166
Macleod, Dennis 68, 166-67, 230
Macleod, Donald 49, 57, 76, 89, 167-69, 196, 219, 239, 264
MacLeod, Lt. Col. Donald 23
MacLeod, Donald of Gleanies 169-70
MacLeod, Finlay 13
MacLeod, John 101
MacLeod, John (historian) 244
MacLeod, Margaret 73
MacLeod, Mary 170, 251
MacLeod, Murdo 170
MacLeod, Murdo (photographer) 231
MacLeod, Neil 170, 206
Macmillan, Daniel 13
Macmillan, Harold 13
MacMillan, James 25
MacNeacail, Aonghas 170-71, 194, 222
MacNeil, Donald 39
MacNeill, Daniel 12
MacNeill, Sir John 215
MacNeill Report 169
MacPhail, Calum Campbell 206
MacPhee, Catherine-Anne 148-49, 171, 177, 210
MacPherson, Hugh 66
MacPherson, John 86-87, 171-72, 223, 262. *See also* Glendale Martyrs
Macpherson, John ("the Coddy") 37
MacPherson, Mary (Màiri Mhòr nan Oran) 109, 151, 172-73, 177, 186, 205-206, 232
Macrae, Alasdair 35
MacRae, Allan 14
Macrae, Rev. David 73
MacRae, Donald 173
MacRae, Donald (schoolmaster) 174
Macrae, Iain 35
MacRae, John 108, 173, 206

Mac-Talla (The Echo) (newspaper) 11, 25, 30, 150, 173
Malcolm, Rev. David 130
Malcolm, Neil 12
Malthus, Thomas Robert 173, 197, 248
Manifest Destiny 191
"Manitoba" (MacLean) 207-206
Mao Zedong 173
Martin, Abraham 23
Martin, Donald 261
Maryland 140
Marx, Karl 174, 234
Massacre of Glencoe 78, 86, 97
Matheson, Donald 73
Matheson, Donald (poet) 108
Matheson, Sir James 28, 132, 164, 174, 249
Matheson, Karen 40
Mayhew, Henry 46
McAden, Hugh 195
McCulloch, Horatio 175, 182, 218
McDonald, Father Allan 175
McDonald, Archibald 229
McDonald, Ellice Jr. 176
McDonald, Steve 175-76
McDonell, Alexander 19
McEachern, D. P. 73
McGillivray, Lachlan 60
McGrath, John 13, 42-43, 92, 176-77
McIllwain, Jeffrey Scott 71
McIntosh, Alastair 80
McIntosh, Lachlan 60
McKean, Thomas 204
McLean, Allan Campbell 177
McLean, Hugh 229
McLean, Marianne 88-89, 133, 202
McLeod, John 229
McLeod, Rev. Norman 177-79, 202, 252
McMillan, Archibald 133
McNeill, Sir Malcolm 52
McPhee, John 47-48, 179-80
McQueen, Alexander 180-81

McTaggart, William 155, 181-82
Meade, George G. 134
Meek, Donald 182, 203, 207, 264
Memorabilia Domestica (Sage) 121, 225
Memories of a Northern Childhood (Maclean) 154
Meyer, Duane 195
Miller, Hugh 57, 182, 234, 236, 255, 263
Mingulay 250
Mitchell, Joseph 100, 183
Mòd 48
Moffat, Alexander 13, 183
Mohawk Valley (New York) 119
Moidart 199
Moir, David Macbeth 38
The Monarch of the Glen (Landseer) 129
Montcalm, Louis-Joseph, Marquis de 23, 158
Montgomery's Highlanders 79
Moore's Creek Bridge, Battle of 23, 146, 173
Morgan, Edwin 183
Morrison, Alexander 262
Morrison, John 263
Morvern 199
Mounsey, Paul 211, 222
Muck 199
Muie 199
Muir, Edwin 115, 183-84, 240
Muisel 184
Mulgrew, Gerry 35
Mulock, Thomas 57, 184-85, 196, 220
Mull 32, 120, 151
Munro, Donald 28
Munro, Donnie 92, 144, 185-86, 212, 221
Munro, Hugh of Novar 59, 257
Munro, Hector of Novar 257
Munro, John Farquhar 185
Murdoch, John 128, 186
Murray, John 13

Museum of the Isles 46
"My Fair Young Love" ("Mo rùn geal òg") (song) 117
My Heart's in the Highlands (McCulloch) 175
Mylne, Robert 113
Na Fògarraich 210
Nairne, Lady Carolina 116, 187
Napier Commission 41, 46, 79, 171-72, 187-90, 197, 204, 207, 218
Napier, Lord 187-88
Napoleonic Wars 19, 69-70, 120
Nasmyth, Alexander 123, 175
National Theatre of Scotland 35-36, 107
Native Americans 11, 109, 112, 150, 190-92, 218
Neat, Timothy 94, 96, 192, 224
New Brunswick 13, 114, 127, 140
New England 31
New Lanark 139, 192-93
Newton, Michael 39, 111, 116, 135-36, 210, 225, 228
New York 23, 140
New Zealand 7, 16, 102, 165, 179, 197, 219, 226-27, 252
Nicol, John Watson 193
Nicolson, Alasdair 153, 193-94
Nicolson, Alexander 188, 263
Nicolson, Donald 21
Nicolson, James 21
A Night of Islands (Maclean) 155
Noble, Sir Iain 194
No Great Mischief (MacLeod) 24, 38, 159, 163, 194
North America 16; Highland songs in 107-108. *See also* Canada; United States
North British Daily Mail (newspaper) 57, 193, 220, 236
North Carolina 11, 23, 140, 145, 194-95, 252; failed 1884 emigration to 73-74; Highland songs in 108. *See also* Argyll Colony; Cape Fear, "Fort Bragg Clearances"

Northern Association of Gentlemen and Farmers, Breeders of Sheep 196
Northern Ensign (newspaper) 57, 113, 185, 196
Northern Friends (ship) 39
North Uist 40-41, 101, 113, 120, 143, 146, 188, 235-36; North Uist Clearances 196, 261
North West Company (NWC) 24, 228-30
Norton, Alex 176
notice of removal 196
Nova Scotia 23, 31, 39, 69, 96, 140, 207, 240, 249; Highland songs in 108. *See also* Cape Breton Island
Novick, Peter 59

Oates, Joyce Carol 159
Oglethorpe, Gen. James 60, 254
Oh Why I Left My Hame (Faed) 72, 176
On the Origin of Species (Darwin) 197, 237
Ontario 132, 140, 164, 240, 247, 249; Highland songs in 108. *See also* Upper Canada
Orkney 73, 189, 197
Otago 197
Oughton (ship) 18
Outer Hebrides 200
Owen, Robert 192
Owen, Wilfred 115

Pairc Deer Raid 61, 155, 201, 206
Passenger Vessels Act (1803) 201
Paterson, Bill 176
Pearl (ship) 119
Peguis, Chief 229
Pennant, Thomas 201-202
"People's Clearance" 202
Perrotta, Guy 103
Perth Constitutional (newspaper) 193
Perthshire 192, 202

Philadelphia Land Company 96
Pickett, George 134
Pictou (Nova Scotia) 96-97, 178, 202, 249
Pinkerton, John 202-203
Plains of Abraham, Battle of the 23, 79, 158
Platt, Joseph Arthur 201
Poets' Pub (Moffat) 183
Poett, Lucy 104
Poland 226
Prebble, John 8, 20, 55, 57, 59, 65, 80, 84, 87-88, 91, 96, 106, 120, 149, 167, 211, 238-39
Prestonpans, Battle of 24, 115
Prince Edward Island (PEI) 47, 208, 212, 249, 264; Highland songs in 108
Prince of Wales (ship) 121
The Private Memoirs and Confessions of a Justified Sinner (Hogg) 85
Proclaimers 131, 193
Proscription, Act of (1746) 9
Protestant work ethic 212
Purser, John 25, 212

Quarantine Passage/Grosse-Île (Maclean) 154
Québec 13, 19-20, 23, 87, 89, 127, 132, 140, 154, 158, 164, 235, 249

Raasay 93, 148, 151-55, 164-66, 207-208, 213, 215
Raasay House 213-14
Rachmanism 214
Rachman, Peter 214
racism 214
rack-renting 214
Raeburn, Sir Henry 88, 214-15
Rainy, George 93, 213, 215, 260
Ramsay, Allan 214
Ramsey, John 114
Rannoch 199
Ray, Celeste 228

Red River Colony 18, 122, 228-29, 247. *See also* Winnipeg (Manitoba)
Rent Act (1965) 214
Rent Day 215
Rent Day in the Wilderness (Landseer) 129
Report to the Board of Supervision in Scotland 215
resistance 215-17
Revolutionary War 23, 140
Rhymer, Thomas the 217
Richards, Eric 8, 11, 14, 19, 30, 46, 54, 55, 61, 65, 70, 89, 95, 97, 99, 102-103, 132, 134, 168-69, 174-75, 198, 216-18, 240
Riddell, James Milles 11
The Right Madness on Skye (Hugo) 111, 209
rigs 218
ring-net fishing 218
Rinzler, Ralph 253
Rio de Janeiro (Brazil) 46
Ritchie, Bill 14
Rixson, Denis 8, 125, 128
Robertson, Charles of Kindeace 54, 267
Robertson, Colin 229
Robertson, Ewen 204, 218, 266
Robinson, Fred Norris 95
Robinson, Mary 48
Rob Roy (film) 219
Rodger, Willie 218
Rogart 199
Rona 164, 215
roots tourism 219
Rosal 219-20, 230, 264. *See also* Strathnaver
Rose, Eugene 72
Ross, Allan 176
Ross, Sir Charles 198
Ross, Donald 51, 57, 92, 124-25, 167, 196, 220-21, 239, 261
Ross, John 96
Ross, William 151, 207

Rothiemurchas 199
Rousay 197
Rousseau, Jean-Jacques 218
Rowe, Lyn 214
Rum 39, 221
Runciman, Alexander 215
Runrig (band) 92, 103, 144, 147-49, 153-54, 166, 171-73, 185, 191, 210-11, 221-24, 232
runrig (method of farming) 137-38, 221
Russell, Charles 191
Russell, Michael W. 123, 167, 184
Russell, William 220

Sabbath of the Dead (Maclean) 155
Sabhal Mòr Ostaig 48, 120, 155, 170, 185, 194, 225, 235
Sage, Rev. Alexander 121-22, 225
Sage, Rev. Donald 121-22, 225
The Sailing of the Emigrant Ship (McTaggart) 181
Salmond, Alex 67-68, 184, 255
Sand Creek Massacre 191
Sandy (superstorm) 46-47
Sandy Grove Presbyterian Church 78
Saskatchewan 51
"Satire on Patrick Sellar" (Baillie) 265-66
School of Scottish Studies 26, 37
"Scots Wha Hae" (song) 116
Scott, Dave 253
Scott, Sir Walter 38, 83, 100, 104, 109, 116, 124, 130, 135, 147, 184, 219, 225-26
Scottish Centre for Diaspora Studies (SCDS) 62, 226
Scottish Centre for Island Studies 226
Scottish Crofting Federation (SCF) 226-27
Scottish diaspora 165, 227; long memory of 134, 227-28. *See also* individual countries

Index

Scottish Journey (Muir) 183-84
Scottish National Heritage 126
Seachd: The Inaccessible Pinnacle (film), 35
Seil 11
Selkirk, Lord (Thomas Douglas, Fifth Earl of Selkirk) 14, 18, 25, 121-22, 134, 212, 228-29, 255
Selkirk Settlers 122, 134, 224, 228-30, 233
Selkirk Settlers Monument 230
Sellar, Patrick 14, 26, 32, 43, 49, 54, 66, 72, 74-76, 111, 167-68, 209, 214, 218, 230, 235, 239, 241, 246-47, 260, 264-66
Semple, Robert 229
septs 231
Sevastopol, Siege of 20
Seven Oaks, Battle of 24, 229
7:84 Theatre Company 171, 177-78
Seven Men of Knoydart 125-26, 231
78th Fraser Highlanders 23, 158
Seven Years War 23. *See also* French and Indian War
Shaw, Donald 40
Shaw, Margaret Fay 37, 231, 256
Sheep Clearances. *See* Highland Clearances
Sheridan, Gen. Philip 191
Sheriffmuir, Battle of 115
Shetland 189, 199, 232
Shuna 11
Shiaba (Isle of Mull) 199
shielings 232
shinty 232-33
Siege of Sevastopol 20
Sileas na Ceapaich (Julia MacDonald) 251
The Silent Ones: A Legacy of the Highland Clearances (Macleod) 133, 163, 209
Silly Wizard 238
The Silver Darlings (Gunn) 218
Sim, Duncan 228

Sinclair, Rev. Dr. Alexander MacLean 30, 233
Sinclair, Sir John of Ulbster 17, 42, 215, 233-34
The Singing (Beamish) 25, 209
Sismondi, Jean Charles Léonard de 234
Skene, W. F. 234
Skye 12, 32, 39, 73, 82, 97, 106, 111, 120, 131, 146, 152, 172-73, 188, 209, 212, 250. *See also* individual Clearance sites on
Skye Museum of Island Life 234
Sleat Community Trust 120
Smith, Adam 234-35 237
Smith, Iain Crichton 35, 49, 76, 94, 103, 152, 183, 207-209, 230, 235, 246
Smith, John 206
Smith, Sydney Goodsir 184
Smith, Tommy 58
Soillse 235
Sollas 217-18; Sollas Clearances 196, 235-36
So Many Partings (Silly Wizard) 238
Somersaults (MacLeod) 36
Somers, Robert 57, 174, 236-37
"A Song of the Battle of Falkirk" (Macintyre) 115
South Africa 165, 227
South Carolina 23
Southey, Robert 237
South Uist 19-20, 26, 39, 48, 70, 89, 101, 120, 188, 231, 239
Spencer, Herbert 197, 237
squatters 237
SS *Politician* (ship) 70
St. Ann's (Cape Breton) 177-78, 202, 252
Statutes of Iona 237-38
Steen, Carl R. 77
Stevenson, John 12
Stewart, Alexander 207
Stewart, Andy M. 57, 76-77, 210-11, 238

Stewart, Angus 188, 262
Stewart, Gen. David of Garth 99, 238
Stone, Jamie 11
The Storm (McTaggart) 181
Stornoway 9
Stowe, Harriet Beecher 169, 238-39, 264
Strand, Paul 231, 239-40
Strathaird Clearances 240
Strathconon Clearances 240
Strathglass Clearances 240
Strathmore Clearances 240-41
Strathnaver 74, 219; Strathnaver Clearances 75, 97, 111, 122, 167, 241, 247, 264. *See also* Rosal
"Strathnaver" (Thomson) 155, 208, 246
Strathnaver Museum 241-42
Strathnaver Trail 242
Strath Oykel 200
Strathrusdale 200
Strathspey 242
Stuart, Charles Edward ("Bonnie Prince Charlie") 21-22, 58, 64, 70, 87, 115-17, 136, 140, 145, 243-44, 254
Stuart, James Francis Edward 87, 115, 243
"Stuarts of Appin" (song) 117
Suishnish (Skye) 82-83, 208-209, 244
Sunny Memories of Foreign Lands (Stowe) 169, 239
Sutherland 121, 131, 189, 192, 198, 255; Sutherland Clearances 101, 133, 167, 244, 258-59. *See also* Strathnaver
Sutherland, Alexander Robert 17
Sutherland, David 17
Sutherland, John (of Badbea) 17
Sutherland, John (writer) 159
Sweden 226
Sweeney, William 94, 170, 209, 244

tacks 245
tacksmen 18, 31, 103, 245
Taylor, Sue Jane 171
Telford, Thomas 34, 139, 237, 245-46, 249
Theakston, Joseph 26
"Thin Red Line" 20-21, 220
The Thin Red Line (Gibb) 17
Thom, Robert 39
Thomson, Derick S. 28, 155, 207, 246
Three Fires, Achnahaird (Maclean) 154
Thurso 139
Tiffany, John 107
Timespan Heritage Centre 97, 246-47
Tiree 247
Tobar an Dualchais (Kist-o-Riches) 247
Tolbooth Steeple 247
Tomintoul 139
Torosay 11
townships 247
Traill, George William 197
transhumance 248
Treaty of Paris 24, 79
Trevelyan, Charles 16, 19, 41, 91, 248
Two Sights of the Sea (Maclean) 154
Two Solitudes (MacLennan) 156

Uig Clearances (Lewis) 249
Ullapool 102, 139, 249
Ullapool Museum 249
Ulva 249
Union, Act of (1707) 60
United States 7, 102, 165, 219, 226-27
University of the Highlands and Islands (UHI) 42
Upper Canada (Ontario) 12, 18, 20, 69, 89, 133, 259
Upper Deeside 200
Urbain, Jean-Didier 109

Valtos 250
Vatersay 250

Index

Vatersay Boys 250
Vatersay raiders 250
Victoria, Queen 101, 110, 184
village bards 250-51
Virginia 140-41
Voices over the Water (documentary) 103

Wade, Gen. George 33, 252
Waipu (New Zealand) 178-79, 202, 227, 252
Waipu Heritage Trail 179
Wales 69
Wallace, Alexander 257
War of 1812 18, 147
Watkins, Peter 57-58
Watson, Arthur 154
Watson, Doc 252-53
Watson, W. J. 204
Waverley (Scott) 88
Weber, Max 253
Wellins, Bobby 58-59
West, Benjamin 60
West Greenyards 200
West Highland Free Press (newspaper) 253-54
West Highland Museum 254
West, John 122
Whisky Galore (film) 70
whiteness 254
Whyte, Henry 76, 238
Whyte, John 172, 205
Wick 139, 216
The Wicked Generation (Johnson) 56, 117
Wilkie, David (artist) 35, 83, 254-55
Wilkie, David (musician) 104, 211
Wilkie, Jim 253
William III 86
Wilson, Brian 80, 253-54
Wilson, George Washington 231, 255
Wilson, John 38

Winnipeg (Manitoba) 18, 24, 67, 69, 122, 134, 166, 227-28, 230, 247, 255. *See also* Red River Colony
Witherspoon, Rev. John 96, 141
Witness (newspaper) 57, 182, 236
Wishart, Peter 222
Wolfe, Gen. James 23-24, 60, 158
"The Woods of Raasay" (Maclean), 170, 207
Wounded Knee Massacre 191
Wylie, Gus 231, 256

Year of the Sheep (Bliadhna Nan Caorach) 257-58
York boats 258
York Factory (Manitoba) 228-29, 258
Young, William 14, 72, 258

Zorra 259

Born in Glasgow, Scotland, June Skinner Sawyers is the author or editor of more than twenty books, many with a Celtic theme, including *Celtic Music; Dreams of Elsewhere: The Selected Travel Writings of Robert Louis Stevenson; Praying with Celtic Saints, Prophets, Martyrs, and Poets; The Road North: 300 Years of Classic Scottish Travel Writing;* and *The Scots of Chicago: Quiet Immigrants and Their New Society*. Her essays, "Weeping Willows and Long Black Veils: The Country Roots of Rosanne Cash, from Scotland to Tennessee" will appear in the forthcoming *Walking the Line: Country Music Lyricists and American Culture* and "Celtic Music in America" in the *Encyclopedia of Music and American Culture*, respectively. In addition, her work has appeared in *Scottish Tradition*, the *Chicago Tribune*, the *San Francisco Chronicle, Sing Out!, Dirty Linen, Booklist,* and the *Common Review*. In 2013, she was the recipient of the Flora Macdonald Award from St. Andrews University in Laurinburg, North Carolina, which is given to a woman of Scots birth or descent who has made an outstanding contribution to the human community.

www.ingramcontent.com/pod-product-compliance
Lightning Source LLC
Chambersburg PA
CBHW030135170426
43199CB00008B/66